ROUTLEDGE LIBRARY EDITIONS:
LANDMARKS IN THE HISTORY OF
ECONOMIC THOUGHT

Volume 1

I0891136

A REVIEW OF ECONOMIC THEORY

A REVIEW OF ECONOMIC THEORY

EDWIN CANNAN

Routledge
Taylor & Francis Group
LONDON AND NEW YORK

First published in 1929 by P. S. King & Son Ltd
Reprinted in 1964 by Frank Cass and Co. Ltd.

This edition first published in 2017
by Routledge
2 Park Square, Milton Park, Abingdon, Oxon OX14 4RN

and by Routledge
711 Third Avenue, New York, NY 10017

Routledge is an imprint of the Taylor & Francis Group, an informa business

British Library Cataloguing in Publication Data
A catalogue record for this book is available from the British Library

ISBN: 978-1-138-21086-8 (Set)
ISBN: 978-1-315-40933-7 (Set) (ebk)
ISBN: 978-1-138-21812-3 (Volume 1) (hbk)
ISBN: 978-1-138-21816-1 (Volume 1) (pbk)
ISBN: 978-1-315-43837-5 (Volume 1) (ebk)

A REVIEW OF ECONOMIC THEORY

Edwin Cannan

With a new introduction by
B. A. CORRY

FRANK CASS AND CO. LTD.
1964

This edition published by
Frank Cass and Co. Ltd., 10 Woburn Walk, London, W.C. 1
by arrangement with P. S. King & Son.

First Edition 1929
Second Edition 1964

PREFACE

In the Preface to the 1917 issue of my *History of the Theories of Production and Distribution in English Political Economy from 1776 to 1848* I expressed a hope that "within the next few years" I might be able to supplement that book by one in which the period dealt with in it might be "put in its proper relation both with what preceded it and with what followed it." The present work may perhaps be accepted as a somewhat tardy fulfilment of the half-promise, but, to use the perfect frankness which becomes a preface-writer, it is much less a supplement to the earlier work than a rendering in book form of the substance of the course of about sixty lectures entitled "Principles of Economics, including the History of Economic Theory," which I gave to second and third year students at the London School of Economics for many years down to June 1926.

That course covered two years, and lectures repeated only every second year are much more easily altered than those repeated every year, so that faithful note-takers of the earlier part of the period are likely to find many things omitted and others added, and even those who attended in 1924–6 will find changes which I might have introduced if I had been lecturing in 1927–9 with the advantage of a sabbatical—or rather a belated semi-jubilee—year's release from oral teaching.

Of the buzzing *φροντιστήριον* or "thinkery," as Aristophanes would have called it, which in my time moved from two rooms in John Street to five in Adelphi Terrace, and then leapt to what we thought magnificence in Clare Market, and gradually fought its way from there through a wilderness of old bricks and mortar and dirt to a front door in Houghton Street, I have many pleasant recollections, but none sweeter than that of what

Professor Lilian Knowles, in her kindness of heart, told me a few months before her untimely death :

" A student talking to me the other day about you said, 'There's one thing about him; he always makes you want to go on.' Wasn't that nice? "

It was; and it encourages me to hope that this book, in spite of all the deficiencies of which I am painfully aware, and all the others which will be found out by reviewers and readers, may yet make a few more students " want to go on." There is no finality in economic theory, and indeed, until it makes more impression on the vulgar mind than it has so far done, it must be regarded as only in its infancy.

The title, " A Review of Economic Theory," has been chosen to disarm the criticism of those who would complain of omissions. A reviewer always does well to say what he wants to say and leave the rest out.

June, 1929.

NOTE TO SECOND IMPRESSION

In this impression some half-dozen misprints and slips of the pen have been corrected; any careful reader will have observed all of them except the erroneous insertion of " his " before " possession " in the quotation from Walker on p. 358, l. 7, and perhaps the confusions about Hume's views on the rate of interest, p. 252, ll. 20–23, and the alternative supposititious gifts to J. S. Mill, p. 403, l. 24. On p. 11 I have modified the statement that Adam Smith " invented " or " devised " the term " Mercantile System," as it seems likely that he took it from Quesnay and Mirabeau (see Oncken, *Geschichte der Nationalökonomie*, p. 335).

My thanks are due to the kind friends who have contributed most of these corrections, Mr. L. L. Price, Dr. F. Hayek, and Professors Arnold Plant and Lionel Robbins.

October, 1930.

CONTENTS

CHAPTER I

THE ORIGINS OF ECONOMIC THEORY

CHAPTER II

THE NAME OF ECONOMIC THEORY

CHAPTER III

THE THEORY OF PRODUCTION

CHAPTER IV

THE INFLUENCE OF POPULATION ON PRODUCE

CHAPTER V

THE INFLUENCE OF CO-OPERATION ON PRODUCE

CHAPTER VI

THE INFLUENCE OF ACCUMULATION ON PRODUCE

CHAPTER VII

THE THEORY OF VALUE IN GENERAL

CHAPTER VIII

THE THEORY OF THE VALUE OF LAND

CHAPTER IX

THE THEORY OF THE COMPARATIVE VALUE OF CAPITAL AND INCOME

CHAPTER X

THE CLASSIFICATION AND "DISTRIBUTION" OF INCOME

CHAPTER XI

INCOMES FROM LABOUR: THEIR GENERAL LEVEL

CHAPTER XII

INCOMES FROM LABOUR: THEIR INEQUALITIES

CHAPTER XIII

INCOMES FROM PROPERTY

CHAPTER XIV

ASPIRATIONS AND TENDENCIES

New Introduction

by

B. A. CORRY

READERS coming to this reprint of Edwin Cannan's famous *Review* for the first time and perhaps even to Cannan for the first time, will probably find themselves rather puzzled by the contents of the book. It is not just that this book was first published in 1929—even for that period it has a particular slant. In this short introduction I want to explain why this is so rather than write at length about the book which speaks for itself.

The author of this book, the late Edwin Cannan, was professor of economics in the University of London at the London School of Economics and Political Science from 1907 until his retirement in 1926. His teaching connections with London ante-date his professorial appointment by some ten years. In fact he was invited to lecture at L.S.E. from its very inception in 1895.[1] His active interest in the world of economics did not end with his official retirement from office; he contributed a steady flow of books, articles and reviews right up to his death in 1935. If, for reasons of simplification, we think in terms of rough chronological divisions of the development of economic science, Cannan's very active and influential career spans two of these divisions. The earlier part of his career is concerned with the consolidation of marginalism as an alternative to the classical schema of consumption, production and distribution, whilst the latter—post 1918 era—is concerned primarily with the various attempts to integrate the theories of money and output in a more satisfactory manner than the orthodox, classical attempt. This latter controversy was even more striking from Cannan's point of view because, in England at least, the major competing groups were the emerging "Keynesian" school at Cambridge and the bitterly opposed "Austrians" at the London School of Economics. Yet it is a fact that Edwin Cannan took no part in these developments.[2]

[1] For further biographical information see: *Dictionary of National Biography*: article on Cannan by Professor Lionel Robbins. *Times Newspaper* obituary notice.

[2] Of course Cannan retired in 1925 and the real animosity between London and Cambridge did not develop until after this date. However, Cannan did remain active in economic discussions after his retirement but did not participate in this controversy. Rivalry, if not open warfare, seems to have existed between the two centres before the clash of the late Twenties and early Thirties. See Sir Roy Harrod's *Life of John Maynard Keynes*, *p.* 319.

In general, he stood outside the main controversies which took place during his active lifetime—and he had by any comparison a long and highly productive life. His first publication—the *Elementary Political Economy*—appeared in 1883 and his last book review in 1934 in the *Economic Journal*. Probably he will be remembered in the future as he is perhaps even today, as the great interpreter of the classic period and in particular of, surely his first love, his fellow Scot—Adam Smith. Students of the history of economic thought will always be indebted to him, of this there can be no question. However, when we come to assess Cannan's positive contribution to the development of economics—to his understanding of the theoretical analysis which guides us in our interpretation of the economic systems that we see around us—then doubts as to his place in the hall of fame must inevitably creep in.

Many readers will doubtless associate the name of Cannan with a series of *simpliste* solutions to the most complex of economic problems. Students of money and banking are all familiar with Cannan's dogmatic opinions on the inability of banks to create credit.[1] Perhaps even better known are Cannan's views on the causes of unemployment and the efficacy of certain suggestions for its amelioration.[2]

I have picked out these two examples not because they are both grossly mistaken ideas, nor simply because belief in them and their policy implications could be and was well-nigh disastrous, but because I think that they both stem from the central characteristic of Edwin Cannan's economics, and this characteristic was his great strength and yet at the same time his fundamental weakness. It was his essentially commonsense view of economics. Such an approach had its advantages, it challenged the sophisticated, involved view of an economic process, with the everyday understanding of it, and this is often a useful thing to do although it is never sufficient, as Cannan was wont, only to look at the common-

[1] See e.g. E. Cannan, "The Meaning of Bank Deposits", *Economica*, Vol. I. (1921).

[2] ". . . general unemployment is in reality to be explained almost in the same way as particular unemployment. In a particular employment, provided demand for its product is elastic, more persons can be employed if they will work for less remuneration. In all employments *taken together*, demand is indefinitely elastic, and consequently indefinite numbers can be employed if they do not ask for too high a remuneration. General unemployment appears when asking too much is a general phenomenon." "The demand for Labour", *Economic Journal*, Vol. XLII. (1932, p. 367).

sense view. It also enabled a rapid communication with the intelligent lay public to take place and Cannan found his audience very often among business men, trade unionists, political groups and so on.

Professor Jacob Viner summed up this central feature of Cannan's thinking extremely well in his review of the *Review* where we read:

> "The exercise of a soundly critical commonsense avoidance of technical concepts unintelligible to the intelligent layman, distrust of long chains of abstract reasoning and of highly technical refinements of concepts and procedure, freedom from any yearning to construct a formal and elaborate doctrinal 'system,' these are the outstanding characteristics of his method. With the paraphernalia of economic inquiry developed since the classical period—demand and supply curves, utility analysis, the translation of economic process into algebraic equations, the concept of general equilibrium, systematic induction by statistical methods, the comprehensive study of the influence of institutional change on economic process, and so forth—he will have commerce at arms length or not at all. If the book is a faithful transcript of the lectures, his students could have received from him little stimulus to become master of any of these techniques, and must have been led to an undue degree of contentment with common sense as an adequate instrument of economic investigation . . ." [1]

It may perhaps be a cause of some surprise to contemporary readers of this book to discover (as they will on reading Cannan's preface) that this book was a course of lectures in economic principles given to non-specialist undergraduates at the London School of Economics and Political Science. It was a two-year course and was given, on and off, from his first appointment at the School in 1895 until he retired in 1926. Even though we must remember that it was a course of lectures delivered in the 1920s and not the 1960s it still differs quite fundamentally from similar non-specialist textbooks at the time such as those by Taussig, Cassel or Marshall.

Apart from its belief in the ultimate efficiency of the application of common sense to an understanding of economic systems it has

[1] J. Viner, *Economica*, Vol. 28 (1930). A defence of Cannan's position is to be found in his "The need for Simpler Economics", *Economic Journal*, Vol. XLIII. (1933).

two other outstanding features which immediately strike the reader today.

In the first place it is clear that the main target of criticism and inspiration is the English Classical School. There are certainly references to Marshall, Jevons and Wicksteed (although none e.g. to Walras, Wicksell or J. B. Clark) but the re-occurring names are Smith, Ricardo, Malthus and J. S. Mill.

In part, as I have already mentioned, this is explicable in terms of Cannan's own well-known interest in this field. The lecture course was after all entitled " Principles of Economics," including the " History of Economic Theory." But why this interest ? To answer this we must look at the second outstanding feature of the book. The central focus of this course of lectures is not an elaboration of the working of the price system as we would expect from a survey course of economic theory. It is instead a re-examination of Adam Smith's central theme—" *the origin and causes of the wealth of nations.*" This problem, with greater concern over the distribution of wealth than occupied Smith, was dominant in the whole of Cannan's work. The central concept of Economic Science was material wealth. His well-known textbook—*Wealth*—is essentially an introduction to economics from this point of view.

It is also significant that the sub-title of this book reads " A brief explanation of the causes of economic welfare ". Cannan was quite prepared, and indeed took it to be the job of the economist, to expound propositions leading to improvement in economic well-being. It was for this reason that he refused to accept the modifications to his definition of economics suggested by Lionel Robbins in his *Nature and Significance of Economic Science.* Cannan reviewed that book and included the following revealing sentence : " Benefactors endow Chairs of Economics, audiences listen to economic lectures, purchasers buy economic books, because they think that understanding economics will make people better off. Is it really necessary for professors of economics to destroy this demand for economic teaching by alleging that they do not know what ' better off ' means ? " [1]

For Cannan then, the division between economic policy and economic science was not one to be countenanced. The economist

[1] *Economic Journal*, Vol. XLII. (1932), p. 426.

qua economist was, or should be, committed to the improvement in the material standards of living of mankind. Economists today are more circumspect but, I suspect, secretly long to cross the river that Cannan bridged so easily.

I have suggested certain criticisms of Cannan's approach to economics but it would be dishonest to end on such a note. On the credit side we cannot but admire the well of humanitarianism from which he drew his inspiration and concern over the economic well-being of mankind. Perhaps we may feel that he was over-confident that general social improvement was drawn along with economic improvement (for example his views on the lessening of class divisions in society), but at least he was on the side of the angels.

It is unlikely that a bust of Edwin Cannan will be commisioned for the Economist's Hall of Fame, equi-probably he will never be exhibited in the Rogue's Gallery. He did not have what Schumpeter called "vision", but as Schumpeter himself suggested, merely to say this "entirely fails to do justice to the teacher and the man, his commonsense, his lovable outspokenness, the strength of his convictions—virtues that, from standpoints other than our own, more than compensate for the lack of analytic refinement."[1] In the contemporary world of economics where technical facility is taken for granted and models appear with the frequency of branded detergents, it is a salutary experience to savour, if only *en passant*, the virtues of Edwin Cannan.

Finally, we must remember that Cannan was a great teacher and the greatest memorial to a teacher is to be found in the generations of students he produced. Cannan was no exception to this observation.[2]

[1] J. Schumpeter, *History of Economic Analysis*, p. 832.
[2] See *London Essays in Economics in Honour of Edwin Cannan* ,a volume of contributions by some of his ex-students.

March, 1963.

BIBLIOGRAPHY

This bibliography is not exhaustive. It includes all of Cannan's books and articles published in the major economic journals.

BOOKS

Cannan, David Alexander: Trade unions . . . a paper read in Manchester, 1851. Note by Edwin Cannan.

Elementary Political Economy, London, 1888.

A scheme for at once relieving tenants for being rated for the permanent improvement of their landlord's property . . . offered to the House of Commons Select Committee on Town Holdings. Market Weighton 1890.

A History of the Theories of Production and Distribution in English Political Economy from 1776 to 1848. London, 1893, 1894; 2nd ed. London, *King*, 1903; 3rd ed. London, 1920, 1924; London, *Staples*, 1946.

The History of Local Rates in England; five lectures (L.S.E Studies in Economics and Political Science No. 1), London, 1896; 2nd ed. London, *King*, 1912, 1927.

Mr. Edwin Cannan's answers to the questions submitted to him by the Royal Commission in Local Taxation [United Kingdom. Royal Commission on Local Taxation, 1898].

Notes on the population of Oxford, 1901.

King, Joseph (M.P.) and others: The management of private affairs, Oxford, *Clarendon Press*, 1908.

The Economic Outlook, London, *King*, 1912.

Wealth: a brief explanation of the causes of economic welfare. London, 1914; 2nd ed. 1916, 1924; 3rd ed. 1928, 1930, *Staples*, 1946.

Lectures . . . on the theory of public finance: notes arranged in accordance with order of lectures given in 1915–16.

Copy of letter (to the Committee on Prices), 1916.

Furniss, Henry Sanderson, and others: Some economic aspects of international relations. (Ruskin College, Oxford. Reorganization of industry, Series 3), Birmingham, 1917.

Money: its connexion with rising and falling prices. London, *King*, 1918; 2nd ed. London, 1920; 3rd ed. London, 1921; 4th ed. London, 1923; 5th ed. London, 1926; 6th ed. 1929; 7th ed. 1932; 8th ed. 1935.

Coal nationalisation: précis and evidence offered to the Coal Industry Commission. London, 1919.

Ed. The Paper Pound of 1797–1821: a reprint of the Bullion Report, London, 1919; 2nd ed. 1925., 3rd ed. 1963.

An Economist's Protest, London, *King*, 1927.

A Review of Economic Theory. London, *King*, 1929, 1930.

Balance of trade delusions . . . Sidney Ball Lecture . . . 1931 (Oxford. Barnett House. Barnett House Papers. No. 15) London, 1931.

The Changed Outlook in Regard to Population, 1831–1931 (British Association Centenary Meeting, London, 1931 : Section F). London, 1931.

Modern Currency and the Regulation of its Value, London, *King*, 1931.

Economic Scares, London, *King*, 1933.

ARTICLES

ECONOMIC JOURNAL

1894. Vol. IV. " Ricardo in Parliament ", June, pp. 249–61.
" Ricardo in Parliament ", Sept., pp. 409–23.
" Growth of Manchester and Liverpool ", March, pp. 111–14.

1895. Vol. V. " Inequality of Local Rates and its Economic Justification", March, pp. 22–34.
" The Probability of a Cessation of the Growth of Population in England and Wales during the Next Century ", Dec., pp. 505–14.

1897. Vol. VII. " What is Capital ? " June, pp. 278–84.

1898. Vol. VIII. " The Proclamation of 1717 Reducing the Rating of Gold Coins ", March, pp. 135–8.
" Two Letters of Adam Smith's ", Sept., pp. 402–4.

1899. Vol. IX. " Aught Municipal Enterprises to be Allowed to Yield a Profit ? " March, pp. 1–9.

1901. Vol. XI. " Equity and Economy in Taxation "; Dec., pp. 469–80.
" The Census ", June, pp. 230–4.

1902. Vol. XII. " The Practical Utility of Economic Science ", Dec., pp. 459–71.

1903. Vol. XIII. ' The Financial Relations between English Localities ", March, pp. 6–19.

1907. Vol. XVII. " The Proposed Relief of Buildings from Local Rates ", March, pp. 36–46.

1908. Vol. XVIII. " The Principle of Rating : A Reply ", June, pp. 314–19.

1914. Vol. XXIV. " Report of Committee on Local Taxation ", p. 329.

1915. Vol. XXV. " Report of the Committee on Coal Prices ", June, pp. 262–9.

1915. Vol. XXV. Obituary of William Smart, p. 300.

1916. Vol. XXVI. " Report on British Industry after the War ", p. 97.
" A Study in Malthusianism", p. 218.
" The Report on Food Prices ", p. 472.

1917. Vol. XXVII. " Industrial Unrest ", p. 453.

1918. Vol. XXVIII. " Reports on National Expenditure ", p. 101.

1919. Vol. XXIX. " The National Income ", p. 207.

1920. Vol. XXX. " South African Currency ", p. 519.

1921. Vol. XXXI. " The Application of the Theoretical Apparatus of Supply & Demand for Units of Currency ", p. 453.

1922. Vol. XXXII. " Prof. Cassel on Money and Foreign Exchange ", p. 506.
" Recent Memoirs on Currency Policy ", p. 58.

1923. Vol. XXXIII. " The Agricultural Inquiry ", p. 172,

1924. Vol. XXXIV. " Limitation of Currency or Limitation of Credit ? " p. 52.
1928. Vol. XXXVIII. "Report of the Industrial Transference Board ", p. 14.
1930. Vol. XL. " The Problem of Unemployment ".
1931. Vol. XLI. " The Changed Outlook in Regard to Population, 1831–1931 ", p. 519.
1932. Vol. XLII. " The Demand for Labour ", p. 357. " Saving and Usury " : A Symposium ", p. 123.
1933. Vol. XLIII. " The Need for Simpler Economics", p. 367.

ECONOMICA

1921. Vol. I. " Meaning of Bank Deposit ", p. 28.
1922. Vol. II. (Cannan et. al) " Who said ' barren metal '?" p. 105.
1923. Vol. III. " Adam Smith on Twentieth Century Finance ", p. 93.
1924. Vol. IV. " Alfred Marshall, 1842–1924 ". p. 257 " ' Total utility ' and ' consumer's surplus ' ", p. 21.
1926. Vol. VI. " Adam Smith as an economist ", p. 123.
1934. Vol. I (New Series). " Capital and the Heritage of Improvement ", p. 381.

REVIEW OF ECONOMIC THEORY

CHAPTER I

THE ORIGINS OF ECONOMIC THEORY

§ 1. *Ancient and Mediæval Philosophy.*

ECONOMIC matters must have been of great interest to the most primitive man. Even a somewhat unintelligent baboon must have some recognition of the law of diminishing returns from successive accretions of labour, and of the law of diminishing utility from successive additions of any commodity. The story of Adam and Eve is very old, and it suggests the advantage of capital invested in the improvement of land when it pictures Adam as having an easy and pleasant job so long as he was required only to " dress and keep " the " garden " of Eden, and a very hard one when he was thrown out of it and driven to contend with a " cursed " ground all covered with " thorns " and " thistles " or their Eastern equivalents.

The Hebrew scriptures and other ancient records would perhaps repay more economic study than they have yet received. How unintelligently most people read the Old Testament is shown by the fact that few, if any, of us can remember wondering why there is no account in the historical books of an actual year of Jubilee. According to Leviticus, chapter xxv, every fiftieth year should have been marked by an immense reversion of property to owners who had temporarily alienated it up to that date, and yet we hear nothing of forcible evictions or leasehold enfranchisement associations. But though much of economic interest might be found in those old legends and records, I doubt if the most patient research even if combined with a fairly active imagination would find in them much with which to fill a doctoral dissertation on " Ancient Jewish Economic Theory."

We might suppose that the Greek philosophers, who spent

their whole time in thinking and talking, would be sure to drop, from time to time at least, into interesting economic speculation. But we should be disappointed. From the compendious account of the economic ideas of Plato and Aristotle given by D. G. Ritchie under their names in Palgrave's *Dictionary of Political Economy*, a reader is likely to get an impression which is more favourable than it should be, because translation into modern language inevitably gives a certain flavour which is absent in the original. But even thus the total looks small. Plato had some idea of the advantage of division of labour which arises from differences of natural talents. "All things are produced in greater abundance and better in quality and more easily when one man does one thing which is natural to him and does it at the right time and leaves other things alone." In relation to foreign commerce, he says of his citizens, "What they produce at home must be not only enough for themselves, but such both in quantity and quality as to accommodate those from whom their wants are supplied," which shows appreciation of the fact that the real purpose of exports is to procure imports.

Aristotle classified industries into natural and unnatural; the natural industries are the raising of cattle and sheep, agriculture and hunting, which last includes war as a sort of hunting of "men who, though intended by nature to be governed, will not submit; for war of such a kind is naturally just"; the unnatural industries are those which depend on the existence of exchange, namely, trade, money-lending, and working for wages, while wood-cutting and mining fall between the natural and unnatural. On the origin, value, and use of money Aristotle is more advanced, telling us why gold and silver are commonly used, how they were exchanged by weight before the invention of coins was hit upon, and that money is not, as some said, valueless nor, on the other hand, the only valuable thing.

Engaging in its simplicity is his suggestion that it would be useful to those who value the art of making money if someone—some ancient Greek Samuel Smiles—would write histories of the ways in which individual fortunes have been acquired. For example, he says there was Thales the Milesian, who, knowing by meteorology that there would be a great harvest of olives, hired all the olive presses in Chios and Miletus, and then let them out again at high rates. But this does not suggest to him any economic reflections on the power of monopoly—he only remarks that Thales "thus showed to the world that philosophers could easily be rich if they like, but that their ambition is of another sort" (*Politics*, I. 4).

The fact is that these ancient philosophers were not and could not be economists in our sense of persons who are interested in and think and perhaps talk or write about the material welfare of mankind. They professed to be concerned with higher things, and if they were not always so in fact, it was because they thought of themselves rather than because they thought of their fellow-men. Their State, of which they made so much, covered a contemptible little district with one small town in it and a population of which the great majority were not citizens but slaves. It was impossible for economics to develop in such an environment.

Rome was an even more unfavourable situation for economic theory. The Roman Empire, in spite of the great work which it did for its subjects, remained outside them, and we might as well expect economic theory to emerge from the offices of the old East India Company as from ancient Rome.

The European Middle Ages show some progress. Economic matters came under the consideration of theologians who had to decide what actions were allowable and praiseworthy in a Christian man. Sometimes they are supposed to have been considerably influenced by Aristotle, as, for example, in following his condemnation of interest, but we must beware of the danger of supposing certain writers to have been influential merely because their views were much discussed and frequently adopted. We always turn those of our predecessors with whom we happen to agree into "the best authorities," and people have done so in all ages. The mediæval theologians' ideas were really the product of their own environment, as the Greek philosophers' were of theirs.[1]

To us it looks as if there was a very close association between discussion of what is permissible to a Christian man and discussion of what is economically desirable. Can we really make

[1] Instructive accounts of them may be found in Ashley's *Economic History*, in his article on Aquinas in Palgrave's *Dictionary*, and also in Bonar's *Philosophy and Political Economy*.

up our mind whether we *ought* as Christians to give money to a beggar without raising the question whether he will buy whisky for himself or food for his alleged starving children? Can we recommend indiscriminate almsgiving in spite of the universal poverty and degradation to which it is certain to give rise? The mediæval mind, however, was inclined to concentrate its attention on the effects of actions on the soul of the actor, and not to think of the ultimate and general effects likely to follow such action. This was largely the result not of simplicity or childishness, but of the fact that purchases and sales and loans were so much more casual and occasional than they are now, so that it was less obviously necessary to think of the effects of one transaction on future transactions than it is now. This makes an immense difference, as may be illustrated by Ashley's story,[1] taken from Augustine of Hippo, about the honest book-buyer who gave "the just price" for a book although in his ignorance the seller had asked for less. Ashley says, "this to moderns will seem an extreme example" of honesty. Will it? If a new student at the School of Economics—an old one would know better—offered the professor who teaches economic theory the original edition of Cantillon's *Essai* for 7*s.* 6*d.*, would anyone think the professor "extremely" honest if he told the student what the real value was? On the other hand, if a bookseller near the British Museum, who has bought and sold economic books for more than a generation, did not recognise Cantillon, and put the *Essai* at 7*s.* 6*d.* in his catalogue, would not quite honest buyers telegraph for it without any scruple of conscience? Why this difference? Obviously for the reason obscurely implied in the aphorism, "Business is business." The first transaction would be a casual one between persons neither of whom is in the business. In the second the bookseller is carrying on the business of bookselling, and must be taken to understand his business. Business simply could not be carried on if buyers had to go about considering whether they were giving enough as well as whether they were giving too much. The theory of the advantages of division of labour suggests that it is the buyer's duty to look after his side and the seller's to look after his, just as in a court of law we hope that truth will be arrived at by

[1] *Economic History*, Vol. I. p. 133.

one counsel speaking for one party and another for the other party.

But though the mediæval theologians scarcely arrive at economic discussion proper, their writings do indicate the existence of a more favourable atmosphere for the emergence of economics than that in which the ancient philosophers lived. They are more humane in their interests, and their idea of society —the whole Christian Church, if not all mankind—is wider.

They reflected the change, the improvement, I think we may justly say, which had taken place during the "Dark Ages," as they used to be called.

The extent of the change or improvement will be obvious if we look at Sir Thomas More's *Utopia*, 1516, and W. S.'s *Discourse of the Commonweal of this Realm of England*, 1581. The contrast between More's Utopia and Plato's Republic in regard to humanity is great, and there is a very modern ring about the "common greifs" described by W. S., such as rural depopulation and the "dearness of all things, though there be scarceness of nothing." We may perhaps regard modern economics as beginning to emerge about this time, the sixteenth century, though it did not get a name and a recognition of its separate existence till long afterwards.

The principal contributors to the science in the seventeenth century may be classed as the philosophers, ethical and juristic, the mercantilists and the cameralists, including the political arithmeticians.

§ 2. *Seventeenth-century Philosophy.*

I do not propose to trespass into the province which Dr. James Bonar has occupied in his *Philosophy and Political Economy*, 1893. I will only say that the discussions of the juristic and political philosophers of the sixteenth century bear much more directly on economic theory than those of the mediæval theologians. Hugo of Groot, the Dutchman known to the scholarly world as Grotius, in his great treatise *De jure belli et pacis* (*On the Laws of War and Peace*), 1625, quickened thought about the institution of property, contracts, and other economic subjects. The German, Samuel Pufendorf, though apparently despised as a philosopher and a jurist, put a large quantity of useful economics into his *De jure naturæ et gentium* (*On the Law of Nature and Nations*), 1672, and *De officio hominis et civis* (*On the Duty of the Man and the Citizen*), 1673. Our own John Locke in his *Two Treatises on Government*, 1689, explained the origin of property in a way which went far towards suggesting the theory of value which long held the field.

§ 3. *Mercantilism.*

Though the philosophers had no little importance, Espinas is right when he says in his brief but brilliant *Histoire des doctrines économiques*, 1892 :

> " But it was not philosophical interests which prevailed in the realist politics of the sixteenth and seventeenth centuries. Great States were being formed. Uplifted by a new-found consciousness of their unity and their strength, each of them strove for complete independence. . . . Standing armies provided with artillery were being organised, and demanded pecuniary sacrifices such as no nation had been obliged to make since the time of the Roman Empire. The luxury of their courts gave princes a new field for rivalry and prodigality. These enormous expenses were supported by taxes, and it was industry and commerce, carried to a higher degree of activity than ever before, which paid the bill. . . . Religion became nothing but an obstacle to be removed or an instrument to be used. The Church became in France an organ of the State. History entered on an age of gold and iron, and Europe appeared like the scene of a tournament in which every kind of covetousness appeared in conflict " (pp. 135–7).

Mediæval Europe had perhaps tried to believe in the saying, " Blessed are the poor," as applied to individuals, and had not thought much about the aggregations of persons living within certain boundaries : the new Europe believed in the blessedness of rich nations. The mercantile theory—" mercantilism " as it has been the fashion to say since English economic historians took to the study of German—professed to tell how nations could be made rich.

Uninstructed public opinion everywhere and in all ages about which we know anything has always been alarmed by money going out of the country and delighted when it comes in ; and whenever metallic money is used, both the alarm and the pleasure are felt also when the bullion out of which money is made is exported or imported. Throughout the Middle Ages accordingly we find a perpetual attempt by each country to prevent coin and gold and silver bullion from being exported. But this was not mercantilism, for it has nothing specially to do with merchants. Mercantilism proper arose about the beginning of the seventeenth century as the merchants' protest against the prohibition of the exportation of coin and bullion. Those who traded with the East were stimulated to protest by self-interest. Silver was a commodity produced in the West and desired in the East, and its continuous export from the West to the East was consequently profitable. The East India merchants, therefore, very naturally argued against this trade being prohibited, pointing out that to increase the stock of precious metals, coined and uncoined, within a country which contains no natural source of those metals, the only plan is to import more of them than is exported—to have, in other words, " a favourable balance " of imports over exports of precious metal. The prohibition of export, they said, would not help to secure this balance, since in the first place it would be evaded, and in the second place it often happened that an export of precious metal was necessary to start a series of exchanges which would eventually bring in more of that metal than went out. All that was wanted was " a favourable balance of trade," that is, exports of goods (other than precious metal) exceeding in value the imports of goods. If the goods exported were worth more than the goods imported, the balance must be imported in precious metal.

Once propounded by interested merchants, this " balance of trade " theory carried conviction to the mind of every merchant, interested or uninterested. To a merchant trade is profitable, not when he pays out nothing, but when he receives more than he pays out; and as he conceives the nation in his own image, it is very natural for him to think that what is true of his trade must be true of the trade of the whole nation.

One of the earliest and quite the finest expositor of this theory was Thomas Mun, born in 1571. He became a director of the East India Company in 1615, and published in 1621 *A Discourse of Trade unto the East Indies* in defence of the exportation of silver, but his masterpiece was *England's Treasure by Forraign Trade, or the Ballance of our forraign Trade is the Rule of our*

Treasure, which he wrote about 1630, though it was not published till 1664. Adam Smith a century later said that its title "became a fundamental maxim in the political œconomy not of England only, but of all other commercial countries,"[1] which may remind us not to fall into the stupid mistake of supposing that England was alone in adopting the mercantile system.

As is appropriate in a book setting forth the mercantile gospel, *England's Treasure* begins with a glorification of the merchant, who must be "a principal agent" in the great business of enriching the kingdom and supplying the king with treasure, and is "the steward of the kingdom's stock." The "perfect merchant" must not only know all the things we might expect him to know in the present age, but in those pre-specialist days a great deal more. He should be skilled in shipbuilding and navigation, and "although there be no necessity that such a merchant should be a great scholar; yet is it (at least) required that in his youth he learn the Latine tongue, which will the better enable him in all the rest of his endeavours."

After this we come to the enunciation of the mercantile system in Chapter II, entitled, "The means to enrich the Kingdom, and to encrease our Treasure":

> "Although a Kingdom may be enriched by gifts received or by purchase[2] taken from some other Nations, yet these are things uncertain and of small consideration when they happen. The ordinary means therefore to encrease our wealth and treasure is by *Forraign Trade*, wherein wee must ever observe this rule; to sell more to strangers yearly than wee consume of theirs in value. For suppose that when this Kingdom is plentifully served with the Cloth, Lead, Tinn, Iron, Fish, and other native commodities, wee doe yearly export the overplus to forraign Countries to the value of twenty-two hundred thousand pounds; by which means we are enabled beyond the Seas to buy and bring in forraign wares for our use and Consumptions, to the value of twenty hundred thousand pounds; By this order duly kept in our trading, we may rest assured that the Kingdom shall be enriched yearly two hundred thousand pounds, which must be brought to us in so much Treasure; because that part of our stock which is not returned to us in wares must necessarily be brought home in treasure" (pp. 7, 8 in the reprint in Ashley's Economic Classics, 1895).

[1] *Wealth of Nations*, Cannan edition, Vol. I. p. 401.
[2] *I.e.* by forcible acquisition.

Chapter IV seeks to prove, "contrary to the common opinion" (p. 19), that "the Exportation of our Moneys in Trade of Merchandise is a means to encrease our Treasure." If £100,000 be sent to buy 100,000 quarters of wheat in the East, and then the wheat is sold to Spain or Italy for £200,000, "the Kingdom hath doubled that Treasure" (p. 21). It is as good as sowing seed. "If we only behold the actions of the husbandman in the seed-time[1] when he casteth away much good corn into the ground, we will rather accompt him a mad man than a husbandman: but when we consider his labours in the harvest which is the end of his endeavours, we find the worth and plentiful encrease of his actions" (p. 27).

The last chapter of the book consists of an emphatic restatement of the thesis that

> "so much Treasure only will be brought in or carried out of a Commonwealth as the Forraign Trade doth over or under ballance in value. And this must come to pass by a Necessity beyond all resistance. . . . Behold then the true form and worth of forraign Trade, which is The great Revenue of the King, The honour of the Kingdom, the Noble profession of the Merchant, The School of our Arts, The supply of our wants, The Employment of our poor, The Improvement of our Lands, The Nurcery of our Mariners, The walls of the Kingdoms, The means of our Treasure, The Sinnews of our wars, The terror of our Enemies" (p. 119).

In itself and without the erroneous corollaries which were attached to it, the balance of trade theory was and is perfectly correct. A country which does not itself produce gold and silver and which is not in a position to compel other countries to give it gold and silver for nothing, must either go without those metals or give other commodities or services for as much of them as it wants. It is true, of course, that the sum of the value of all exported goods other than the gold and silver at the national frontier (even if correctly recorded by the custom house), minus the sum of the value of imported goods other than gold and silver, will not give the value of the net imports of gold and silver unless allowance is made for freight and various other things dealt with in the modern text-books. But Mun, as his Chapter XX shows, and the more intelligent of his followers,

[1] The long *s* in the original unfortunately led to this being printed "feed-time" in Ashley's edition.

were alive to this fact, and prepared to take account of all the items which were of any importance in their time.

Nevertheless, the theory had its bad side both in regard to general economic thought and in regard to political practice.

As to general economic thought, the effect of the prominence given to the question of how to get more gold and silver into a country was to strengthen the vulgar view that what is wanted in economic matters is "plenty of money," and so to obscure the fact that what is really wanted is not a large quantity of the medium of exchange, but a large supply of goods of all kinds. It is no use to say that every intelligent person must always have known that money is only wanted in order to procure food, raiment, house-room and other goods. In fact, quite recently we have seen some of the most intelligent peoples in Europe allowing their Governments to flood them with a plethora of money and complaining at the same time of shortages of currency. The great majority of people are not intelligent—at any rate in economic matters—and they were certainly no better in the seventeenth century than they are now.

"Money, in common language," Adam Smith observed, "frequently signifies wealth; and this ambiguity of expression has rendered this popular notion so familiar to us, that even they who are convinced of its absurdity are very apt to forget their own principles, and in the course of their reasonings to take it for granted as a certain and undeniable truth. Some of the best English writers upon commerce set out with observing, that the wealth of a country consists, not in its gold and silver only, but in its lands, houses and consumable goods of all different kinds. In the course of their reasonings, however, the lands, houses and consumable goods seem to slip out of their memory, and the strain of their argument frequently supposes that all wealth consists in gold and silver, and that to multiply those metals is the great object of national industry and commerce." (*Wealth of Nations*, Vol. I. pp. 415–16.)

The bad side of the balance of trade theory in practical politics is suggested by Mun's own statement: "We must ever observe this rule, to sell more to strangers than we consume of theirs in value." It was supposed that some pains must be taken by the Government of the country to secure that this "favourable balance of trade" should exist. Ordinary unfettered trade might be trusted to bring in ordinary commodities which were wanted, but not to bring in gold and silver. Hence came a mass of duties, bounties and regulations intended to discourage importation of goods and to encourage exportation. Each country was regarded as a unit, and the interest of each was supposed to be opposed to that of all the rest, as the great object of each of them was to get as much gold and silver as possible at the expense of the others. Trade between nations was looked on very much as some barbarians are said to have regarded trade in general, not as a method of co-operation but as a sort of tolerated robbery. The paramount aim of a statesman seemed to be the making of ingenious arrangements for cheating the foreigner out of some of his gold and silver.[1]

I cannot conclude this section without entering a protest against the misuse of the term "mercantile" which has crept into modern economics under the influence of the German "historical" school. Adam Smith brought the term "Mercantile System" into common use by writing his chapter, "Of the Principle of the Commercial or Mercantile System." He gave his Book IV the title, "Of Systems of political Œconomy," and in the Introduction to it he says, "Political œconomy considered as a branch of the science of a statesman or legislator proposes two distinct objects. . . . It proposes to enrich both the people and the sovereign." Different circumstances have given rise to "two different systems of political œconomy with regard to enriching the people. The one may be called the system of commerce, the other that of agriculture." He will endeavour to explain both, beginning with the system of commerce, and he proceeds to head Chapter I with the words, "Of the Principle of the Commercial or Mercantile System." After this we can scarcely doubt that, finding that the Physiocrats had what was called in French a "système" which laid unusual stress on agriculture, he devised the name "commercial or mercantile system" for the prevailing policy which laid great stress on commerce. It is noteworthy that at first he seems to prefer "commercial" to "mercantile" (see Vol. I. pp. 437 and 452): later he drops into "mercantile system," and the name was adopted by his followers, and in recent times

[1] For a scathing but just denunciation of the evil effects of the mercantile theory see W. A. S. Hewins' *English Trade and Finance*, 1892, p. xxxiv.

transformed into the German "mercantilismus" and English "mercantilism."

Now what did Smith mean by the commercial or mercantile system?

He begins the chapter on its "Principle" with the words, "That wealth consists in money, or in gold and silver, is a popular notion," and goes on to ridicule this popular notion, which may suggest to a careless reader that he intended it to be the principle of the commercial or mercantile system. But he does not say that it is, and there seems little reason to doubt that the first five paragraphs are merely introductory, and that he intended the description of the mercantile system to begin at the sixth paragraph. He has told us that "anciently" the practice of most European nations was to prohibit the exportation of the precious metals, and then the sixth paragraph begins: "When those countries became commercial, the merchants found this prohibition upon many occasions extremely inconvenient." The words "commercial" and "merchants" in this sentence are clearly intended to introduce "the commercial or mercantile system," and we must look to what follows for Smith's interpretation of his own term. He says the merchants argued (1) that exportation of gold and silver ought to be allowed, because it often eventually led to the importation of more than had gone out, since goods were bought from the East with gold and silver by English merchants and then sold to some other country for a larger quantity of gold and silver. And (2) they also argued that prohibition could not be actually enforced. So they said that prohibition of export was useless, and what was wanted was a favourable balance of trade securing a net importation. After criticising this idea at some length Smith says:

> "The two principles being established . . . that wealth consisted in gold and silver, and that these metals could be brought into a country which had no mines only by the balance of trade . . . it necessarily became the great object of political œconomy to diminish as much as possible the importation of foreign goods for home consumption and to increase as much as possible the exportation of the produce of domestic industry" (Vol. I. p. 416).

It is obvious that Smith could not have meant either or both of "*two* principles" to be "*the* principle" of the mercantile system, and there can be little doubt that he understood the principle to be that to which those two lead up, namely, the encouragement of exportation and discouragement of importation.

In accordance with this, the "mercantile theory" should be the doctrine that States must not leave the balance of trade to take care of itself, but must encourage exportation and discourage importation, and "mercantilism" should be (according to the context) either this theory or the practice which it recommends. This is quite a convenient sense for the term, and I fail to see any convenience whatever in the sense which some German writers and English writers following them have given to mercantilism by treating it as equivalent to economic nationalism inspired by military considerations.

§ 4. *Cameralism and Political Arithmetic.*

The name Cameralist is derived from *Camera*, the King's chamber, in which he was thought to spend his time discussing with his Ministers the ever-present problem of how to make ends meet. It is the "counting-house" of the old rhyme,

> "The King was in his counting house, counting out his money,
> The Queen was in the parlour eating bread and honey."

Cameralists are those who wrote from the point of view of Ministers of State.

The mercantilists were not wanting in patriotism and loyalty and believed that the policy they recommended would be good for their respective States; but State revenue was not their immediate concern. The cameralists, on the other hand, thought of the State in the first place. Antoine de Montchrétien may be taken as an extreme example. His *Traicté de l'Œconomie politique*, 1615 [1] is divided into Book I, "Of the utility of the mechanical arts and the regulation of manufactures"; Book II, "Of Commerce"; Book III, "Of Navigation," and Book IV, "Of the example and principal duties of the Sovereign." If the language were modernised, a reader might glance over many pages without hitting on anything very obviously suggesting

[1] A reprint was published in 1889, edited by Th. Funck-Brentano, who put forward on Montchrétien's behalf claims which were vigorously contested by W. J. Ashley in the *English Historical Review*, Vol. VI. p. 779.

that the book is three hundred years old. France is to be, as she easily could be, self-supporting, and to cease importing nasty cheap things from Germany of which scarcely two or three per cent. were good for anything, and which draw a large sum of money out of the country every year. Improvements in transport have brought imported articles to places which were not formerly incommoded in that way, and are now "smothered" by them. Imported books poison the French genius and corrupt French morals, and so on. But the ruling motive is not quite the same as that of modern economists, whether good or bad. The book is addressed to the King and the Queen-Mother. It censures Aristotle and Xenophon for not having recognised that the science of acquisition is as useful to States as to families, and then expresses surprise that these writers have forgotten this part of public administration "to which the necessities and burdens of the State require us to give our chief attention" (p. 32). The State is the King, and while the King ought to "regard nothing except the welfare, repose and contentment" of his people (p. 338), this is thought of from the King's end, so to speak. It is not that the people must have a good king who will serve them well, but the King must do his best for them, so that he may have a good reputation on earth and escape "eternal damnation" when he dies (p. 340).

In England the monarch was of less account than in France and the German States, and few of his subjects took much interest in his prospects in the next world. But towards the end of the seventeenth century a good deal of attention was given by servants of the Crown to "Political Arithmetic," or what we should call economic statistics, in consequence of their connection with the public revenue. "Political Arithmetic" was so called because "things of government . . . the glory of the Prince and the happiness and greatness of the people are by the ordinary rules of arithmetic brought into a sort of demonstration." [1]

The inventor of the term, and by far the greatest genius among the political arithmeticians, was Sir William Petty, born at Romsey in Hampshire in 1623. The son of a clothier there,

[1] Lord Shelbourne's dedication prefixed to Petty's *Political Arithmetick*. In C. H. Hull's edition of *Sir William Petty's Economic Writings*, 1899, p. 239.

he went to sea as an apprentice at the age of fifteen, but after ten months he luckily broke his leg and was therefore put ashore in Normandy, where his scholarly attainments and commercial ability led to his receiving further education from the Jesuit fathers at Caen. After a short service in the navy he went back to the Continent and studied in the Netherlands and France. In 1646 he returned to Romsey and carried on his father's business, but at the same time busied himself with mechanical inventions, one of which was a letter-duplicator. In 1649, on the strength apparently of some study of anatomy at Paris, three or four years earlier, he went to Oxford and was almost immediately made a doctor of physic. In the next year he showed his skill by resuscitating a woman who had been hanged at Oxford for murdering her child.[1] Early in the following year he was made Professor of Anatomy, and at once obtained leave of absence for two years, before the end of which he was appointed Physician-General to the Army in Ireland, but soon took in hand the Down Survey for the forfeited lands. This led directly to his first work, *A Treatise of Taxes and Contributions, showing the Nature and Measures of Crown-Lands, Assessements, Customs, Poll-Moneys, Lotteries, Benevolence, Penalties, Monopolies, Offices, Tythes, Raising of Coins, Harth-Money, Excize, &c., With several intersperst Discourses and Digressions concerning Warres, The Church, Universities, Rents and Purchases, Usury and Exchange, Banks and Lombards, Registries for Conveyances, Beggars, Ensurance, Exportation of Money, Wool, Free-Ports, Coins, Housing, Liberty of Conscience, &c. The same being frequently applied to the present State and Affairs of Ireland,* 1662. Some of these subjects may seem rather irrelevant to political arithmetic, but it is well not to judge them too hastily.

[1] Though it is quite irrelevant, I cannot forbear quoting from Lord E. Fitzmaurice's *Life of Sir W. Petty*, 1895, p. 19, the contemporary account of what happened before Petty found poor Ann Green in the dissecting-room. "She seemed to take an unconscionable time in dying, so her friends went to assist her in getting out of this world, some of them thumping her on the breasts, others hanging with all their weight upon her legs, sometimes lifting her up and then pulling her down again with a sudden jerk." In spite of this treatment, she showed signs of life when the coffin was opened in the dissecting-room, "which being observed by a lusty fellow who stood by, he, thinking to do an act of charity in ridding her out of the reliques of a painful life, stamped several times on her breast and stomach with all the force he could." At this point Petty and a colleague appeared and undertook the resuscitation.

"The Church," for example, is a proper public charge because it is so easy "to elude the Laws of man, to commit unproveable crimes, to corrupt and divert Testimonies, to wrest the sense and meaning of the Laws, &c.," that it is necessary to have "a publick Charge wherewith to have men instructed in the Laws of God, that take notice of evil thoughts and designs and much more of secret deeds, and that punisheth eternally in another world what man can but slightly chastise in this." (*Economic Writings*, ed. Hull, p. 19.)

For our present purposes the interesting part of the *Treatise* is the mention of the small proportion which money bears to the whole mass of material goods. On one page we find that "of all the wealth of this Nation, *viz.* Lands, Housing, Shipping, Commodities, Furniture, Plate, and Money," only one-hundredth is in coin, and "perhaps there is scarce six millions of Pounds now in England, that is but twenty shillings a head" (*Ibid.*, p. 34).

This idea is further worked out in *Verbum Sapienti*—A Word to the Wise—which Petty published as an appendix to the *Political Anatomy of Ireland* in 1691, though it must have been written in 1666. Its first chapter is headed "Containing several Computations of the Wealth of the Kingdom" (England and Wales), and gives us a complete account of what we should call the national capital and income. The population of about six millions is calculated to have an annual expense "for food, housing, cloaths and all other necessaries" of £40 millions. Then the capital value of the land is put at £144 millions, that of the houses at 30 millions, the shipping at 3, the cattle at 36, the "wares, merchandise and utensils of plate and furnitures" at 31, and the coined gold and silver at 6 millions, making a total capital of £250 millions. The 144 millions' worth of land "yields 8 millions per annum rent," and as the other property may be taken to yield a somewhat higher percentage, "suppose it to yield 7 [millions], making the whole annual proceed 15" millions. This 15 millions is what we should call the whole income derived from property. It remains to compute the income derived from labour, and this Petty goes on to do in the next chapter:

"Now if the Annual proceed of the Stock or Wealth of the Nation yields but 15 millions, and the expence be 40, then the labour of the People must furnish the other 25; which may be done, if but half of them, viz. 3 millions, earned but £8 6*s*. 8*d*. per annum, which is done at 7*d*. per diem, abating the 52 Sundays and half as many other days for accidents, as Holy days, sickness, recreations, &c." (*Econ. Writings*, ed. Hull, p. 108).

Inquiring in Chapter V "how much money is necessary to drive the trade of the nation," he supposes that as wages are paid weekly and rents quarterly, the whole stock of money may be taken to circulate about once in seven weeks, and that 5½ millions will be enough for an annual expense of 40 millions. He thinks it possible to have too much money: "For money is but the Fat of the Body-politick, whereof too much doth as often hinder its Agility as too little makes it sick." [1]

In face of so clear a conception of the national capital and income and of the smallness of the aggregate stock of money compared with the whole of the capital, the modern reader may feel surprised that general economic theory did not spring into existence in Petty's lifetime or soon afterwards. It seems to us, in our environment, so natural and easy to visualise this "40 millions" of "expense" as a collection of commodities and services valued at £40 million, and to discuss intelligently the general causes of its increase or decrease. But in fact there was still a long row to hoe before the idea of a "real income" could be formed and the causes of its increase and decrease could be intelligently discussed.

Dr. Charles Davenant (1656–1714) advanced matters a little. He was commissioner of excise from 1683 to 1689 and Inspector-General of exports and imports from 1705. His work and influence are inextricably mixed up with those of Gregory King (1648–1712), who let him have the free use of his manuscript, *Natural and Political Observations and Conclusions upon the state and condition of England*, 1696, which was not printed and published till 1801.[2] King was Lancaster Herald, and was employed by Ogilby, the producer of the earliest and the finest

[1] He goes on to admit, however, "'Tis true that as Fat lubricates the motion of Muscles, feeds in want of Victuals, fills up uneven Cavities, and beautifies the Body, so doth Money in the State quicken its Action, feeds from abroad in the time of Dearth at Home; even accounts by reason of it's divisibility, and beautifies the whole, altho more especially the particular persons that have it in plenty."

[2] As an annex to George Chalmers' *Estimate of the Comparative Strength of Great Britain*, new ed., 1801.

road-book of England, so that he had probably seen with his own eyes far more of the country than many did in those days. Davenant, following King, improved upon Petty by adding the idea of national "income" to that of national expense and explaining the relation between the two.

"By Annual Income," he says, "we mean the whole that arises in any Country from Land and its Product, from Foreign Trade and Domestick Business, as Arts, Manufactures, &c. And by Annual Expence we understand what is of Necessity consum'd to Cloath and Feed the People, or what is requisite for their Defence in time of War or for their Ornament in time of Peace. And where the Annual Income exceeds the Expence, there is a Superlucration arising, which may be call'd Wealth or National Stock." [1]

In England the income exceeded the expense by about £2,400,000, and this was the annual addition to "the general Stock of England." [2]

Protesting against a critic's desire to confine "the riches of a people" to gold and silver, Davenant says:

"With submission to better judgments we think it has a signification far more extensive. We understand that to be wealth which maintains the prince and the general body of his people in plenty, ease, and safety. We esteem that to be treasure which for the use of man has been converted from gold and silver into buildings and improvements of the country; as also other things convertible into those metals, as the fruits of the earth, manufactures, or foreign commodities and stock of shipping." [3]

Moreover, he quotes King's calculations of "the product" of the land of England, which not only specify the different kinds of agricultural produce and their respective values, but in most cases give the quantities as well, thus tending towards the later conception of a national produce or income. But he gets no further than this. He was really far from recognising the important part that produce or "income" was going to play in the economics of the future. He spoiled his proposition that "even perishable goods may be held the riches of a nation"

[1] *Discourses on the Public Revenues and of the Trade of England*, 1698, Pt. I. Disc. v. (in *Political and Commercial Works*, ed. Sir Chas. Whitworth, 1771, Vol. I. pp. 251–2), quoted by Davenant himself in *An Essay upon the Probable Methods of making a People Gainers in the Ballance of Trade*, 1699, pp. 140–1 (in *Works*, Vol. II. pp. 264–5).

[2] *Ballance of Trade*, p. 53 (in *Works*, Vol. II. p. 204).

[3] *Discourses*, Pt. II. i; in *Works*, Vol. I. p. 381.

by adding the condition, "if they are convertible, though not converted, into gold and silver."[1] He ruined the effect of the discussion of the product of the land by embedding it in an essay on how to make a nation gain in the balance of trade, thus subordinating what was substantial to the mercantile will-o'-the-wisp.

§ 5. *Cantillon's Essay on the Nature of Commerce in General.*

The next great landmark is the somewhat mysterious *Essai sur la Nature du Commerce en général,* published anonymously in Paris in 1755 with a false imprint (a thing not unusual at that time and place), "*à Londres, chez Fletcher Gyles dans Holborn,*" and always attributed to Richard Cantillon, a financier of Irish extraction who had business in Paris, and was murdered by his servant in London in 1734. The last note of time it contains is 1730, and it appears to have been read and used by some persons before publication in 1755. Mirabeau is known to have had it in manuscript, and several of the articles in Postlethwayt's *Dictionary of Commerce,* 1751, contain long unacknowledged extracts from it.[2] Its language is a kind of French which suggests at once that it was either written in French by an author whose own tongue was English, or written first in English and then translated into French by the English author or some other English-speaking person.

Someone has called Cantillon "the economists' economist," meaning that his influence was on the leaders of thought rather than on the rank and file. In fact the Essay had several editions within a few years of 1755, and was very highly thought of at the time, but, probably in part owing to its mongrel Franco-English character, it soon sank into oblivion. Neither the old *Dictionnaire d'économie politique,* 1852, nor the *Nouveau Dictionnaire* of Say and Chailley, 1894, thought Cantillon worthy of inclusion, and it is highly improbable that any of the great English economists of the nineteenth century before Jevons knew more of him than that he is once quoted by Adam Smith.

[1] *Discourses,* Pt. II. i; in *Works,* Vol. I. p. 382.

[2] See the article in the *Contemporary Review,* January 1881, reprinted in Jevons' *Principles of Economics,* 1905; Henry Higgs' article in the *Economic Journal,* June 1891; articles on Banking, Barter and Interest in Postlethwayt's *Dictionary.* An exact reprint of the *Essai* was published by Harvard University in 1891.

Jevons rediscovered him and wrote an account of his work in the *Contemporary Review* for January 1881, from which the following passage may be taken, as it can scarcely be improved upon:

"The book . . . is divided into three Parts. . . . The First Part is to some extent a general introduction to Political Economy, beginning with a definition of wealth, and then discussing the association of people in societies, in villages, towns, cities and capital cities; the wages of labour; the theory of value; the par between labour and land; the dependence of all classes upon landed proprietors; the multiplication of population; and the use of gold and silver. The Second Part takes up the subjects of barter, prices, circulation of money, interest, etc., and is a complete little treatise on currency, probably more profound than anything of the same size since published on the subject. The Third Part treats of foreign commerce, the foreign exchanges, banking, and 'refinements of credit.' Judged by the knowledge and experience of the time, this third part especially is almost beyond praise, and shows that Richard Cantillon had a sound and pretty complete comprehension of many questions about which pamphleteers are still wrangling and blundering, and perplexing themselves and other people. The *Essai* . . . is a systematic and connected treatise, going over in a concise manner nearly the whole field of economics with the exception of taxation. It is thus, more than any other book I know, the first treatise on economics. Sir William Petty's *Political Arithmetic* and his *Treatise of Taxes and Contributions* are wonderful books in their way and at their time, but, compared with Cantillon's *Essai*, they are mere collections of casual hints. . . . Cantillon's essay is, more emphatically than any other single work, 'the Cradle of Political Economy.'

"The opening sentence of the first chapter, '*De la Richesse*,' is especially remarkable, and is as follows: '*La Terre est la source ou la matière d'où l'on tire la Richesse ; le travail de l'Homme est la forme qui la produit : et la Richesse en elle-même n'est autre chose que la nourriture, les commodités et les agrémens de la vie.*'

"This sentence strikes the keynote, or rather the leading chord, of the science of economics."[1]

All this is true, and the praise is not in the least overdone. We may add that it is in the *Essai* that we first find the undertaker of business (translated *entrepreneur*) playing the great part which he is given in subsequent treatises of what the socialists love to call "bourgeois economics."

[1] Pp. 164–5 in the reprint in Jevons' *Principles of Economics*.

It is curious that a business man, and one too who by all accounts was remarkably successful in his business, should have produced so academical a treatise—academical in the sense that the author seems to have had no axe to grind, no pet policy to advocate, but to have been actuated solely by a desire to explain economic organisation to his readers.

§ 6. *Academic Teaching in Scotland.*

About the time that Cantillon was showing that a purely didactic treatise could be written on general economics, Francis Hutcheson, Professor of Moral Philosophy in the University of Glasgow, was showing that academic instruction could be given on the subject. He found it desirable to explain to his class the advantages of social life arising from the specialisation of persons to particular kinds of labour. He told them that industry was necessary, and that men must be stimulated to industry by self-interest and family affection. He discussed money, and put forward a cost of production theory of value and a fructification theory of interest. Moreover, he vigorously opposed the doctrine that luxury, intemperance and other vices made people work and were therefore to be regarded as beneficial from what we should call the economic point of view. Bernard Mandeville had taught this doctrine in doggerel verses which he called *The Grumbling Hive: or Knaves Turn'd Honest*, in 1705, and republished with a prose addition in 1714 as *The Fable of the Bees: or Private Vices, Public Benefits.* He very naturally scandalised the moralists, and his work was ordered to be burnt by the common hangman—"publicity" which any modern author or publisher would be glad to secure.

Hutcheson exercised great influence over his students, and one of his greatest admirers among them was a boy from Kirkcaldy in Fife, named Adam Smith, who was born in 1723, and attended the Glasgow classes from 1737 to the spring of 1740, when he was sent to Oxford with one of the Snell exhibitions given at Glasgow and tenable at Balliol College. John Rae in the *Life of Adam Smith*, 1895, has collected all that has so far been discovered about his six-year stay at Balliol. He seems to have read travels and other books voraciously, but probably got little or no instruction from either the College or the University.

Oxford was then at a very low intellectual ebb, fully justifying the condemnation Smith passed upon the English universities long afterwards.[1] In some way which has never been explained, he obtained a reputation which led to his being able to lecture in Edinburgh, first on English literature and then in 1750–1 on some subject which in his hands included the advocacy of "natural liberty" and freedom of commerce.

In 1751 he was elected to the professorship of Logic in his own university of Glasgow, and just as he entered into office the illness of the Professor of Moral Philosophy caused him to be asked to take the duties of that professorship as well. In April 1752 he was translated from the Logic to the Moral Philosophy Chair, but for the whole session he was doing the work of two professors at once. I mention this detail because it excuses or explains (if either excuse or explanation is needed) the closeness with which in his moral philosophy lectures he followed Hutcheson, and also perhaps the prominence which economics assumed in them.[2] Being much pressed for time, he would very naturally make great use of his notes of the lectures of his admired predecessor and master, and throw in as much as possible of his own Edinburgh lectures. What he was teaching a few years after this hurried beginning may be gathered in part from the *Theory of Moral Sentiments* which he published in 1759, and from the student's notes of his lectures on Jurisprudence which I was lucky enough to be able to edit in 1896.[3]

His Jurisprudence lectures were divided between Justice, Police, Revenue and Arms, and the two middle parts, Police and Revenue, cover what we call economics and public finance.

"But how in the world," the modern reader asks, "did economics come to be dealt with under 'Police'?" It came about in this way. Police is the French form of the Latin *politia*, which is nothing but the Greek πολιτεία, government, but in its French form had become specialised so as to signify the province of government which has to do with security, markets and sanitation. A book which is known to have been included in Adam

[1] *Wealth of Nations*, Vol. II. pp. 250 ff.
[2] See on this W. R. Scott, *Francis Hutcheson*, 1900, pp. 230–43.
[3] *Lectures on Justice, Police, Revenue and Arms, delivered in the University of Glasgow by Adam Smith, reported by a Student in* 1763, edited with an introduction and notes by Edwin Cannan, 1896.

Smith's library,[1] Bielfeld's *Institutions politiques*, 1760, tells us that when the Chief of the Paris Police was being admitted to office in 1667, he was told that the King required of him security, cleanliness and cheapness (*sûreté, netteté, bon-marché*), which three things, Bielfeld says, " comprise the whole of police " (vol. i. p. 99). So Smith told his Glasgow class :

> " Police is the second general division of jurisprudence. The name is French, and is originally derived from the Greek πολιτεία, which properly signified the policy of civil government, but now it only means the regulation of the inferior parts of government, viz., cleanliness, security, and cheapness or plenty " (*Lectures*, p. 154).

But he had very little to say about cleanliness and security. They were " too mean to be considered in a general discourse of this kind." Cleanliness he seems to have regarded as merely the " proper method of carrying dirt from the streets," about which he had nothing to suggest, though it was a thing certainly not unimportant when the streets were still largely receptacles for what now is put in the dust-bin or the sewer. Security he did think worth a few words. Safety, he says, cannot be secured by a multitude of regulations, and the best police for preventing crimes is the introduction of commerce and manufactures, which make the population independent instead of consisting of a crowd of retainers or menial servants. This leaves the field clear for " cheapness." Now if cheapness is to be attained by police regulation of prices, by putting profiteers in the pillory, stopping speculation, and other devices of that nature, a treatise on cheapness might come tolerably near our modern idea of a treatise on " police." But Smith thought that cheapness was secured by plenty, and that plenty was better secured by letting people provide for themselves in their own way than by making police regulations, so that whatever it may have been when he began to lecture at Glasgow, by the time he left off, the " police " part of his lectures contained very little about police in any sense of the word. He expanded " cheapness " into " cheapness or plenty," and the consideration of " plenty " led him to endeavour to explain the natural wants of mankind, the division of labour and how opulence arises from it, the nature of prices and money, the absurdity of regulations intended to secure a favourable balance

[1] See James Bonar, *Catalogue of the Library of Adam Smith*, p. 13.

of trade, the theory of interest, the foreign exchanges, the causes why wealth increases so slowly, and the influence of commerce on manners.

Under " Revenue " Smith's lectures included a discussion of taxes and also, in consequence of their connection with national debts, an explanation of stocks and stockjobbing.

We may perhaps hazard a guess that the " causes of the slow progress of opulence " and the " influence of commerce on manners " were the whole or part of the Edinburgh economic lectures, served up again with little alteration.

The " Police " and " Revenue " lectures are much more like a modern treatise on general economic theory than Sir James Steuart's *Principles of Political Economy*, published in two great quarto volumes in 1767. This was divided into Book I, " Of Population and Agriculture," 160 pages; Book II, " Of Trade and Industry," 360 pages; Book III, " Of Money and Coin," 219 pages; Book IV, " Of Credit and Debts," 381 pages, and Book V, " Of Taxes and the proper application of their amount," 165 pages. Steuart was a thorough believer in the old mercantilist beggar-my-neighbour-nation policy. In chap. xv of Book II he says that in Book I,

> " luxury was looked on with a favourable eye, and every augmentation of superfluity was considered as a method of advancing population. We were then employed in drawing mankind, as it were, out of a state of idleness, in order to increase their numbers and engage them to cultivate the earth. We had no occasion to divide them into societies having separate interests, because the principles we treated of were common to all. We therefore considered the industrious, who are the providers, and the luxurious, who are the consumers, as children of the same family, and as being under the care of the same father.
>
> " We are now engaged in a more complex operation; we represent different societies, animated with a different spirit; some given to industry and frugality, others to dissipation and luxury. This creates separate interests among nations, and every one must be supposed under the government of a statesman who is wholly taken up in advancing the good of those he governs, though at the expence of other societies which lie round him."

There is nothing even in the First Book of Steuart's *Principles* so like a modern discussion of the nature and causes of the wealth of society in general as we find in Smith's lectures when he treats of the manner in which division of labour improves productive power and of the causes of the slow progress of opulence.

But though Smith's lectures went far towards what was afterwards called a theory of production, they failed to put forward anything like what was afterwards called the theory of distribution. They said a good deal about general wealth—the wealth of society as a whole—but very little about the differences in the wealth enjoyed by different classes within the society. For the origin of this side of general theory, as well as for the particular form taken by the theory of production, we have to look across the Channel to France on the eve of her Revolution.

§ 7. *Physiocracy in France.*

Restrictions and regulations had hampered internal commerce in France much more than in England, and protests had long been made. Turgot says, "In all ages the desire of commerce in all nations has been embodied in these two words: liberty and security (*protection*), but especially liberty. We know the saying of M. Le Gendre to M. Colbert: *laissez-nous faire.*"[1] The phrase, shortened to *laissez-faire*, has been incorporated into the English language because even the full form of it is incapable of terse translation: the literalist's suggestion, "Let us do," is quite unacceptable: "let us be" or "let us alone" suggests inactivity; and "let us get on with our business in our own way," which gives the sense very well, is too long and flat.

Men and women and children have always protested against interference with their activities, and we can well imagine that some equivalent of "*laissez-nous faire*" was frequently heard in the family circle of Adam. The specialisation and popularisation of the maxim is attributed to Vincent de Gournay, a merchant who lived from 1712 to 1759. He was not an author of any importance, but he exercised considerable influence over subsequent thought by conversations with the economic writers of his time, especially Turgot, who, perhaps idealising him a little, says in a passage which gives a good idea of the state of things prevailing when de Gournay was made an intendant of commerce in 1751:

[1] *Éloge de Gournay* in *Œuvres de Turgot*, ed. Daire, Vol. I. p. 288.

" He was astonished to find that a citizen could neither make nor sell anything without having bought the right to do so by getting at great expense his admission into a corporation. . . . He thought that a worker who had made a piece of cloth had added something real to the aggregate riches of the State, and that if this cloth was inferior to some other cloth, there would be found among the multitude of consumers someone whom this very inferiority would suit better than a more costly perfection. He was very far from believing that this piece of cloth in default of complying with certain regulations should be cut every four yards and the unfortunate man who made it condemned to pay a fine sufficient to reduce a whole family to beggary. . . . He did not think it desirable that the manufacture of a piece of cloth should involve a plea and a tiresome discussion to ascertain whether it conformed to a long and often obscure regulation, nor that this discussion should take place between a manufacturer who could not read and an inspector who could not manufacture. . . .

" Nor had he imagined that in a kingdom where the order of succession was only established by custom, and where the application of the death penalty for several crimes is still left to the discretion of the courts, the Government would have condescended to regulate by express laws the length and breadth of each piece of cloth, and the number of threads of which it must be composed, and to consecrate with the seal of the legislature four quarto volumes full of these important details; and also to pass innumerable statutes dictated by the spirit of monopoly, of which the whole object is to discourage industry, to concentrate commerce in a small number of hands by the multiplication of formalities and expenses, by the requirement of apprenticeships and journeymanships of ten years for trades which can be learnt in ten days, by the exclusion of those who are not sons of masters, of those who are born outside certain limits, by the prohibition of the employment of women in textile manufactures, etc., etc.

" He had not imagined that in a kingdom subject to one and the same prince, all the towns would regard each other as enemies, would arrogate to themselves the right of preventing Frenchmen called foreigners from working inside their boundary, of opposing the sale and free passage of the commodities of a neighbouring province, and of thus fighting, for the sake of a trifling interest, the general interest of the State, etc., etc.

" He was no less astonished to see the Government occupy itself with regulating the price of each commodity, proscribing one kind of industry in order by that to make another flourish; putting particular hindrances in the way of the sale of the provisions which are most necessary for life; prohibiting the accumulation of stores of a thing of which the harvest varies every year while its consumption is always much the same; prohibiting the export of a thing subject to extreme depressions of price, and fancying that it ensured abundance of corn by making the condition of the cultivator more uncertain and unhappy than that of all other citizens, etc." (*Éloge de Gournay* in *Œuvres*, Vol. I. pp. 266–9).

He knew, Turgot adds, that some of these abuses had once prevailed over a great part of Europe, and that "vestiges of them still remained in England," but he knew also that for the last hundred years "all enlightened persons, whether in Holland or in England, regarded them as the remains of Gothic barbarism and of the feebleness of all governments, which had neither known the importance of public liberty nor how to protect that liberty from the attacks made by the spirit of monopoly and personal interest."

So, as another of his admirers, Du Pont de Nemours, tells us, he decided that commerce should "never be ransomed or regimented": he adopted "this maxim, *Laissez faire et laissez passer*," "Let people do what they want, and let them and their goods go where they please."

The merchants and manufacturers of France do not seem to have been attracted by de Gournay's slogan, but the cry for freedom from regimentation went very well with the cult of Nature which was becoming prevalent among the political thinkers; and as, of all the arts, agriculture seems nearest to Nature and was in France particularly oppressed by regimentation it is not surprising that the cry for freedom became coupled with the championship of the economic importance of agriculture as compared with other industries. Freedom and agriculture were both championed by the little band known to later generations as the Physiocrats (because they believed in the rule of Nature), but to their contemporaries as the *économistes*, of whom the revered head was François Quesnay (1694–1774), the Court physician. Du Pont de Nemours, who had better opportunities of knowing the doctrines of this band than anyone else, says that about 1750 de Gournay and Quesnay, approaching from different directions, arrived at the same conclusions. De Gournay, the merchant, thought of the merchant's side: Quesnay, "born on a farm, the son of a landowner, and a good farmer himself," thought of agriculture, and, "inquiring whence come the riches of nations, found that they spring (*naissent*) only from the kinds of labour in which *nature* and THE DIVINE POWER combine with the efforts of man in producing or collecting new productions; so that increase of these riches can only come from cultivation, from fishing (he reckoned hunting as of little account in civilised societies), and from the working of mines and quarries." The most respectable of other kinds of labour only made productions more usable, or gave their value a duration which facilitated their accumulation. None of them added to the value of the material employed anything more than the value of the things consumed by the workers, together with the repayment or the interest on their advances.

"He saw nothing in this but a simple, though useful, exchange of services against productions and an opportunity of earning a wage, where this wage, deserved by those who receive it, is inevitably paid out of riches already produced and belonging to somebody else;—whereas the kind of work which is assisted by the fecundity of Nature and the bounty of heaven produces itself the subsistence and remuneration of those who do it, and gives, in addition to this remuneration and subsistence, all the raw goods and materials which are consumed by other men of all professions.

"He gave the name of net product (*produit net*) to that portion of the harvest (*recoltes*) which exceeds the repayment of the cost of cultivation and the interest on the advances which it requires." [1]

It is always easy for anyone impressed with the importance of a particular kind of income—generally his own kind—to persuade himself that it alone is the real thing, and that those from whom he buys goods and services are "paid out of" it. Thus even at the present day an absolutely idle person drawing his income from government stock or private mortgages will often believe that he "supports" not only his domestic servants but his butcher and his tailor: he forgets that all these people may with at least equal justice hold that they support him by providing him with what he consumes. But the doctrine is most easily held of the kind of income obtained by producing the more tangible products: since a physician gets food, clothes and other tangible objects in return for his services, it always seems at first sight

[1] "Notice sur les Économistes" prefixed by Du Pont to Turgot's *Éloge de Gournay*. In Daire's *Œuvres de Turgot*, Vol. I. pp. 258–9.

more reasonable to think of him as being supported by his patients than to think of them as being dependent on him, even if he has quite unquestionably saved all their lives.

It is especially easy for an agriculturist to fall into this form of error. He is urged into it by the admitted importance of agriculture in providing food, which is regarded as the first necessary of life: this is suggested in the sign of "The Five Alls," in which it is the farmer who "pays for all." His descent into it is hastened by the use of the word "produce" and its derivatives: it is true that even in classical Latin *producere* could be used of making any article of commerce, but in the eighteenth century a strong flavour of the more literal sense (Latin, *ducere*, to bring; *pro*, forth), in which it is particularly appropriate to the earth bringing forth vegetables and animals bringing forth their young, still clung to its English and French forms. Hence we need not be surprised that Quesnay, "the son of a landowner, born on a farm," held that agriculture and a few other industries which appear to draw tangible objects forth from the earth were the only really "productive" industries and supported all those who worked at the other and "sterile" industries.

More peculiar was the idea of a net product of agricultural and other extractive industry and the importance attached to the idea. Part of the whole product of this kind of industry was regarded as being over and above the cost of production, and therefore available to form the income of the King by way of taxes and of the landlords by way of rents. Quesnay was probably inspired here, directly or indirectly, by three chapters in Part I of Cantillon's *Essai*. In chap. xii Cantillon had sought to prove that "All classes and all men in a State subsist or grow rich at the expense of the landlords"; in chap. xiv, that "The tastes, fashions and mode of life adopted by the Prince and still more by the landlords settle the use to which the land of the country is put, and cause the variations which take place in the market prices of everything"; and in chap. xv, that "The increase and decrease of population in a country depends chiefly on the will and the fashions and mode of life of the landlords." In the first of these chapters, after dividing society into two classes, the Prince with the landlords, who "live in independence," and the wage-earners with the undertakers, he says:

"The farmers usually have two-thirds of the produce of the land, one for the pay and maintenance of those whom they employ, the other for the profit of their business; out of these two-thirds the farmer generally provides directly or indirectly the subsistence of all who live in the country, and besides this also the subsistence of some artisans or undertakers in the town, in consequence of the fact that town merchandise is consumed in the country.

"The landlord usually has the remaining third of the produce of his land, and out of this third he provides the subsistence not only of all the artisans and others whom he employs in the town but very often also of the carriers who bring the country stuff to the town.

"It is usually supposed that half the inhabitants of a country make their living and reside in the towns, and the other half in the country; this being the case, the farmer, who has two-thirds or four-sixths of the product of the land, gives, directly or indirectly, one sixth of it to the town-dwellers in exchange for the merchandise which he gets from them; which sixth, together with the third or two-sixths which the landlord spends in the town, makes three-sixths or one-half of the produce of the land."

Something of this kind was depicted in Quesnay's *Tableau Œconomique*, which we may follow tradition in translating "Economic Table," if we understand "table" in the sense in which the word is used in the phrase "Multiplication Table," though quite modern usage would suggest "Economic Chart." This was printed by the press in the palace of Versailles for the use of Quesnay and his friends in 1758, and again in 1759, and was given to the public in 1760 by Mirabeau in a Continuation of the Sixth Part of *L'Ami des Hommes*, entitled *Tableau Œconomique avec ses explications*, of which an English translation appeared in 1766.[1] A facsimile of the 1759 edition was published by the British Economic Association (now the Royal Economic Society) in 1891, and a copy sufficiently accurate though not in facsimile will be found in the Editor's Introduction to my edition of Smith's *Wealth of Nations* (p. xxxii). On the opposite page I give in English the essential part of it, which caused hostile contemporaries to ridicule it as "the zigzag."

[1] *The Œconomical Table, an Attempt towards ascertaining and exhibiting the source, progress and employment of riches, with Explanations, by the Friend of Mankind, the celebrated Marquis de Mirabeau, translated from the French*, 1766.

PRODUCTIVE EXPENSES	EXPENSES OF REVENUE	STERILE EXPENSES
Annual advances to produce a revenue of 600*l*. are 600*l*.	Annual revenue of	Annual advances for articles of sterile expenses, are 300*l*.
600*l* produce net............	600*l*	
PRODUCTIONS	half passes this way / half passes this way	ARTICLES &c.
300*l* reproduce net............	300*l*	300.
	half passes this way / half passes this way	
150 reproduce net............	150.	150.
	half &c. / half &c.	
75 reproduce net............	75.	75.
37..10s reproduce net............	37..10.	37..10
18..15 reproduce net............	18..15.	18..15
9...7...6 reproduce net.........	9...7...6*d*	9...7...6*d*
4..13..9 reproduce net.........	4..13..9.	4..13..9
2...6..10 reproduce net........	2...6...10.	2..6..10
1...3...5 reproduce net.........	1...3...5.	1...3...5.
0..11...8 reproduce net........	0..11...8.	0..11...8
0...5...10 reproduce net.........	0...5..10.	0..5..10
0...2...11 reproduce net.........	0...2..11.	0...2..11
0...1...5 reproduce net.........	0...1...5.	0...1...5

&c.

The idea of the zigzag seems to be that any given sum, say 600 livres or 600,000,000 livres, expended on agriculture, under the circumstances which ought to exist in a well-regulated state, will cause a net produce of equal amount to appear, which goes to the landlords as net product or revenue. What afterwards becomes of this revenue is shown by the zigzag lines. As the first two lines, sloping downwards from the middle to left and right, indicate, half goes to pay for articles (*ouvrages*) made by—we must on no account say "produced by"—the sterile class of workers, and half goes to pay for "productions" of the productive class. The 300 l. which go to the left or productive class are spent, half in buying productions of that class, such as bread, wine and meat, and half in buying clothes, utensils and tools from the sterile class; this is 300 l. towards restoration of the annual advances. But besides merely restoring advances of that amount, the 300 l. causes a net reproduction of the same amount, as shown in the middle column.

The 300 l. which goes from the landlords to the right or sterile class is spent by that class, half of it among themselves for their maintenance (*entretien*) and for the restoration of the sum advanced until they finish and sell their work, while the other half goes to the productive class to pay for bread, wine, meat and raw materials.

Successive splittings of the amounts passing are shown by the figures and dotted lines in the Table down to 1 sou and 5 deniers, and that the splittings go on indefinitely is indicated by the "&c." in the left-hand bottom corner. When this process is complete, the annual PRODUCTIONS in the right-hand column will add up to 600 l. (less an infinitely small amount which is neglected), and the ARTICLES [1] or output of the sterile class will add up to the same amount. But there is this great difference between the two classes, that the productive class has not only produced that amount of productions to restore advances, but has also produced a further 600 l. worth, which is the total of the middle column of net produce or *revenu*; the sterile class has only restored its advances and maintained itself.

Besides being considered useful for exhibiting this supposed

[1] In reprinting the Table I have followed Mirabeau, who puts PRODUCTIONS and OUVRAGES in capitals, rather than the original, which puts them in less noticeable italic small letters.

truth, the Table was believed to furnish proof of the bad effects of wrong conduct. If the proper scheme of things was disordered by improper taxation or by improper expenditure of the *revenu*, the figures in the Table could be altered so as to show insufficient replacement of advances and consequent ruin of agriculture. In addition to the Table which we have just been discussing, Mirabeau has another with different figures bringing in taxes and tithe, and then four others with figures which he supposes to result from different kinds of disorders.

The veneration with which Quesnay's disciples regarded the Table far exceeded that which the Israelites displayed for the tables of stone which Moses brought down from Sinai. Mirabeau said of it in his *Philosophie Rurale*, 1766 (Vol. I. pp. 52–3) :

> "Three great primary inventions have given stability to society beside the large number of others which have enriched and adorned it. These three are : (1) The invention of writing, which alone gives man the power of handing down without alteration his laws, his contracts, his annals and his discoveries. (2) That of money, which binds together all relations in civilised societies. The third and last, which belongs to our age and of which our descendants will enjoy the fruit, is derived from the other two and completes each of them equally by perfecting their object : it is the discovery of the Economic Table which, becoming henceforth the universal interpreter, embraces and harmonises all the correlative fractions or proportions which should enter into every general calculation of the economic order."

Wildly extravagant as this praise appears, the Table really did form an important stepping-stone in the progress towards the modern conception of an income of goods and services as the principal subject-matter of general economic theory. The political arithmeticians had calculated national incomes from the data of quantities and values available, but had not seriously inquired what these incomes really were. They had brought the profits of trade into their computations alongside the products of agriculture without any attempt to show either that products and profits were homogeneous, or that their want of homogeneity formed no objection to their being added together. The question had to be tackled, and the fact that Quesnay's answer is unacceptable must not be allowed to deprive him of the great credit of having been the first to compel serious consideration to be given to it.

Further, while the political arithmeticians had thrown some light on the actual distribution of national incomes, and a large amount of disconnected discussion about the interests of particular classes had taken place from time to time, no general view of the national income as a whole to be divided, and of the causes which govern the division had been put forward. The Table, no doubt, did not do this very well, but it did at any rate suggest that it is a thing to be done. We are not to dismiss the Table as merely the crazy invention of a cranky physician; it marked a step in progress and had considerable influence.

By far the best economic work produced in France for a long time after it was Turgot's *Reflexions sur la Formation et la Distribution des Richesses*, written in 1766, and first published in the *Éphémérides du Citoyen* in 1770. Like Cantillon, Turgot was a genius: like Cantillon's *Essai*, his *Réflexions* are academic in character: he intended them originally for the instruction of two Chinese students who had come to France to absorb the learning of the West. The title of the treatise is much more suggestive of nineteenth-century economics than Cantillon's Essay on the Nature of Commerce in General, especially when we find that "formation" is pretty obviously a mere synonym for "production," used because "production" had acquired a strong physiocratic flavour, and Turgot, with very little reason, believed himself not to belong to the sect.[1] The style of the *Réflexions* is attractive; they are perhaps the most brilliant of all the short expositions of general economic theory which have been produced down to the present time. Yet they fell rather flat, and exercised no great influence on the progress of economic thought. For this the chief reason, I believe, is that Turgot's "*richesses*" are not the annual produce. He did not take hold of and develop the suggestion of the Economic Table, that the annual produce was the real subject-matter of economics. To perform this service was left to the Scotchman, Adam Smith.[2]

[1] See *e.g.* Turgot's letter to Du Pont, February 2, 1770, in Schelle, *Du Pont de Nemours et l'école physiocratique*, 1888, p. 128, partly quoted in Ashley's translation of Turgot's *Réflexions*, p. 111.

[2] For the physiocrats generally see A. Oncken, *Œuvres Économiques et Philosophiques de F. Quesnay* (Frankfort-s.-M. and Paris), 1888, G. Schelle, *Du Pont* (see preceding note), and biographies of Quesnay, Turgot, Le Trosne and La Rivière, as well as his article *Physiocrates* in Say et Chailley's *Nouveau Dictionnaire d'économie politique*, 1891–2: Henry Higgs, *The Physiocrats*, 1897.

§ 8. *Smith's "Wealth of Nations."*

In 1763, after twelve years at Glasgow, Smith was persuaded to give up his professorship and become tutor to the young Duke of Buccleuch, who, after the fashion of that time, was to complete his education by travelling abroad. The duties of the post were not heavy enough to prevent Smith from being introduced into Quesnay's circle and making himself thoroughly acquainted with the sect and their doctrines.

He and they were commended to each other by their common belief in the maxim of *laissez faire*. Long ago, in his Edinburgh lectures of 1750–1, he had preached the doctrine that things should be left to Nature, and that peace, low taxation and good administration of justice were all that was wanted for economic progress, and throughout his tenure of the Glasgow chair he had always denounced the restrictions imposed by the mercantile system, and had held up all sorts of exclusive privileges as impediments to the progress of opulence. In this province he had little to learn from the physiocrats, though to find them so entirely on his side must have confirmed him in his view. Of the "arithmetical formularies," as he calls them, of the Economic Table, he speaks somewhat disparagingly, and he quotes Mirabeau's panegyric merely to amuse his readers, but he owed more to the general effect of the Table than he realised. In his lectures, delivered before he went to France, "produce" plays a very small part, and "distribution" none at all. But in the *Wealth of Nations*, written afterwards, the "annual produce" is the chief subject-matter, and its "distribution" between different classes is in form at any rate, if not in substance, made one of the principal topics of general economic theory.

The "Introduction and Plan of the Work" opens with a statement that the degree in which the nation is supplied with necessaries and conveniences depends on the magnitude of the produce of its "annual labour" and the value of that portion of it which is exchanged for foreign goods; it ends with a sentence in which "the annual produce of the land and labour of the society" is treated as identical with its "real wealth," and this identification is frequently repeated in the body of the work.[1]

[1] See Vol. I. pp. 237, 240, 320, 417; Vol. II. p. 176 gives the credit of the identification to the physiocrats.

Though economists later than Smith often inadvertently fell back into the old conception of the wealth of society consisting of an accumulation of things existing at one and the same point of time, we may take it that from 1776 such an accumulation was recognised as merely a means to an end, the end being the provision of a continuous supply of the "necessaries and conveniences of life." "Annual produce," "real revenue," or "income," appear as the end of economic endeavour and the principal subject-matter of general economic theory.

CHAPTER II

THE NAME OF ECONOMIC THEORY

§ 1. *The Ancient Meaning of "Economics."*

In the words which begin with the three syllables " econom," the " eco," formerly spelt with a diphthong, " œco," is the Greek for house (οἶκος), and the " nom " is the Greek for law (νόμος) in the sense in which it is used in " astro*nomy*," when we treat of the law and order followed by the stars, rather than in the sense in which it is used in " deutero*nomy*," which is the second set of ordinances laid down for the Hebrew people.

In the Greek of the period now commonly studied in schools and universities outside Greece, *οἰκονόμος*, which was the nearest equivalent of our " economist," meant a person who managed a house; *οἰκονομία*, our " economy," was then management of a house, and *οἰκονομικός* was a person skilled in that management. The neuter plural of this last word, namely, *οἰκονομικά*, which we use in the form " *Economica* " as the title of a periodical, and in the English form " Economics " as the title of our science, naturally meant things having to do with the management of a house, and the feminine singular, with the word for " art " understood, *ἡ οἰκονομική*, *scil.* *τέχνη*, meant the art of household management.

But we are not to jump to the conclusion that our " economics " is just what the Greeks meant by it slightly enlarged in scope so as to make it apply to all households in the community taken together instead of only to the individual household. " Household management " has to us a more material ring than its Greek equivalent had to the Greek philosophers who talked about it. To our minds it brings thoughts of the milk which failed to be forthcoming at breakfast-time, of the difficult choice between the butcher whose meat is often high and the other butcher whose meat is always tough, or between the nervous cook who spoils the food when there is company and the lazy cook who does very well then and badly all the rest of the time.

The Greek philosophers had higher thoughts than these. Aristotle included in household management not only the management of the slaves but also the management of wife and children. The household to him was like a little kingdom, so that its management formed a part of Politics. And it was thus, as a part of politics, that the earlier eighteenth-century philosophers in Great Britain still understood their "Œconomicks." Francis Hutcheson, Adam Smith's teacher and model, divided his *Short Introduction to Moral Philosophy*[1] into three Books: "I. Elements of Ethicks," "II. Elements of the Law of Nature," and "III. Principles of Œconomicks and Politicks." It is in the second of these Books that he deals with what we call the economic subjects of property, value and contract, while in the third Book, the "Principles of Œconomicks" are dealt with in three chapters, "Concerning Marriage," "The Duties of Parents and Children," and "The Rights of Masters and Servants." Of these the first is principally concerned with divorce, and the third with the injustice of slavery, and there is scarcely any economics in the modern sense in any of them except a slight reference in the second to the fact that sums spent on the education of children are ordinarily regarded as a donation and not as an investment. It is clear that Hutcheson took "Œconomicks" in the old Greek sense. It is not by this road that we are to trace the origin of the modern Economics.

§ 2. "*Economy*" *and* "*Political Economy.*"

We must go back and make a fresh start by following the fortunes of "economy" rather than of "economics" for at any rate the first part of the journey. "Economy," at first the management of a household, came to be used more loosely of any sort of management, it might be even the arrangement of the different parts of a poem. When the word was adopted into Latin and subsequently modified into the French *économie*, it was used in this wide sense, so that Hatzfeld and Darmesteter's *Dictionnaire générale* says the meaning *gestion intérieure d'un*

[1] The Latin version of this was published as *Philosophiæ moralis institutio compendiaria* in 1742, the translation in 1747.

maison is obsolete, and goes on at once to *ordre avec lequel les choses sont administrées*. Then, as if to show how completely this general sense has superseded the old sense, it gives as the first example, *économie domestique*, which would be tautological if the old sense had not gone completely out of use. In English the same wide use of the word still exists, though we are apt to forget it in our preoccupation with things economic in the modern sense. The "Divine economy" is still sometimes spoken of, and any of us, when inclined to be a little archaic in diction, might say that a very unwholesome lunch had quite upset our "internal economy."

When "economy" was used in this wide sense, nothing would be more natural than to speak of the "economy of the State" in the sense of public administration, and this was done in Greek —often by Polybius, as Liddell and Scott's *Lexicon* records. In French "the economy of the State" would be "*économie politique*," and it was probably with this sense of *économie politique* in his mind that Antoine de Montchrétien in 1615 called his book *Traicté de l'Œconomie politique*,[1] though his interest in the economic side of administration was so great that his book deals with little except what we should call economic subjects. As late as 1755, nearly a century and a half after Montchrétien wrote, the actual subject of Rousseau's article *Économie politique* in the *Encyclopédie* was not what we should call economics but politics.

In England Sir William Petty's *Political Anatomy of Ireland*, 1691, must have only just escaped being the "Political Economy of Ireland," as Petty meant by "anatomy" just the same as "economy" in the phrase "the animal economy," and he was very near using "political economy" in the more modern sense when he spoke in that work of "the most important consideration in political Œconomies, viz. how to make a Par and Equation between lands and labour, so as to express the value of anything by either alone" (*Economic Writings*, ed. Hull, p. 181).

During the middle quarters of the eighteenth century "economy" became more specially used in the sense of economic organisation,

[1] See above, p. 13. The book seems to have passed the censor under the title of *Traicte œconomique du Trafic ;* see p. 371 of the 1889 ed.

and "political economy" in the sense of the science of economic organisation. In 1736, Quesnay, then only a physician, wrote an *Essai physique sur l'économie animale*, in which *économie* is used in the old wider sense, but in 1758, having become an economist, he brought out *Maximes générales du gouvernement économique d'un royaume agricole*, and added to it the famous *Tableau économique*, in both of which *économique* has its modern sense. Towards the end of his Explanation of the Table, Mirabeau, in 1760, spoke of *économie politique* as if it consisted of a dissertation on agriculture and public administration as well as on the nature of wealth and the means of procuring it,[1] and in 1763 he published *Philosophie rurale ou économie générale et politique de l'agriculture*, thus coupling the adjective "general" along with "political" in a way which shows that the technical sense of *économie politique* was not yet well established.

In that year 1763, however, in Italy, Count Pietro Verri began the preface to his *Memorie storiche sulla economia pubblica dello stato di Milano* with the words, "La scienza dell' Economia Politica."

Three years later the unknown English translator of Mirabeau's Explanation of the Table makes him speak of "the principles of true political œconomy," where in fact Mirabeau only mentions "principles of economy,"[2] and at last, in 1767, "Political Economy" appeared in the title of an English book, Sir James Steuart's *Inquiry into the Principles of Political Œconomy, being an Essay on the Science of Domestic Policy in Free Nations, in which are particularly considered population, agriculture, trade, industry, money, coin, interest, circulation, banks, exchange, public credit and taxes.* In the preface Steuart says, "I have read many authors on the subject of political œconomy," as if the term was quite commonly used. But the explanation with which he begins the text of the work shows that the ancient Greek sense of economy was curiously blended with the modern sense in his mind. He says:

"Œconomy in general is the art of providing for all the wants of a family, with prudence and frugality.

"If anything necessary or useful is found wanting, if anything

[1] *L'Ami des Hommes, suite de la vi partie*, p. 227.
[2] P. 199; cp. with the original, p. 210.

provided is lost or misapplied, if any servant, any animal, is supernumerary or useless, if any one sick or infirm is neglected, we immediately perceive a want of œconomy. The object of it in a private family is therefore to provide for the nourishment, the other wants, and the employment of every individual. In the first place, for the master, who is the head, and who directs the whole; next, for the children, who interest him above all other things; and last for the servants, who, being useful to the head, and essential to the well-being of the family, have therefore a title to become an object of the master's care and concern.

"The whole œconomy must be directed by the head, who is both lord and steward of the family. It is, however, necessary that these two offices be not confounded with one another. As lord, he establishes the laws of his œconomy; as steward, he puts them in execution. As lord, he may restrain and give his commands to all within the house, as he thinks proper; as steward, he must conduct with gentleness and address, and is bound by his own regulations. The better the œconomist, the more uniformity is perceived in all his actions, and the less liberties are taken to depart from stated rules. He is no ways master to break through the laws of his œconomy, although in every respect he may keep each individual within the house in the most exact subordination to his commands. Œconomy and government, even in a private family, present, therefore, two different ideas and have also two different objects.

"What œconomy is in a family political œconomy is in a state; with these essential differences, however, that in a state there are no servants, all are children: that a family may be formed when and how a man pleases, and he may establish what plan of œconomy he thinks fit; but states are found formed, and the œconomy of these depends upon a thousand circumstances. The statesman (this is a general term to signify the head, according to the form of government) is neither master to establish what œconomy he pleases, or in the exercise of his sublime authority to overturn at will the established laws of it, let him be the most despotic monarch upon earth.

"The great art, therefore, of political œconomy is first to adapt the different operations of it to the spirit, manners, habits and customs of the people, and afterwards to model these circumstances so as to be able to introduce a set of new and more useful institutions.

"The principal object of this science is to secure a certain fund of subsistence for all the inhabitants, to obviate every circumstance which may render it precarious; to provide everything necessary for supplying the wants of the society and to employ the inhabitants (supposing them to be freemen) in such a manner as naturally to create reciprocal relations and dependencies between them, so as to make their several interests lead them to supply one another with their reciprocal wants."

In the next paragraph he seems to use "political economy" in rather a different way, since he says that when we consider the variety of institutions, laws and customs, we can see that "the political economy in each" country must be different, though "principles" are "universally true."

Progress in the use of the term was not confined to England; in France in November of the same year, 1767, Du Pont gave to the Second Part of his *Physiocratie* the title of "*Discussions et développements sur quelques-unes des notions de l'économie politique,* and in the 1769 numbers of his periodical *Éphémérides du Citoyen,* he had a *Notice abrégée des différents écrits modernes qui ont concouru en France à former la science de l'économie politique.*

And in Italy in 1771 Count Pietro Verri published *Meditazioni sull' economia politica.* In the preface to the 1772 edition of this he says that everyone knows what a mental and moral revolution has taken place since the discovery of America:

"States feel they have new connections: the riches of kingdoms are estimated in order to discover the degree of security and prosperity which they enjoy. Commerce comes to be regarded as a matter of public concern, and finance as a province of legislation. Reason attempts to throw light on these subjects; their importance and the influence which they exercise on the happiness of the human race becomes generally recognised, and a department of knowledge is created under the name of political economy (*economia politica*). Isolated facts, local knowledge of the different states come first: then follow the general theories to which the human mind rises after a long series of well-known facts: later, someone appears who happily links theories together and leads the attention safely, gradually, from the more simple to the more complicated and important ideas. Such is the history of every science, such is the origin of every truth.

"The moment seems to me to have come when political economy is developing into a science; there was only wanting that method and that linking up of theorems which would give it the form of a science."

After this it may seem a little surprising that Adam Smith in 1776 did not use the term political economy in the title of his great work. But it is clear that the title he actually chose, "*An Inquiry into the Nature and Causes of the Wealth of Nations,*" was intended by him as a mere synonym for political economy, since he says that certain writers "treat not only of what is properly called Political Œconomy, or of the nature and causes of the wealth of nations, but of every other branch of the system of civil government" (Vol. II. pp. 176–7). We may conjecture with some plausibility that he refrained from using the term simply because it had already been appropriated by Steuart. As it was still rather a new term, to use it as the title of a book which was intended to supersede Steuart's would have seemed discourteous.

§ 3. "*Economics*" *and* "*Economists.*"

"Political Economy" became the usual name of the science from Smith's time till it was displaced by "Economics." That term is very modern. The "*New*" or Oxford *English Dictionary* records that Emerson spoke of "Chemistry—natural history and economics" in 1841, but there is conclusive proof that the term was unfamiliar as late as 1856. The British Association for the Advancement of Science had a section for "Statistics" from 1835 to 1856. Yet in spite of that, when, in 1856, it was desired to add what we call economics, the section was not re-christened "Economics and Statistics," but "Economic Science and Statistics."

Not, I believe, till the late eighteen-seventies did "Economics" appear in the title of books on the science. In 1877 a little known American writer, J. M. Sturtevant, brought out *Economics or the Science of Wealth;* in 1878 H. D. Macleod followed with *Economics for Beginners,* and in 1879 Marshall with his wife published *Economics of Industry.* On p. 2 of that work the authors say it is best to drop the term "political economy" because "political" is misleading, since "political interests generally mean the interest of some part or parts of the nation," from which I suppose that we must gather that they were thinking of "political parties." Jevons, writing the preface to the second edition of his *Theory of Political Economy* in May 1879, said he had discarded "the old troublesome double-worded name of our science" on the surer ground of convenience. No one could long talk of "politic-economic" things: the adjective universally employed was "economic" or "economical," and there was obvious convenience in calling the science which deals with economic things "economics" on the analogy of Mathematics, Ethics, Æsthetics. "Mr. Macleod," says Jevons, "is, so far as I know, the re-introducer of the name in recent years, but it appears to have been adopted also by Mr. Alfred Marshall at Cambridge. It is thus to be hoped that Economics will become the recognised name of a science which nearly a century ago was known to the French economists as *la science économique*" (p. xiv).

Jevons was unable to alter the title of his own *Theory of Political Economy*, and it cannot be said that "Political Economy" was superseded generally by "Economics" till Marshall brought out his *Principles of Economics*, Vol. I, in 1890. Moreover, in spite of Jevons' suggestion in the passage just quoted, that the French were ahead of the English in this matter, *Économie olitique* still holds the field in France. Landry's *Manuel 'Économique* is, so far as I know, the only French treatise with the shorter name.

The term "*Économiste*" came into use in France in the middle of the eighteenth century, but was then and for a long time afterwards applied exclusively to the followers of Quesnay, subsequently rechristened "Physiocrats." Even in 1814 Jean-Baptiste Say used it in that sense in his *Traité d'économie politique*. The word was absent from the Dictionary of the Academy in 1814, and was admitted in the modern sense in 1828. The *Journal des Économistes* was founded in 1841.

In English "economist" was at first commonly used in the earlier French sense. The first instance which the Oxford Dictionary can give of its use in the modern sense is in Whateley's *Logic*, 1827, as the example which it quotes from Lauderdale is really of its use in the older sense.[1]

[1] Much of the earlier history included in this chapter is drawn from two articles by Joseph Garnier, *De l'origine et de la filiation du mot économie politique* in the *Journal des Économistes* of 1852, Vols. XXXII and XXXIII.

CHAPTER III

THE THEORY OF PRODUCTION

§ 1. *The Nature of Produce.*

It was found easier to agree with Adam Smith in regarding annual produce as the main subject-matter of general economic theory than to discover what sense should be put upon the term.

The physiocrats, as we have seen, held that all labour was sterile unless it extracted something from the soil, and this doctrine necessarily excluded from produce every kind of output except raw materials. Smith wished to enlarge the conception of produce, but only did it in a half-hearted and illogical way. He said "the capital error" of the physiocratic system lay "in its representing the class of artificers, manufacturers and merchants as altogether barren and unproductive." He saw that the work done by these classes was just as necessary for the maintenance of the people, or at any rate for providing them with the "necessaries and conveniences of life," as that done by the agriculturists, and therefore he regarded them as productive labourers, and included the results of their labour in his conception of annual produce, but he refused to go further than that, so that he excluded not only "menial servants" and some of the "most frivolous professions," such as "players, buffoons, musicians, opera-singers, opera-dancers," but also some of the "gravest and most important," such as "churchmen, lawyers, physicians, men of letters of all kinds," even economists, presumably. He tried to distinguish the productive from the unproductive by two criteria, without noticing that the two do not give the same results. One is that to be productive the labour must "fix or realise itself" in some "particular subject which" endures after the labour is done; and the other is that the labour must fix or realise itself in a "vendible commodity." To put the matter in another way, he thinks and speaks as if all persons who are employed in what we call " making " something " produce " something which their employer can sell, and all those who produce or perform what are called " mere services " fail to produce anything which he can sell. The illustration given is, " A man grows rich by employing a multitude of manufacturers: he grows poor by maintaining a multitude of menial servants " (Vol. I. pp. 313–14). This quite overlooks the fact that a man may quite easily grow poor by employing others to make things for his own consumption, that an hotel-keeper may grow rich by employing a multitude of " menial servants," and a provider of public entertainments by employing " players, buffoons, musicians and opera-singers."

Smith's doctrine on this matter found very little acceptance. The physiocrats objected to any extension of their idea of the content of productive labour; other people thought his extension did not go far enough. Even the French translator of the *Wealth of Nations* thought it necessary to append a hostile note of over thirty pages. He notices *inter alia* Smith's inconsistency in holding some wage-paid labourers unproductive while at the same time declaring the produce of labour to be the natural wages of labour.[1] J.-B. Say in 1803 observed that " immaterial products," such as a good stage-play, were just as real as material products such as fireworks.[2] Lauderdale laughed at Smith for having made a distinction between products which last and products which immediately perish, after having himself made fun of people who thought it better to accumulate pots and pans indefinitely rather than drink good wine.[3] McCulloch remarked that Smith's " menial servant " who brought coal up from the householder's cellar was raising coal just as much as the miner; [4] and finally Senior cleared the matter up by pointing out that whether we think of a person as producing a thing or as performing an " immaterial " service depends upon trifling circumstances. A bootmaker makes leather and thread into boots: a shoeblack makes dirty boots and blacking into clean boots. We think of the bootmaker as having produced boots because we buy the boots from him:

[1] Germain Garnier, *Recherches*, etc., par Adam Smith, 1802, Vol. V. p. 171.
[2] *Traité d'économie politique*, Vol. II. p. 362.
[3] *Inquiry into the Nature of Public Wealth*, 1804, pp. 152–3.
[4] *Principles of Political Economy*, 1825, pp. 406–7.

we think of the shoeblack as having performed a " mere service " because the chief material on which he works belongs to us, so that we do not have to buy it from him.[1] This ought to have been enough, but the obstinacy of James and John Stuart Mill kept the semi-physiocratic doctrine from complete disappearance till the nineteenth century was far gone. Even in 1888 the author of an elementary manual classed schoolmasters, actors, musicians and domestic servants along with the idle rich, the idle poor, and even "thieves," as living "on what the directly productive classes produce."[2] But in general economists regarded the physiocratic and semi-physiocratic doctrines as obsolete, and were content to treat "produce" as including "services" as well as "commodities."[3]

This was a simple matter compared with another question which received astonishingly little attention but really was of the greatest importance. Given that the produce included services as well as commodities, did it include all commodities and services, and if not, how should those to be included be distinguished from the others?

The explanation of the small attention given to the question seems to be found in the fact that Adam Smith virtually answered it when he boldly alleged that the " price or exchangeable value " of " all the commodities which compose the whole annual produce of the labour of every country, taken complexly, must resolve itself" into three parts which together make up the total " revenue " of the inhabitants of the country (*Wealth of Nations*, Vol. I. p. 54.

The word " revenue," which by its derivation suggests something which comes again or periodically, though now used almost exclusively of the periodical receipts of states, in Smith's time was commonly applied to the periodical receipts of individuals and was equivalent to the modern " income," which has replaced it. " Revenue " was in his time, and " income " is in our own,

[1] *Political Economy*, 1836 in 8vo. ed., pp. 51–2.

[2] J. E. Symes, *Short Text-book of Political Economy*, p. 11.

[3] After writing this I received the October 1927 issue of the *Belgrade Economic Review*, and read on p. 206 that "a group of experts" in the Jugo-Slavian Ministry of Finance has calculated the national income at 69 milliard dinars, " reckoning in this only actually productive and original sources of income." To this sum they add another 10 milliard as derivative income, such as the salaries of public servants, the income of the professions, etc.

commonly thought of and spoken of as a sum of money—so many pounds sterling per annum—coming in to a recipient, and not at all as things and services produced by workers and going out from those workers. What goes out from the workers is "output"; not "income." The individual worker does not under modern conditions receive much of what he himself has produced, and the individual owner of property does not get much of what is produced with the instrumentality of that property. Both workers and owners of property are paid in money, and buy in the general market things produced by other workers with the instrumentality of other persons' property. The consequence is that when the economist, following his usual practice, "goes behind" the money-income of an individual, he asks what is bought with the money, and speaks and thinks of the commodities and services bought by the individual as his "real income" as opposed to his "money income." Now these commodities and services exclude all such as are what may be called merely instrumental in the sense that they are used in the course of providing other commodities and services which form the "real incomes," thus conceived, of the individuals. Grain kept for seed, guano, pig iron, wool, for example, are all certainly "produce of land and labour," but they form no part of anyone's "real income."

But, as Smith himself said, "Consumption is the sole end and purpose of all production" (*Wealth of Nations*, Vol. II. p. 159). Production is carried on not for the sake of the intermediate or instrumental products, but in order to get the ultimate products. There does not seem to be any sense in trying to add into a total (1) the food of the ox so far as it nourishes his skin, (2) the leather made of his skin, and (3) the boots made of the leather; the idea of a total or aggregate of products or "gross produce" seems chimerical. Compilers of censuses of production are at great pains to exclude what they call double reckonings.[1]

Possibly the ambiguity of the word "commodity" played some part. It had come to signify any article of commerce, but a little of the old flavour of commodiousness lingered about it,

[1] Smith himself in *Wealth of Nations*, Vol. I. p. 315, seems to feel there is something in "produce" besides "real revenue," though on p. 52 he seeks to dispose of any difficulty by saying that persons receive income for producing.

so that the produce of commodities suggested the things which reached the final consumer rather than things used up in producing them.

Whatever the precise explanation may be, there is no doubt about the fact that the "produce" of which general economic theory investigated the production and distribution came to be treated as identical with the income of society.

This income, considered as the subject of general economic theory, had the enormous advantage, too often lacking in the conceptions of professional economists, of being something already familiar to and well understood by ordinary middle-class persons. Every member of that class had a fairly definite knowledge of the amount of his own money-income and of the kind and quantity of commodities and services which he could buy with it. He had also some knowledge of the amounts of many of his neighbours' money-incomes and of what they were in the habit of buying. He could understand estimates of the total income of a whole society being formed by adding together the individual money-incomes of all its members, and could appreciate inquiries into the causes of increase and decrease of this total money-income which, when the purchasing power of money was stable, would mean increase and decrease of the amount of commodities and services which could be bought with it.

At this point we must beware of identifying the largest possible produce per head, the ideal of Production, with the highest possible economic welfare, the ideal of economic endeavour taken as a whole. There are several reasons why produce per head and economic welfare do not in fact always vary together.

In the first place, though labour is not in itself an evil but a good, it may be excessive or disagreeable even when not excessive. A population of overworked and badly treated slaves might produce as much or more per head as a population of free persons working under agreeable conditions, and yet be much worse off from an economic point of view. Our own produce might be increased while economic welfare was reduced if we resumed employing young children in factories and mines.

Secondly, the manner in which the total produce is distributed between those who get it causes a difference in the amount of economic welfare resulting from it. Among persons of equal needs and equally good judgment in regard to their demand and consumption, equal distribution will make a given amount of produce "go further" than unequal distribution. If needs are unequal, as they always are, the general rule of equality requires to be modified by these differences in order to get the most out of a given produce. If good judgment is unequally distributed among those who receive the produce, something may be gained by giving the persons who have the better judgment more than those who have the worse—it is easy to see that a distribution which gave larger amounts to those who had the worst judgment would be inexpedient.

Thirdly, given any particular amount and distribution of produce, the goodness of the general or average judgment with regard to demand, which settles the form the produce shall take, and, with regard to consumption, which determines what shall be done with the particular produce which comes into existence in response to demand, has much to do with the amount of economic welfare resulting from it. It is difficult to get any two persons to agree about what is the best way for any particular individual to spend his income, but everyone agrees that there are better and worse ways of spending it, and that the whole population may improve or deteriorate in its judgment in the matter. War furnishes us with a glaring example of this. After every war it is generally admitted that one side lost economic welfare by it, and very often it is rightly believed that both sides lost, and that the world in general lost. But modern war increases rather than diminishes produce per head. In the war of 1914–18 whole populations worked harder than they had ever done before, and methods of production were enormously improved over wide fields of industry in consequence of the general eagerness to produce as much as possible. The output of shells and other munitions rose to an amount which would have seemed perfectly incredible in 1913; no doubt the output of many things and services fell off, but not nearly in the same proportion as that in which the other things increased.

It is useless to suggest that munitions of war should not be reckoned as produce. Even the services of the actual fighting men must be reckoned as such. If we once begin to exclude goods and services which do not appear to us to promote economic welfare, we shall never know where to stop. It would be extremely awkward and cause endless confusion and inconvenience to hold that persons who produce munitions of war are not producers at all, or only produce when they work for what the speaker regards as the right side. What is wrong with war is not that produce is diminished by it, but that the wrong things and services are produced, and that the right ones are largely wasted by application in wrong directions. If anyone says that war is anomalous, abnormal and not worth considering (all of which is untrue), we must ask him what he has to say about the carpenter's or the glazier's tools bought by the burglar. We cannot conveniently say that the makers of centrebits and of glasscutting tools are producers at one moment and not at another according as they are employed on a tool which will be used by an honest carpenter or glazier, and not producers at the next moment when they are employed on one which will be used by a burglar.

We must hold in the theory of production to the ordinary sense of products and produce, without inquiring at this stage whether or how far the things included will in fact minister to material welfare. All valuable goods and services must be included—whisky, even if drunk by a delirium tremens patient, as well as the most innocent lemon squash; cocaine whether to ease the extraction of a hopeless tooth or to satisfy an abandoned drug-taker; the services of the military and munition makers even in a civil war. But while we include all valuable goods and services whether they are real goods and real services in the judgment of some infallible outsider or not, we must not exclude any goods or services simply because they are not bought and sold and therefore do not appear to have value. A householder who clears snow from his private approach and the public sidewalk is producing just as truly as the municipal employee who clears it from the carriage-way; a medical man who discovers the prophylactic against some disease and publishes it for the free use of all the world is producing as well as the inventor of some gadget who secures a profitable patent.

The really difficult question seems to be not, What are products? but, How can we measure a total of unhomogeneous products? If we talk of produce per head being greater or less, we must have in our minds some system of measurement. It is no use to propose value as the measure, since the value of things is purely relative; we can say that one thing has more value than another, but it is futile to say that the whole produce of the whole of society or the produce per head of all the members constituting society is greater when its total value is greater, since there is nothing outside it wherewith to compare it. If we compare the total value of the produce with that of some particular commodity included in it, we may always be confronted with the objection that the greater value of the total as shown by this method may be due not to an increase in the quantity of the total produce, but to an increase in its value as reckoned in the particular measure chosen, and this increase of value may be due to a diminution in the quantity of things in the total other than the commodity chosen as a measure.

But though there is difficulty about the measurement of produce as a whole, it is obviously possible to measure large portions of it. Large portions of it will be almost unchanged except in quantity, and here we can measure simply by quantity. Other portions will be changed in character so as to make comparison by yards or tons impossible, but there will be some standard, such as the "candle-power" by which we compare the illumination resulting from the use of oil, gas and electricity, and this will serve in place of measurement by the more obvious standards of weight and bulk. In still other cases the fact that of free choice men have substituted variety for monotony, as in that of food, entitles us to say that the produce is greater, not because its quantity is greater but because the quality has been improved. And when we find that the produce per head of what we regard as the more necessary articles has increased in this way, and that in addition we manage to have a large amount of other things previously unthought of, we may be sure that the produce per head has increased, though we may be quite unable to say by how much per cent. it has increased.

It must be admitted that the whole of this subject requires more elucidation than it has yet received. It is only recently that it has been thought worth while to attempt to construct something which should do for the volume of production what index-numbers of prices have done for value. Pending further progress in this direction we must be content with the fact that while we may find it difficult to be sure whether produce per head has increased or diminished in some short period, such as that between 1913 and 1929, we are nearly all agreed that it is much greater now than in 929 B.C. or even A.D., and a thousand years is not very long in the history of mankind.

§ 2. *The Requisites of Production.*

Whether produce be taken to mean income or anything else which is measurable, I think anyone unsophisticated by knowledge of the actual course of the development of economic science would naturally expect that the theory of production would be concerned with the explanation of the causes which render produce greater or less. Adam Smith seems to have had this conception in his mind before he familiarised himself with the bepuzzlements of the physiocrats on productive and sterile labour. Early in his lectures he showed how " division of labour occasions a multiplication of the product, or, which is the same thing, how opulence arises from it " (*Lectures*, p. 163); later on he examined " the causes of the slow progress of opulence " (*ib.*, p. 222). And even after beginning the *Wealth of Nations* he had not altogether abandoned the idea, although the " Causes of the slow Progress of Opulence," converted into Book III, " Of the different Progress of Opulence in different Nations," drop out of the theory and become a chapter of economic history to which readers pay little attention. The first sentences of the " Introduction and Plan of the Work " hold out great hope of a systematic theory of production conceived on these lines. They suggest that the ideal economic condition is that the produce should be as great as possible " in proportion to the number of those who are to consume it," and that how far this ideal is approached " must be regulated by two different circumstances: firstly, by the skill, dexterity and judgment with which " the nation's " labour is generally applied; and secondly, by the proportion between the number of those who are employed in useful labour and that of those who are not so employed."

But Smith's performance falls far short of his promise. About the first of the two " circumstances," which he himself considers the most practically important of the two, he only tells us that "the greatest improvement in the productive powers of labour" has been the effect of division of labour, and then, after three luminous but short chapters on this point, he slips from the subject, by way of a discussion of the origin and use of money, back into the theory of prices which had been evolved in the course of his lectures on Police. About the second circumstance, all he had to say is comprised in the dissertation on productive and unproductive labour in Book II, chapter iii, where he allowed himself to be fogged by the peculiar doctrine of the physiocrats, and became completely confused between labour which is "useful" in the sense which both he and others ordinarily attach to that term, and labour which is "productive" in the special and entirely different sense which he thought an improvement on the physiocratic interpretation.

Jean-Baptiste Say in his *Traité*, 1803, seems to be largely responsible for the elevation of Production into a great department worthy of a "Book" or other principal division in treatises on general economic theory. Like Turgot, he seems to have been a little shy about using the term, since in the title of his treatise he puts *se forment* instead of *se produisent*, just as Turgot had put *formation* instead of *production* (above, p. 34) making it *Traité d'économie politique ou simple exposition de la manière dont se forment, se distribuent, et se consomment les richesses.* But Book I is boldly entitled *De la Production*, and even in the first edition (in which it does not include Money) this occupies 412 pages out of a total of 1057. To Say also production seems to owe the form which the theory took during the nineteenth century. He not only brushed aside the physiocratic doctrine by declaring that what is produced is not matter but utility, so that production is merely giving things the quality of being useful, but also introduced into the discussion a classification of requisites corresponding with the threefold classification, wages, profit and rent, in distribution. Adam Smith had declared all income to be originally derived from labour, stock and land, but it had not occurred to him to build a theory of production on this classification of sources of income. But Say at the outset of his discussion of Production shows "how industry, capital and land contribute, each its own part, towards production," and " how these three things are all indispensable for the creation of products." [1]

In the chapters which follow he provides a good deal of useful discussion of particular points in the organisation of production, but does not succeed in taking a comprehensive view of the whole. He makes, for example, no attempt to show the part played by the various social institutions, with the one exception of Property. And that he treats in what seems to us, at this day, inspired as we all are more or less with the " historical spirit," a curiously absolute and consequently misleading way. For example, instead of regarding such rights, and such only, as a master actually possesses over his slave, where slavery is established, as part of the property of the master, he assumes that slavery always means, or ought to mean, that the master has absolutely unlimited power to do what he likes with his slave, and any limitations of this power are " interventions " of the State between the individual and his property (ed. 2, Vol. I. p. 139).

The 1803 edition of Say's *Traité* was probably little known in England, and Ricardo and Malthus, each of whom wrote his *Principles of Political Economy* after 1814, when Say's second edition was published, and who were well acquainted with the work, were too unsystematic and too much interested in passing controversy to put forward any coherent theory of production. But in 1821 Robert Torrens brought out *An Essay on the Production of Wealth*, and in the same year James Mill published his *Elements of Political Economy*, divided into four parts, Production, Distribution, Interchange and Consumption. Both Torrens and James Mill used the idea of the three requisites of production being labour, land and capital, and from this time forward it became usual for systematic treatises on general theory to represent Production as a great department of the subject, and to give the classification of requisites into labour, land and capital the most prominent place in that department.[2]

The prominence given to this classification seems to have been

[1] Ed. 1, p. 32. In ed. 2, p. 35, " land (*fonds de terre*) " becomes " natural agents (*agents naturels*)," and the three " things (*choses*) " become " three elements of production (*éléments de la production*)."

[2] McCulloch is a notable exception to the rule as regards the classification, as he makes no use of it.

rather an obstacle in the way of the emergence of a comprehensive and illuminating theory of production. It tended to make the discussion take the form of remarks on Labour, followed by remarks on Land and concluded by remarks on Capital, which, put, as they were, in separate compartments, were likely to cause writers and readers to ignore or forget the question which Adam Smith had formulated when he spoke of the magnitude of the produce in proportion to the number of those who are to consume it.

J. S. Mill, trying to sum up the wisdom of the Ricardian age in 1848, arranged his treatment of production in three parts, of which the first, a "general survey of the requisites of production,"[1] fills half of the whole number of pages, and the last, an inquiry whether aggregate (not *per capita*) production "has practically any limits, and what these are,"[2] fills nearly a quarter, thus leaving little more than a quarter for "the second great question in political economy, on what the degree of productiveness of" the three "agents depends."[3] Productiveness, Mill says, depends on natural advantages of locality, energy of labour, skill and knowledge, intelligence and trustworthiness, security, and co-operation, but he does not say it is affected by the magnitude of capital or of population. The effect of the accumulation of capital, very much misunderstood, is dealt with in the general survey of the requisites of production, and the influence of the magnitude of population is treated in the third part. This third part—the inquiry into what, if anything, limits aggregate production—is oddly divided between three chapters setting forth three "laws" and a fourth exhibiting the consequences of these laws. The laws are themselves suggested by the threefold classification, the first being "the law of the increase of labour," the second, "the law of the increase of capital," and the third, instead of being the law of the absence of increase of (area of) land, being "the law of the increase of production from land." The magnitude of population is regarded, not as something which may be either excessive or insufficient for the purpose of securing the highest productiveness, but merely as something which would readily increase indefinitely if it were not restrained by the limitation of the quantity of

[1] *Principles*, ed. Ashley, p. 101. [2] *Ib.*, p. 155. [3] *Ib.*, p. 101.

land—which thus appears as the villain of the piece in Production, just as the landlord does in Distribution.

Mill deprived himself of all chance of dealing intelligibly with production by his strange belief that while the " laws " of " Distribution are partly of human institution, since the manner in which wealth is distributed in any given society depends on the statutes or usages therein obtaining," the " laws of Production," on the other hand, are independent of human institution, being derived from " facts of outward nature " combined with " other truths relating to human nature " (p. 21). It may seem incredible that Mill or anyone else should ever have believed that the amount of wealth which could be produced in any given society did not depend partly upon the " statutes or usages therein obtaining," but Mill was at any rate so much influenced by this belief that he excluded from Production his consideration of slavery, custom and competition, and different systems of landholding, and crammed all he had to say about these things under Distribution, while he put " the influence of the progress of society on production " in a separate Book along with the influence of progress on distribution.

Later writers seem to be struggling without decisive success to emancipate themselves from the thrall of the traditional three requisites or agents of production. In Marshall's *Economics of Industry*, 1879, Book I is headed " Land, Labour and Capital." Chapter ii of this is on the " Agents of Production," and ends up with, " We have now seen how land and labour are two of the requisites of production, the third requisite is capital." Chapter iii, on " Capital," is followed by three chapters on the " Law of Diminishing Return," " The Growth of Population. Malthus. Poor Laws," and the " Growth of Capital." These are introduced by the following paragraph :

> " We have seen that the requisites of production may be classed as land, labour and capital. We have now to seek for the Law of fertility of land, the Law of the increase of population, and the Law of the growth of capital. The latter two Laws depend on the first, which goes by the name of the Law of Diminishing Return."

These three chapters are merely new versions of Mill's chapters on " the law of the increase of production from land," and the laws of the increase of labour and capital.

After this, however, Marshall breaks away from the tradition. Chapter vii begins:

"The last chapter finished the discussion of the three requisites of the production of wealth—natural agents, labour and capital. Before proceeding to examine the modern methods of production and exchange it will be well to see how these methods have gradually grown up."

Accordingly, Chapter vii, entitled "Organisation of Industry," undertakes a survey of "Uncivilised tribes," the "Agricultural state," "Greeks, Romans and German races," "Mediæval Gilds," the "Transition to modern times," and the "Circulation of Capital." The next chapter, on "Division of Labour," includes in its purview "production on a large scale," and "localisation of industry," and it identifies "the Law of the Division of Labour" with the "Law of Increasing Return." It leads up at the end to Chapter ix, the last in the Book, on the "Tenure of Land."

As time went on, Marshall did not get further away from the traditional acceptance of labour, land and capital as the foundation of an exposition of Production, but rather the contrary. In the first edition of the *Principles* he says, "The total efficiency of production depends on many conditions," of which the first is "the aid which Nature gives to man: which we shall find to be such that though she scarcely ever ceases to respond to his increased efforts, she often affords them only a diminishing rate of return"—this is the old "Land" with Mill's "law of the increase of production from land" taken along with it instead of illogically separated from it. "Next we have to discuss the growth of numbers and the average strength and industrial skill of each class of workers"—this is the old "Labour" together with Mill's "law of the increase of labour." "Next, after looking at the growth of wealth in general, and in particular those parts of it which aid and support future production"—this is the old "Capital" with Mill's law of its increase—"we must examine the causes and effects of industrial organisation; for the collective efficiency of production depends on its organisation almost as much as it does on the numbers of those who work, or on their individual efficiency" (p. 189). The appearance of Organisation here, as in the *Economics of Industry,* suggests an important departure from the traditional treatment, but our hope is dashed by the first words of the next paragraph, " Having thus taken a broad survey of the factors of production," which make us ask, Can it be that Organisation, instead of being the arrangements by which men are able to carry on efficient production, is to be only a fourth " requisite," " agent " or " factor," added to the traditional three?

The contents of the chapters on organisation seem indeed to answer this question in the negative. They deal with the survival of the fittest, the division of labour, the influence of machinery, the localisation of industry, production on a large scale and business management. But in the third edition Marshall altered the title of Book IV from " Supply or Production " to " The Agents of Production : Land, Labour, Capital and Organisation," thus distinctly making Organisation a fourth wheel to the productive chariot. The Book is made to begin with a statement that " the agents of production are commonly classed as Land, Labour and Capital," but soon adds that " capital consists in a great part of knowledge and organisation," and then " partly " because the distinction between " public and private property in knowledge and organisation is of great and growing importance," Marshall thinks "it seems best sometimes to reckon Organisation apart as a distinct Agent of Production " (ed. 3, pp. 214–15, much the same in ed. 8, p. 139).

When after this we read at the end of Chapter xii. that the supply price of business ability in command of capital consists of the supply prices of three things—first, capital, second, business ability and energy, and third, the " organisation by which the appropriate business ability and the requisite capital are brought together " (ed. 3, p. 392, ed. 8, p. 313), it is difficult to avoid suspecting that Marshall's " industrial organisation " owes its appearance as a fourth agent of production to the recognition of the entrepreneur's profit as a fourth share in Distribution. To have four shares in Distribution and only three agents in Production would have spoilt the symmetry of J.-B. Say's arrangement.

§ 3. *Causes of Variation in* per capita *Produce.*

Seven years, however, before the publication of the first edition of Marshall's *Principles*, Henry Sidgwick had broken loose from tradition and had given an account of variations in productive power without using the old trio. The first fundamental question, he thought, for the Theory of Production to answer was, " What are the causes that make the average annual produce per head of a given community at a given time greater than that of another whose primary wants are not materially different, or greater than its own produce at a previous stage of its history? " (*Principles*, 1883, pp. 96–7). He manages to perform the task without any list of requisites or agents of production, and only comes to Capital as an aid to productiveness after dealing with Co-operation and Invention. His influence may be seen in my own *Elementary Political Economy*, 1888, in which I enumerated three " immediate causes " of the historical increase in the productiveness of industry: (1) the growth of knowledge, (2) the accumulation of useful things (*alias* capital), and (3) the growth of co-operation, adding cautiously that increase of population might affect productiveness favourably or unfavourably according to circumstances.

In more recent years the tendency has been for " Organisation of Production " to supplant rather than merely to supplement the old rambling dissertations on the three requisites. Taussig's *Principles*, 1911, starting, as it does boldly with " Book I. The Organisation of Production," is a prominent example of this tendency. But this phrase does not cover all that we should reasonably expect to be covered by " Production." Taussig is obliged to put his discussion of diminishing returns into his Book on Value and Exchange, and to find a place for his theory of population in his Book on Distribution, though surely the effect of variations in the number of producers upon the produce per head is one of the most important of all questions in any general theory of Production. Moreover, " organisation of production " is suggestive of the detailed account of actual institutions and practices which we sometimes call " descriptive economics " rather than of the search for generalisations about causes and effects of given institutions and practices which we are accustomed to expect in general theory.

It certainly seems as if we should do well to follow Sidgwick in harking back to Adam Smith's unfulfilled intention of explaining what the factors are which determine the magnitude of the whole produce of society in proportion to the number of its members, or, more shortly, what regulates the amount of produce per head.

So, but without committing myself rashly to the assertion that there are no other causes, or even that there are no other more important causes, I propose to deal now, in Chapters IV, V and VI, with the traditional subjects of Population, Co-operation and Accumulation as causes of variation in produce per head.

CHAPTER IV

THE INFLUENCE OF POPULATION ON PRODUCE

§ 1. *The Emergence of Theory.*

One of the simplest and apparently most obvious of all economic truths is that the number of producers has some influence upon the magnitude of the produce per head, and that this influence is such that it depends upon the particular circumstances whether produce per head will be increased or diminished by a change of population in either direction. It is clear that the larger the number of producers the greater the possibility of reaping the advantages of co-operation or division of labour. But, on the other hand, it is equally clear that the smaller the number the more relatively plentiful will be space to work in, raw materials to work on, and tools and instruments to work with. Dispute should only be possible about the question whether the circumstances of any particular moment are such as to make increase or decrease desirable.

But till quite recent times consideration of the subject with a view to the economic interest of the whole of society was scarcely possible. The interests of the family, the interests of the State, and the interests of religion were thought of, but the economic interests of society as a whole were not grasped, and would not have been regarded if they had been. Primitive parents in the prime of life supported their young children and their own old fathers and mothers or killed them off according as they thought best in the interest of the family—which meant chiefly themselves—without thinking or caring whether the course taken would benefit or damage outsiders. The governors of the little States of early times encouraged or discouraged the growth of population according as they thought it good or bad for the State—which meant again chiefly themselves—in regard to internal order and security from outside attack; the worse the policy was for the outside world, the better they thought it. The Spartans, for example, were entirely in favour of the increase of Spartans, but were apprehensive about the increase of helots. In republican Rome, Quintus Metellus, as Censor, recommended marriage as an inconvenience which should be endured for the sake of national safety:

> "If, Romans," he said, "we had the power of living without wives, we should all be free from that trouble; but nature has so disposed it that we can neither live very commodiously with them, nor without them exist at all; and we must then provide rather for perpetual security than for transient pleasure."

Later, it was still anxiety for "the perpetuity of the State" which led Augustus to promote the legislation encouraging marriage which was known as the *lex Papia et Poppæa*, Papius and Poppæus being the two consuls of the year—both, by the way, unmarried and childless.

The priesthood of most religions has generally been in favour of the procreation (at any rate by others than themselves) of new human beings to worship the Deity on earth and perhaps to go to heaven afterwards, without regard to their welfare here below. Even Luther thought every man should marry not later than his twentieth year, and every woman between the ages of fifteen and eighteen, "and let God provide the way and means by which their children shall be nourished." Obviously the belief that our future state is destined to be infinitely longer and much more definitely happy or miserable than our present state is bound to prevent attention being given to the economic effects of procreation. I have been told that in the City Council of York, under the shadow of an Archbishop's cathedral, a councillor, somewhere about the year 1900, objected to steps being taken to diminish infant mortality on the ground that "Jesus said, 'Suffer the little children to come unto me.'"

From the sixteenth century onwards, however, we find the economic ideal gradually coming into competition with the political and religious. War and pestilence begin to get some credit, or at any rate to find some excuse, and emigration begins to get some recommendation, from the fact that they prevent a superabundance of population. But this superabundance is for a long time spoken of in metaphorical terms which show it was very vaguely conceived. Raleigh, for example, thought that "when any country is overlaid by the multitude which live upon it, there is a natural necessity compelling it to disburden itself and lay the load upon others." The Virginia Company, animated no doubt by a desire for more workers for the colony, and devoid of a sense of humour, wrote to the Secretary of State in 1616 that Virginia was an admirable country for the "emptying of the full body of England."[1] Bacon was only a little more definite when he thought precaution necessary so that "the population of a kingdom do not exceed the stock of the kingdom which should maintain them."[2]

Such slight impressions of over-population as these had little chance of prevailing against the political advocacy of large population by statesmen and patriots who wanted to provide for the defence, or more likely the aggrandisement, of their respective countries. Even the philanthropic Vauban held that "the grandeur of kings is measured by the number of their subjects." The popular cry became, as Joseph Townsend complained in 1786, "Population! Population at all events!"[3] Goldsmith illustrates the earlier eighteenth-century view when he makes his Vicar of Wakefield "ever of opinion that the honest man who married and brought up a large family did more service than he who continued single and only talked of population" (*Vicar of Wakefield*, 1776, Vol. I. p. 1). To "talk of population" was to descant on how to increase it. The philosophy of the period, as usual, backed up the opinion of the multitude, replacing the old Christian idea of the desirability of large numbers of persons to praise God by the proposition that a larger number of persons are at any rate likely to have a bigger aggregate of happiness than a smaller number. On this the highly respectable Paley agreed with the less respectable Hume. Hume believed it to be "the general rule that the happiness of any society and its populousness are necessary attendants,"[4] and Paley believed

[1] P. A. Bruce, *Economic History of Virginia*, 1896, Vol. I. p. 60.

[2] Down to this point I have in this chapter done little more than rifle the rich store of information collected by Dr. C. E. Stangeland in his *Pre-Malthusian Doctrines of Population*, 1904 (Columbia Studies in History, etc.), Chaps. i–iii.

[3] Joseph Townsend, *Dissertation on the Poor Laws*, 1786, repr. 1817, p. 62.

[4] *Essay of the Populousness of Ancient Nations*, footnote near beginning.

that "a larger portion of happiness is enjoyed amongst ten persons possessing the means of healthy subsistence than can be produced by five persons under every advantage of power, affluence and luxury."[1]

That extraordinary genius, Cantillon, was quite exceptional when he put his finger on the spot by putting the question, "whether it is better to have a great multitude of poor and ill-nourished (*mal entretenus*) inhabitants or a number less considerable but much better off (*bien plus à leur aise*); a million of inhabitants consuming the product of eight acres or four millions living on that of two acres each."

And he dismisses it as not belonging to his "subject," but presumably to that of the philosophers.[2]

§ 2. *The Inevitability of Checks.*

While all the patriotic members of each nation wished the population of their own country to increase without limit, students of what may be called the arithmetic of human multiplication could not help seeing that if the population of the whole world were to increase as fast as human fecundity, coupled with the amount of mortality which was regarded as normal, would allow, the earth would soon be too full.

As far back as 1682 Petty assisted "a worthy divine" in his quarrel with certain "sceptics" who said that there would not be enough matter in the whole globe to provide material "for all the bodies that must rise at the last day," nor space for them to stand upright. Petty calculated that half of Ireland would give them all graves, and two Irish mountains would provide all the requisite matter for their bodies. In trying to make the increase of population over the whole period of 5630 years supposed to have elapsed since the Creation fit in with the little that was known (or supposed to be known) about the actual population of different portions of the world at different times, he found it necessary to estimate the rapidity of increase to have been diminishing as time went on after the Flood: at first

[1] *Moral and Political Philosophy*, 1785, Book VI. chap. xi.

[2] *Essai*, p. 113. The actual figures in the French text are 6 and 1½ arpents. As an arpent is about 1¼ acres, this rather suggests that the French version is that of a translator rather than of Cantillon himself, who would not be likely to use a fractional figure in a supposition of this kind.

the period of doubling might, he estimated, have been ten years, it gradually rose till in his time it was 1200 years, and he foresaw that it must diminish still further or the world would become " overpeopled " (*Econ. Writings*, ed. Hull, pp. 465–7 and n.).

Eighty years later this idea began to get into economic politics. Dr. Robert Wallace some time in the late seventeen-forties read a paper to the Edinburgh Philosophical Society in which he showed that, on what he thought moderate assumptions with regard to fecundity and mortality, population could be doubled every 33⅓ years, so that at the end of 1233 years it might increase from 2 to 412,316,860,416 (which is, we may remark, about 13 to the acre of land excluding the Polar Regions), and it occurred to him to add, rather casually, that " had it not been for the errors and vices of mankind and the defects of government and education, the earth must have been much better peopled, perhaps might have been overstocked, many ages ago."[1] In his *Various Prospects of Mankind, Nature and Providence*, 1761, he built up an argument against the possibility of a " perfect government," by which he meant a communistic Utopia, on the basis of this idea of " overstocking " the earth with people.

> " For though," he says, " happily such governments should be firmly established, though they should be found consistent with the reigning passions of human nature, though they should spread far and wide; nay, though they should prevail universally, they must at last involve mankind in the deepest perplexity, and in universal confusion. For how excellent soever they may be in their own nature, they are altogether inconsistent with the present frame of nature and with a limited extent of earth.
>
> " Under a perfect government the inconveniencies of having a family would be so entirely removed, children would be so well taken care of, and everything become so favourable to populousness, that though some sickly seasons or dreadful plagues in particular climates might cut off multitudes, yet, in general, mankind would increase so prodigiously that the earth would at last be overstocked, and become unable to support its numerous inhabitants " (p. 114).

Rather mildly, it seems to a reader who remembers his demonstration of the possibility of Adam and Eve having over four hundred milliards of living descendants early in the thirteenth

[1] *Dissertation on the Numbers of Mankind in antient and modern times*, 1753, pp. 1–13.

century after the Creation, he pronounces it merely " not probable " that under the conditions supposed the earth would not have been " overstocked " before A.D. 1761. But however that may be, he thinks it obvious that the earth could not provide nourishment for the population

" for ever, unless either its fertility could be continually augmented, or by some secret in nature, like what certain enthusiasts have expected from the philosopher's stone, some wise adept in the occult sciences should invent a method of supporting mankind quite different from anything known at present " (p. 115).

And if some means of supporting the increasing population were found out, there would still be a limit in the want of space for containing the bodies of the people on the surface of the earth. He thought it certain that the animal frame could not be supported without food, and " equally certain that limits are set to the fertility of the earth, and that its bulk, so far as is hitherto known, hath continued always the same and probably could not be much altered without making considerable changes in the solar system." Therefore, he concludes,

" the earth would be overstocked at last, and the greatest admirers of such fanciful schemes must foresee the fatal period when they would come to an end, as they are altogether inconsistent with the limits of that earth in which they must exist " (p. 116).

He supposes the catastrophe would be sudden : " while there was room for increase, mankind must have been happy; the earth must have been a paradise in the literal sense, as the greatest part of it must have been turned into delightful and fruitful gardens " (p. 117). Knowing what a highly cultivated kitchen garden is like, we may wonder at his " delightful." To prevent the catastrophe he can think of no expedients except restraint on marriage, celibacy of priests and others, sterilisation, infanticide, and killing off of persons on their reaching a certain age varying with the plenty of provisions. " Mankind would never agree about such regulations. Force and arms must at last decide their quarrels, and the deaths of such as fall in battle leave sufficient provisions for the survivors and make room for others to be born " (p. 119).

Malthus, nearly forty years later, contending against his father's view that mankind is capable of indefinite progress—or, as it was then put, is "perfectible"—adopted Wallace's argument, but thought Wallace "had not applied it to the subject with its proper weight or in the most forcible point of view" (*Essay on the Principle of Population*, 1798, p. 8). He complained that "all writers on the perfectibility of man and of society who have noticed the argument of an overcharged population . . . invariably represent the difficulties arising from it as at a great and almost immeasurable distance," and that even Wallace "did not seem to be aware that any difficulty would occur from this cause till the whole earth had been cultivated like a garden, and was incapable of any further increase of produce." If that were all,

> "An event at such a distance might fairly be left to Providence; but the truth is that . . . the difficulty so far from being remote, would be imminent and immediate. At every period during the progress of cultivation, from the present time to the time when the whole earth was become like a garden, the distress for want of food would be constantly pressing on all mankind, if they were equal. Though the produce of the earth might be increasing every year, population would be increasing much faster; and the redundancy must necessarily be repressed by the periodical or constant action of misery or vice" (p. 144).

Malthus' belief that the "difficulty" was a thing not of the remote future but something which is and always must be present, whatever the arrangements of society, was based on a theory that population tends to increase faster than food, or, to put the same thing in plainer terms, that the annual or daily produce of food cannot be made to increase as fast as population could and would easily increase if plenty of necessaries were forthcoming. If this is true, it is obviously inevitable that the growth of population must and will be checked, that is, the population must and will always be prevented from growing as fast as it could and would easily grow if plenty of necessaries were forthcoming.

Malthus imagined that he had proved his theory by an early and most unfortunate attempt to substitute mathematics—or, as the University of London would say, arithmetic—for the usual logical processes of economic thought. Having pictured population as tending to grow every twenty-five years by duplication, he said that " the most enthusiastic speculator " could not expect the daily produce of food to be increased every twenty-five years by an addition greater than the total produced in 1798. " Yet this ratio of increase," he said, " is evidently arithmetical," and he thought this justified the proposition that " Population when unchecked increases in a geometrical ratio. Subsistence increases only in an arithmetical ratio " (pp. 14, 22).

Even the most determined apostles of the faith that mistake was impossible to the more prominent of the English economists of the period 1776 to 1848 have been obliged to admit that there was nothing in the geometrical and arithmetical argument. Malthus cannot have had in his mind any clear idea of a geometrical ratio. An increase is in geometrical ratio even if it is only one-millionth every billion years, and Malthus, as well as everyone else, would have thought it absurd to contend that the production of food could not be increased at *that* rate. He was really thinking not of geometrical rates in general, but of the particular rate which he supposed would be a safe estimate of the rate at which an unchecked population would increase, namely, about 3 per cent. per annum.[1] His idea of food increasing only in arithmetical ratio was even more confused. Taking " the first twenty-five years " quite arbitrarily as the twenty-five following 1798 (in the first edition—later dates in the later editions), he supposes the daily or annual production may be increased 100 per cent. in that period, but cannot be increased by more than 50 per cent. in the second twenty-five years, 33⅓ in the third, 25 per cent. in the fourth, 20 per cent. in the fifth, and so on with a perpetual decrease of percentage. He quite forgets that if he put the " first " period back only 2475 years before his time he would have to hold that the production of food could not be increased more than 1 per cent. in the twenty-five-year period from 1798 to 1823, which is obviously inconsistent with his being willing to admit that it might conceivably be increased as much as 100 per cent. in that period.[2]

[1] Doubling every twenty-five years is a little less than an increase of 3 per cent. per annum, as reference to a table of compound interest will show.

[2] In 99 periods of twenty-five years (*i.e.* 2475 years) the production would have increased from 1 to 100 by equal additions of 1 in each of the 99 periods; the addition of 1 to this total in the " next twenty-five years " would be only 1 per cent.

His position is rendered the more indefensible by the fact that he founded his estimate of unchecked population doubling itself in twenty-five years on figures showing that the population of a certain portion of North America had actually increased at that rate for several centuries. Now unless the people of this area were worse fed at the end of the period than at the beginning, which he never suggests, this obviously gives us an example of the production of food being increased not only in geometrical ratio, but also in the particular geometrical ratio which he adopts in the example which he gives to show the impossibility of the production of food keeping pace with an unchecked population. He might, of course, have adopted the vulgar method of escape by alleging that the law he was attempting to establish was only a general rule liable to exceptions, and that the portion of North America referred to, being a "new colony," was exceptional. But he scorns this miserable expedient:

> "In instances of this kind," he says in a footnote (ed. 1, p. 106), "the powers of the earth appear to be fully equal to answer all the demands for food that can be made on it by man. But we should be led into an error if we were thence to suppose that population and food ever really increase in the same ratio. The one is still a geometrical and the other an arithmetical ratio, that is, one increases by multiplication and the other by addition."

This is absolute nonsense. To cover its absurdity Malthus takes refuge in an inapplicable simile:

> "Where there are few people and a great quantity of fertile land, the power of the earth to afford a yearly increase of food may be compared to a great reservoir of water supplied by a moderate stream. The faster population increases, the more help will be got to draw off the water, and consequently an increasing quantity will be taken every year. But the sooner, undoubtedly, will the reservoir be exhausted and the streams (*sic*) only remain."

The simile would have been effective if the Americans had started with a large store of food and had lived partly on this during the earlier part of the period in question, but as they had no such store, this talk of a "reservoir of water" is quite out of place. It does not in the least show that the Americans did not double their production of food as fast as they doubled their population. So it is not surprising that the portion of the footnote so far quoted did not reappear in the second edition. The note proceeds:

"When acre has been added to acre till all the fertile land is occupied, the yearly increase of food will depend upon the amelioration of the land already in possession; and even this moderate stream will be gradually diminishing. But population, could it be supplied with food, would go on with unexhausted vigour, and the increase of one period would furnish the power of a greater increase the next, and this without any limit."

In the second edition this passage is transferred to the first chapter. There, after having considered the experience of America and other countries, Malthus says:

"It may safely be pronounced, therefore, that population when unchecked goes on doubling itself every twenty-five years, or increases in a geometrical ratio.

"The rate according to which the productions of the earth may be supposed to increase, it will not be so easy to determine. Of this, however, we may be perfectly certain, that the ratio of their increase must be of a totally different nature from the ratio of the increase of population. A thousand millions are just as easily doubled every twenty-five years by the power of population as a thousand. But the food to support the increase from the greater number will by no means be obtained with the same facility. Man is necessarily confined in room. When acre has been added to acre till all the fertile land is occupied, the yearly increase of food must depend upon the amelioration of the land already in possession. This is a stream which, from the nature of all soils, instead of increasing, must be gradually diminishing. But population, could it be supplied with food, would go on with unexhausted vigour; and the increase of one period would furnish the power of a greater increase the next, and this without any limit."

In the later editions, "stream," no longer appropriate without the omitted portion of the 1798 footnote, is replaced by "fund," and in the sixth edition "in a limited territory" is inserted between "ratio of their increase" and "must be of a totally different nature."

It is fairly clear from this that Malthus' belief in the necessary, immediate and perennial "difficulty" arising from "the principle of population" was founded on the difference between quantities increasing in geometrical progression and quantities increasing in arithmetical progression, which may perhaps be most easily indicated by saying that if plotted out on a chart, the first ascends in a curve and the second in a straight line. The annual increases of the first are always increasing and the increases of the second remain always the same. It follows from this that if of two equal quantities one starts increasing in geometrical progression and the other in arithmetical progression, *and the rates chosen are such that the two quantities will still be equal at the end of some "first period,"* say twenty-five years, then the first quantity will increase more than the second in all subsequent periods and more and more as time proceeds. On this supposition, therefore, it is extremely plausible to say that geometrical increase is always much more "powerful" than arithmetical increase, and that to keep two quantities equal when one tends to increase in geometrical and the other in arithmetical progression it is always necessary that the first should be "checked" in its growth. And the supposition of equality at the end of the "first period" (and indeed any other period) was applicable to population and food, since it might be assumed that people were approximately equally well fed and do not produce any surplus of food to throw away. Consequently Malthus felt himself justified in pronouncing that population always required to be "checked," at any rate after the conclusion of the "first period," which might have been put at any time.

Where he went wrong was in treating the increase of food production as if it were a kind of natural phenomenon with which the amount of human industry had nothing to do, and in trying to get a general rule of growth from a speculation about the future rather than from past history. The most obvious factor in the production of human food is the number of persons there are to consume it, and to produce it because they want to consume it. The population of the moment has produced the amount of food which it consumes, and if the increase of production of food has always been in arithmetical ratio in the past, the increase of population must have been so as well, which is entirely contrary to all historical evidence, sacred and profane, and is never claimed by Malthus.

His apologists have sometimes alleged that he attached no importance to his contrast of geometrical and arithmetical increases, but there is no shadow of justification for this. In the Appendix to the third and later editions he speaks of "the different ratios of increase on which all" his "principal conclusions are founded," and in a note a little further on he says that it "is not quite true" to say, as some critic had said, that he had "written a quarto volume to prove that population increases in a geometrical and food in an arithmetical ratio." Not because the geometrical and arithmetical ratios were unimportant or unessential, but because, he says,

> "The first of these propositions I considered as proved the moment the American increase was related, and the second as soon as it was enunciated. The chief object of my work was to inquire what effects these laws, which I considered as established in the first six pages, had produced and were likely to produce on society."

The whole of Malthus' case against Wallace—his contention that the difficulty foreseen by Wallace must necessarily be present immediately and not only in a possibly remote future as Wallace supposed—depended on the proposition that the production of food can only be increased in arithmetical ratio, and fails when that proposition is withdrawn.

Soon after the publication of the first edition of the *Essay on the Principle of Population as it affects the future Improvement of Society, with remarks on the Speculations of Mr. Godwin, M. Condorcet, and other writers,* Malthus' mind underwent a considerable change. Instead of being merely the exponent of a theory that there is an insuperable obstacle to communistic and equalitarian schemes, he became a reformer himself, desirous of showing that a particular policy would greatly conduce to "the future improvement of society." At the end of the second edition he "hoped that the general result of the inquiry is such as not to make us give up the cause of the improvement of society in despair." There is a striking contrast between the last two chapters of the first edition, in which "the sorrows and distresses of life" are rather welcomed as aids to higher things, and Book IV, chapter ii, in the second, on the effects which would result to society from the general practice of moral restraint. If moral restraint were generally practised, the "picture of society" would "present a very different scene from that which we now contemplate." No man whose earnings were only sufficient to maintain two children would have four or five; the price of labour would be raised by the restriction on its supply; "the period of delayed gratification would be passed in saving the earnings which were above the wants of a single man and in acquiring habits of sobriety, industry and economy which would enable him in a few years to enter into the matrimonial contract without fear of its consequences," and "all squalid poverty would be removed from society, or, at least, be confined to a very few who had fallen into misfortune against which no prudence or foresight could provide" (p. 495).

But this change of view, which converted Malthus from a mere stonewall obstructionist of equalitarian schemes into an ardent advocate of late marriages as a cure for poverty, does not seem to have been based on any improvement in his view of the relationship between population and production. He still thought of the two things as tending to grow at their two different ratios, that of population being the more rapid, and his hope of improvement lay merely in the possibility, which he now recognised, of the tendency of population to outstrip the production of food being repressed without the intervention of vice and misery formerly supposed by him to be necessary. He does not, any more than before, give any definite reason, except the geometrical and arithmetical ratio argument, why an "unchecked" population should not produce as much per head as a "checked" one.[1]

§ 3. *The "Law of Diminishing Returns."*

The law of diminishing returns had been stated by Turgot thirty years before Malthus wrote, and that too in a form much superior to that in which it became current in England after the Napoleonic war. In comments upon a prize essay, Turgot had said:

> "Granting to the writer of the essay that, where ordinary good cultivation prevails, the annual advances bring in 250 to the hundred, it is more than probable that if the advances were increased by degrees from this point up to that at which they would bring in nothing, each increment would be less and less fruitful. In this case the fertility of the earth would be like a spring which is forced

[1] For discussion of Malthus' plans for reform, see below, Chap. XI. § 3.

to bend by being loaded with a number of equal weights in succession. If the weight is light and the spring not very flexible, the effect of the first load might be almost *nil*. When the weight becomes sufficient to overcome the first resistance, the spring will be seen to yield perceptibly and to bend; but, when it has bent to a certain point, it will offer greater resistance to the force brought to bear on it, and a weight which would before have made it bend an inch will no longer bend it more than half a line. The effect will thus diminish faster and faster. This comparison is not perfectly exact; but it is sufficient to show how, when the soil approaches near to returning all that it can produce, a very great expense may augment the production very little.

" If, instead of the advances being increased by equal additions beyond the point where they give the largest return, they are, on the contrary, diminished, the same change in the proportion will be found. It is not only conceivable but certain that very small advances give a much smaller profit than very large advances, and not merely that but one which is also smaller in proportion to the advances. If £100 bring a return of £250, £50 will perhaps not bring in £75, and £25 will not bring in £30.

" Seed thrown on a soil naturally fertile but totally unprepared would be an advance almost entirely lost. If it were once tilled the produce will be greater; tilling it a second, a third time, might not merely double and triple, but quadruple or decuple the produce, which will thus augment in a much larger proportion than the advances increase, and that up to a certain point, at which the produce will be as great as possible compared with the advances.

" Past this point, if the advances be still increased, the produce will still increase, but less, and always less and less until the fecundity of the earth being exhausted, and art unable to add anything further, an addition to the advances will add nothing whatever to the produce." (*Observations sur le Mémoire de M. de Saint-Péravy*, written about 1768, in *Œuvres*, ed. Daire, Vol. I. pp. 420–1; cp. also p. 436.)

Turgot very properly goes on to explain that the farmer need not stop at the point of maximum return, since the returns beyond that point, though smaller, may still be large enough to be profitable.

But the remarks of an adjudicator on essays submitted for a prize seldom attain wide publicity. I do not know that these observations of Turgot were published at all till they appeared in Du Pont's collection of Turgot's Works, 1808–11, and I doubt if any notice was taken of them till I quoted them in *Production and Distribution*, 1893, whence Marshall introduced them into the third edition of his *Principles*, 1895 (pp. 249–50). They are an interesting anticipation of later doctrine, and that is all.

Of course every practical farmer, and indeed every gardener, has always known that it is impossible to get an infinite amount of produce off a definite area of land by any increase of the labour expended on it; and probably most farmers and gardeners have realised that the limitation on production was not of such a character that if the labour were increased, it would be found all of a sudden that not a single atom more could be produced by any amount of additional labour. No doubt they would say, " By putting some more labour in we could get a little more produce, but so little that it would not pay." This clearly implies that the return to any given quantity of additional labour, say another hour of weeding, would be less than the return actually obtained from the least productive hour of labour which it has in fact " paid " to apply. In other words, it implies that a " diminished return " would be got from the additional labour.

But the more vocal of agricultural theorists have always been ardent advocates of the view that too little labour is put into the soil, at any rate by the average farmer, and their enthusiasm led them to talk as if there was no limit to the profitable employment of labour in improving and working the soil. That well-known and prolific writer on agricultural subjects, James Anderson, though, as we shall see below in Chap. VIII, he anticipated the " differential " part of the Ricardian theory of rent, remained even in 1801 a profound believer in the indefinite continuance of proportionate returns and the consequent possibility of maintaining an indefinite increase of population. In his *Recreations in Agriculture, Natural History, Arts and Miscellaneous Literature* he said:

" Man, when he once betook himself to the cultivation of the soil, became an agriculturist; and in process of time he made discoveries that were of infinite consequence to him as an inhabitant of this globe. Instead of finding his subsistence, as before, limited to a certain extent which it was beyond the reach of his power to exceed, he found himself endowed with faculties that enabled him to augment the quantity of subsistence for man to an extent to which he hath never been able as yet to assign any limits. At the first, he no doubt conceived that it was only those spots which were naturally of the most fertile kind that could afford him abundant crops of corn; but experience taught him, that if the dung of the animals that were fed by the native produce of the soil were preserved and laid upon those parts of the ground that were cultivated, and properly dug into it, and judiciously managed, even barren fields could be rendered productive, and not only for a time but even for a perpetuity; for the forage that was produced by these crops enabled him to sustain more cattle, which, of course, afforded a greater quantity of manure; and this extra manure, when conjoined with others that he found in the bowels of the earth itself in inexhaustible quantities, if blended with the earth in a proper manner by labour under the guidance of skill, tended still to add more and more to the fertility of the soil the longer it was continued; so that thus he saw it was in his power to form at will, as it were, a new creation. He could not, indeed, add to the extent of his fields, but he could add to their productiveness from year to year, so as to make it keep pace with his population, whatever that might be; allowing him still to enjoy plenty to an inconceivable amount." (Vol. IV. pp. 373–4.)

No one, Anderson thinks, can "pretend to say that it is beyond possibility to furnish subsistence to one hundred people from the produce of one acre of land which was originally in that infertile state that would have required the produce of one thousand acres to subsist one person" (p. 375), and a page later he says:

"The melioration of the soil must ever be proportioned to the means that are made use of to augment its productiveness; and this will ever depend upon the quantity of *labour* and manure that is judiciously bestowed upon it. I mean to say that no permanent or general melioration to any considerable extent can ever be effected but by labour; and that, under skilful management, the degree of melioration will be proportioned to the *labour* that is bestowed upon the soil, and the attention that is paid to the proper use of manures, those especially which arise from the soil itself. In other words, the productiveness of the soil will be proportioned to the number of persons who are employed in active labour upon the soil, and the economy with which they conduct their operations."

In *A Calm Investigation of the Circumstances that have led to the present Scarcity of Grain*, 1801, Anderson put forward the same view:

"Wherever population increases," he says, "the produce of the country must be augmented along with it, *unless some moral influence is permitted to derange the economy of nature.*

"The natural conclusion then from this undeniable fact is that no legislator need ever be afraid, in a country which is not destitute of soil, that an augmentation of population will decrease the means of subsistence for the people, unless it shall be his desire that it should be so, by favouring such arrangements as shall prevent it from becoming the interest of individuals to attend to the cultivation of the soil in a proper manner" (p. 41; Anderson's own italics).

To suppose, as many writers about Malthus have done, that his *Essay* enunciated the law of diminishing returns in opposition to the agricultural enthusiasts' view and founded its main argument on that law is a mistake. It is true that even the earliest edition of the *Essay* does here and there rather vaguely suggest that the obstacle in the way of population is to be found in the nature of land. "Nature," we are told, "has scattered the seeds of life abroad with the most profuse and liberal hand," but "has been comparatively sparing in the room and the nourishment necessary to rear them" (pp. 14, 15). This certainly suggests that the obstacle is to be found in the limited area of land and the limited quantity of matter available for the nourishment of living things. In the second edition we may notice the proposition, "Man is necessarily confined in room" (quoted above, p. 71), which is made the more significant by the insertion in the sixth edition of the words "in a limited territory" in the proposition that the rates of increase of food and population are of a different character. References to "fertility" embody the same idea, since an acre of good land may easily be regarded as a larger quantity of a productive instrument than an acre of bad land. But Malthus never resorts to calculations of the amount of land per head like that of Senior, who took the trouble to reckon that if the population of England doubled itself every twenty-five years for five centuries, there would be only a single square inch of land for each family.[1] What Malthus always had in mind was not the idea that with increasing numbers there must be less and less land per head, but that as time goes on it will be more and more difficult to make the necessary changes or "improvements" within each

[1] *Two Lectures on Population*, 1829, p. 9.

twenty-five years. To make the improvements necessary to provide for a perpetually *increasing* addition to the produce every twenty-five years he regards as most obviously impossible in the future, though it has been done in the past, and he does not himself think it possible to make enough improvement to provide even an equal addition every twenty-five years.[1]

The "law of diminishing returns," on the other hand, in none of the numerous forms in which it has been framed, has ever said anything about the annual or the quarter-century additions to produce; it has always related to the additions which can be made by given additional quantities of labour, or of capital or of some compound of "capital and labour." We are not entitled to say that Malthus founded the *Essay* on the law of diminishing returns merely because he sometimes uses the word "diminishing" in speaking of something else than the subject of the law. Though he himself played an important part in the emergence of the law of diminishing returns in 1814 (see below, Chap. VIII), he never introduced it into the later editions of the *Essay*. But by the other economists of the age it was immediately recognised as an excellent substitute for his geometrical and arithmetical ratios. Instead of relying on those ratios for the purpose of proving that population tended to increase faster than subsistence, or than "capital," which they confusedly identified with subsistence, they argued that as increase of population either diminished or tended to diminish the productiveness of labour, it tended to diminish the rapidity of the increase of the supposed fund of subsistence or capital from which the earnings of labour were derived. A kind of race, they thought, took place between population and "capital" in which each of the two competitors "alternately took the lead."[2] Not much could be done to accelerate the rate at which capital progressed, and the hope of humanity lay, therefore, rather in the diminution of propagation. The practical conclusion arrived at was the same as that of

[1] See the passages quoted above, pp. 67 ff., and also the following from ed. 2, p. 7: "The improvement of the barren parts would be a work of time and labour; and it must be evident to those who have the slightest acquaintance with agricultural subjects, that in proportion as cultivation extended, the additions that could yearly be made to the former average produce must be gradually and regularly diminishing."

[2] Ricardo, *Essay on the Influence of a low price of Corn on the Profits of Stock*, 1815 in *Works of David Ricardo*, ed. McCulloch, p. 379: in *Economic Essays by D. Ricardo*, ed. Gonner, p. 236.

Malthus though the argument was different. J. S. Mill represents the new line of thought very well when, mindful that the proverb, "With every mouth God sends a pair of hands," might be brought up against an opponent of propagation, he says:

"It is in vain to say that all mouths which the increase of mankind calls into existence bring with them hands. The new mouths require as much food as the old ones, and the hands do not produce as much" (*Principles*, ed. Ashley, p. 191).

Increase, Mill thought, would do no harm in some very early stage of civilisation because it might then be necessary to allow the benefits which arise from division of labour to be obtained, but,

"After a degree of density has been attained sufficient to allow the principal benefits of combination of labour, all further increase tends in itself to mischief so far as regards the average condition of the people" (*ib.*, pp. 191–2).

This degree was supposed to have been attained, at any rate in "all the most populous countries" (*ib.*, p. 750), before 1848, so that their populations were even then excessive and ought not to have increased any more.

Later economists have for the most part taken a much less unfavourable view of the effects of growth of population.

In the first place, living in a richer age, they have been more awake to the fact that man does not live by bread alone or even by food alone. Consequently they have seen that even if a growth of population did tend to diminish agricultural produce per head, it might still be desirable in consequence of its increasing other produce per head. The food expenditure of a modern civilised community is not so large a proportion of its whole expenditure—the proportion of its labour devoted to the acquisition of its food is not so large a proportion of all its labour—that there is little chance of a diminution of returns in agriculture being outweighed by an increase of returns in all other industries.

Secondly, recent years have been marked by a striking application of machinery and organised scientific research to agriculture which has made it impossible to ignore the fact that agriculture as well as other industries can and does have its productiveness increased in consequence of changes made possible by the growth of population. Therefore the budding student is now no longer taught that from some very early stage in the history of man every increase of population has always tended to diminish the productiveness of labour in agriculture. He is told that without the bigger population the agriculturist would have had neither the machinery nor the knowledge which are now at his command.

Thirdly, it has been realised that the point in the growth of population where increasing returns end and diminishing returns begin, both in agriculture alone or in agriculture and other industries taken together, is not fixed at a date either some thousands of years ago or a few years before 1850, but is continually being moved by the progress of knowledge.[1] The movement may be in either direction; discoveries are conceivable, though it is difficult to think of an actual example which would make a smaller population desirable, but in general the progress of knowledge has been rather in the other direction, making increase of numbers more likely to increase productiveness.

As a result of this the attempt has been made to re-state the law of diminishing returns in a form which would eliminate any suggestion that increase of population either actually diminishes returns or tends to diminish them. It has been suggested that we may say that at any given time, or, what comes to the same thing, given any particular conditions or other things being equal, there is what may be called a point of maximum return attained when the population is so exactly fitted to the circumstances that returns (or productiveness of labour) would be less (" diminished ") if it were either less or more than it is. This population has been christened the " *optimum* " population.[2]

§ 4. *The " Optimum."*

But unfortunately the usual cheap expedient of providing that other things shall be equal cannot properly be applied to increases and decreases of population. We cannot usefully speculate on

[1] This was clearly stated by Sidgwick in 1883, *Principles*, pp. 150–1; in 2nd ed., pp. 151–2.

[2] I am myself responsible for adopting the idea of a point of maximum return in *Elementary Political Economy*, 1888, and the first edition of *Wealth*, 1914. In the 1928 edition of *Wealth* considerations mentioned in the next section are introduced. Professor Carr Saunders is, I think, responsible for the term " optimum density of population " (*Population Problem*, 1922, p. 200).

what would be the condition of the world if its population were greater or smaller than it actually is, *other things being equal,* since it is perfectly certain that they would not be equal. J. S. Mill made a prodigious blunder when he said that the world would have been better off if population had been more restrained "*and the same improvements taken place.*"[1] It might be argued that the improvements would have been greater or less in quantity, but it is totally impossible that they could have been the *same* in character. Not only knowledge, but also material equipment or capital must be considered. If the population had been greater or smaller, invention and discovery would have taken a somewhat different direction; and we must remember to consider not only knowledge but also material equipment or "capital." A rapidly growing population will find out different things and make different things from those which a slow-growing or stationary population will find out and make: the accumulated knowledge and the accumulated material equipment will both be different. Consequently, if the population of the world had remained at the level Mill thought desirable, other things, so far from being equal, would have been so different from what they actually are, that it is quite useless to say that if they had been the same as they are, the smaller number of people would now have been more productive than the larger number now in existence actually are.

From this it seems to follow that the idea of there being at any and every point of time (or given any particular conditions) a certain magnitude at which population ought at that time to stand in order that the maximum possible productiveness may be then attained, is not so useful as it looks at first sight. The number of mankind is not determined by the wave of a conjurer's hand, but is increased by births and diminished by deaths. Unless there is pestilence or slaughter, the deaths will follow a fairly steady course, dependent chiefly on the numbers born a lifetime earlier; the number of births is largely dependent on the number of persons born from twenty to forty years earlier, and persons born do not begin to work, at any rate to much purpose, till they are about fifteen years of age. Consequently, population, and still more the population of workers, at any one

[1] *Principles*, ed. Ashley, p. 193.

moment of time cannot be dissociated from the population which preceded it nor from the population which is to follow after it, and the "optimum" or best possible population, conceived in the way suggested, of one moment, say 1848, may be quite incompatible with the optimum conceived in the same way for 1828 or 1868 or even, though in less degree, of 1798 and 1898, and in still less degree with that of still earlier and later dates. Therefore, in conceiving the optimum population of any particular time, we must not confine ourselves to that date without looking before and after, but remember that the population is the result of the existence of previous populations and will be the cause of subsequent populations, and that the best is what is best in the long run, so that the best population for any particular moment is that which is compatible with population taking the best possible line of movement, whether that be increase or decrease, slow or rapid.

This perhaps seems to make the theory of the subject more difficult, but it makes its application to practical life much easier. In practical life the existing population has to be taken as a starting-point, and whether it is above or below the optimum from the point of view of the whole of mankind, past, present and future, is of no importance, since we cannot alter the past. Moreover, in modern civilised life we cannot even alter that immediate future which we call the present; we cannot deliberately reduce the population by murder, and to increase it by the addition of babies in excess of the number of deaths or decrease it by keeping the births below the deaths is a slow process. Thus all we can do is to alter, and that only very gradually, the population of the future by some action which will increase or diminish either mortality or natality—the converse of mortality.

In considering at any time the desirability in the interest of future mankind of increasing or decreasing population, we have to weigh on the one side the advantages which may be expected from the greater possibilities of gain from co-operation if people are more numerous against the advantages which may be expected from the greater relative plentifulness of land surface, natural forces and materials, and man-made material equipment, if people are less numerous.

About the advantages derivable from the co-operation of larger numbers it is difficult to say anything, except that it seems clear that they must diminish as the number already present grows. If, by virtue of co-operation, 200 can produce three times as much as 100, we should not infer from this that 2000 will produce three times as much as 1000, and still less that 2000 millions will produce three times as much as 1000 millions. J. S. Mill was no doubt wrong in thinking the advantages of co-operation had been fully attained with the population rather less than it was in 1848, but he would have been right if he had said that they were diminishing as the world became fuller, and would eventually become unimportant if it went on getting fuller and fuller.

About the disadvantage arising from the larger number of mankind having less surface of land and less natural forces and materials per head than the smaller, we can say pretty confidently that the English economists of the first half of the nineteenth century took far too gloomy a view. Doubtless in course of time, if numbers went on increasing, the disadvantage would become as important as they supposed it. But the world had certainly not become so thickly peopled by their time that an enlargement of the terrestrial globe would then have been of any great benefit. There were still immense unused territories of "fertile land" in every way as good as, or even better than, most of the land already "occupied."

It is not a sound objection to this to urge that the unoccupied land was "more distant" and consequently "worse" than that already occupied although it was equally or more "fertile." Distant from what? From the existing location of mankind? But that location would be altered by the occupation. The sites of New York and Chicago seemed very distant a few generations ago, the sites of London and Berlin seemed very distant in the time of Julius Cæsar—are they distant now? We may therefore say with some confidence that in all the earlier stages of human history it was not the "niggardliness of Nature," the shortage of land-surface, natural forces and natural materials that created the possibility that if natality were high and mortality low, the resultant increase of population would have been too rapid in the sense of causing a diminution of returns or productivity.

What really created this possibility was the shortage of the material and non-material equipment required for utilising the unused "gifts of Nature." (Nature was supposed to be a "giver," although a "niggardly" one.) The new lands, whether they were an addition to the occupied area of an early English township or manor,[1] or a colony in North America, could not be occupied effectively and productively without a certain amount of knowledge, organisation and material machinery and implements which could not be accumulated at all except by people who had more than a bare subsistence, and could not be accumulated even by them unless they were given time.

This makes it certain that there always was some limit to the rapidity with which population could advantageously grow, but of course it does not tell us what that limit was. We can only guess that in early times the desirable rapidity must have been for the world at large a rate which we with our nineteenth-century European and American standards would call very low.

At this point we are forced to take notice of the fact that all sections of mankind need not and do not increase together at the same rate. Rapid increases in some sections may be accompanied by standstill or even decrease in others. The rate for the whole is the result of putting together a number of different rates. Consequently, the fact that the desirable rate for the whole was very low may have been often quite compatible with a very rapid increase of particular sections. When locomotion over long distances was impossible or very difficult, the sections with easy access to "new" or unoccupied lands could increase rapidly with advantage to themselves and the whole, while the sections more in the middle of the old occupied area could not. And everywhere, whether on the borders or in the centre, sections which possessed more ability to accumulate knowledge and material instruments, and to use them both when accumulated, could, with advantage to themselves and the whole, increase more rapidly than the inferior sections.

This actually happened. In modern recorded history we have it illustrated by the great example of the increase of the European section, which was situated immediately opposite almost unoccupied America, and was also more capable. But an explana-

[1] "Newlands" is a common name in English topography.

tion may be demanded; it may be asked why this convenient result came about.

Malthus, of course, explained it by the fact that in the case of the conveniently placed and capable sections, what he called positive and preventive checks were both relaxed; there was not so much starvation, and there was less reluctance to produce and bring up a large family. Professor Carr Saunders is inclined to deny that starvation played nearly so large a part as Malthus imagined in keeping down population; he thinks of it as kept down at all times by prudential motives leading to practices which prevented conceptions or destroyed the infants, before or after their birth, or killed the children at a somewhat later stage when it became more obviously inconvenient to support them. But it is a little difficult for him to hold that the well-placed and capable sections increased simply owing to a relaxation of their preventive checks, inasmuch as he suggests that the adoption of these checks, however abominable some of them may seem to us, are the real explanation of the human race being able to raise itself above the lower animals.

My own suggestion is that the required explanation is to be looked for in facts concerning infant mortality. Neither Malthus nor Professor Carr Saunders seem to me to have realised what an overwhelming part infant mortality can play and probably did play in the regulation of population. In the absence of records of births such as are provided by the modern system of registration, infant mortality is apt to be greatly under-estimated. The traveller who uses only his eyes sees the living children, and either forgets the dead altogether or rashly supposes them to bear about the same proportion to the living as they do in the superior country from which he himself comes. He then reports that "families are not large" or that "women do not have many children." The traveller who is not content with what he sees, but proceeds to question parents about the number of children they have actually had, is given numbers far below the truth, because the parents have no records and neglect or forget such trifling incidents as the birth and death of an infant who only lived a few hours or days. Commentators are then misled into concluding that the people observed do not increase in numbers, or do not increase rapidly, because natality is low, while in fact it may be quite high but is counteracted by high infantile mortality.

Now even in countries sufficiently advanced to have registration of births and deaths, infant mortality has been recorded of between three and four hundred per thousand, that is to say, between three and four children out of every ten born have died before reaching the age of twelve months. Double this mortality, and suppose seven out of ten to die in the first twelve months, and you could not have an increasing population unless the mortality at later ages was extraordinarily low or each woman on the average had more than ten children. And would there be anything surprising in even mediæval Western Europeans, to say nothing of barbarians at all times, having an infant mortality double of that which prevailed in a large area of India in 1902–11?

It thus appears extremely probable that in early times infantile mortality required very little assistance in keeping population stationary or increasing at a very slow rate. If this is so we get a very reasonable explanation of the manner in which what Malthus called "the difficulty arising from the principle of population" was actually overcome. The tribes or peoples who had sufficient energy and skill to take better care of their children than the others would, of course, increase in numbers relatively to the others as well as absolutely. But this greater will and capacity for tending their offspring would be likely to be accompanied by greater energy and capacity in other directions; those whose numbers become a larger proportion of the whole would be also those who could best utilise all opportunities of planting out additions to the human race either by intenser cultivation of already occupied territory or by pioneer occupation of territory which before was lying either entirely waste or only slightly used. Whatever doubts we may have about the Israelites taking possession of Canaan, we can have none about the Europeans who took what is now the United States and Canada. On the whole we may be sure that the peoples which increased relatively because they were more capable of caring for their offspring were just the peoples which could increase without any diminution, but rather with an increase of productivity on the part not only of themselves but of the world at large.

§ 5. *The Future.*

While we may look back on the past with some complacency, we may be troubled by doubts with regard to the future.

It is true that the introduction and popularisation of modern methods of preventing conceptions make it much more unreasonable than it was to fear that the population of the whole world will increase too rapidly—faster than the optimum rate. The population can be kept down without more of Malthus' "vice and misery" than is necessarily connected with these methods. How much that is will be a matter of dispute, but few will think it as great as that which was involved in the primitive methods of getting rid of human offspring already in being, or even as great as what would have been involved in Malthus' recipe of "postponement of marriage," if that were carried as far as it would have to be carried in order to have a considerable effect in checking the growth of a healthy population.

It is true also that there is not much reason to fear the extinction or even the reduction of the whole human race in consequence of the adoption of the new method of control. As children become scarcer, they will, like other things in similar case, come to possess greater marginal utility—not only will they evoke greater paternal pride, but they will be able to earn more in the early stages of working life and thus be less of an economic burden on their parents. States as well as parents will be affected and less inclined to burden families with taxation and more inclined to adopt "family endowment" and other schemes for reducing this burden.

The real danger seems now to be not that the total of population will be much too great or much too small, but that the growth of the more capable and efficient sections may be so checked relatively to that of the less capable and efficient by the new method of control that the effect on the total productivity may be bad.

That there will for some time be a relatively larger growth of the sections which are at present the less capable and efficient seems to be inevitable. It is the advanced sections which have adopted the new method first, and its use will only spread gradually to the rest of the world. Meantime the rest of the world will be learning from the advanced sections how to care better for its infants and will also be acquiring greater means of supporting them, so that its population is likely to grow much faster for a time than it has done in the past. This relative growth of the less advanced sections must be unfavourable to the general productivity, so long as it lasts. But when the transition period is passed and the new control has become universal, it would seem reasonable to expect that the old state of things in which the more capable and efficient races increased relatively to the others will be restored. Those who see good openings for their children will have more children than the others. It will, of course, not be necessarily true that those which are at the top of the tree now will continue to be so, and therefore such races as are so now must beware of supposing that the world will be less capable and efficient if they become a smaller proportion of the whole population or even die out altogether.

It does not appear that the economist will get much help in considering the future by toying with the doctrine of natural selection or survival of the fittest.

Marshall in a fine flight of imagination says of Adam Smith that

> " after insisting on the advantages of division of labour and pointing out how they render it possible for increased numbers to live in comfort on a limited territory, he argued that the pressure of population on the means of subsistence tends to weed out those races who through want of organisation or any other cause are unable to turn to the best account the advantages of the place in which they live " (*Principles*, ed. 1, p. 300, ed. 8, p. 240).

Future editors of Marshall will be puzzled to find this argument in the *Wealth of Nations*. But ten years after that work was published Joseph Townsend did suggest something of the kind in his attack on the poor-law :

> " By establishing a community of goods, or rather by giving to the idle and vicious the *first* claim upon the produce of the earth, many of the more prudent, careful and industrious citizens are straitened in their circumstances and restrained from marriage. The farmer breeds only from the best of his cattle; but our laws choose rather to preserve the worst, and seem to be anxious lest the breed should fail." (*Dissertation on the Poor Laws*, 1786, repr. 1817, p. 62.)

Malthus, though his insistence on the geometrical ratio appears to have been of some assistance to Darwin (see the Preface to the *Origin of Species*), does not seem to have concerned himself about breeding from the best stock, and his antidote to over-rapid increase of population, the postponement of marriage by the careful and prudent, is obviously open to the objection urged by Townsend against the poor-law.

Later on we find Herbert Spencer taking up Townsend's line. In *The Man* versus *the State*, 1884, p. 69, after saying that natural selection was shown by Darwin to be the chief cause of the "evolution through which all living beings . . . have reached their present degrees of organisation and adaptation to their modes of life," he adds:

> "Yet, strange to say, now that this truth is recognised by most cultivated people—now that the beneficent working of the survival of the fittest has been so impressed upon them that, much more than people in past times, they might be expected to hesitate before neutralising its action—now, more than ever before in the history of the world, are they doing all they can to further the survival of the unfittest!"

He is arguing, like Townsend, against State action in favour of the poor, and he endeavours to support his position by referring to Margaret Jukes and her descendants. She was a disreputable person who lived somewhere up the Hudson and had a great many descendants equally or more disreputable, including 200 criminals, and Spencer, without distinctly saying so, desires his readers to understand that if there had been no legal system of poor relief in New York State, Margaret would have had at any rate fewer descendants. But, as he would not forbid private charity (as appears from p. 66 of the work quoted), he really required to prove, not only that the New York State system contributed something to the existence and number of Margaret's descendants, but also that it contributed more than private charity would have done in the absence of any State system of relief. This he made no attempt to do, and in view of the fact that State systems have been adopted and are maintained because private charity is too lavish and indiscriminate, we may well doubt it. Our doubt will be intensified when we remember that charitable gifts can be made by will, and that if the State is never to regulate such gifts, an enormous mass of endowments absurdly ill-adapted to the needs of the moment will gradually come into existence and do more harm than any State poor relief is ever likely to do.

Going a little deeper than this, we may question the soundness of the idea on which all arguments like that of Herbert Spencer rest. This is, that economic competition, bounded only by such conditions as are supposed to be consistent with a policy of strict *laisser faire*, is a struggle for existence.

That tribes of mankind have struggled for existence, and that some have been exterminated by others, is doubtless true, though the conquerors, who alone tell the tale, have generally been led by their pride in butchery to exaggerate rather than to conceal the extent of their success in wiping out the enemy.[1] Optimists may hope that the butchers were "fitter" than the butchered. But economic competition is not war, but rivalry in mutual service. The pressure which it exercises is not directed towards the extermination of the "unfit," but towards inducing everyone, whether "fittest" or "unfittest," to do the kind of work which will pay him best. We say, loosely, that a blind or legless man is at a disadvantage in competition, but such a man has far more chance of being able to support himself by labour in a society of men co-operating by way of "competition" than he would have in a state of isolation. In short, competition has no tendency to weed out the "unfit"; it rather provides situations in which they can manage to live.

While rejecting the eighteenth-century view that a particular set of arrangements in regard to property, marriage, parental power, and other institutions are natural, and also rejecting the simple belief of Townsend and Spencer that these arrangements must be untouched in order to allow of natural selection producing the best variety of human beings, we need not rush off to the opposite extreme and advocate the establishment in each State or Empire of a Ministry of Propagations charged with the

[1] Sihon, king of Heshbon, like the government of Belgium in 1914, refused to allow an army to cross his neutral territory on its way to invade another country. The chronicler of the invaders quite proudly reports, "The Lord our God delivered him before us; and we smote him, and his sons, and all his people. And we took all his cities at that time and utterly destroyed the men, and the women, and the little ones, of every city, we left none to remain" (Deuteronomy ii. 26–34).

task of selecting couples for matrimony and prescribing how many children each couple are to have. "The best" of the cattle, from which, as Townsend says, the farmer breeds, are the best from his point of view, which is determined by market values. There is no such easy criterion for settling what is "the best" human being—not even a Conference of representatives of all the national Ministries of Propagation, sitting at Geneva, could be trusted to make no mistake about this.

While we cannot say that we could not have been bred better than we have been, we can, like Homer's Greeks, boast that we are much better than our remote ancestors,

ἡμεῖς τοι πατέρων μέγ' ἀμείνονες εὐχόμεθ' εἶναι,

so that although it may be true that we might have been bred better, it is also true that we might have been bred much worse than we are. This rather suggests that we should not attempt to turn things quite topsy-turvy on the chance of making an improvement, but content ourselves with small changes, such as a further hampering of propagation by persons with undoubted hereditary defects or diseases.

CHAPTER V

THE INFLUENCE OF CO-OPERATION ON PRODUCE

§ 1. *The Advantages of Division of Labour.*

THE number and quality of the people being given, the next thing to consider is their Co-operation or working together.

That the aggregate produce of a number of persons would be greater if they joined their forces and allotted work to each in such a way that each one did not have to produce for himself all things which he wanted, must have been observed at a very early stage in history. The learned Roscher in his *Principles of Political Economy* (Vol. I. p. 189 in Lalor's translation) gives a number of references to Xenophon, Plato, Aristotle, Thomas Aquinas and Luther. But we may content ourselves here with the immediate ancestry of Adam Smith's famous exposition of the subject.

Sir William Petty, writing his *Political Arithmetic* in 1672, argues that a big shipping trade can work cheaper than a small one because it makes it possible to have different kinds of ships for different purposes, just " as cloth must be cheaper made when one cards, another spins, another weaves, another presses and packs, than when all the operations above-mentioned were clumsily performed by the same hand " (*Econ. Writings*, ed. Hull, p. 260). And in his defence of the possibility of London having at some date in the future 4,690,000 inhabitants, he says :

" in so vast a city manufactures will beget one another, and each manufacture will be divided into as many parts as possible, whereby the work of each artisan will be simple and easie ; as, for example, in the making of a watch, if one man shall make the wheels, another the spring, another shall engrave the dial-plate and another shall make the cases, then the watch will be better and cheaper than if the whole work be put upon any one man. And we also see that in towns, and in the streets of a great town, where all the inhabitants are almost of one trade, the commodity peculiar to those places is made better and cheaper than elsewhere" (*ib.*, p. 473).

Mandeville, in the second part of the *Fable of the Bees*, makes Cleomenes, one of the speakers in his dialogue, say that people who have peace and security will soon learn to "divide and subdivide their labour." The other speaker, Horatio, says he does not understand, and then the dialogue proceeds :

"CLEO. Man, as I have hinted before, naturally loves to imitate what he sees others do, which is the reason that savage people all do the same thing; this hinders them from meliorating their condition, though they are always wishing for it; but if one will wholly apply himself to the making of bows and arrows, whilst another provides food, a third builds huts, a fourth makes garments, and a fifth utensils, they not only become useful to one another, but the callings themselves will, in the same number of years, receive much greater improvement than if all had been followed promiscuously by every one of the five.

HOR. I believe you are perfectly right there; and the truth of what you say is in nothing so conspicuous as it is in watch-making, which is come to a higher degree of perfection than it would have arrived at yet, if the whole had always remained the employment of one person; and I am persuaded that even the plenty we have of clocks and watches as well as the exactness and beauty they may be made of are chiefly owing to the division that has been made of that art into many branches" (Dialogue vi).

Francis Hutcheson, Adam Smith's teacher and predecessor in the Glasgow chair of Moral Philosophy, said :

"Nay, 'tis well known that the produce of the labours of any given number, twenty for instance, in supplying the necessaries and conveniences of life shall be much greater by assigning to one a certain sort of work of one kind in which he will soon acquire skill and dexterity, and to another assigning work of a different kind, than if each one of the twenty were obliged to employ himself by turn in all the different sorts of labour requisite for his subsistence without sufficient dexterity in any. In the former method each procures a great quantity of goods of one kind, and can exchange a part of it for such goods obtained by the labours of others as he shall stand in need of" (*System of Moral Philosophy*, 1755, Vol. I. p. 255).

Next comes the disquisition on "*Art*" in the *Encyclopédie*, 1751, which adds rapidity of work and likelihood of the invention of machinery to "skill and dexterity":

"As to the rapidity with which the work can be executed and the goodness of the article, these depend entirely on the number of workmen brought together. When a manufacture is conducted by a large number of persons, each operation is performed by a different man. One workman throughout his life has done and will do only one single thing; another only does some other thing; the result of which is that each thing is well and quickly done and, moreover, that the best-made article is the cheapest. Further, taste and artistic sense are necessarily become more perfect among a great number of workmen, since some are then sure to be found who are capable of thinking, of making the proper combinations and eventually discovering the only means of putting them in front of their neighbours; finding the means of saving material, or of making the time or the labour go further, whether by the invention of a new machine or the discovery of a more suitable method." (Vol. i. p. 717, quoted in the French in Smith's *Wealth of Nations*, ed. Cannan, vol. i. p. 9, n. 4.)

The *Encyclopédie* also has an article on pins (*Épingle*) which describes their manufacture as being divided into eighteen separate operations.

Joseph Harris, in his *Essay on Money and Coins*, 1757, added the advantage which comes from persons and countries being specialised to occupations which are suitable to their different natural qualities. "Men," he says, "are endued with various talents and propensities which naturally dispose and fit them for different occupations," and "all countries differ more or less either in the kinds or goodness of their products, natural or artificial" (Pt. I, § 11, p. 15). In a section (Pt. I, § 12) headed "Usefulness of distinct trades further illustrated" he says:

"The advantages accruing to mankind from their betaking themselves severally to different occupations are very great and obvious: for thereby, each becoming expert and skilful in his own particular art, they are enabled to furnish one another with the products of their respective labours performed in a much better manner and with much less toil than any one of them could do of himself" (p. 17).

Even the farmer, he points out, could not get on without the aid of the smith and the carpenter, and

"in building and furnishing a house the business becomes still more complex, and more variety of arts are necessary. And should anyone undertake to provide a coat only, by going himself through the various operations of shearing the wool, carding, spinning, weaving, tucking, etc., half the labour and toil in his own particular profession would not only have equipped him with a better garment, but also procured him other necessaries. Besides the great incumbrance of tools that would be requisite for the finishing of most things from the beginning, it would be next to impossible for any one man either to find time or to acquire skill sufficient for the making of all those tools; he would soon find himself at a loss, and under a necessity of seeking the aid of others" (pp. 17–18).

Adam Smith's account of the division of labour, though so famous, is not remarkable for originality nor even for completeness in the exposition of what had already been discovered. Both in the lectures and in the *Wealth of Nations* only three advantages of division of labour are given: (1) the increase of dexterity in the specialised workman, (2) the saving of time spent in passing from one kind of work to another, and (3) the increase of invention owing to work being simplified. Smith damaged his exposition of the first of these by a too exclusive insistence on mere manual dexterity in the performance of simple operations, although he was aware that the specialisation of persons to different occupations and even to different sciences was important. Similarly in regard to the third advantage, he greatly overstressed the importance of invention by manual workers who see that their simple jobs might be done by a machine, forgetting that the invention of such a machine is anything but popular among those whose labour it is to supersede. He omitted altogether the economy of tools and the possibility of localising industries so as to get the most good from the different qualities of different places. And he not only omitted but actually denied the existence of the advantage which is got by sorting persons out among different kinds of labour according to their natural qualities. It was the fashion of the time to believe that all men are born much alike, and Smith only fell in with the fashion of his time in making the modest suggestion that his own natural abilities were no better than those of any street porter:

"The difference between the most dissimilar characters, between a philosopher and a street porter, for example, seems to arise not so much from nature, as from habit, custom and education. When they came into the world, and for the first six or eight years of their existence, they were perhaps very much alike, and neither their parents nor playfellows could perceive any remarkable difference. About that age, or soon after, they come to be employed in very different occupations. The difference of talents comes then to be taken notice of, and widens by degrees, till at last the vanity of the philosopher is willing to acknowledge scarce any resemblance" (Vol. I. pp. 17–18).

Even if it were true, however, that there is no advantageous sorting out of persons to the various occupations according to the suitability of their natural talents, the obvious advantage of a certain distribution of occupations between the three great categories of men, women and children would still remain.

The British mind loves the certainty and precision of simple arithmetic, and what chiefly contributed to the enormous success of Adam Smith's exposition of the advantages of division of labour was the way in which he caught the imagination of his readers by describing the eighteen operations of pin-making, each performed by a different workman, and by calculating that even in a factory which he had seen, where only ten men divided the work among them, the output per man was 4800 pins per day instead of the twenty or less which it might have been if they had each worked alone. This was backed up by the magnificent passage at the end of Chapter I, in which, taking his cue from Mun, Locke and Mandeville, he contrasts the "accommodation of the most common artificer or day-labourer in a civilised and thriving country" with "that of many an African king, the absolute master of the lives and liberties of ten thousand naked savages," and attributes the whole difference to the "co-operation of many thousands" in supplying the civilised labourer's wants.

Owing to the popularity of its form, Smith's exposition was amended in a somewhat desultory and half-hearted manner.

His omission of the saving of tools was pointed out by John Rae in his *New Principles on the Subject of Political Economy*, 1834, who is quoted by J. S. Mill (*Principles*, ed. Ashley, p. 129): "If any man had all the tools which many different occupations require, at least three-fourths of them would constantly be idle and useless."

His denial of the advantage of sorting out persons of different natural qualities according to their suitability for various occupations was to some extent rectified by Babbage in his *Economy of Machinery and Manufactures*, 1832. Babbage at any rate saw that factory work could be advantangeously divided between persons of different natural strength as well as of different acquired skill (pp. 132 ff.).

Smith himself, in a later passage of the *Wealth of Nations*, repaired to some extent his omission of the advantage arising from the fact that co-operation of persons living in different countries enables different kinds of production to be suitably sorted out between countries with various natural qualities. It would, he says, be obviously absurd for the Scotch to grow grapes for wine-making at enormous expense in hothouses instead of procuring the wine from southern countries by offering in exchange something which can be easily produced in Scotland.

> "It is," he says, "the maxim of every prudent master of a family never to attempt to make at home what it will cost him more to make than to buy. The tailor does not attempt to make his own shoes, but buys them of the shoemaker. The shoemaker does not attempt to make his own clothes, but employs a tailor. The farmer attempts to make neither the one nor the other, but employs those different artificers. All of them find it for their interest to employ their whole industry in a way in which they have some advantage over their neighbours, and to purchase with a part of its produce, or, what is the same thing, with the price of a part of it, whatever else they have occasion for.
>
> "What is prudence in the conduct of every private family can scarce be folly in that of a great kingdom" (Vol. I. p. 422).

This exposition is wanting in generality, occurring, as it does, in the discussion of mercantile restraints on foreign trade and dealing expressly with "kingdoms," although co-operation between persons living in different parts of the same country or kingdom is advantageous for exactly the same reason as international co-operation. Subsequent writers tended to follow Smith in this respect and so to tuck away the advantage arising from "territorial division of labour," as Torrens called it, in their discussion of international trade, and, falling in with the pernicious practice of treating international trade as different in principle from internal trade, they embarrassed the subject by preposterous attempts to illustrate the gains resulting from international division of labour by arithmetical examples which would have been seen at once to be absurd if they had been applied to the gains arising from division of labour between, say, calico producers living in Lancashire and milk producers living in Cheshire. William Ellis, in his *Outlines of Social Economy*, 1846, was a notable exception to the rule (pp. 25–7), but had no influence.

Much later the economists began to discuss the matter under the new title of "Localisation of Industry." Marshall in the earlier *Economics of Industry*, p. 47, says that the "collection into the same locality of large numbers who are engaged in the same trade is called the Localisation of Industry." The name is not a very satisfactory one, because any trade which is established in a place may be said in the natural sense of the word to be localised there, whereas localisation of a trade in the sense intended requires that the trade should be carried on in the locality to a greater extent than will satisfy the local demand for its products. In the *Principles*, Marshall headed Book IV, chap. x, "The Concentration of Specialised Industries in Particular Localities," and "concentration" seems an improvement on "localisation."

We must notice that differences in the natural characteristics of different areas are not the only reasons which make some concentration of industries desirable. Even if all areas were alike in situation, climate and other natural characteristics, there would be reasons for some, though doubtless a less amount of, concentration.

In the first place many things can only be produced, or can be produced more easily, when large quantities are produced in the same town or district. Even if no situation is any better than another for it, a country will do well to put its seat of government somewhere. Even if all considerations of situation, climate and other natural features are absent, it will be well for some manufactures to be carried on in some towns and others in other towns. A single big factory involves a considerable amount of concentration, since it can supply a large area with the articles it produces; biscuits cannot be made in a factory as large as Huntley and Palmer's without concentrating the industry to a large extent in the place where such a factory is situated. But besides this we have to reckon with the fact that factories and works of each particular kind are constantly in need of things, such as machinery and parts of machinery, which can be supplied to them more easily when they are massed together in considerable numbers than if they are scattered widely over the area which they serve; for example, even if all parts of Great Britain were alike in climate and other natural characteristics and all were equally accessible from the sources from which the material is drawn, it would still be desirable that the cotton manufacture should be concentrated somewhere, because it would be easier to deliver the material to factories concentrated in one district than to hundreds of single factories spread all over the country. Even in agriculture a certain amount of concentration is made desirable not only by differences of soil and climate but also by the concentration of population. When, in consequence of the advantages which we have just been describing or for any other reason, people have become concentrated in certain towns and districts, it is desirable to concentrate the production of table-vegetables, milk, butter, eggs and other things which are rapidly perishable and difficult to transport, in the neighbourhood of the more thickly peopled areas, and to grow grain and other things which are neither rapidly perishable nor difficult to transport in the more distant areas. It is certainly desirable to do this to some extent if the near and the distant areas are exactly similar in natural characteristics, and it may even be desirable to some, but a less extent, if the natural characteristics of the areas would by themselves suggest the reverse arrangement.

Secondly, so long as people are not perfectly mobile, the difference in the characteristics of the inhabitants of different areas is a good reason for concentration of many industries; the inhabitants of Central Africa and of North America being what they are at present, the difference between them would be sufficient reason for making the motor vehicles for both in North America even if there were no other good reasons.

We should notice also that when particular characteristics have once been acquired either by the areas themselves or by the inhabitants of the areas, the fact that the characteristics have been given by man and not by Nature makes no difference.

It is quite possible that if a choice had to be made now between Lancashire and South Wales, both denuded of all that has been done to them by man and also of their present inhabitants, South Wales might be adjudged the better area in which to concentrate the English cotton manufacture. But, as things are, it would be ridiculous to attempt to move the manufacture from Lancashire.

§ 2. *The Stimulus to Industry.*

It is one thing to explain the advantages which a number of persons will derive from working together and distributing the different kinds of labour among them; it is another to get them to do it. Isolated Man, if we may be allowed to refer to a person of such doubtful antecedents, works in order to get the produce of his own labour, and Society as a whole works in order to get the produce of *its* own labour. Even at the present time a good deal of work is done by individuals because they expect to get, and do actually get, what they themselves produce—we have only to look at a great mass of the work done by women and men within the household and at men toiling on "allotments" for examples.

But when people co-operate and divide labour, each individual can no longer get his own particular produce. Politicians and professors are sometimes said to eat their own words, but this is metaphor. Even the farmer nowadays eats little of what he has produced on the farm. Instead of getting what he himself has produced, the individual usually gets little bits of what thousands of other people have combined to produce. It is obviously impossible under the present system to give each worker the whole of what he himself produces or any considerable part of it. The diamond-cutter cannot live on cut diamonds, nor the navvy on cubic yards of embankment.

This being so, and free labour being the rule, the organisation must be such that each potential worker is offered more if he comes into the scheme than if he elects to stand outside it and support himself without assistance from others. And he is offered more. People come into the scheme and work in it because it promises them amounts of money such that they will be able to buy far more of what they want than they could get by working independently by themselves, trying to produce all they want directly for themselves and without help from others. I doubt if the " hardest " of poor-law reformers ever proposed that each able-bodied pauper or unemployed person should be fenced in on a suitable area of land and allowed to support himself without intercourse with the world outside. It is recognised that such isolation would mean what modern civilised man calls starvation. The worst terms that the individual could get by entering the general scheme of co-operation would be better.

The general theory of value, outlined below in Chapter VII, may suggest a difficulty in making co-operation produce as much as it might do. As each section of workers sells to the other sections and depends for its remuneration on the value of what it sells, will not the dependence of value on quantity cause the value of its product to fall, and so discourage it from producing?

If this were true to any serious extent, some change would long ago have been forced on the world by declining production. Fortunately, the difficulty is not quite as great as it looks at first sight.

Firstly, a diminution in the value of a product means a diminution of the value of any given unit of the product, and not necessarily of the aggregate product when that aggregate has increased. From a greater aggregate production the producers may receive more, although the value of the unit has declined. Hence it frequently happens that the discovery and adoption of some easier way of making an article actually benefits the existing body of producers because it enables them to sell a great deal more of the article at a price per unit which, though reduced, is not so much reduced as to diminish the aggregate amount received for the whole quantity sold by that body of producers. Consequently, it is in these cases advantageous to the producers, even considered as a single body, to introduce the easier method of production and produce more. The increased production, owing to improved methods, of motor-cars, for example, has greatly reduced their price, but so far at any rate the reduction has been counterbalanced by the increased number sold, so that there has been no tendency for the remuneration of producers to be cut down. It seems too that the elasticity of demand for commodities is on the whole mass somewhat increasing in consequence of more and more substitutes being introduced for each particular thing. Are we not even told that a particular sort of glass which admits ultra-violet rays is a substitute for butter?

Secondly, even where the elasticity of demand is so small that it does happen that an increase of output will diminish the aggregate value of the whole output, and not merely the value of the unit, this will not cause individual producers working in competition with one another to reduce or keep down their output. It may be the interest of all the persons engaged in a particular trade or manufacture, say the production of calico, that the total output should not be increased, but it will remain the interest of each of the competing producers to increase his own particular output. To restrain him from doing so, a binding agreement between all the producers is necessary, and this is difficult to obtain, and difficult to enforce when it is obtained. And if it is obtained and enforced, the combination is not safe from new competitors. What may happen in the future is uncertain, but so far as the history of the world has yet gone, consumers of particular commodities have suffered only trifling damage from such restrictions of production.

No institution is perfect, but no institution which serves its purpose at all is to be swept away before we are sure of something better to put in its place. The present incentive to industry is not at all times as effective as is desirable, but do we know of a better one?

Fear of punishment has been tried. One set of persons have been made slaves to others and induced to work by fear of beating and other torture. But, though this method has worked fairly well with horses, it has failed with most other animals, and especially with human beings. Emancipation of slaves took place because it was gradually recognised that more was to be got by paying the worker for free labour than by beating him, and then the chief incentive to labour became the money to be got in exchange for it. The discovery of the superiority of free labour, it must be remembered, applied to forced labour for the local and the national group of persons as well as to forced labour for individual slave-owners. Most *corvées* for public purposes were gradually replaced by free paid labour. Forced labour only lingers in Western civilised countries in cases where it is supposed a levy of the whole able-bodied population is required, as for war, and in a few survivals which are interesting rather than important, such as jury service, and clearing snow from the pavements.

The nature of the transition from slavery to free labour is flagrantly misrepresented in Rodbertus' well-known epigram, "Hunger was found a good substitute for the lash." Hunger is not a good substitute for the lash and never will be. If it had been, the slave-owners would have tried it. They did not, any more than the horse-owner tries to make his horses work by refusing them oats. It is not hunger, nor even the fear of hunger, which is the great incentive to industry. Even in the Middle Ages it was not so; beggars were often "sturdy" then, and it is impossible to be sturdy without food. Private and State charity stands between the idle and starvation, and for everyone that works because he is afraid of not having the necessaries of life there are ten thousand who work in order to get money over and above what will supply them with those necessaries—money which they can spend as they please on things other than the necessaries of life.

Fear of punishment being clearly of no use, a sense of duty may be suggested as an incentive to work, and no doubt this is often very effective. But among reasoning beings the strength of this motive will always depend greatly on an estimate formed by the worker of the consequences of his action. Men will do their duty regardless of toil, inconvenience and danger when it is obvious to them that important consequences hang on the punctual performance by everyone of his duty, but they will quite cheerfully neglect their duty when they think the consequences of neglect are unimportant. In war the important consequences of flinching in face of the enemy are very obvious to soldiers, and so we find that they generally have a powerful sense of duty in regard to "going over the top" or sticking to their post; but in the matter of abstention from pilfering stores and avoidance of waste, armies of the highest reputation have been notoriously sadly wanting in sense of duty. In the late war I knew a highly respected member of Parliament of distinctly socialist opinions who sometimes lectured on elementary economics. He happened to be a corporal in the army, and instead of returning unused bread to the stores, he was compelled by the public opinion of his company to bury it for fear their ration might be reduced.

In order to make the small economies which can be effected by single individuals belonging to the rank and file seem worth some inconvenience to themselves, the results must not be spread over a very wide area. The corporal's company did not mind wasting the bread, because the loss when spread over all the British tax-payers appeared very trifling to them compared with the possibility of their own ration being reduced to something less than what they might some time require. We can easily see that it would be hopeless to expect the rank and file in industry to work hard and well and intelligently in order to do their duty to mundane society as a whole:

"Work hard, my good fellow, put your back into it, and bring your brains to bear on your job. As you are the average man, and there are about fourteen hundred million workers in the world, if you can manage to increase your output by twenty per cent., the income per head of all the world will be increased by one seven-thousand-millionth!"

If the appeal could be made not to one person at a time but to a whole group of workers in some particular line of production let us say that of providing coal, for example, it would sound a little better:

"Oyez! Oyez! All ye who are engaged in getting coal out of the ground and carrying it to wherever it is wanted! Work harder and better! Remember that if you all increase your output by twenty per cent., the whole world will have twenty per cent. more coal, or, by shifting some of you off into other employment, it will be able to take the advantage partly in more coal and partly in other things."

Here the good to be got would seem more striking; the additional produce would be appreciable. But the magnitude of the body appealed to causes difficulties from which the appeal to a single individual was free. The work is carried on in different parts of the world under very different climatic and other conditions; the workers in some parts will be certain to think that they are already doing all that is required and that the gingering up should be applied only to certain other quarters.

"But," some reader will object, "why all this talk of duty to the world at large? Of course no one is going to bother about mundane duty; it is civic duty that we must preach, duty to the nation."

By " the nation " he means the inhabitants of the areas which happen to be within a single customs boundary—Great-Britain-and-Northern-Ireland, the Union of South Africa, Jamaica, Latvia, for examples—and has to imagine arrangements quite different from the present for co-operation between the inhabitants of each of these areas and the inhabitants of the other areas. If we overlook that difficulty we must certainly admit that duty to the nation is a more promising incentive than duty to the world. An individual American average worker would by increasing his output 20 per cent. (if the benefit was confined to the United States) increase the average income of the inhabitants of the United States about one four-hundred-millionth; and an average worker in Esthonia would in similar circumstances increase the average income of Esthonia by about as much as one four-millionth, which figures compare very well with the one seven-thousand-millionth suggested in the case of mundane duty. But why are these figures better? Simply because the area is smaller. Anyone who thinks that duty to the persons who live within the same customs area is a more powerful incentive than duty to the world at large, should consider whether duty to persons living inside the same local taxation area may not be still more powerful, and then, after thinking over the difficulties of defining and segregating these persons in such a way that duty can be performed to them without getting mixed up with advantages given to others, let him further consider whether there is not a good deal to be said for letting people work, not for the world, not for the nation, not for the " locality," but for the tiny circle of self, spouse, children, relations and friends whose interest the ordinary man and woman is able to see and is consequently willing to serve.

Let us have no nonsense about ignoble motives. Superior persons—of whom some are incapable of earning anything, and others quite willing in private life to grind the poor—are fond of denouncing " money-getting " or " acquisitiveness " as " sordid " or even " immoral." They would have us believe that everyone who wants to earn money wants it in order to spend on whisky and cigars consumed in gloomy seclusion. In fact, the great majority of the money-getters are getting it not for themselves, but for others for whom they have some regard. To say that their motive is self-interest is misleading. It is interest not in self, but in something considerably wider, though not so wide that it cannot be clearly grasped by the imagination of the ordinary person. And even the minority who work for themselves alone are doing it because they are not willing to become a burden on their fellows. It is not the worker under the present system who is immoral, but the work-shy.

Moreover, the fact of the ordinary work of the world being done for the sake of a little circle need not and does not stand in the way of work inspired by civic and mundane duty. It does not prevent crusades being carried on without hope of money payment against such things as drunkenness or monetary inflation. That great devotion may be shown in such causes only enforces my argument, for here the benefit to be conferred by the success of the crusade appears enormous to the crusader. Pussyfoot cheerfully even loses an eye because he is borne up by the hope of conferring the benefit of sobriety on the whole world for ever and ever; the anti-inflationist fulminated in 1918 in hopes of preventing, for his own and other countries, the enormous troubles which actually came on them in various degrees dependent inversely on the strength of the protests made against the course on which they had embarked.

The exaggerated estimate which such people form of the probable effects of their action helps them; they would be much discouraged if the actual effects were daily weighed up as accurately and indisputably as the output of the coal-hewer—but fortunately they are not.

§ 3. *The Distribution of Labour between Occupations.*

It is easy to descant on the enormous advantages of distributing persons between the various occupations and to get everyone to admit the existence of the advantage, but it is quite another and much more difficult matter to distribute them in such a way as to secure the maximum advantage possible. Modern civilisation is still a long distance from this ideal.

There are two great requirements: first, the total labour force must be correctly distributed between the different occupations

—there must not be too many persons in some occupations and too few in others—and secondly, the individual members of the labour force must be allotted, so far as possible, to the occupations for which they are most suitable. The two requirements interlace in an embarrassing manner, since, to use a current metaphor, putting the square persons into the square holes and the round into the round holes may be interfered with by there being more square holes than square persons or more round persons than round holes.

A single person does not find the distribution of his labour force between different employments a very serious problem. He knows, or thinks he knows, how much of each product he requires after taking into account how much he likes or dislikes the exertion involved in getting different quantities of the different products, and distributes his hours accordingly. Nor does the problem appear very difficult when we think only of the work carried on in a single establishment like Adam Smith's pin factory. Whoever controls the factory will see that it would be silly to have two men putting heads on the pins when there were only enough other men to supply pins for one man to put heads on. But there is no such direct personal control of the whole of industry. What the people want, and how much they like or dislike the different kinds of work involved in getting the different things is decided by the composition of many hundreds of millions of individual preferences, and no single authority has the power of saying how many persons are to be drafted into the pin factories, how many to the pig-killing, and so on.

Yet somehow or other the people are distributed between the various occupations in proportions which in ordinary times seem so nearly correct that the world was recently both surprised and puzzled when it was told by those who had carefully inquired into the subject that, owing to a series of untoward events, the number of coal-miners was perhaps 20 per cent. above what it would be on a reasonable distribution of labour force. In a usual way the world is quite content to think of occupations as Topsy thought of herself when she "s'posed she growed."

Sometimes people think of the distribution of persons between occupations as being an hereditary matter, and of course it is true that in purely rural districts, and also in highly specialised manufacturing or mining districts, the proportion of persons following the same trade as one or other of their parents is usually large, but that is clearly due to environment rather than heredity. Often too the hereditary transmission of property carries with it a certain tendency of at least one in the family to follow the occupation of one of his parents. Beyond this there seems little trace of hereditary transmission of employments in the modern Western world. Persons with the surnames of Smith, Carpenter, Slater and such like presumably all had ancestors who practised the trades suggested by their names, but we find it "funny" if Mr. J. Carpenter is actually a carpenter, and much more natural that he should be a smith or a slater. New occupations arise and grow with no assistance from parentage. No aviator or broadcast transmitter follows the occupation of his father to-day, and an army of typists and telephonists had come into existence before a single typist or telephonist was the daughter of a typist or telephonist.

The fact is, of course, that the distribution of the workers between the various occupations is varied, and on the whole easily and smoothly varied, by changes in the comparative demand for the different kinds of occupations, and by changes in the productiveness of the labour involved. Perhaps the biggest blunder made in economic theory in modern times was J. S. Mill's last and worst "fundamental proposition respecting capital," namely, "a demand for commodities is not a demand for labour." No truth in economics could well be more fundamental than that a demand for a particular kind of commodity either is or immediately gives rise to a demand for labour to make that commodity. When horse-drawn vehicles began to be demanded, makers of such vehicles appeared and increased in number; when navigable canals and barges were demanded, "navigators" or "navvies" and barge-builders appeared and increased in number; when railways and trains were demanded, navvies increased still further, and Swindon and Crewe testified to the appearance and growth of train-builders; and when the invention of the internal combustion engine and rubber tyres led to a demand for automobile vehicles, the makers of horse-drawn vehicles almost disappeared, and an enormous army of makers of automobile vehicles grew up in quarter of a century.

Improvements in the productive power of labour in any particular occupation, such as are occasioned by the invention of better machinery or better methods, may cause an increase in the proportion of persons employed in it if the demand for its product is sufficiently elastic, and this is very often the case. There is no doubt, for example, a larger proportion of persons employed in producing books than if printing had never been invented and all books were still hand-written. But we more often have our attention drawn to cases where the demand is such that the improvement causes a reduction in the number of persons employed in an occupation, or at any rate is expected to do so.

Changes in demand and changes in productive power both exercise their influence on the distribution of labour between the various occupations, partly by varying the distribution of the young recruits to industry, and partly by redistributing adults who have already adopted some particular occupation.

The possibilities of frictionless change which can be made by the first method are considerable. The average duration of human life is well under sixty years, and the duration of working life is, of course, much shorter than that, in consequence of the years of childhood at one end and the years of infirmity and old age at the other. If we take the average working life to be as high as forty years, the annual recruitment necessary to maintain a permanently stationary number of workers in an occupation would obviously have to be 2½ per cent. on that number in order to counterbalance the 2½ per cent. wastage. If recruitment were stopped altogether, the employment would be wiped out in about sixty years (if we suppose the last survivor to go on to seventy-five years of age) without a single person having to be driven out of it while still fit to work in it. On the other hand, if we could direct all the recruits into a single new industry, that industry might comprise nearly half the whole working population in twenty years' time.

Very great changes in the distribution of labour are, in fact, continually being slowly made without hardship to anyone by diversions of the stream of young recruits. Though, as will be explained in Chapter XII below, there are obstacles to the exercise of free choice among occupations which prevent young people entering them in just such numbers as will reduce their total advantages to an equality, any departure of an occupation from the place it has usually taken among the rest will affect the proportion of the young recruits to industry which it gets. When a trade is hit by some change in demand or supply which makes it impossible for as many persons to be employed in it as before at the same rate of remuneration, employers have less desire to take on fresh boys or girls, and the boys and girls themselves, with their parents, friends and schoolmasters influencing and guiding them in various ways, do not desire to be taken on in that employment. Conversely, when a trade is doing well, employers in it are willing and able to make it more attractive to the potential recruits, and these recruits are accordingly attracted in greater numbers.

But for obvious technical reasons a new industry cannot be started by boys and girls, and for the same reasons, or some of them, even an established industry is not likely to be able to increase the number of persons employed in it very rapidly if it can get only boy and girl recruits. Moreover, family life, coupled with the concentration of industries in particular localities, and trade-union or other restrictions on the number of apprentices or learners which may be employed in a trade, hamper to a considerable extent the flow of young people into the most promising industries.

Conversely, an old industry can never have its personnel reduced at all rapidly simply by not taking in young recruits. In no case would this extinguish the industry in less than forty or fifty years, and in many cases it would be impossible to dispense altogether with young workers, so that if the industry was to be carried on at all, it would need to attract some young recruits.

Therefore to secure the rapid changes in the proportion of persons engaged in different occupations which are often required, especially in an age of rapid progress in knowledge, it is frequently necessary that a considerable number of changes of occupation should be made by adults. In order that a new industry should come into existence or an old one have its personnel very rapidly increased, and in order that an existing industry may be rapidly extinguished or reduced without throwing its personnel or some of it into idleness, it is necessary in the first case that the new or rapidly increasing industry should be able to draw adult recruits from all or some of the others, and in the second case that the declining industry should have its superfluous personnel absorbed by the other and more prosperous industries.

About the movement into the rising industry, little difficulty is felt. In all employments the persons employed are of various degrees of mobility: some are scarcely capable of doing anything else than what they have learnt to do in the employment, while others are, in varying degree, capable of doing something else; and besides this, some are extraordinarily well adapted by nature to the employment and others in various degrees less well adapted. Consequently, there is on the fringe or margin of each employment a certain number of persons who can change over to different employment without much difficulty, while as you cut, so to speak, more deeply into the mass, you come further and further into a region of increasing difficulty.

The result of these facts is, firstly, that there is no hardship involved in the change of occupation required by the rise of a new or the rapid increase of an old employment. The new or increasing employment attracts persons who form the extreme fringe in a large number of other employments, persons who by temperament or accidents of training see, probably rightly, more prospects of success in the new or rising trade than that in which they have been so far occupied. In general, they do pretty well and nobody pities them for having left the old occupation. Anyone of mature years can think of examples for himself. For my own part, with a recollection going back to 1870, I can recall how in the early days of the bicycle the trades of making and repairing cycles were filled by plumbers, gasfitters and all sorts of other artisans; one large shop which I remember was run by an ex-coachman. The early part of the present century has seen something of the same kind take place in the rise of the motor trade. A miscellaneous body of this kind is likely to contain many incompetents, but, on the other hand, it will also contain more geniuses than an old-established trade which goes steadily on its way without much change of magnitude; and the personnel will introduce its own children and attract other boys and girls, who will eventually bring about more ordinary conditions as they grow up and take the place of the pioneers. Nobody complains of all this.

But, secondly, when what is required is the extrusion in a few years of the whole or a large proportion of the persons specialised in some particular occupation, much more difficulty, friction and hardship is often inevitable. To get the fairly mobile fringe to move is easy, but the further the reduction has to go, the more it reaches persons whom a change of occupation will not suit. If the reduction is to be only 5 per cent., nobody will be much hurt, if the right people are induced to go; a 10 per cent. reduction will cause some hardship, a 20 per cent. reduction more than twice as much as a 10 per cent. one, and an 80 per cent. reduction a great deal more than four times as much as a 20 per cent. one.

In cases where considerable hardship is likely to be caused by transfer to other occupations, the persons employed and their friends are likely to think of expedients for avoiding it. One expedient often recommended, especially by the employers in the trade, is that the persons employed should agree to accept lower remuneration than before. This recommendation is founded on the expectation that selling the product somewhat cheaper will so increase the demand for it that the whole of the existing personnel can continue to be employed at the reduced rate. Sometimes, no doubt, this may be so, but even then, unless the occupation was before in a better position than others, and the reduction of remuneration merely puts it on a level with them or even leaves it somewhat higher, the situation is eminently unsatisfactory to the individuals who have to submit to the reduced remuneration. As a temporary measure to tide over a temporary reduction of demand or a temporary fortuitous increase of product, it may be advisable. If the personnel is very highly specialised and immobile, it may even be advisable in their interest when the unfavourable circumstance is not likely to pass away; to hang on at the reduced rate till they die or till natural wastage and the absence of recruits to the industry brings about a recovery of their remuneration is the best that they can do. Even so, we must notice that the end, after all, is reduction of the number employed.

When the difficulty is caused by an increase of output due to some improvement in production, a shortening of the hours of labour looks very attractive to the personnel. "If we are producing more, and the price of what we are producing is falling in consequence, why should we not rectify things by cutting down our hours and producing only the same as before?" To the rest of the community, however, this solution would appear a thoroughly bad one. Applied in this one instance it would mean that instead of the consumers of the product getting the benefit of the improvement in production, this particular class of producers would get more leisure than their fellows in other occupations. If we can stretch our imagination so far as to suppose the principle to have been applied all round, it would mean that all improvements in production had always been, so to speak, frittered away in increased leisure to the producers of the commodities concerned, so that there was no greater plenty of anything than if these improvements had never taken place. Fortunately the producers seldom have it in their power to adopt the plan. If some local body of them did reduce their hours, their happy state with the old remuneration and less labour would be observed, and competitors springing up in the same place or elsewhere would, by adding to the product, reduce its price.

When it is proposed in order to meet a reduction in the demand for the product, reduction of hours is even more hopeless. Unaccompanied by a reduction of remuneration, it means that in face of a reduction in the demand for their services, the personnel is to improve its position relatively to that of other occupations, and to that which it itself formerly occupied, by cutting down the output to such a degree that, it is hoped, the smaller quantity will sell for as much as the larger did before the demand fell off. Say, for example, that the demand for coal has fallen off so that at the old price only 80 per cent. of the old quantity of labour can be employed in producing it if the incomes of the workers who continue to be employed are not to be reduced. Cutting down the hours of work to 80 per cent. will obviously retain all the old number in employment if the pay per hour and the total earnings are reduced in the same proportion; but the proposal is to cut down the hours more than this, say to 60 per cent. of the old number of hours, in the hope that restriction of the supply to 60 per cent. of the former output may raise the price to 166⅔ per cent. of the old price, so that the 60 per cent. output will be worth as much as the 100 per cent. output used to be worth. But in view of the given fact that an 80 per cent. output could only be sold at the same price as the 100 per cent. output used to be (that is, for 20 per cent. less in the aggregate), it seems highly improbable, though not altogether inconceivable, that the elasticity of demand would be such that the 60 per cent. output could be sold at a price equal to $166\frac{2}{3}$ per cent. of the old price. And in that very improbable case the arrangement could scarcely fail to be broken up by the cupidity of new competitors, who would work for a normal day and secure at first, till they substantially increased the output, nearly 66 per cent. more than those who restricted themselves to the shorter hours.

In both these cases the sympathy of the rest of the community would properly go with the outside competition. It is obviously not in the interest of the rest of the community to pay for extra leisure enjoyed in an occupation chosen by chance. The interest of the whole community obviously is that the labour power set free, whether by diminution of demand or by improvement in production, should not be wasted, but should be applied to some other form of production. So the only proper course is a reduction in the number of those employed in the occupation.

The actual extrusion of the required percentage from a declining occupation is commonly effected in two different ways. (1) In cases where changes in earnings follow quickly on changes in the value of products, increases in the amount of a particular product in consequence of improvements in its production or decreases of demand for it will cause a general fall in the earnings of its producers. The immobile mass will submit to this indefinitely, but the more mobile fringe in the occupation will be induced to move out of it by the fact that it is now less well paid in comparison with other occupations into which it is possible for them to move. (2) Where earnings do not respond quickly to changes in the value of products, as very often happens in the most recent of historical periods owing to the prevalence of collective agreements between large bodies of employees on one side and of employers on the other, persons will be extruded, whether they are willing to go or not, by being dismissed from employment in the declining occupation.

When the first of these methods is in vogue, the individuals to move are selected by themselves, and will therefore be those to whom the prospect of transfer presents most attraction and least terror. Where the second method is in vogue, the selection is made by the employers, who are likely to select those who are worst at their employment without any reference at all to their capacity for other employments. The second method is consequently more likely to cause unemployment than the first. On the other hand, it has the advantage of not requiring the immobile mass to suffer reduced earnings: if anyone doubts this advantage, he should study the history of the handloom weavers at the beginning of the nineteenth century, and consider whether the rapid extinction of an occupation with a rigid standard wage could cause as much suffering as was caused by the lingering death of handloom weaving.

§ 4. *The Selection of Individuals for Occupations.*

We may now proceed to consider what was enumerated at the beginning of the last section as the second requirement of a good distribution of the people between the various occupations, namely, a correct selection of individuals with regard to their suitability for the occupation they are to adopt.

The problem of sorting out persons among the occupations in accordance with their natural characteristics is made very difficult by the fact that the allotment must be made at least to some extent at a very early period in the lives of the persons. According as they are to go into this or that occupation they must have different kinds of education and training, which must be begun not only long before it is at all easy to tell for what kind of work each of them is best fitted by his or her natural qualities, but also long before it is possible to decide at all accurately how many persons will be required for each particular kind of work by the time the child has reached working age.

In our actual world the selection is effected roughly as follows. First, the circumstance of the birth and early surroundings of the individual make it impossible for a very large body of persons to get into any of those occupations which require long and expensive training; they cannot pay for such training themselves, and there is nobody who both can and will pay for it for them. Secondly, within the restricted limits indicated by this free choice of occupation, young persons are allowed a choice which is hampered only slightly by the legal rights of parents, and much more seriously influenced by the advice and assistance of parents, schoolmasters and other counsellors. The parents as well as the others are usually on the look-out for the occupation which they think will be "the best" for the particular young person, making his probable earnings their principal consideration; the young person himself does not know very much about earnings, and thinks more of other conditions, such as whether he likes the kind of work. From this rather confused welter of views, which are often in sharp conflict, it results that there is at any moment a certain number of young candidates for admission to each of by far the greater number of occupations. To anyone who thinks that the levelling effects of competition have been over-estimated or that they have much diminished in modern times, it must seem rather a wonderful thing that the candidates' preferences are so widely distributed. It is usually believed that all healthy small boys want (or did want before air-craft were invented) to become engine-drivers; but by the time they are old enough to work and have a little more discretion, they spread their desires over nearly the whole field. A very small number of occupations never attract young recruits and are filled solely by older persons who have failed in or somehow or other been thrown out of the other occupations, and, on the other hand, only a very small number of occupations, and those chiefly Government appointments, are so attractive that entrance into them can only be secured by "influence" or examination or the payment of premiums.

Individuals born into better circumstances than the mass can, if they have average natural ability or even a little less, choose occupations which those born into worse circumstances cannot aspire to unless gifted with considerably more than average natural ability; but in spite of that undoubted disadvantage even the poorer individuals in a modern Western country have usually a fairly free choice between a large number of occupations, and it is probable that a very large proportion of them manage to get their first preference.

So far as it goes this is satisfactory. The choice made in the way described is by no means completely successful in arranging the allotment of individuals to occupations in the best conceivable manner; mistakes must be frequent, and there are doubtless many carpenters who would have been happier and better workmen as fitters and *vice versa*. But it is not at all probable that any very revolutionary change would under present circumstances be an improvement. Certainly no placing of the allotment in the hands of national or local governments would be an improvement; governments allot conscripts to the different branches of military and naval service, but this is a comparatively simple matter, and their success in allotting each conscript to the right service has not usually been conspicuous. One shudders to think of all boys and girls leaving schools and universities being allotted to all the different occupations by the teachers acting in accordance with the directions given by the Ministries of Education and Labour.

What is wanted is merely a continuation of improvement on its present lines. There is already better advice and influence available for the mass of boys and girls than there ever was before, but both are probably capable of considerable further improvement. It is more possible than it ever was before for a person born in humble circumstances to find his way up the ladders provided for him if he has exceptional ability, but it is at any rate very probable that the general efficiency of many of the higher paid occupations would be considerably higher if the field from which they are recruited was wider than it is. These occupations seem generally to contain a large contingent of rather incompetent persons who have been able to get into them owing to inherited advantages other than that arising from inherited ability. The extrusion of these persons by others of more ability would be very advantageous to society.

§ 5. *The Local Distribution of Occupations.*

Just as it is easy to see the advantage of distributing the people between the various occupations, but difficult to distribute them so as to get the utmost possible advantage from the plan, so it is easy to see the advantage of different industries being more or less concentrated in particular areas, but difficult to arrange where this concentration should be, and how far in each case it should be carried.

The attitude of the public towards the existing concentration is most remarkable. The concentration which exists inside any "country" (a term which is seldom defined, but appears to be identical with any area which is to some extent divided from the rest of the world by a boundary at which customs duties are levied) is usually regarded with absolute complacency even by the stoutest opponents of the policy which they call *laisser faire*. I know of no protectionist who thinks the cotton industry and the woollen industry should change places between Lancashire and Yorkshire or even should be equally divided between the two counties, and I know of no socialist who claims that the position of Coventry is a monstrous mistake and that a wise, far-seeing Government would have concentrated the motor industry at, say, Burton or Buxton.

What has been written on this part of the subject has generally taken the form of discovering and explaining good reasons—or reasons supposed to be good—for concentrations which have actually taken place. Taking an example at random we find John Kennedy, long eminent among Manchester manufacturers, speaking to the Literary and Philosophical Society of Manchester in 1815 as follows:

"I have not been able to obtain any information respecting the circumstances that first led to the establishment of the cotton manufactory in this part of the island. After it was once commenced, however, its extension in this quarter appears to have been promoted by various circumstances. The abundance of excellent fuel could not fail to encourage it. The humidity of the climate and the unfitness of the soil for agriculture would induce the inhabitants to seek, in preference, for employment within doors. But I believe the rapid growth and extension of the trade in this particular district is chiefly to be ascribed to the great ingenuity and the persevering, skilful, laborious disposition of the people. In these qualities I believe they surpass the inhabitants of every other part of this island, or of the whole world." [1]

[1] *Miscellaneous Papers on Subjects connected with the Manufactures of Lancashire*, reprinted from the *Memoirs of the Literary and Philosophical Society of Manchester*, 1849 (privately printed), pp. 20–1. Kennedy was the third son of a small landowner and farmer in the Glenkens, Kirkcudbrightshire, who in 1784, following boy-friends from the same district, Adam Murray and James McConnell, became apprentice to William Cannan and James Smith at Chowbent (now called Atherton); Cannan being a carpenter who had migrated from the Glenkens to Lancashire some years before and established a business in making the machinery then used in the cotton mills. Descendants of these particular immigrants have played and still play a large part in the industry of Lancashire. That Kennedy's eulogy was intended for the employed rather than the employers is shown by the paragraph which follows the one quoted above:—"We have the satisfaction of observing also, that they are gradually becoming better informed, and more regular in their conduct. Their employers see the advantage of this, and many of them take great pains to promote the welfare of the people and the education of their families. The people themselves begin to take a pride in this, and value themselves on the proficiency of their children in education."

It is interesting to observe that neither when speaking in 1815 nor when reprinting the paper in 1849 does Kennedy say that the " humidity of the climate " was specially suitable for piecing thread, which is the reason which is now usually put in the forefront. Nor does he mention the availability of water-power in East Lancashire and the convenient position of South Lancashire for imports of the raw material and exports of the finished article, both of which reasons are also commonly adduced. Modesty perhaps caused him to omit mention of what Lancashire owed to immigrants like himself who managed to take command of the natives of whom he spoke so highly.

" The circumstances that first led to the establishment " of a particular industry in a particular area are generally a matter of merely antiquarian interest. In most cases it will have been established there before it was concentrated there in any considerable degree; concentration comes because the industry established there gradually extends its market, and the true causes of concentration are the causes which enable it to do so. Marshall tells us that " the mechanical faculty of Lancashire is said to be due to the influence of Norman smiths who were settled at Warrington by Hugo de Lupus in William the Conqueror's time." [1] Whether Lupus' smiths had any influence or not is of very trifling importance compared with the large demand for machine makers and repairers caused by the concentration of the cotton factories in quite modern times.

If we ask, as any serious inquirer into general economic theory ought to ask, how it happens that the good reasons for concentration have actually in our past and present organisation brought about the concentrations which have taken place, the answer is that the good reasons caused additional people to be attracted to the trade in the district by offering them more remuneration or better conditions of work than they could get by carrying on the same trade elsewhere or by carrying on other trades in the same district. John Kennedy and his friends came to Chowbent and Manchester to better themselves, and even the poor-law apprentices were sent to Lancashire to improve their position, and they did so. And what woollen industry there was in Lancashire faded away because the recruits

[1] *Principles*, ed. 8, p. 269.

it might otherwise have received were attracted into cotton mills.

All this is pretty well understood and nobody complains about it. But when we come to concentration of industries not in different parts of the same " country " but in different " countries," we find the public of each country displaying a strange hostility to the concentration of any industry in any country but their own. Yorkshire does not think itself ruined because the cotton factories are in Lancashire, and Dorset quite calmly acquiesces in having to buy textiles from Lancashire and Yorkshire : no state or town in the United States believes itself injured because all the cash-register machines are made in one city. The people of the places where a particular industry is not concentrated know that they get the product of the industry cheaper because it is concentrated, and recognise that they would gain nothing by trying to produce it themselves. But when we come to consider concentration of industries not in different parts of the same country but in different " countries," we find the people of each country displaying the utmost animosity against the concentration of industry in any of the other countries. They do this even when some industries are largely concentrated inside their own country, although that very fact necessitates a certain concentration of other industries outside; a large majority of the people of Great Britain and Northern Ireland simply hate to think of the industries of producing cash-registers, type-writers and sugar being concentrated outside their own country, while at the same time they would like to see that country supplying the whole world with cotton and artificial silk goods. That the only object of exporting these goods is to get others in exchange, they seem incapable of realising.

CHAPTER VI

THE INFLUENCE OF ACCUMULATION ON PRODUCE

§ 1. *The Accumulation of Knowledge or Non-material Equipment.*

It would seem natural to suppose that economists desirous of explaining the causes of greater or less productiveness would give a very prominent place to changes in knowledge. Is not the fact that we know so much more than our immediate and our primitive ancestors a most obviously potent cause of our superior productiveness?

But for several reasons knowledge has not till recently been given the prominent place which it should have occupied. One, and probably the principal, reason was that economists have seldom been sufficiently alive to the fact that the most apparently obvious things are often the least noticed, and that it is consequently desirable for teachers to insist on them, even if they are liable to be told that "everyone knows that." A second reason was that Adam Smith tucked away increase of knowledge under the wings of his exposition of the advantages of the division of labour, saying that division of labour encouraged the invention of machinery and promoted science by specialising particular persons to particular kinds of industry or research. Subsequent writers were often induced by this to forget that the progress of knowledge, though certainly enormously assisted by division of labour, is not wholly dependent on it. A perfectly isolated person can observe, investigate, remember and record, and thus increase his knowledge, and with it his productiveness; and persons who are not isolated can hand on their accumulated knowledge to the next generation without practising any division of labour. A third reason for the common neglect of knowledge was that most accumulated knowledge is free for the use of all in unlimited quantity, so that it has no value, and economists have generally been inclined to neglect things of no value, however important they may be.

How complete the neglect of knowledge was about 1840 we may gather from the fact that McCulloch, collecting all the wisdom of the Ricardian school in the third edition of his *Principles*, 1843, deals with "Means by which the Productive Powers of Labour are increased" in three sections entitled, "I. Right of Property, II. Division of Employments, III. Accumulation and Employment of Capital." There is no section for the accumulation or increase of knowledge, and it is scarcely referred to at all in the sections which exist. Senior, too, could only think of four "causes on which the productiveness of labour depends," and did not make knowledge one of the four.[1]

J. S. Mill is entitled to some credit for having broken this tradition. He put "Causes of Superior Productiveness" under five heads: "Natural advantages, greater energy of labour, superior skill and knowledge, superiority of intelligence and trustworthiness in the community generally, superior security."[2] The coupling of knowledge with skill is not very happy, but the specification of knowledge at all is a great step in advance. It is something to have a plain statement like the following:

> "That the productiveness of the labour of a people is limited by their knowledge of the arts of life is self-evident; and that any progress in those arts, any improved application of the objects or powers of nature to industrial uses, enables the same quantity and intensity of labour to raise a greater produce" (*Principles*, ed. Ashley, p. 107).

Later writers have failed to develop the subject. Possibly there is not very much to add to Mill's statement that the advantage of knowledge is "self-evident," but there may be something to be done in the direction of inquiry about the exact manner in which different changes in knowledge affect productiveness. At any rate attention might be drawn to the fact that some increases of knowledge can only have their effect on productiveness when

[1] See Contents in the 8vo ed. of *Political Economy*; the four causes are—"1. The corporeal, intellectual and moral Qualities of the Labourer; 2. The assistance of Natural Agents; 3. The assistance of Capital; 4. The existence or the absence of government interference." The omission of division of labour is remarkable.

[2] See Contents (of Book I, chap. vii) in Ashley's ed. of *Principles*, p. xxxv.

the machines and other instruments required to utilise them have been added to the existing stock of useful things, whereas other increases of knowledge enable something or other to be done, or done more easily, without requiring the provision of any more instruments.

But there is certainly a good deal, and a good deal that is important, to be said about the relation between the existing economic organisation and the increase of knowledge.

In modern times a belief that more encouragement should be given to the discoverer of new knowledge has caused the maintenance, if not exactly the establishment, of the limited legal monopoly known as patent right, and perhaps has had a little to do with the establishment and maintenance of the somewhat similar limited monopoly called copyright. Copyright, however, protecting the form rather than the substance of a statement, does nothing for a discoverer unless the public want to hear his own account of his discovery rather than any other person's. Patents are rather more successful in rewarding, if not the inventor, at any rate the person or body which brings the invention into use.

But little really depends on these monopolies. By far the greater part of invention and discovery is made without the least hope of patents and copyrights. There is usually something to be gained in other ways. The advantage of being first in the field is great for those who are in business on their own account; expectation of promotion or other improvement in position or emolument encourages the salaried worker.

Sometimes the advantage of being first in the field in regard to an invention becomes mixed up with the acquisition of patents of minor and subsidiary inventions. There was no patent in the pneumatic tyre, but the enormous success of the company which first exploited that invention was largely due to patents subsequently acquired in regard to details in the application of the principle.

The "poor inventor" used to be a stock subject of pity. He was supposed to be at first unable to market his invention at all, and then to be reduced to selling it for a miserable trifle, after which he died in penury in a garret. But nowadays this sad picture seems out of date. Edison and Marconi are not exactly begging in the street, and even Dunlop, who seems to have been extraordinarily unbusinesslike, made far more out of his invention than he did or ever could have done out of his medical practice. On the whole there seems little reason for anxiety about the future of invention so far as immediately marketable things are concerned.

But invention and discovery are just as economically important or more important in regard to some things which are not marketable and cannot well be made marketable. The discovery that some destructive disease could be prevented by some trifling and inexpensive change in diet would be worth an enormous sum to the world, but it could not be patented, and a man might have spent twenty years upon it and not get a penny of material reward for it. If he had other means of support, he might well think the satisfaction of achievement and such gratitude as he got quite sufficient reward, but a man must live, and as things are at present, it does not seem safe to expect that a sufficiency of this kind of research and discovery will be made by those who have already acquired a competence either by work and thrift or by inheritance or marrying rich spouses. The want is relieved to a great extent by the benefactions of private donors and testators for "the endowment of research," and in quite recent times States have supplemented these benefactions. Then we get a whole class of persons, supposed to be suitable, provided with fixed salaries on condition of engaging in particular branches of research. If it is asked whether more might not be done in this field with advantage—whether it would not be better to give more of the world's time to it and less to something else, for that is what the question means—I think the answer is certainly in the affirmative. It does not follow, however, that any very rapid increase of the amount is desirable. Some industrious and well-meaning researchers are prone to lose themselves in paths which are interesting to them but lead nowhere; a few are slackers. Direction and supervision of original research is by the nature of the case very ineffective. We have to proceed, boldly indeed, but with considerable caution, in creating new endowments and we must be careful to bring the old ones under frequent scrutiny.

§ 2. *The Accumulation of Material Equipment.*

That productiveness is assisted, that is, made greater at any moment than it otherwise would be, by the presence of useful animals and inanimate material objects which have been adapted by man to suit his purposes out of materials furnished by nature, and have been accumulated by one generation after another, is as "self-evident"—to use Mill's phrase again—as that it is assisted by the accumulation of useful knowledge. The world is obviously benefited by the fact that a large portion of the surface of the earth has been made much more suitable for agriculture than it was before it was touched by the hand of man, and that a stock of greatly improved cattle and other domesticated animals, as well as of tools and machinery, has been accumulated. The farmer has always known that he could produce more if his land was improved; the artisan that he could produce more with good tools; and the trader that he could serve his customers better if he had a suitable stock of goods in hand.

There is some difficulty in finding a name which will conveniently indicate the whole of what we desire to deal with here. Things in a natural state and situation, however useful, are not to be included, and we may try to express this by using the word "accumulation," but this is scarcely satisfactory, since we want to include such things as drained fields and excavated docks, which we would not naturally speak of as accumulated. Perhaps "material equipment" will serve as well as any other term. "Equipment" suggests something made or looked for and found by human effort, and excludes what is purely natural. For example, we say that the mines on the Rand are equipped with powerful machinery, but not that South Africa is equipped with rich sources of gold and diamonds. The word also suggests that the things indicated are of prospective use. We are well equipped with a store of grain to last from this harvest to the next, and well equipped with ploughs to prepare the land for future sowings; we do not say that we are well equipped with bread merely because we have up to now had plenty of it, though we might say we were well equipped with bread and cake if we were threatened with an irruption of friends to tea and happened to have plenty.

Moreover, the term may help to make us realise the fundamental likeness between the accumulation of useful knowledge and the accumulation of useful material things. The one is the acquisition of non-material equipment, and the other the acquisition of material equipment. Man equips himself with useful knowledge and with useful tools, machinery and stores for exactly the same purpose. The acquisition of both takes up time which will not be devoted to the purpose unless some advantage over other employment of the time is expected to be gained in the long run.

Whatever name be adopted, it is important to emphasise this fundamental likeness between the two kinds of equipment. At first sight we are too apt to think that while useful knowledge is vague, impalpable and non-measurable, material equipment is simple and easily measurable. A spade, we think, is a much more palpable object than a knowledge of how best to grow cauliflowers, and as two spades are double of one spade, two spades must give twice as much assistance to productiveness as one spade. But this appearance of greater simplicity is delusive. Even simple instruments like spades are of diverse size and quality; two that look very much alike will be found very different in actual use, and the difference will vary with the particular purpose to which the spade is applied. Exactly similar spades may be used for very different periods in each week or year, so that some " do much more work " than others. Doubling the number of spades owned by spade-users will certainly not double the assistance rendered by the existence and use of the stock of spades. The discovery of some new method in agriculture or the increase of ploughs and digging machines may throw many spades out of use till the stock is reduced.

It is not really any easier to measure material equipment than it is to measure useful knowledge. There are no cubic feet or pounds avoirdupois of material equipment any more than there are of useful knowledge. We cannot say material equipment has increased 10 per cent. since, say, 1900, any more than we can say useful knowledge has done so. We make a shift to measure the increase of spinning machinery by number of spindles, to measure the increase of engines by horse-power, and so on, but such measures are not only very imperfect as regards the particular things measured, but are no help at all when we have to add things imperfectly measured by one of the measures to things imperfectly measured by another. Measurement of material equipment by valuation is almost as delusive as similar measurement of knowledge; the aggregate valuation of the stock of houses might fall when house-room and comfort had been actually increased.

In regard to the organisation by which it is provided, material equipment does indeed offer some contrast to non-material equipment. The accumulation of material equipment is much more largely due to the "magic of property" than the accumulation of useful knowledge. Useful knowledge, as we have seen, can only be property in exceptional cases; in general, accessions to knowledge have to be shared with an unlimited number of people. Material things, on the other hand, at least when they are either bits of the outer crust of the earth or what man can get by manipulating those bits either by agriculture or excavation, are for the most part kept in the exclusive ownership of individuals and groups of individuals, and that ownership carries with it the exclusive right to any improvements which the owners may choose to effect in the things. This secures that a more powerful motive than desire to benefit mankind at large shall be brought to bear on the accumulation of material equipment. The owners of land, whether groups or individuals, know that if they improve their land, it will still belong to them; the owners of materials extracted from the earth or raw produce grown upon it know that these things will not cease to be theirs if they fashion them into buildings, tools, machines and other useful instruments or add them to stocks of things required for future use.

If persons thought only of themselves, accumulation would be greatly hampered by the shortness of human life. "Why trouble about it when I shall be dead in a few years?" But property has always been more or less groupal, and groups of persons continually recruited with young lives regard themselves as immortal. And further, when property is purely individual, the common sense of mankind has allowed the proprietor large rights in the disposition of his property after his death, and the lure of exercising these rights either in favour of his own posterity or in favour of some other objects chosen by himself is an encouragement to accumulation which makes up to a large extent for the lack of immortality.

Until the complications of exchange and money are introduced, there is no mystery about the causes or effects of the accumulation of material equipment. A man in exclusive possession of some land and living on what he himself can get from it decides whether or not to spend time in improving it in such a way that it will give him a better return to the same labour in future years by weighing this advantage against that which would result from some different employment of his time; if he builds himself some shelter from the elements it is because he thinks it worth while, *i.e.* better worth doing than something else or than the leisure he might enjoy if he did nothing instead. His decision between action which will be of present or early benefit and action which will only be of later benefit is, of course, influenced by the urgency of his immediate needs. The future advantage to be gained by means of some improvement or tool may be enormous, but he will have to forgo it if he cannot "spare the time" to make the improvement or the tool; it is no use to preach to him about the advantage of improvements and tools if he can only just manage to keep alive and well without attempting to accumulate anything.

In the absence of exchange and money there can be little difficulty in seeing in what the advantage of accumulating material equipment consists. It obviously consists in the simple fact that the equipment either enables larger quantities of what is wanted to be got with equal ease or enables the same quantity to be got with greater ease. In reckoning we have, of course, to remember that material equipment is seldom permanent, and generally requires repair. Repairs and renewals must be covered before the advantage begins to accrue. To take from Roscher [1] the classical example of the primitive fisherman who can catch three fish a day with his hands as he wades or swims in the water and thirty when he has made himself a boat and a net, we must not reckon the advantage as twenty-seven fish per day unless we are sure that the framer of the example means that the fisherman can catch thirty fish every day and also maintain his boat

[1] *Volkswirtschaftlehre*, § 189, Vol. II. p. 126, in J. J. Lalor's trans. Quoted by Böhm-Bawerk, for which see below, Chap. IX at end.

and net by proper repairs and renewals without working longer hours than before. If the thirty fish are only caught in a full working day and every tenth day has to be devoted to maintaining the equipment, we must reckon the advantage as only twenty-four; and if the boat and net are so badly constructed or made of such poor materials that nine days out of ten have to be devoted to maintenance, there will be no advantage at all—in ten days the man will catch only thirty fish, or three per day, the same number as he used to catch without having the boat and net.

If he foresaw that he would not be able to do better than that, it is certain that he would never accumulate the boat and net in the first place. In order to make the accumulation he would have either to work additional hours as well as those necessary for catching his three fish a day, or to pinch off some of the hours given to catching fish, and therefore to submit for a time to a smaller consumption—and in doing either of these things he would feel he was "wasting his time," as nothing would be got by it. He would be depriving himself either of leisure or of fish and getting nothing in return. This points the way to an explanation of what has puzzled some persons, the fact that for the most part accumulations do bring in a return. There is no law of nature that they must do so, and in fact there is an infinite number of conceivable accumulations which would not bring in a return; but man does not, except by mistake, waste his time on those which do not, but confines himself to those which do.

The fact that the fisherman expects accumulation of boat and net will bring in *some* return is not sufficient to make him accumulate them. He must expect that it will bring in a better return than any other accumulation which he can think of; he will not spend hours in making a boat and net if he believes that the same hours would be more profitably spent in making a rod and line. And, secondly, he must be satisfied that the gain in the future is sufficient to outweigh any disadvantage in the present. If it happens to mean starvation or something approaching starvation, the disadvantage of having to live on two fish a day for some time instead of three may easily outweigh the advantage of having four instead of three for ever after the period of privation is over.

The introduction of division of labour and exchange of services does not alter the essentials of the subject. The principle is the same (1) whether each of three fishermen makes a boat and net for himself by giving one-third of his time to that work and subsisting on two fish per day instead of three, or (2) the three fishermen co-operate by two men continuing to fish and catching three fish per day and giving two out of the six fish to the third man, who for the time gives up fishing and works altogether at boat and net making; in both cases one-third of the labour-force is allotted to the boat and net making and the accumulation is the same..

And any economist can see that it will be all the same whether the two men who fish all the time arrange with the third man to give him two fish per day for his services in making a boat and net for each of them,[1] or pay him the money value of two fish which he can spend in buying two fish from them.

But while it makes no real change, the intervention of money disguises the actual process of the accumulation of material equipment by suggesting to the ordinary mind that the thing accumulated is not, at any rate at first, the material equipment itself but a sum of money. Fishermen unfamiliar with monetary transactions, and accustomed to construct their own boats and nets for themselves, would have no doubt that what the accumulating fisherman does is to add a boat and net to the material equipment possessed by himself and the community of which he is a member. But fishermen familiar with monetary transactions, and accustomed to buy their boats and nets with money procured by the sale of fish, will be apt to think of this money being " saved " or accumulated before the purchase, and thus to imagine that an accumulation of money is a necessary preliminary to the acquisition of material equipment.

Now the economists of Adam Smith's time and long afterwards, though they were above the simple delusion of supposing a previous accumulation of money to be necessary before boats and nets or other material equipment could be accumulated, were not above a rather more subtle delusion which was founded on a confusion between the " stock " or " capital " in the sense of money-value involved in the accumulation and in the sense

[1] Which occupies two-thirds of his time; in the other third he is making his own boat and net.

of the things accumulated themselves. This confusion led them to believe that though money was not necessarily accumulated "beforehand," something else, other than the resulting material equipment itself, something known as "stock" or "capital," must be accumulated before the accumulation could take place or even begin.

In this very example of the fisherman, Roscher, one of the greatest of German economists in the middle of the nineteenth century, actually makes the fisherman accumulate, at the rate of one a day, a stock of one hundred fish, and then knock off fishing altogether for a time while he makes the boat and net and lives upon this stinking, putrid mess! Even Jevons, acute as he was, in his earlier period had the same idea. Approving the Japanese maxim, "Dig a well before you are thirsty," he adds, "But you must have capital to live upon while you are digging the well." [1]

In order to explain the origin of this extraordinary belief, that before anything can be accumulated something else must be accumulated, we must go rather deeply into the history of the terms stock and capital.

§ 3. *The Commercial and Ordinary Conception of "Capital."*

In Adam Smith's examination of the "Causes of the Slow Progress of Opulence" in his *Lectures* he is reported to have said that "it is no wonder" that a savage "continues long in an indigent state," seeing that he has "no stock to begin upon, nothing to maintain him but what is produced by the exertion of his own strength," while "the meanest labourer in a polished society has in many respects an advantage over" him; "he has more assistance in his labour; he has only one particular thing to do, which by assiduity he attains a facility in performing; he has also machines and instruments which greatly assist him" (p. 223). Slaves

"have no motive to labour except the dread of punishment, and can never invent any machine for facilitating their business. Free men,

[1] *Primer of Political Economy*, 1878, p. 27; cp. his *Theory*, Chap. vii. Later Jevons knew better; in the fragment of *Principles* published too long after his death, he says, "the saving is not in the commodities consumed but in the durable work produced. If a farmer makes a new road to his farm, the food of the labourers is unquestionably consumed, and tools and barrows may be worn out. But the saving is in the road" (p. 125).

who have a stock of their own, can get anything accomplished which they think may be expedient for carrying on labour. If a carpenter thinks that a plane will serve his purpose better than a knife he may go to a smith and get it made; but if a slave make any such proposal, he is called a lazy rascal, and no experiments are made to give him ease. . . . In the ancient world, as the arts were all carried on by slaves, no machinery could be invented, because they had no stock; after the fall of the Roman Empire, too, this was the case all over Europe" (p. 231).

Another cause of the slow progress of opulence, Smith said, was the want of improvement of land, caused by the fact that a villein tenant had no stock, and if he had had any, would have had no inducement "to lay it out on improvements" (p. 226), and by the fact that primogeniture, entails and cumbrous and expensive forms of transfer prevented land from getting into the hands of commercial persons.

"A merchant who buys a little piece of land has it in his eye to improve it and make the most of it he can. Great and ancient families have seldom either stock or inclination to improve their estates, except a small piece of pleasure-ground about their house" (p. 228).

The absence of good highways and rivers made fit for navigation was also an obstacle.

This shows a proper appreciation of the advantage of having material equipment, but no clear apprehension of the way in which it is obtained. The invention of machinery is not distinguished from the acquisition of the machines in which the invention is embodied, and without which the invention is not an addition to material equipment, but only an addition to knowledge of which no use has yet been made. The existence of "stock" is treated as something which must come *before* machinery is accumulated, and it is supposed that "stock" must be in existence and "laid out" before improvements of land can be made.

Smith was no doubt primarily misled by the fact that the ordinary person thinks of himself as first accumulating money when he wants material equipment, but, being always acutely conscious that money was not the real thing, and being desirous of "going behind it" to the real thing, he substituted "stock" for money, probably without having at the moment any clear idea what he meant by it, and certainly without grasping the fact that the things really accumulated were the machines and the improvements of land themselves.

He was greatly assisted to misunderstand the process by the fact that the word "stock" was in the language of commerce applied to the money laid out in enterprises as well as to the things bought with that money. The "stock" of a company might be the actual things possessed by it, but it could also signify, and was coming more and more to signify, the amount of money put into the concern—a number of pounds sterling rather than machinery and stocks of materials and finished goods.

But "Capital" played a larger part than "stock" in the confusion, and is worth more detailed examination.

[1] It would not have been at all surprising if the adjective *capitalis*, formed by the Romans from their substantive *caput*, which is the Latin for our substantive "head," had been applied by them to many different things. We ourselves, using "head" adjectivally or in composition with a hyphen, talk of head-keepers, head-offices, head-quarters, and many other head things. But, if the dictionaries are to be trusted, Latin writers of the classical period generally confined their use of *capitalis* to the sense in which we, following them, use the adjective "capital" in applying it to crimes and punishments—the sense of "having to do with life." But they did sometimes use it in what to us, with our belief that the head is the seat of personality, seems the more obvious sense of "most important." In later ages this use became common, so that the French speak of "*la ville capitale d'un pays*," "*le point capital de l'affaire*," and the English used to speak of "the capital messuage," and still speak of "the capital city of a country," and "the capital merit" of a work, and many other things.[2] In this sense it is synonymous with "chief," which is itself nothing but the French *chef*, a softened form of *caput*.

[1] The next nine pages are reprinted from the *Quarterly Journal of Economics* for May 1921, and are copyright in the United States of America. In the February 1926 issue of the same journal, Mr. R. D. Richards brought up further evidence of the introduction of the term capital into England from Italian accountancy.

[2] A "capital letter" is, however, not a most important letter, but originally one that stood at the head of a sentence or word, and subsequently any letter similar in form.

Now if we ask ourselves what is the chief sum of money dealt with in any particular business, whether that business is carried on by an individual or by a small number of partners such as we call a firm, or by a larger number of partners such as we call a company? the answer is, "the sum which is the foundation of the business, the total of money on which the individual, firm or company carries on trade." At first this is, of course, the amount on which the business is started; later, it is that amount plus any additions which may have been made to it, and minus any subtractions which may have been made from it. What additions and subtractions should properly be made is constantly a matter on which opinions differ, and the rules generally accepted differ to some extent between different kinds of business and even within the same kind of business according as it is carried on by an individual or a firm or a company. But though dispute may arise about the correct amount of the sum, there is never any doubt about its identity. Critics of the accounts may say that the sum is really greater, or that it is really less, than it is represented; they may even say that it is "all lost," while the managers assert equally confidently that it is not; but there never is any question about there being such a thing, even if it is alleged that its amount is now *nil* or a minus quantity. It is the "chief" sum because it originally started the business, and because it is ordinarily bigger than the sums obtained by means of the business—"the profits" for the short periods such as a year or half-year for which they are likely to be calculated. The kind of pre-eminence which it possesses is the same as that which a sum lent has over the interest upon it and which leads us to call that sum "the principal" sum, or, for short, "the principal."

My linguistic attainments are not sufficient to enable me to speak positively on the subject, and an effort I once made to enlist foreign assistance (in the *Revue d'économie politique*, May 1893, pp. 178, 179) was a failure, but I believe that whatever was the modern equivalent of the Latin *capitalis* was used in several of the continental countries as a substantive to indicate this chief sum in a business by at least the middle of the sixteenth century. The way was very probably smoothed for it by Low Latin usages; Böhm-Bawerk says, without giving any authority, that *capitalis pars debiti* meant the principal of a debt.[1] Irving Fisher[2] quotes from Du Cange's *Glossarium*, "*capitale dicitur bonum omne quod possidetur*," i.e. "capital is a name for all the goods possessed." Anyway, the first examples of the use of capital, or rather "capitall," in this sense which have been unearthed in English literature are in books which seem to be attempting to teach the English merchant how to keep accounts with the aid of the superior methods practised abroad. Professor W. R. Scott tells us that James Peele, who taught "the art of Italian merchants accounts," writing in 1569, described "an inventorie for trafique" as "a note to be taken in writinge of all thinges, founde and remayninge in the house apperteyninge to trade of merchaundise, thereby to know a mans estate, and doth consist of ii kindes; the one whereof, is that a man hathe or ought to have in possession, to saye in readye monie, debtes and goodes; and thother kinde, is that which he oweth to other men being his creaditours, and by comparinge of the totall somme of the readye monie, debtes and goodes, with the totall somme of creaditours, the estate of that accompte is presentlye perceyved (that is to saye) so muche as the monye debtes and goodes sormounte the creaditours, so muche apperteyneth to thowner of that accompte for his proper stocke or capitall, in traffique."[3] Professor Scott gives from the *Briefe Instr.* of J. Mellin, published in 1588, "The remaine is the net rest substance or capitall of the owner." Richard Dafforne, on whom the effect of foreign influence is sufficiently suggested by his giving his examples in guilders, in *The Merchant's Mirrour; or Directions for the perfect ordering and keeping of his accounts*, 1635, gives this instruction: "No. 96. to booke the capitall which each partner of a joint company promiseth to bring in:

Simon Sands promiseth into the company for his stocke, ...	gl. 11,400
And Richard Rakes for his stocke intendeth, ...	gl. 7,800
	gl. 19,200"

[1] *Positive Theory of Capital*, 1891, p. 24.

[2] *Nature of Capital and Income*, 1906, p. 62.

[3] "The Pathwaye to Perfectnes, in th' accompte of debitour and creaditour; in manner of a Dialogue, very pleasaunte and profitable for Merchauntes"; quoted in Scott's *Constitution and Finance of English, Scottish and Irish Joint Stock Companies to 1720*, Vol. I. p. 60 n., 1912.

The Oxford Dictionary quotes Cotgrave's *Dictionarie of the French and English Tongue*, 1611, as negative evidence suggesting that capital was not at that date in familiar use in England, since Cotgrave, who was by no means superior to the common lexicographer's practice of translating a word by itself (as *riche* by "rich," *généralité* by "generality," *large* by "large"), does not say that the French *capital* is "capital," but "wealth, worth, a man's principall or chiefe substance." He gives as an example of its use, "*en argent soit le capital de celuy la qui te veut mal.* Prov. Let money be thy enemies whole stocke."[1]

Three years after Cotgrave's *Dictionary* was published, capital, we are told by Professor W. R. Scott, began to be used in the records of the East India Company to indicate what we should now call the nominal amount of the holding of a shareholder, not "in the company," for the company had not yet arrived at the stage of having a permanent stock or capital, but in one of the undertakings called a "voyage." When the shareholders in one of these "voyages" were to receive a sum equal to 50 per cent. on their holdings, on September 20, 1614, the records call this a division of "fifty on the hundred," but on December 6 they call it a division of a "half-capital," and a fortnight later they speak of "capital in money" being divided where we should speak of a dividend of 100 per cent. "After 1614," says Professor Scott, "payments expressed in terms of one or more 'capitals' are frequent." Here the term "capital" is used, just as in the example quoted above from Dafforne, for the capital subscribed by the shareholder (or held by him if he has obtained his shares otherwise than by being an original subscriber). Moreover, in 1621 an English translation of Orders of the States-General of the United Provinces for the establishment of a West

[1] Those who consult the Oxford Dictionary should make themselves acquainted with the symbols it employs. Several good writers, failing in this, have imagined Cotgrave's to be a dictionary of English, and have therefore quoted his translation of the French word capital as if it were a definition of the English word capital. They would have avoided this error if they had noticed that the quotation from Cotgrave is preceded by the symbol intended to indicate negative evidence; the N.E.D. quotes Cotgrave's translation to show that capital was *not* familiar to lexicographers as an English word in 1611. This negative evidence may be supplemented. The 1632 edition of Cotgrave's work has an English-French part which gives "*Capitall*, capital, capitulaire, a great capitall (or text) letter, cadeau." And Henry Hexham's copious *English and Nether duytch Dictionarie* 1660, gives "*Capitael*, The Principle or Chief Summe."

Indian Company mentions the " capital or stock " of the members of the company and the " capital sums " subscribed into the company by them. Professor Scott thinks that the new term was introduced because the " stock " of the company in the sense of the things which it possessed included what it had bought with borrowed money, so that when it was expressed in terms of money the total stock of the company would be what was subscribed by the shareholders plus what was borrowed, and therefore a division of fifty on the hundred (or, as we should say, 50 per cent.) " on the stock " might be misunderstood.[1] It is clear that the various significations of " stock " in connection with companies would require to be distinguished somehow, and the rather exotic " capital " was called in for the purpose.

From calling the holdings of the individual members of a company, when thought of as amounts of money, their " capitals," it is a very short step to calling the aggregate of these holdings " the capital of the company "; a short step which is made easier by the fact that this aggregate is the thing upon which all operations of the company are founded—it is the most important or chief stock of the company. We can almost see the working of the seventeenth-century mind in this matter in the Bank of England's 1697 Act of Parliament (8 and 9 W. and M., chap. 20). Sect. 20 first wedges the adjective " capital " in between " common " and " principal," speaking of the " common " capital, and " principal " stock of the company, and then drops both " common " and " principal " by referring to the same thing as " the said capital stock." The term " common " suggests the idea of aggregating the individual " capitals," and " principal " suggests the idea of the pre-eminence of the particular stock.[2]

The Act shows that the idea of the capital of the company as a sum of money with nothing but an historical connection with the actual possessions of the company at the moment had as yet made little progress, since " for the better settling and adjusting the right and property of each member " of the company, the

[1] *Constitution and Finance of English, Scottish and Irish Jointstock Companies to 1720*, Vol. I. pp. 157–8.

[2] As there are no commas in the original, the word " capital " in " common capital and principal stock " might be taken to be a substantive, but this interpretation seems excluded by the use of " capital stock," and would make no difference to the argument above if it were adopted.

capital stock was to "be computed and estimated by the principal and interest owing to them from the king or any others and by cash or by any other effects whereof the said capital stock shall then really consist over and above the value of the debts which they shall owe at the same time." The idea evidently is that the "real" capital stock is the assets less liabilities, not the sum originally subscribed plus additions and minus subtractions made in some formal manner. But we may safely say that in the region of company finance capital was fairly established by the end of the seventeenth century in the two senses in which it is still understood there. When the company started, and shareholders provided the money, they were said to provide "capital," and this, once obtained, became the "capital stock," or shortly "the capital" of the company, and was the sum on which profits were reckoned and dividends declared at so much per cent., its ownership being regarded as distributed among the members or shareholders in proportion to the number of pounds held by each of them.[1]

Starting thus in company finance, the term gradually won its way into the fields of individual finance, "political arithmetic," and economics.

In earlier times the individual could feel no want of such a term in his own affairs. The primitive agriculturist, feeding himself and his family almost entirely on what he and they have won from the ground with their own hands, might recognise, like Abraham and Lot, that his stock of cattle had increased, or that he had got his soil into better condition, but he certainly never dreamt of saying that he had put a certain number of shekels or pounds into the business and was getting 10 per cent. or any other percentage upon that number. The early artisan knew when his stock of tools was improving or deteriorating and when his stock of materials or finished goods was greater or less, but it did not occur to him that he ought to know what profit he was making on the sum of money which he had—very gradually in all probability—"put into the business."

[1] I am not forgetting that companies' capitals are often divided into shares, that dividends are declared at so much per share, and that each member is regarded as holding a number of shares. In fact the shares are always described as "— pound shares," and the holder of a £10 or £1 share is in just the same position as the holder of £10 or £1 of "stock" in a company which does not allow division below £10 or £1.

But by the time the term capital came into general use in connection with companies, there were many individuals, chiefly merchants, who could make some estimate of the amount of money embarked in their business, and who would find it convenient to calculate what percentage upon that amount they were making, inasmuch as the percentage would tell them whether they were doing well or ill compared with their neighbours at the same time, and compared with themselves in earlier periods, and also whether it would be better to drop the particular line of business and take up some other. "Stock" was not a very convenient term for the amount of money put into the business, since it properly signified the actual things owned, though sometimes used of the money put into them. A man's "stock-in-trade" would be that part of his goods which was used in his trade, but what was wanted was a name for the amount of money invested in this stock-in-trade. It was very naturally found in the term which had come into use for the amount invested in the stock-in-trade of a company, and men began to talk of "putting capital into" their own individual business just as they spoke of putting capital into such and such a company.

So Postlethwayt's *Universal Dictionary of Trade and Commerce* in 1751 gives us this:

> "CAPITAL, amongst merchants, bankers, and traders, signifies the sum of money which individuals bring to make up the common stock of a partnership when it is first formed. It is also said of the stock which a merchant at first puts into trade, for his account. It signifies likewise the fund of a trading company or corporation, in which sense the word stock is generally added to it. Thus, we say the capital stock of the bank, etc. The word capital is opposed to that of profit or gain, though the profit often increases the capital, and becomes itself part of the capital, when joined with the former."

Johnson, whose attitude towards finance is shown by his explaining "stockjobber" as "a low wretch who gets money by buying and selling shares in the funds," had not got so far in 1755 as to recognise capital as a substantive at all. "Capital Stock" he explains as "The principal or original stock of a trading company."

Postlethwayt thinks of the merchant's capital as the stock, by which he evidently means money, first put into his trade.

There is something prior and something subsequent to this. Before the merchant first puts the sum into trade it is there ready to be put in. The merchant "has capital to employ." When he has put it in it does not cease to exist; he still has capital unless it is lost, which normally it will not be. The term was already used of money to invest. After being once put in, the merchant's capital would be analogous to the capital of the company, with this very important exception, that there was no need to stereotype it in the same way.

In company finance it is convenient that the capital should have a great measure of fixity. It may indeed from time to time be increased by the addition of new subscriptions or formal appropriations from profits, or be decreased by some rather solemn process of "writing down." But the whole or most of the convenience which is obtained from the use of the conception would be lost if the capital was continually varying with every fluctuation in the money value of the stock-in-trade and goodwill owned by the company minus its liabilities. Imagine the confusion which would be wrought in the payment of dividends in stock exchange dealings and elsewhere if the capital of every bank and railroad were adjusted every six months or even every year on the principle of the 1697 Act of Parliament! The capital of the company, sometimes called even now the "nominal capital" owing to the continuance of a hankering after a "real capital," cannot be frequently altered without inconvenience. But an individual has no such need for a "nominal capital," because he has no stock or shares to be dealt in, and no shareholders among whom profits are to be divided. Consequently he is more likely to think of the capital in his business as the money value of the stock-in-trade and goodwill of the business at the moment when the accounts are made up. If it is less than it was last time the accounts were made up, the capital in the business is less by the amount of the difference and *vice versâ*. Thus the capital of the merchant or manufacturer came to mean, not, like the capital ot the company, a stereotyped figure having some historical connection with the amount of money originally invested, but the money value at the moment of the stock-in-trade and goodwill less debts; or shortly the assets less the liabilities.

I do not think any one in the eighteenth century proposed to extend the conception of the capital of the merchant or manufacturer so as to make it cover the whole of his assets less the whole of his liabilities as a man. It was confined to so much of his assets and liabilities as belongs or appertains to that side of him which is merchant or manufacturer. When a company is formed to carry on a business, the question here involved cannot be asked with regard to it. The funds which it employs in its business are necessarily separated from the rest of the property of its individual members. It is true that the separation disappears if the company is one with "unlimited liability" and is insolvent. But all the more important of the old companies, like all modern companies, had limited liability; and after all solvency is more usual and normal than insolvency. So the capital of a company was never difficult to distinguish from other property owned by its proprietors. But when an individual carried on business on his own account, there is no corresponding distinction of ownership between property belonging to his business and property outside that business. All is his, and all is liable for all his debts; misfortune in business may deprive him of his furniture and dwelling-house, and extravagance in living may ruin his business by depriving it of necessary funds. Some of his material possessions may be used partly for his business and partly for the comfortable maintenance of himself and his family; his house may be partly a workshop or a "front shop," his carriage or cart and horse may sometimes be employed in the business and sometimes otherwise.

The difficulty may require different solutions according to the purpose in view, but it is always possible in some way or other to distinguish the capital in the business from the rest of the man's property. If, for example, the purpose is to discover how much, if anything, the man will lose by abandoning his business, we may divide his house between its two uses by asking how much a house to live in would cost him if he retired from business, subtract this from the selling value of his present dwelling and shop house, and say the remainder is capital in the business. For answering questions about the success of the business some estimate of the capital employed in it is necessary and can be made, though often with considerable doubt.

The question, often discussed in recent years, whether land "is to be included in capital," did not present itself so long as capital was thought of as money to invest or as money which had been invested. A capital of £10,000 might be invested in the purchase of land as well as in the purchase of other movable commodities; no one would think of then reducing its amount to £8000 if £2000 of it had been spent on buying land. In the case of a company the semi-stereotyped figure of its capital would be unaffected by any subsequent change in the value of the land bought; in the case of an individual re-valuing his possessions from time to time, changes in the value of the land included in them would be either ignored or recognised just like changes in the value of other things—sometimes the land would be put "at cost" and sometimes at market value. We must remember that the capital was always conceived as the money invested, not as the things themselves in which the money was invested.

As for the application of the term to the affairs of the nation, at least two pre-Smithian writers, and probably others, summed up a total which they regarded as the national capital. The author of a *Discourse of Money*, 1696, p. 198, talks of "the capital stock of national treasure," and Andrew Hooke, in his *Essay on the National Debt and National Capital*, 1750, treats the "national capital" as consisting of (1) "cash-stock or coin," (2) "personal stock" or "wrought plate and bullion, jewels, rings, furniture, apparel, shipping, stock-in-trade, stock for consumption, and live-stock of capital," and (3) "land stock," *i.e.* "the value of all the lands in the kingdom."

To sum up, then, it appears that when Adam Smith took possession of the conception of capital in the *Wealth of Nations*, the term capital was already used very much as it is to-day in ordinary English outside the works of the economic theorists.

The answer to the question, "What is the capital of such and such a firm or company?" would always have been, as it is to-day, a figure in pounds sterling. The relation between this figure and the actual valuable possessions of the firm or company was a perfectly simple one. According as the context indicated the one meaning or the other, the number of pounds was either the money which was conventionally reckoned to have been "put into" the concern and consequently "invested in" the actual possessions of the concern, or else the money which these possessions would "realise" if sold. If anyone did say that the capital of any firm or company was "really" its actual possessions, he would have been understood to be speaking metaphorically, and merely to mean that the sum of money said to be the capital should be put at the true value of those possessions.

The question, "What is the capital of the country?" was answered, as statisticians answer it to-day, by giving a sum of money reckoned up by estimating the value of the possessions of the people of the country, including in those possessions all their valuable land.

There was only one important difference between the language of that day and this. The question, "What is the capital of So-and-so?" if So-and-So was regarded as not engaged in business, was not asked. In our own day the term has been found convenient as applied to private persons as well as to firms and companies, and all well-to-do private persons are familiar with arguments in which their "capital" as well as their "income" appears, and in which their capital means the money-valuation of their possessions at the moment. But Smith's age was not sufficiently commercialised for this, and when his contemporaries desired to mention the amount of money which a private person's possessions were worth, they said his or her "fortune" was so much. If a banker possessing nothing outside his bank, which was worth £60,000, left the bank in equal shares to two otherwise penniless sons who proceeded to carry it on, they would be said to have a capital of £30,000 each; but if he left the property in equal shares to a son and a daughter and the daughter left her share with the bank at interest, while the son carried it on alone, she would have a "fortune" of £30,000 while her brother alone had a capital of £30,000.

And if the banker or any other person engaged in business, had property which was not used in the business, he was not spoken of as having a capital reckoned by adding the value of this property to the value of what was engaged in the business.

§ 4. *The Economists' Conception of "Capital."*

In the student's notes of Adam Smith's *Lectures* the word capital occurs only once, and then it is used simply of a sum of money lent as opposed to interest on the loan :

> " When a sum of money is lent to a private person, the creditor can come upon the debtor when he pleases for both capital and interest; but it is not on this footing that the Government borrows money; they give you a right to a perpetual annuity of three or four per cent., but not to redemand your capital " (p. 248).

And even in Book I of the *Wealth of Nations,* composed as it doubtless was before Smith had come under physiocratic influences, the word is seldom used, and when it does occur, it is almost always used as any business man might use it, and not as a term belonging specially to economic theory. It is the " profits of stock " not the " profits of capital " which are one of the three sources of revenue (p. 54); chapter ix is entitled " Of the Profits of Stock " and chapter x " Of Wages and Profit in the different Employments of Labour and Stock "; and in neither of these chapters is there any suggestion that only a part of stock, called capital, brings in profit.[1]

The title of Book II, " Of the Nature, Accumulation and Employment of Stock," raises hopes which, like those raised by the title of Book I, are destined to be disappointed. The short " Introduction " prefixed to it may perhaps be said to suggest, though rather confusedly, that the stock of individuals and society consists of " goods of different kinds " which are " stored up," or accumulated, and that these consist, firstly, of things which " maintain " workers from the time when they begin till they have " not only completed but sold " their product; secondly, of the " materials and tools of " their work, and, thirdly, of " a particular branch " called money. This may perhaps be regarded as covering the " nature and accumulation "

[1] In Vol. I. pp. 50–1, " the capital annually employed " by a master-manufacturer is his expenditure on labour and materials for twelve months, which is not distinguished from his " stock " (compare with this p. 53). On p. 110 capital employed in insurance is said to bring in no more profit than that obtained in any common trade. On p. 158 tobacco plantations are said to be worked " by the capital " of absentees. The " stock " and " capital " of a grocer are treated as synonyms on p. 114, and so are the stock and capital employed in a mine on p. 166. The " capital stock of Great Britain " and of " the society " is mentioned on p. 95.

of stock. But even the Introduction says the Book will examine, not the employment of stock pure and simple, but the employment of " the stock which is accumulated into a capital," and when we come to look at the Book itself, we find that nearly the whole of chapter i, " Of the Division of Stock," concerns the part which Smith calls capital; chapter ii, in the first place entitled, " Of Money considered as a particular branch of the General Stock of the Society," has an alternative title, " or of the Expense of maintaining the National Capital"; chapter iii is " Of the Accumulation of Capital or of Productive and Unproductive Labour," and chapter v is " Of the Different Employments of Capitals." Chapter iv, indeed, is " Of Stock lent at Interest," but it begins with the sentence, " The stock which is lent at interest is always considered as a capital by the lender."

The fact is that Book II does not deal with the comparatively simple idea of a stock, or stored-up or accumulated body of goods, but with a very hazy conception to which Smith gave the name of capital, and which he had created by combining a misunderstanding of English commercial language with a partial acceptance of the prime physiocratic misconception of the nature of production.

If he had approached the subject from the side of accountancy applied to firms and companies, he would have seen that the relation between the stocks of things possessed by them and their capital was not that their capital was only a part of these things, but that it was the conventional or actual valuation in money regarded as representing the whole of them; and it would not have occurred to him to think of any part of the things as not expected to afford or yield a profit.

Unfortunately he did not approach from this side, but began with the case of the individual owner of stock and that at a time when, as we have seen, the term capital had not been introduced into everyday individual accountancy:

" When the stock which a man possesses is no more than sufficient to maintain him for a few days or a few weeks, he seldom thinks of deriving any revenue from it. . . . But when he possesses stock sufficient to maintain him for months or years, he naturally endeavours to derive a revenue from the greater part of it; reserving only so much for his immediate consumption as may maintain him till this revenue begins to come in. His whole stock, therefore, is distinguished into two parts. That part which he expects is to afford him this revenue is called his capital. The other is that which supplies his immediate consumption, and which consists either, first, in that portion of his whole stock which was originally reserved for this purpose; or, secondly, in his revenue, from whatever source derived, as it gradually comes in; or, thirdly, in such things as had been purchased by either of these in former years, and which are not yet entirely consumed, such as a stock of clothes, household furniture, and the like."

The "revenue," which immediately after becomes "revenue or profit," is clearly conceived as money, and the basis of the distinction between the non-capital and the capital is to be that while the non-capital is useful directly (or, in Smith's phrase, "immediately") to the owner, the capital is only useful to him indirectly in consequence of its bringing in money revenue. If I live in my own house and use my own furniture, the house and furniture are, according to Smith, not part of my capital and are "reserved for my immediate consumption." But if I let the house and furniture to somebody else, and "derive a revenue" from them, and hire for my use another person's house and furniture, my own will "serve in the function of a capital" (Vol. i. p. 264) to me, and the other house and furniture will do the same to the other owner.

This is awkward enough, but may perhaps be said to be not very important. But when the same criterion is applied, as Smith at any rate professes to apply it, to the stock of society as a whole,[1] it causes difficulties which are both insuperable and important. Machines, instruments of all kinds, buildings, and improvements of land become capital if or when they are used for producing things not for their owner's consumption but for the consumption of other persons to whom the owner sells. If the things produced are for consumption by the owners they are not capital but stock for immediate consumption. Society's "stock of provisions," of materials and finished work, so far only as all three are still in the possession of producers who expect

[1] "The general stock of any country or society is the same with that of all its inhabitants or members" (Vol. I. p. 263; cp. p. 320). But in the enumeration on p. 264 the "acquired and useful abilities of all the inhabitants or members of the society" are included, though nothing had been said about such abilities being capital to the individual members.

to sell them to other persons, are part of the capital of the society; but so far as they are in the possession either of producers who intend to consume them themselves or of persons who have bought them from the producers, they are not part of the capital but of the stock reserved for immediate consumption.

Smith himself seems to have felt there was a difficulty, at any rate with regard to some things, in the criterion which he proposes. In regard to dwelling-houses, furniture, clothes and the "furniture of funerals" let out on hire, he coolly adopts a totally different criterion—the criterion of productivity in the physiocratic sense in which it is judged by capacity to produce a tangible material object. These things, he says, can never be part of the capital of the society because they themselves "produce nothing," the revenue derived from them by their owner being drawn from some other source of revenue (p. 263). He makes no attempt to explain the relation between this view of houses, furniture and clothes let out on hire and the statement which he makes within a page or two that both the materials for such things and "the work which is made up and completed" are part of the capital of society while they are "still in the hands of the merchant or manufacturer and not yet disposed of or distributed to the proper consumers" (p. 265), though if such things themselves "produce nothing" when they are let on hire, it certainly seems difficult to see how they can "produce something" when not yet sold or let. And if a house is built in order to be let by the builder and so remains in his ownership indefinitely, does it then produce something or nothing?

Smith's unconscious attempt to deprive capital of its well-established meaning and to give it a new one would thus have failed even if he had always adhered to what seems his general intention of making it signify certain things themselves which form a portion of the stocks of individuals and society. But the usual associations of the word were too powerful to allow him to keep that intention steadily in view. Even in his actual description of the different parts of the stock and the capital phrases keep occurring which are appropriate to the usual meaning of the word and inappropriate to that which he is trying to adopt. The capital is often spoken of as if it were something other than the goods themselves. "*It*," for example, "may be employed in raising, manufacturing, or purchasing goods, and selling them again with a profit," although it is "the goods of the merchant" which "yield him" the profit (p. 261). "*It*," again, "may be employed in the improvement of land" and "in the purchase of useful machines or instruments of trade." "*The price or value* of" the farmer's "labouring cattle is a fixed capital in the same manner as that of the instruments of husbandry" (p. 262). "Both *the price and the maintenance* of the cattle which are bought in and fattened, not for labour, but for sale, are a circulating capital" (pp. 262–3). The third "article" of the fixed capital of society consists "of the improvements of land, of *what has been profitably laid out* in clearing, draining, enclosing, manuring and reducing it into the condition most proper for tillage and culture" (p. 264). The inclusion of "the acquired and useful abilities of all the inhabitants or members of society" as a fourth article of the fixed society's fixed capital is justified on the ground that their acquisition "always costs *a real expense*, which is a capital fixed and realised as it were" in the persons of the acquirers. In all these cases Smith is drifting back into the ordinary use of the term capital in the sense of money invested in the things rather than the things themselves.

In the later chapters of Book II he fails much more completely to hold tight to his formal conception of the capital as consisting of a portion of the things themselves which constitute the stock. The capital degenerates into a kind of expenditure, and is greater or less according as this kind of expenditure is greater or less per annum. The "accumulation" of capital, though the result of "parsimony" saving and storing up (Vol. I. p. 320), is somehow not the result of more being produced than is consumed, because what is saved is not unconsumed (as every stock, we should imagine, must be), but is consumed by "productive" labourers.

Smith's successors for over a century completely failed to clear the matter up, and there are writers of popular text-books and lecturers at this day who blindly follow most of his confused and contradictory doctrine. It is still quite common to "define capital" as "wealth productively employed," without making it in the least clear what is meant by "wealth" and without discarding either of the two incompatible interpretations of "productively"—one, "so as to bring in money profit to the owner," and the other, "so as to assist in making useful material objects."

§ 5. *Inappropriateness of Capital as a Name for Accumulated Material Equipment.*

Towards the end of the nineteenth century Irving Fisher, who kindly treated me as an anticipator of his doctrine, tried to induce economists to speak of the capital of individuals and societies as the whole of the things owned by them at some particular moment or point of time, so that capital should be simply the correlative of income, which comes in over a period or length of time. Insistence on the capital existing at a point of time and income covering a length of time was certainly useful and tended to clear up a good deal of confusion.[1]

But capital in Fisher's sense was not quite what the economists were groping for in the theory of Production. They wanted to explain differences in productiveness, and were in search of some comprehensive term to cover the whole of what may be perhaps best described as the legacy left by each generation of mankind in the shape of useful—that is, *still* useful—alterations made by man in his material surroundings. One generation hands on to the next a certain amount of accumulated knowledge which is favourable to production; it also hands on land which has been improved for agriculture and other industries as well as for residence, buildings of all kinds, furniture, machinery, tools and stocks of improved domesticated animals.

The object of the creation of the concept is to facilitate explanation of the effect of man's work in the past upon the productiveness of man's work in the present. Just, it has to be shown, as the productiveness of the present day is enormously assisted by what has been done in the past to improve knowledge, so it is enormously assisted by what has been done in the past to improve our material surroundings.

Fisher's concept, on the other hand, is essentially a concept of things which are property, things "owned," as he puts it, and the things which are owned are not always products of past

[1] See Fisher's articles "What is Capital?" and "Senses of Capital" in the *Economic Journal*, December 1896 and June 1897, and his *Nature of Capital and Income*, 1906, *passim*.

labour, and we are so much in the habit of measuring them by their value that it is difficult for us to think of them being greater or less except in the sense of their being more or less valuable.

Property, things owned, includes unimproved land and any natural objects which have not been altered in any way by man's labour. Some of these things have considerable value, and if we measure by value we put them down as important constituents of the whole, whereas they do not enter into the concept of results of past labour at all. Things, on the other hand, which have been affected by past labour in a way which makes them very important aids to productiveness may quite easily become, and in fact often do become, of very little value. Two railways, for example, between two terminal points, but serving different intermediate places, can scarcely be less useful than one, but in unrestrained competition they may easily be less valuable. Or it may be that a quite important product of past labour, as for instance, roads and sewers or the buildings in which the administration of government is carried on, do not come into commerce at all, and consequently do not get valued in the ordinary course. To include such things in a concept called "capital," and to give them due weight there, may be possible, but it is certainly very difficult and not likely to be done.

The best way to avoid all difficulty seems to be to speak of the accumulated material equipment when we mean to indicate the products of past labour which are embodied in material things and are still in existence and useful; to speak of property when we mean to indicate the possessions of persons and institutions, including both the material things possessed and such other things as are valuable possessions; and to use the term "capital" in the perfectly well-defined and useful senses in which it is commonly used by intelligent commercial and ordinary persons whose language has not been corrupted by too great familiarity with the misguided attempts of economists to improve their mother-tongue.

If accumulated material equipment is clearly conceived and not confused either with products which happen to be valuable property, or with sums of money which happen to be the capital of some person or body, many puzzles will lose their intricacy. For example, the trouble which is given by the proposition,

"Capital is the result of saving" or "of abstinence," is avoided altogether. To ascribe the fact that certain persons have valuable property to those persons having "saved" part of their income or having "abstained" from consuming as much as they might have consumed without reducing their property is often correct, though we must not forget that it is often correct when the valuable property is "land" as well as when it is produce of past labour. But to say that nobody has valuable property other than the somewhat ill-defined entity "land" unless he himself has saved or abstained is so obviously incorrect that no one says it. And to say that nobody has this kind of property unless either he or its previous owners have saved or abstained—or to say that this kind of property is the result of its present or previous owners having saved or abstained—is less obviously incorrect, but is still untrue in the only sense in which the words are likely to be taken. Hearers of the words are certain to measure the property by its value, and to assume that what is meant is that every pound's worth of anyone's property is due to his or his predecessor's saving one pound or abstaining from the consumption of one pound's worth of income. But, as every owner of property knows, things rise and fall in value, so that his possession of a thousand pounds' worth of property other than land is no proof that he or previous owners saved £1000. Endless misunderstandings between those who attack and those who defend a particular type of economic organisation have resulted.

On the other hand, there is little doubt or difficulty about the relation of saving and abstinence to material equipment. The actual products of man's labour in the past have all been saved in the only possible sense which can be attributed to the word in this context, that is, they have been produced and have not been consumed; they are all the result of abstinence again in the only possible sense, namely, that some person or persons and all persons taken together abstained from consuming either the things themselves or something which could have been made instead of them. And since we are not accustomed to measure material equipment by its value (as we measure property and "capital") we shall not be troubled by anyone supposing that the saving or abstinence must somehow equal the material equipment which comes into existence in consequence of it, or that the whole of the savings of the past must be still with us in the form of material equipment.

However, neither saving nor abstinence are very satisfactory words for the purpose of explaining the origin of material equipment. "Abstinence" suggests a kind of intended-to-be-virtuous privation, such as that practised by monks and teetotallers, and this is misleading, since for very rich people it is scarcely what the ordinary person calls privation to invest a portion of their income rather than to spend it all, and in case of small incomes saving may on occasion be wicked rather than meritorious, as when a parent starves his children of food and education in order to add to his capital. The older and more usual expression, "saving," is a little unfortunate in the fact that it suggests the preliminary accumulation of money, which is apparent rather than real. Marshall's suggestion of "waiting" is worse than either saving or abstinence; waiting is inaction, and inaction cannot create material equipment. Material equipment has to be actively collected before it is used, not waited for. On the whole "accumulation" seems by far the best available term.

CHAPTER VII

THE THEORY OF VALUE IN GENERAL

§ 1. *Early Theories*

In modern Western society, in which purchase and sale plays so large a part, the first approximation in any comparison of material welfare, usually begins with an inquiry into the magnitude of incomes, and the measurement of this magnitude is by way of valuation. If we ask which of two persons is the better off, we are likely to be told in the first place, at any rate, that one of them has a better income than the other; and we understand by that not that his income is heavier, bulkier, prettier or sweeter than that of the other, but that it is valued at more pounds, dollars, or some other units which happen to be the national standard of value.

Down to the present point we have staved off the consideration of value, in the hope that productional problems might be made intelligible with no more aid than that furnished by the rudimentary knowledge of the way in which values move possessed by every intelligent adult in civilised countries. But now that we are moving on to questions of the comparative material welfare of individuals and groups at one and the same time, consideration of the theory of value can no longer be delayed.

Discussion of the ethics of value is much older than discussion of the economics of value. Inquiry into the justice of prices seems always to precede inquiry into the causes of prices and price-movements. It is so with children and uneducated adults even in our own time and country. The first thought that anyone has about a price is that it is "wrong." So long as prices are what he has always been accustomed to, he does not think about them at all. If a price moves in his favour, he thanks a bountiful providence and does not deem it necessary to investigate the reasons of his good fortune. But if a price moves against him, whether he is a buyer or a seller, he begins at once to think about it, and what he thinks is that the change is wrong, wicked. It outrages his moral sense; and why not? He loses by it something which he has been accustomed to look on as his own, so it is just the same as robbery, and everyone knows that robbery is wicked. When he complains, the other parties concerned try to throw blame on each other; the middleman says it is the fault of the wicked producers, who have formed a ring, and the producers retort that it is the fault of the middlemen, who are profiteers and give too little and ask too much. It is a sign of great advance in civilisation when these recriminations diminish and people begin to think of changes in price not as something wicked and anomalous but as normal phenomena, "obeying," as they say, "the law of supply and demand" or something like that. When they reach this stage, their moral sense is no longer outraged by alterations of price, and there is much less friction and loss of temper.

The beginnings, at any rate, of the transition from ethical to economic discussion are perceptible in the seventeenth century. The ancient philosophers had done nothing for the theory of value beyond exercising a slight influence on the mediæval theologians who asked themselves what was the just price which a Christian man might charge for a commodity or service. It was this question which gave rise to the first economic theory of value. A very effective defence for a person accused of having "unjustly" raised the price he charges for a commodity or service presents itself if it can be said with any plausibility that the thing sold now costs him more labour than it did. It is inevitable that this justification of a rise of price, universally accepted as it was, should suggest "quantity of labour required" as the cause or at least one of the causes of value. If a thing cost more labour than it did, it might be expected to rise in value; and a corollary of that proposition is that if one thing cost more labour than another, it may be expected to have greater value.

From this then arises the crude semi-ethical, semi-economic theory that the value of things is properly, or "really in the long run," determined by the quantity of labour required to produce them; and most of the early economists' thought on the subject of value was directed either towards modifying this doctrine so as to make it more plausible, or towards explaining why prices fluctuated above and below this proper or permanent price.

Sir William Petty, in consonance with the physiological metaphor which he used in describing labour as the father and active principle of wealth and land the mother,[1] suggested that land as well as labour was taken into account in the determination of value.

"All things," he says, "ought to be valued by two natural denominations, which is land and labour, that is, we ought to say a ship or garment is worth such a measure of land with such another measure of labour; forasmuch as both ships and garments were the creatures of lands and men's labours thereupon: This being true, we should be glad to find out a natural Par between land and labour, so as we might express the value by either of them alone as well or better than by both, and reduce one into the other as easily and certainly as we reduce pence into pounds." (*Treatise of Taxes*, chap. iv, § 18; in *Econ. Writings*, pp. 44–5.)

In a later work he says "how to make a Par and Equation between lands and labour so as to express the value of anything by either alone" is "the most important consideration in political œconomies," but he does not seem to think he has completely solved the question. He supposes an untended calf in a meadow to produce a certain amount of additional eatable flesh in a year, and this addition to be the year's rent of the meadow and interest on the value of the calf, while any surplus over it which could be got by the calf being tended would be the wages of labour so expended. This leads him to the conclusion that "the day's food of an adult man at a medium, and not the day's labour is the common measure of value." [2]

He sees the difficulty of deciding how much labour is required to produce a thing. Is it to be measured by the number of persons actually employed on the job, or by the number really necessary? He does not answer the question, but avoids it by distinguishing between "natural cheapness," which depends on the number of hands necessary for production, and "political

[1] *Treatise of Taxes and Contributions*, 1662, chap. x, § 10; in *Economic Writings*, ed. Hull, p. 68.

[2] *Political Anatomy of Ireland*, 1691, chap. ix; *Econ. Writings*, p. 181. Perhaps Cantillon was thinking of this passage, or some first draft of it, when he said that Petty "in a little manuscript of the year 1685, regards this par in the equation of land and labour as the most important consideration in political arithmetic (*Essai*, p. 54).

cheapness," which may be less than the natural because of the interposition of "supernumerary interlopers," as when two hundred husbandmen are employed in doing what one hundred could do.

Fluctuations of price, for which the merchant has to look out, arise from various circumstances, among which is the existence of "substitutes or succedanea" for almost all commodities.[1]

John Locke, in his account of the origin and foundation of property, attributes value to labour :

"Let us but trace some of the ordinary provisions of life . . . and see how much they receive of their value from human industry. Bread, wine, and cloth are things of daily use and great plenty, yet notwithstanding, acorns, water, and leaves, or skins must be our bread, drink, and clothing, did not labour furnish us with these more useful commodities. For whatever bread is worth more than acorns, wine than water, and cloth or silk than leaves, skins or moss, that is wholly owing to labour and industry." (*Civil Government*, 1690, § 42).

"Wholly owing to labour," he says here, though in the next section he admits that land is a contributor, though a very small one, to value.

There was as yet no serious attempt to bring either the pure labour theory or the labour-and-a-little-land theory into close relationship with the market fluctuations of prices. Though the idea of value being determined by the labour required for production was distinctly predominant, the notion that utility had something to do with value was not absent. Nicholas Barbon, in his *Discourse of Trade*, 1690 (reprinted by Johns Hopkins University, 1905), has a chapter "Of the Value and Price of Wares," in which he says :

"The value of all wares arise from their use ; things of no use have no value ; as the English phrase is, They are good for nothing.

"The use of things are to supply the wants and necessities of man ; there are two general wants that mankind is born with ; the wants of the body and the wants of the mind ; to supply these two necessities all things under the sun become useful and therefore have a value. . . .

"Things rare and difficult to be obtained are general badges of honour : from this use, pearls, diamonds and precious stones have

[1] *Treatise of Taxes*, chap. xiv. §§ 17, 18 ; *Econ. Writings*, p. 90.

their value. Things rare are proper ensigns of honour, because it is honourable to acquire things difficult.

"The price of wares is the present value; and ariseth by computing the occasions or use for them with the quantity to serve that occasion; for the value of things depending on the use of them, the overplus of those wares which are more than can be used, become worth nothing; so that plenty, in respect of the occasion, makes things cheap; and scarcity, dear.

"There is no fixed price or value of anything for the wares of trades; the animals and vegetables of the earth depend on the influence of heaven, which sometimes causes murrains, dearth, famine, and sometimes years of great plenty; therefore the value of things must accordingly alter. Besides, the use of most things being to supply the wants of the mind and not the necessities of the body, and those wants most of them proceeding from inagination, the mind changeth; the things grow out of use, and so lose their value" (pp. 13–15 in the reprint).

The merchant guesses values by "reckoning prime cost, charges, and interest," and the artificer does the same by "reckoning the cost of the materials and the time of working them":

"But the market is the best judge of value; for by the concourse of buyers and sellers the quantity of wares and the occasion for them are best known; things are just worth so much as they can be sold for, according to the old rule, *valet quantum vendi potest*" (p. 16 in the reprint).

Locke, too, in his more distinctly economic work, *Some Considerations of the Consequences of the Lowering of Interest and Raising the Value of Money*, 1696, thinks of scarcity and utility and has some idea of the elasticity of demand:

"The price of any commodity rises or falls by the proportion of the number of buyers and sellers. This rule holds universally in all things that are to be bought and sold, bating now and then an extravagant fancy of some particular person, which never amounts to so considerable a part of trade as to make anything in the account worthy to be thought an exception to this rule.

"The vent of anything depends upon its necessity or usefulness as convenience or opinion, guided by fancy or fashion, shall determine. . . .

"There is nothing more confirmed by daily experience than that men give any portion of money for whatsoever is absolutely necessary rather than go without it. And in such things the scarcity of them alone makes their prices" (pp. 45–7).

So, if there were a great scarcity of wheat and "a proportionable want of all other food," a bushel of wheat might rise from 2*s*. 6*d*. to 25*s*. in a year:

"Things absolutely necessary for life must be had at any rate; but things convenient will be had only as they stand in preference with other conveniencies, and therefore in any one of these commodities, the value rises only as its quantity is less and vent greater, which depends upon its being preferred to other things in its consumption. For supposing that at the same time that there is a great scarcity of wheat and other grain, there were a considerable quantity of oats, men no question would give far more for wheat than oats, as being the healthier, pleasanter, and more convenient food: but since oats would serve to supply that absolute necessity of sustaining life, men would not rob themselves of all other conveniencies of life, by paying all their money for wheat when oats, that are cheaper, though with some inconvenience, would supply that defect" (pp. 47–8).

John Law, who later acquired fame as the originator of the Mississippi Scheme, propounded at the beginning of his *Money and Trade Considered*, 1705, a quantity-and-demand theory of value as follows:

"Goods have a value from the uses they are applied to; and their value is greater or lesser, not so much from their more or less valuable or necessary uses, as from the greater or lesser quantity of them in proportion to the demand for them. *Example*. Water is of great use, yet of little value; because the quantity of water is much greater than the demand for it. Diamonds are of little use yet of great value because the demand for diamonds is much greater than the quantity of them.

"Goods of the same kind differ in value from any difference in their quality. (*Ex.*) One horse is better than another horse. Barley of one country is better than barley of another country.

"Goods change their value from any change in their quantity or in the demand for them. (*Ex.*) If oats be in greater quantity than last year and the demand the same or lesser, oats will be less valuable.

"Mr. Lock says, The value of goods is according to their quantity in proportion to their vent. The vent of goods cannot be greater than the quantity, but the demand may be greater. (*Ex.*) If the quantity of wine brought from France be 100 tun and the demand be for 500 tun, the demand is greater than the vent; and the 100 tun will sell at a higher price than if the demand were only equal to the vent. So the prices of goods are not according to the quantity in proportion to the vent, but in proportion to the demand" (pp. 4–5 in 2nd ed., 1720).

An important book because of its influence in making Adam Smith discard money as a measure of value in long periods, and because it contains the germ of the index-number method of dealing with prices, was Bishop Fleetwood's *Chronicon Preciosum: or an account of English Money, the price of corn and other commodities for the last* 600 *years*, 1707. It says the question has been asked whether in order to qualify for a fellowship in a college founded A.D. 1400 a man may swear that he has not £5 a year when he actually has more. After elaborate investigation it concludes he may, if he has less than about £30. People who lived in the founder's time might with £5 purchase as much "bread, drink, meat, cloth, firing, books, and other necessaries and conveniencies" (p. 12) as could be bought in Fleetwood's time for £28 or £30 (p. 171).

Francis Hutcheson headed Book II. chap. xii of his *Introduction to Moral Philosophy*, 1747, with the words, "Concerning the Values or Prices of Goods." He says that to maintain commerce there must be some way of estimating the values of goods and services:

"The ground of all price must be some *fitness* in the things to yield some use or pleasure in life; without this they can be of no value. But this being presupposed, the prices of things will be in a compound proportion of the *demand* for them and the *difficulty* in acquiring them. The *demand* will be in proportion to the numbers who are wanting them, or their necessity to life. The difficulty may be occasioned many ways: if the quantities of them in the world be small; if any accidents make the quantity less than ordinary; if much toil is required in producing them, or much ingenuity or a more elegant genius in the artists; if the persons employed about them according to the custom of the country are men in high account, and live in a more splendid manner; for the expence of this must be defrayed by the higher profits of their labours, and few can be thus maintained.

"Some goods of the highest use yet have either no price or but a small one. If there's such plenty in nature that they are acquired almost without any labour, they have no price: if they may be acquired by easy common labour they are of small price. Such is the goodness of God to us that the most useful and necessary things are generally very plentiful and easily acquired.

"Other things of great use have no price, either because they are naturally destined for community, or cannot come into commerce but as appendages of something else, the price of which may be increased by them though they cannot be separately estimated."

Such, he says in a foot-note, are the air, the light of the sun, wholesome air in certain situations, and "fine prospects." And other things, he adds, such as religious offices, have no price because the buying and selling of them is forbidden by natural or positive law.

Cantillon, writing about 1730, though his work did not become public till 1755, has a chapter headed "The intrinsic price and value of a thing in general is the measure of the land and labour which enters into its production" (chap. x. in Pt. I). The labour is to be measured by its quality as well as by its quantity, since the artisan costs more to bring up than the labourer; and the land too is to be measured by goodness or product as well as by area.

However, he says, things do not always sell on the market at this intrinsic value. A man who has laid out a fanciful garden may get double or only half the expense when he tries to sell the property. Too much or too little corn may be sown, with the result that corn is sold below or above its intrinsic value. Market prices are continually fluctuating, but, in the case of "goods and merchandise of which the consumption is fairly constant and uniform, do not depart far from the intrinsic value" (p. 38). Even gold and silver have a value proportionate to the land and labour which enter into their production. No doubt Locke was right when he said that the consent of men had given them their value, but this is true of all other commodities. "No matter what men produce by their labour, that labour must furnish their maintenance. It is the great principle which we hear every day in the mouth even of the small men who take no part in our speculations and who live by their labour or their undertakings, 'Everyone must live' (*Il faut que tout le monde vive*," pp. 148–50).

In his chapter on "Market Prices," Cantillon is extraordinarily modern:

"Suppose," he says, "the butchers on one side and the buyers on the other. The price of meat will be settled after some higgling;

and one pound of beef will be nearly in value to one piece of money as all the beef exposed for sale in the market is to all the money which has been brought there to buy beef.

"This proportion is regulated by higgling. The butcher holds up his price on the strength of the number of buyers whom he sees; the buyers on their side offer less according as they think the butcher will have less sale: the price set by some is commonly followed by others. Some bargainers are cleverer at making their merchandise go off well, others more expert at crying it down. Although this method of fixing prices on the market has no exact or geometrical foundation, since it often depends on the eagerness or on the slackness of a small number of buyers or of sellers, yet it seems unlikely that the end could be arrived at by any more convenient way. It is always the case that the quantity of raw produce or of merchandise offered for sale in proportion to the demand or the quantity of buyers is the basis on which the actual market prices are fixed, or believed to be fixed, and that in general these prices do not differ much from the intrinsic value.

"To take another hypothesis—several stewards have received orders at the beginning of the season to buy green peas. One master has ordered the purchase of ten quarts at 60 livres, another has ordered ten at 50 livres, a third demands ten at 40 livres, and a fourth ten at 30 livres. For these orders to be executed, there must be on the market 40 quarts of green peas. Suppose there are only 20; the sellers, seeing many buyers, will keep up their prices, and the buyers will go up to the sums laid down for them, so that those who offer 60 livres for ten quarts will be the first served. The sellers, seeing then that no one will go above 50 livres, will let the other ten quarts go at that price, but those who had orders not to go above 40 and 30 livres will return empty-handed" (pp. 155–8).

If there are 400 quarts on the market the price will fall nearly to the intrinsic value and several stewards who had no order to buy will buy some.

Joseph Harris, in his *Essay on Money and Coins*, 1757 (Pt. I. pp. 11–12), cribs from Cantillon without adding much except a curious passage in which he says the price of land is influenced by the price of labour, as the labourers are the principal consumers of the grosser products of the earth.

"It seems then to be no good policy in the rich to deal too hardly with the poor; besides that such treatment must needs greatly check arts and industry, discourage matrimony amongst the lower class, and inspire them with thoughts of quitting their homes, in hopes of bettering their state elsewhere. But the benevolence here hinted at is to be tempered with discretion : the children of the poor should be brought up and inured as early as may be to some useful labour; and be taught with due care the great principles of religion and morality. But all are not agreed that reading and writing are qualifications necessary for the obtaining of those ends; some think that these accomplishments are useful only in higher stations; and that to instruct at a public expence the youth of the lower class in reading, writing, &c. is a kind of intrusion upon the class next above them; that these qualifications, instead of being advantageous to the poor who possess them, serve only to render their state more irksome and to inspire them with notions subversive of society. There must be labourers; and that most useful class of men should be duly cherished and taken care of: but books and pens will not alleviate the weight of the spade, or at all contribute to dry the sweat off the labourer's brow."

One of his sections is headed " The price of labour, the chief standard that regulates the value of all things " (Pt. I., p. 8). The word "chief" is inserted because he admits land has some share in the regulation, though not a large one; " as," he says, " in most productions labour hath the greatest share, the value of labour is to be reckoned the chief standard that regulates the value of all commodities; and more especially as the value of land is, as it were, already allowed for in the value of labour itself " (p. 9). He leaves the nature and method of the allowance in obscurity.

Turgot, from whom we might expect great things, is disappointing. He sees the difficulty of settling terms of exchange in isolated bartering transactions in which each party is a monopolist. But when there is a market, and a number of competitors, the " price which is midway between the different offers and the different demands will become the current price to which all the buyers and sellers will conform in their bargains " (*Réflexions*, § xxxii, in Daire, xxxiv).

Count Pietro Verri in chapter iv of his *Meditations*, 1771, explains that price is the quantity of a thing which is given in order to get a quantity of another thing. Before the invention of money, he says, there were no " buyers " nor " sellers "; afterwards, these terms were used to distinguish him who offered from him who accepted the universal merchandise, money, and " price " was the name given to the amount of money given for other merchandise. The common price is that by which neither of the contracting parties is impoverished. Alone, neither utility nor rarity can give a thing price. Both together are necessary.

Thus we see that before Adam Smith's time a good deal of subsequent theory had been anticipated. There is the labour theory, the labour and other costs theory, and the supply and demand theory; there is also a tendency to think of the cost of production theory as applying to natural or intrinsic value, and of the supply and demand theory as applying to market value.

§ 2. *Adam Smith's Cost of Production Theory.*

Adam Smith in his lectures seems to have defined "natural price" as the price which would pay for the labour at *its* natural price, which he takes to be what is sufficient to maintain the labourer, to defray the expense of his education, and to compensate the risk of his not living long enough or not succeeding in the business (pp. 173–6). Market price he ascribes to (1) the demand or need for the commodity, (2) the abundance or scarcity of the commodity in proportion to the need for it, (3) the riches or poverty of those who demand it (pp. 176–7). Incidentally he remarks that "labour, not money, is the true measure of value" (p. 190).

In the *Wealth of Nations* he says:

"The word VALUE, it is to be observed, has two different meanings, and sometimes expresses the utility of some particular object, and sometimes the power of purchasing other goods which the possession of that object conveys. The one may be called 'value in use'; the other, 'value in exchange.' The things which have the greatest value in use have frequently little or no value in exchange; and, on the contrary, those which have the greatest value in exchange have frequently little or no value in use. Nothing is more useful than water; but it will purchase scarce anything; scarce anything can be had in exchange for it. A diamond, on the contrary, has scarce any value in use; but a very great quantity of other goods may frequently be had in exchange for it" (Vol. I. p. 30).

Then at the beginning of the next chapter (Book I. chap. v) he says that the value of any commodity not intended by the owner for his own consumption

"is equal to the quantity of labour which it enables him to purchase or command. Labour, therefore, is the real measure of the exchangeable value of all commodities.

"The real price of every thing, what every thing really costs to the man who wants to acquire it, is the toil and trouble of acquiring it. What every thing is really worth to the man who has acquired it, and who wants to dispose of it or exchange it for something else, is the toil and trouble which it can save to himself, and which it can impose upon other people."

I think he does not notice that these two measures, what the thing can save to the possessor and what it may impose on other people, may bring out different results.

He continues:

"What is bought with money or with goods is purchased by labour, as much as what we acquire by the toil of our own body. That money or those goods indeed save us this toil. They contain the value of a certain quantity of labour which we exchange for what is supposed at the time to contain the value of an equal quantity. Labour was the first price, the original purchase-money that was paid for all things. It was not by gold or by silver, but by labour, that all the wealth of the world was originally purchased; and its value, to those who possess it, and who want to exchange it for some new productions, is precisely equal to the quantity of labour which it can enable them to purchase or command."

Then he says wealth is power of purchasing labour, but value is not commonly estimated in labour, because labour is difficult to measure and commodities are more frequently exchanged for other commodities, especially money. But, he says, gold and silver vary in value, whereas,

"Equal quantities of labour, at all times and places, may be said to be of equal value to the labourer. In his ordinary state of health, strength and spirits; in the ordinary degree of his skill and dexterity, he must always lay down the same portion of his ease, his liberty, and his happiness. The price which he pays must always be the same, whatever may be the quantity of goods which he receives in return for it. Of these, indeed, it may sometimes purchase a greater and sometimes a smaller quantity; but it is their value which varies, not that of the labour which purchases them. At all times and places that is dear which it is difficult to come at, or which it costs much labour to acquire; and that cheap which is to be had easily, or with very little labour. Labour alone, therefore, never varying in its own value, is alone the ultimate and real standard by which the value of all commodities can at all times and places be estimated and compared. It is their real price; money is their nominal price only."

The effect of this doctrine of real and nominal price was quite arbitrarily to select labour as the one thing in the world which does not change in value: if labour produces more commodities they all become cheaper, of less value, though exchanging among themselves in just the same ratios as before. Quite arbitrarily, I say, because there is no reason for not saying the converse, namely, that commodities have not varied in value, but labour has become of greater value, inasmuch as more commodities will now have to be given in exchange for it. We do, in fact, say that labour is "better paid" because more productive: Smith requires to say (putting aside receipts of other sharers in distribution) that it is receiving the same value, whatever its productiveness.

We should expect from this doctrine that things would exchange in proportion to the labour expended on them, and so does Smith:

"In that early and rude state of society which precedes both the accumulation of stock and the appropriation of land, the proportion between the quantities of labour necessary for acquiring different objects seems to be the only circumstance which can afford any rule for exchanging them for one another. If among a nation of hunters, for example, it usually costs twice the labour to kill a beaver which it does to kill a deer, one beaver should naturally exchange for or be worth two deer. It is natural that what is usually the produce of two days' or two hours' labour, should be worth double of what is usually the produce of one day's or one hour's labour."

But what about the fact that different kinds of labour get unequal remuneration? Smith is amazingly weak on this point:

"If the one species of labour should be more severe than the other, some allowance will naturally be made for this superior hardship; and the produce of one hour's labour in the one way may frequently exchange for that of two hours' labour in the other.

"Or if the one species of labour requires an uncommon degree of dexterity and ingenuity, the esteem which men have for such talents will naturally give a value to their produce, superior to what would be due to the time employed about it. Such talents can seldom be acquired but in consequence of long application, and the superior value of their produce may frequently be no more than a reasonable compensation for the time and labour which must be spent in acquiring them. In the advanced state of society, allowances of this kind, for superior hardship and superior skill, are commonly made in the wages of labour; and something of the same kind must probably have taken place in its earliest and rudest period" (Vol. I. p. 49).

The first of these suggestions gives no reason at all; if labour is the standard, why should "esteem" affect the matter? There is more force, no doubt, underlying "reasonable compensation," since, as Smith explains in chap. ix, if such compensation is not obtained, the supply of entrants to the occupations will be reduced, but this has nothing to do with "esteem."

However, let us ignore the difficulty of different kinds of labour by assuming all labour to be common or ordinary.

Even thus, the theory is only put forward as applicable to primitive conditions:

"In this state of things," says Smith, "the whole produce of labour belongs to the labourer; and the quantity of labour commonly employed in acquiring or producing any commodity is the only circumstance which can regulate the quantity of labour which it ought commonly to purchase, command, or exchange for."

But this state of things does not last. In civilised times the undertaker or employer manages to get a share of the produce:

"As soon as stock has accumulated in the hands of particular persons, some of them will naturally employ it in setting to work industrious people, whom they will supply with materials and subsistence, in order to make a profit by the sale of their work, or by what their labour adds to the value of the materials. In exchanging the complete manufacture either for money, for labour, or for other goods, over and above what may be sufficient to pay the price of the materials, and the wages of the workmen, something must be given for the profits of the undertaker of the work who hazards his stock in this adventure. The value which the workmen add to the materials, therefore, resolves itself in this case into two parts, of which the one pays their wages, the other the profits of their employer upon the whole stock of materials and wages which he advanced. He could have no interest to employ them unless he expected from the sale of their work something more than what was sufficient to replace his stock to him; and he could have no interest to employ a great stock rather than a small one unless his profits were to bear some proportion to the extent of his stock."

And the landlord too comes in for a share:

"As soon as the land of any country has all become private property, the landlords, like all other men, love to reap where they never sowed, and demand a rent even for its natural produce. The wood of the forest, the grass of the field, and all the natural fruits of the earth, which, when land was in common, cost the labourer only the trouble of gathering them, come, even to him, to have an additional price fixed upon them. He must then pay for the licence to gather them; and must give up to the landlord a portion of what his labour either collects or produces. This portion, or, what comes to the same thing, the price of this portion, constitutes the rent of land, and in the price of the greater part of commodities makes a third component part."

It is not very clear what exactly is supposed to happen—whether products acquire an addition to their labour-value for profit and rent or not.[1]

Either by addition or by subtraction from the labour-value, Smith thus admits a gap between earnings and produce, and in the chapter "Of the natural and market price of commodities" he propounds what is really a revised theory for non-primitive times. There are, he says, natural or ordinary or average rates of wages, profit, and rent, and when these are obtained by the producers of a commodity, it is sold at its natural price, or, in other words, "for what it is worth."

"The commodity is then sold precisely for what it is worth, or for what it really costs the person who brings it to market; for though in common language what is called the prime cost of any commodity does not comprehend the profit of the person who is to sell it again, yet if he sells it at a price which does not allow him the ordinary rate of profit in his neighbourhood, he is evidently a loser by the trade; since by employing his stock in some other way he might have made that profit. His profit, besides, is his revenue, the proper fund of his subsistence. As, while he is preparing and bringing the goods to market, he advances to his workmen their wages, or their subsistence; so he advances to himself, in the same manner, his own subsistence, which is generally suitable to the profit which he may reasonably expect from the sale of his goods. Unless they yield him this profit, therefore, they do not repay him what they may very properly be said to have really cost him" (Vol. i. pp. 57–8).

This is a passage which should be noted by all who have not grasped, or are in any danger of forgetting, that there is an important difference between "cost of production" in the

[1] See Cannan, *Production and Distribution*, p. 202, note, and also see how Smith modified the statement of his first edition, *Wealth of Nations*, Vol. I. p. 51, note.

language of the manufacturer or other business man and in the language of the economists. The business men, both in Smith's time and now, mean by the cost of production of a thing what they have to pay out in order to produce the thing, and do not include what they get for themselves; the economists mean by it something which they regard as the whole cost of getting the thing produced and put on the market, including the "normal" remuneration of the profit-takers.

We must always remember that the idea of normal, or, as Smith called them, "natural" or "ordinary" or "average" rates of remuneration is the very basis of the Cost of Production theory of value. To say that the value of a product depended at any moment on what the producers, including the profit-takers, got for it would have obviously been fatuous, as anyone can see that what they actually get is settled by the price the product is sold for.

The "actual" or "market" price of commodities, Smith thinks, may be above or below or equal to the natural price. It cannot, however, continue long below the natural price, as, when it has fallen below, it will soon cease to be produced in such large quantities, and if competition is open, it will not long continue above the natural price, since, when it has risen above, the hope of profit will cause larger quantities to be produced. So the market price may be said to be continually "gravitating" towards the natural when competition is open. But competition is sometimes restricted by monopolies and sometimes by "natural causes," such as the scarcity of land suitable for vineyards producing highly prized wines, so that the actual price may in some cases be kept above the natural "for many years together" by monopolies and "for ever" by "natural causes" (Vol. I. pp. 62–3).

In brief, Adam Smith's theory of value begins by telling us that in primitive times commodities and services exchanged in ratios determined by the amounts of labour which they cost, but promptly destroys the sweet simplicity of this by admitting, firstly, that even in the most primitive conditions the amount of labour cannot be measured by the time immediately occupied in it, since both its intensity and the labour-cost of training the labourer must be taken into account, and secondly, that a highly "esteemed" kind of labour counts for more in the regulation of value than an equal amount of ordinary labour. Moreover, even when thus amended out of all recognition, the theory is not put forward as applicable to modern times after stock has been accumulated and land appropriated. After that has happened, natural or normal value depends not on the amount and intensity of direct and indirect labour and on the esteem which men have for different kinds of labour, but upon the total of wages, profits, and rents which have normally to be paid for their production. Market prices fluctuate above and below these normal values because supply and demand fluctuate, but in consequence of the competition for profitable employments of labour, capital, and land they are continually gravitating towards the natural or "central" values. But this only applies to articles of which the production is open to competition, and these articles do not include things which cannot be produced without using land of rare quality: so the prices of quite a large number of things do not gravitate to the natural or "central" price but remain indefinitely above it.[1]

A theory of value should explain in general terms why commodities and services are exchanged for one another in the ratios in which they are exchanged, and also why from time to time these ratios are subject to alteration.

As an answer to the first of these two questions Adam Smith's theory does not now seem even plausible. Suppose two things, say a pair of slippers of a particular kind and a copy of a particular printed book, are of the same value, do we conclude that they are or can be produced by equal quantities of labour? Certainly not, and Smith himself does not say so. He only says that in primitive conditions, long since passed away, things produced by equal quantities of labour were of equal value, and then qualifies even this by saying that even in primitive times something else besides quantity of labour must be brought into the

[1] Though at the beginning of chap. vii. Smith says the average rates of wages, profit and rent may be called the natural rates, it is clear that neither incomes nor prices "continually gravitate" towards the average when they are continuously rising or falling. If the price of some commodity or service was 10*d.* from 1650 to 1700, and successively 8*d.*, 6*d.*, 4*d.*, and 2*d.* in the following half-centuries, we cannot say that from 1650 to 1900 it was "continually gravitating" towards the average of 6*d.* Half-conscious of the difficulty, Smith on p. 60 substituted "central" for "average" as the synonym for "natural."

account in the shape of the esteem which men have for different kinds of labour. For civilised times he brings into the account not only quantity of labour and the esteem for labour, but also capital and land, but he provides no means by which we can add up the items. He does not tell us that in civilised times things exchange in proportion to the labour plus capital plus land required to produce them, because he knows no way of "converting" two of these into the third. He does not, like Petty, search for a Par between labour, capital, and land, but without argument, or even warning, simply substitutes the remuneration of labourers, capitalists, and landlords for labour, capital, and land. The pair of slippers and the book become worth the same because the same total expense in wages, profits, and rents is required to produce them. This does not seem plausible to us because we can see that the equality of the wages, profits, and rents with the price is no proof that the price is caused by the wages, profits, and rents: it may be the other way round.

Adam Smith's answer to the second question seems much more plausible. If the particular wages, profits, and rents payable for the production of any commodity rise, we expect that commodity to rise in price. Suppose, for instance, that the coalminers of the world were attacked by some disease which reduced their numbers, and at the same time growing refinement caused greater reluctance of new persons to enter the business, coal would rise, and it would be natural to ascribe the rise to the increased wages: or suppose that, frightened by strikes and rumours of syndicalism, no one would put more capital into mining, coal again would rise and it would be natural to ascribe the rise to the increased profits which must be paid to keep some capital in the industry: or suppose that owing to the spread of towns or something else there were more reluctance to allow mining to be carried out at the expense of damaging the surface, coal once more would rise, and it would be natural to ascribe the rise to the increased amount paid as rent or royalty.

But the price of coal could not rise an atom if the same quantity of coal continued to be put on the market: it rises because the quantity coming to market is reduced, and its rise is not in the least dependent on the higher wages, profits, or rents paid. If the number of miners were reduced to one-half, the price of coal would rise just the same if the miners still employed did not get a penny more than they did before. Each of the suppositions involves a rise in the price of coal not because a particular factor of production is better paid, but because that factor is shorter in supply, and its shortness causes a shortness in the supply of coal. There is no harm in saying that the rise of price is due to diminished supply of labour, capital, or land required for the production of coal, but we must not say that it is caused by the rise of the wages, profits, or rents. It is undeniably rather plausible to say so, but it is incorrect.

§ 3. *Ricardo's Attempt to Revive the Pure Labour Theory.*

In spite of its faults, Adam Smith's theory of value was not seriously attacked for more than quarter of a century. Then the great rise of prices during what we used before 1914 to call the "Great War," set people talking about the theory of value. Some people ascribed the rise in the price of food to the rise of rent. Now Adam Smith had himself in a rather casual utterance at the beginning of his chapter on Rent undermined his theory of value by saying that rent was not, like wages and profit, a cause of price, but was itself the effect of price. All three, wages, profit, and rent, were, he said, "component parts of price," but rent "enters into the composition of the price of commodities in a different way from wages and profit. High or low wages and profit are the causes of high and low price; high or low rent the effect of it." When the controversy over the Corn Laws broke out in 1813 we find both the protectionist Malthus and the free-trader Ricardo accepting this view. Malthus, in his *Nature and Progress of Rent,* early in 1815, insisted on it because it cleared the landlords from the charge of having raised the price of food: food would be no cheaper if all rents were transferred to tenants; the effect "would be merely the turning them into gentlemen" (p. 57). Ricardo, immediately after reading Malthus, insisted on it in his *Essay on the Influence of a High Price of Corn on the Profits of Stock,* because the fact that the high price of corn raised rents presented both Protection and landlords who wanted it in a somewhat odious light.

Malthus' part in the controversy is unimportant, so far as the theory of value is concerned. But Ricardo was led on to argue that Adam Smith ought to have held to the theory of value which he put forward for the original, or as we should say, primitive state of things. It seemed to Ricardo that the rise in the price of corn should be attributed to more labour being required for its production. And he generalises as follows:

"The exchangeable value of all commodities rises as the difficulties of their production increase. If, then, new difficulties occur in the production of corn from more labour being necessary, whilst no more labour is required to produce gold, silver, cloth, linen, &c., the exchangeable value of corn will necessarily rise as compared with those things. . . . Wherever competition can have its full effect and the production of the commodity be not limited by nature, as is the case with some wines, the difficulty or facility of their production will ultimately regulate their exchangeable value." (*Essay*, in *Works*, ed. McCulloch, p. 377; in *Econ. Essays*, ed. Gonner, pp. 233–4.)

He thought the growth of capital caused population to grow, and that the consequent increased demand for food could only be met by producing the necessary additional food under more difficult conditions, so that the price of food would have to rise; protection of agriculture would have the same effect as increased population, since it meant that more food would have to be raised within the country than would otherwise suffice, and this extra quantity would have to be produced under more difficult conditions than the most costly part of a smaller produce.

This led him to think more about value, and we get the result in the first few chapters of his *Principles*. He there begins by quoting with approval Adam Smith's distinction between value in use and value in exchange. Utility, he thinks, is "absolutely essential" to exchangeable value, but does not settle *how much* exchangeable value a thing will have.

"Possessing utility, commodities derive their exchangeable value from two sources: from their scarcity, and from the quantity of labour required to obtain them."

This does not mean that each commodity derives its value from those two sources, but that there are two classes of commodities: first, those of which no labour can increase the quantity, so that their value cannot be lowered by an increased supply, and second, those which "can be increased in quantity by the exertion of human industry, and on the production of which competition acts without restraint." But the first class, he says, "form a very small part of the mass of commodities daily exchanged in the market," so that he will neglect them and speak only of the second class.

Then he quotes the passage in which Adam Smith said beavers and deer exchanged on terms settled by the comparative difficulty of catching them, and that it is "natural" that what is the produce of two days' labour should be worth double what is the produce of one day's labour, and pronounces this to be "a doctrine of the utmost importance in political economy; for from no source do so many errors and so much difference of opinion in that science proceed as from the vague ideas which are attached to the word value." But while he approves this doctrine he objects strongly to another doctrine which, he says, Smith holds in contradiction with it, namely, that things are more or less valuable in proportion as they will exchange for more or less labour; the labourer, Ricardo points out, does not get the whole of the "object" he produces, nor at all times [1] the same proportion of it.

This leads him to wander for several paragraphs in search of the chimera of an invariable standard of value, and only then does he come to consider the two obvious objections to the doctrine that things which are the produce of equal labour are of equal value: first, the fact that different kinds of labour are unequally paid, and second, the fact that the proportion of the "object" produced which goes to the labourer is different in the case of different "objects."

As to the first, it is plausible to say that any particular commodity or service goes up in value (relatively, of course, to other things) when its production comes to require more labour (compared again with that required by other things), and goes down in the opposite case, but is it reasonable to ask us to believe that, say, our artificial teeth, which are ten times as valuable as a pair of boots, must have required exactly ten times as much labour to produce as the boots, when we know as a fact that the dentist and his mechanic are much better paid than the bootmakers?

[1] Readers will please note that "at all times" is not the same thing as "in all cases at the same time." The importance of the distinction will soon be obvious.

Ricardo fails completely to give a satisfactory answer. He says:

"In speaking, however, of labour as being the foundation of all value, and the relative quantity of labour as determining the relative value of commodities, I must not be supposed to be inattentive to the different qualities of labour and the difficulty of comparing an hour's or a day's labour in one employment with the same duration of labour in another. The estimation in which different qualities of labour are held, comes soon to be adjusted in the market with sufficient precision for all practical purposes, and depends much on the comparative skill of the labourer and intensity of the labour performed. The scale, when once formed, is liable to little variation. If a day's labour of a working jeweller be more valuable than a day's labour of a common labourer, it has long ago been adjusted and placed in its proper position in the scale of value.

"In comparing, therefore, the value of the same commodity at different periods of time, the consideration of the comparative skill and intensity of the labour required for that particular commodity needs scarcely to be attended to, as it operates equally at both periods." [1]

Here the plausibility of putting forward a change in the labour-cost of a commodity as the explanation of a change in its value is quite illegitimately used to support the want of plausibility of putting forward different labour-costs as the sole explanation of "the relative value of commodities." The value of the pair of boots may fall from a tenth to a twelfth of the value of the artificial teeth in consequence of some occurrence which has reduced the labour of the bootmakers, but that tells us nothing about the

[1] *Principles*, 1st ed., pp. 12–14; 3rd ed., p. 13, chap. i. § 2. The word "estimation" in line 7 is evidently an echo of Adam Smith's "esteem" in the passage quoted above on p. 166. Malthus, in his *Principles of Political Economy*, 1820, p. 245, complained that Smith had here forgotten "the principle of supply and demand." In his annotation of Malthus, written in 1820, Ricardo agrees that it is the scarcity of the skilled labour which "will make men willing to give more for it," but adds that the scarcity depends on the supply, which depends "upon the interest which fathers may feel to give their children this dexterity and ingenuity and the cost of giving it" (*Notes on Malthus*, ed. J. H. Hollander and T. E. Gregory, 1928, pp. 118–19). This practically throws over "estimation," and substitutes the doctrine that the labour of producing the labourer must be included as part of the labour. But no proof is offered of the proposition that the value of things is in proportion to the labour of the immediate producers plus that expended in producing those producers, and it is known to be not in accordance with facts, though not so far out as the simpler doctrine. Ricardo did not alter the passage above after reading Malthus, except by the insertion in the 3rd ed. (p. 13) of the words "almost exclusively" before "determining" in line 2.

relative quantity of labour required for each kind of production, except that it has altered to that extent. So far as "the relative value of commodities" at one and the same time is concerned the quantity-of-labour-required doctrine is really given up by the admission that "the comparative skill and intensity" of the labour "operate equally at both periods."

Ricardo's aberration here is to be explained by his preoccupation with certain causes of changes in value; he himself excuses his neglect of the causes of the "comparative degree of estimation in which the different kinds of labour are held" by saying that his "inquiry relates to the effect of the variations in the relative value of commodities," while the relative remuneration of different occupations does not alter at all, or at any rate alters very little in "short periods."

The second objection to the quantity-of-labour-required doctrine—the objection that the workers get at the same time and place different proportions of different products—gave Ricardo much more anxiety than the first.

Here he had to meet the Smithian doctrine, then generally accepted, that there are three component parts of price: one for the labourer, one for the capitalist, and one for the landlord. How could he dislodge quantity of capital and land from standing alongside quantity of labour as determinants of value?

So far as capital was concerned he was weak from the beginning, and he weakened more and more as time went on and criticism multiplied.

From the first he admitted that the fact of the "fixed capitals employed" being "of unequal value and unequal duration" in the case of different products does sometime affect their values (1st ed., p. 23). In the second edition, 1819, he divided Chapter I for the first time into sections with headings. Section I is headed, "The value of a commodity, or the quantity of any other commodity for which it will exchange, depends on the relative quantity of labour which is necessary for its production, and not on the greater or less compensation which is paid for that labour." The heading of Section II roundly asserts, "The accumulation of capital makes no difference in the principle stated in the last Section," but the headings of the next two sections flatly contradict this, being for Section III, "The principle stated in the foregoing Section considerably modified by the employment of machinery as fixed capital," and for Section IV, " The principle that value does not vary with the rise or fall of wages modified also by the unequal durability of capital and by the unequal rapidity with which it is returned to its employer." In the third edition, 1821, the heading denying that the accumulation of capital makes any difference is abandoned in favour of the comparatively innocuous statement that " Not only the labour applied immediately to commodities affect (*sic*) their values, but the labour also which is bestowed on the implements, tools, and buildings with which such labour is assisted."

Ricardo's correspondence confirms the impression given by his chapter on Value with its emendations, that he was dissatisfied with this portion of his theory. His heart clung to the pure labour theory, but his candid brain showed him that it was weak at this point. His modesty suggested to him that " the fault is not in the inadequacy of the doctrine to account for all difficulties, but in the inadequacy of him who has attempted to explain it." [1]

In the attempt to dislodge land and rent from standing alongside labour and wages, Ricardo enjoyed both in his own opinion and in that of economists for a century at least a success which

[1] *Letters of David Ricardo to J. R. McCulloch*, ed. J. H. Hollander (American Economic Association publications), 1895, p. 48. Cp. *ibid.*, p. 96 and *passim*; also *Letters of Ricardo to Malthus*, *passim*. Much assistance can be found by anyone desirous of disentangling Ricardo's skein of thought in J. H. Hollander's *David Ricardo, a Centenary Estimate* (Johns Hopkins University Studies), 1910, though it is impossible to endorse Professor Hollander's approval of the note on Ricardo's Theory of Value in Marshall's *Principles* (1st ed. pp. 529–36, 8th ed. pp. 813–21). Marshall endeavours to show, in defiance of all evidence, that Ricardo never desired to put forward the pure labour theory of value. He had apparently never looked at the first and second editions of Ricardo's *Principles*, without which the third is scarcely intelligible; he relies largely on the footnote in the third edition at the end of § 6 in chap. i, in which Ricardo implies that value is the same thing as cost of production " including profits," but he overlooks the fact that in the very paragraph to which this note is attached, Ricardo makes the profits on two commodities, whatever they may be, always in the same proportion to the cost of the labour, so that he can " affirm . . . that their relative values will be governed by the relative quantities of labour bestowed on their production." No matter how much profit is included in cost of production, it will make no difference to Ricardo's principle so long as it is in all cases in the same proportion to wages, and Ricardo assumed that it would be so with some " modifications." The assumption was not so unnatural in a period when capital was supposed to be chiefly advanced in wages, as it would be now when capital is thought of as providing machinery, plant, etc.

was in great contrast to his acknowledged failure with regard to capital and interest.

He did the trick by little more than an arbitrary exercise of the right to define terms. The quantity of labour necessary for the production of a commodity is not to be the quantity of labour which has been necessary to produce each particular unit by itself—that (if value is determined by quantity of labour necessary) would lead to the absurd consequence that different bushels of corn of the same quality would have different prices on the same market. Nor is the quantity of labour necessary to be the quantity required to produce the unit which requires the average amount of labour—a price based on that would contain rent. It is to be the quantity required to produce those units of the total supply which yield no rent.

Ricardo arrives at this definition by first putting forward as a general law the proposition that the quantity of labour which settles the value of a commodity is not the average quantity required for the production of a unit of the commodity, but the quantity required for the production of the unit produced with the greatest difficulty :

"The exchangeable value of all commodities, whether they be manufactured, or the produce of the mines, or the produce of land, is always regulated, not by the less quantity of labour which will suffice for their production under circumstances highly favourable and exclusively enjoyed by those who have peculiar facilities of production; but by the greater quantity of labour necessarily bestowed on their production by those who have no such facilities; by those who continue to produce them under the most unfavourable circumstances; meaning, by the most unfavourable circumstances, the most unfavourable under which the quantity of produce required renders it necessary to carry on the production" (*Principles*, 1st ed., p. 59; 3rd, p. 60; chap. ii, middle).

Then in accordance with this general principle, he says :

"That corn which is produced with the greatest quantity of labour is the regulator of the price of corn, and rent does not enter in the least degree as a component part of its price. Adam Smith, therefore, cannot be correct in supposing that the original rule which regulated the exchangeable value of commodities, namely, the comparative quantity of labour by which they were produced, can be at all altered by the appropriation of land and the payment of rent. Raw material enters into the composition of most commodities, but the value of that raw material as well as corn is regulated by the productiveness of the portion of capital last employed on the land and paying no rent; and therefore rent is not a component part of the price of commodities" (1st ed., p. 67; 3rd, p. 67; chap. ii, middle).

"Its price" at the end of the first sentence in this quotation is clearly the price of "that corn," but it seems likely that careless readers have sometimes taken it to be simply the price of corn generally, and that this may be the origin of the common statement that Ricardo said, "rent does not enter into the cost of production." The whole passage is slightly misleading, because in the first sentence "rent does not enter as a component part of its price" means "rent forms no part of its price," while in the last sentence "rent is not a component part of the price" only means "rent is not a determining part of the price." "Rent does not enter into the cost of production" became an unfortunate shibboleth. It seemed absurd to everyone who thought of the whole of any commodity produced; for if rent does not come out of the prices got for products, he would ask, "Where then does it come from?" It would be no use to answer, "From the surplus of produce got from the rent-bearing land," because the objector could retort, "Then you admit that the whole price of that surplus produce is rent?"

There is no need for any such shibboleth. What Ricardo alleges is simply that the price of products is regulated by the quantity of labour required to produce them under the most unfavourable circumstances, and that in the case of agricultural produce the most unfavourable circumstances are those of the units which are so costly to produce that they yield no rent to the landlord. Even if capital and differences of wages could be ignored, this would be open to the objection that we could not say prices are "regulated by" the quantity of labour required under the most unfavourable circumstances in view of the fact that how far down into "unfavourable circumstances" production will go depends on prices. If, for example, demand increases, price will rise, and the rise will make it worth while to produce under less favourable circumstances than those under which it was worth while before. And, on the other hand, if for any reason the production in rent-bearing situations becomes greater while demand remains unaltered, price will fall, and it will no longer be worth while to continue production under the least favourable circumstances under which it was worth while before.

This objection, however, would have been met if Ricardo had written "measured by" or "indicated by" instead of "regulated by." A much more fundamental objection to the whole attempt to show that quantity of labour alone settles values without any assistance from rent is to be found in the fact that rent, the payment made for land, is not the true correlative of labour. The true correlative is land itself. Ricardo would have been puzzled if asked, "When you say that quantity of labour required for the production of a commodity alone determines its value, do you mean to deny that the quantity of land required for its production has any influence on its value?" If it takes the same quantity of labour but six times as much land to grow a ton of greengages as it takes to grow a ton of potatoes, greengages will sell for more per pound avoirdupois than potatoes. If a discovery is made which enables us to produce a ton of greengages with the same labour as before but with only half the land, the price of greengages will fall.

But at the time no one thought of this line of argument.

§ 4. *Ricardo on the Value of Currency.*

When writing his *Principles*, and even when revising them for the third edition after reading Malthus' *Principles of Political Economy* in 1820, Ricardo does not seem to have been at all troubled by the question whether his general doctrine of value applied to currency, about which he had thought much, and had written more that was sound and useful than on general theory.

Uncoined gold and silver he regarded as entirely subject to the quantity of labour rule:

> "Gold and silver, like all other commodities, are valuable only in proportion to the quantity of labour required to produce them and bring them to market. Gold is about fifteen times dearer than silver, not because there is a greater demand for it nor because the supply of silver is fifteen times greater than that of gold, but solely because fifteen times the quantity of labour is necessary to procure

a given quantity of it." (*Principles*, 1st ed., pp. 499–500; 3rd, p. 421; chap. xxvii, beginning.)

Notice in the second sentence the innocent-looking word "procure," which is evidently intended to be equivalent to "produce" in the first sentence.

But coins, Ricardo proceeds to say, may be worth more than the bullion which they contain:

"If the State charges a seignorage for coinage, the coined piece of money will generally exceed the value of the uncoined piece of metal by the whole seignorage charged, because it will require a greater quantity of labour, or, which is the same thing, the value of the produce of a greater quantity of labour to procure it."

Here the word "procure," instead of being equivalent to "produce," as before, quite obviously means nothing but "obtain by way of exchange." The statement that a seignorage will cause the coin to be of higher value because it causes more labour or the produce of more labour to be given for the coin is a perfectly empty one, quite different from the statement that the coin will be of higher value because more labour is required to produce it, but the two statements are made to look alike by the double use of the word "procure."

At the moment Ricardo was so deceived by this treacherous argument that he even applied it to paper money. In the paragraph next but one to that just quoted, he says, "The whole charge for paper money may be considered as seignorage."

But this attempt to bring currency under the quantity of labour theory was merely a temporary aberration. Ricardo's doctrine about paper money was ordinarily based, and firmly based, on an entirely different principle from that which he laid down for ordinary commodities. He was never tired of insisting that "limitation of quantity" is requisite for the maintenance of the value of a currency. The whole of his currency campaign against the Bank of England was founded on the complaint that the Bank did not limit the issue of notes sufficiently to keep them at par with gold. Even immediately after the passage just quoted, he explains that both paper money and debased coins may be kept up to par by limitation of quantity.

When in 1820 Malthus suggested that it was inconsistent to base value in general on cost of production and then to say that the value of currency could be kept up by limitation, Ricardo at first jotted down a note[1] which implied that paper currency stood alone, but soon scratched that out and defended himself on the ground that coin and paper currency did not belong to the class of ordinary commodities " on the production of which competition operates without restraint."[2] They were monopolised commodities, and the rule of cost of production did not apply to such things. But he has so little to say about the values of monopolised things, and that little is so inapplicable to currency,[3] that it seems impossible to avoid the impression that he did in fact keep his theories of the value of currency so to speak in a different side of his head from that occupied by his general theory of value.

§ 5. *Ricardo on the Value of Foreign Goods.*

While apparently reluctant to admit currency to be exceptional, Ricardo quite definitely and explicitly excepted " foreign goods " from his labour-cost of production theory without throwing them into the class of merely " scarce " articles on the production of which competition did not operate. At the beginning of his chapter on Foreign Trade he assumes that it is admitted that the value of foreign goods " is measured by the quantity of the produce of our land and labour which is given in exchange for them." Not by the quantity of labour required by their production under the most unfavourable circumstances nor even by the quantity of labour which they will purchase or command (as Adam Smith, censured by Ricardo, had said), but by the produce of *land* and labour which they command! If this leaves any doubt about Ricardo's intention to make imported goods an excep-

[1] See Ricardo's *Notes on Malthus*, ed. Hollander and Gregory, 1928, pp. 20–1.

[2] *Principles*, 1st ed., p. 3; 3rd, p. 3; chap. i, beginning.

[3] " When a commodity is at a monopoly price it is at the very highest price at which the consumers are willing to purchase it. Commodities are only at a monopoly price when by no possible device their quantity can be augmented; and when, therefore, the competition is wholly on one side—amongst the buyers " (*Principles*, 1st ed., pp. 340–1; 3rd, pp. 289–90; chap. xvii, middle).

" Commodities which are monopolised, either by an individual or by a company, vary according to the law which Lord Lauderdale has laid down: they fall in proportion as the sellers augment their quantity, and rise in proportion to the eagerness of the buyers to purchase them " (*ib.*, 1st ed., p. 548; 3rd, p. 465; chap. xxx, end).

tion from the general theory of value, it must be set at rest by the very explicit statement,

"The same rule which regulates the relative value of commodities in one country does not regulate the relative value of the commodities exchanged between two or more countries" (1st ed., p. 156; 3rd, pp. 138–9; chap. vii, beginning).

The rule referred to is, of course, the doctrine that values are regulated by labour-cost of production. Ricardo has not the least difficulty in showing that this doctrine is not true of commodities exchanged between countries. Nobody supposed it was. Who in possession of his senses ever supposed that Ford cars exported to Hong Kong would be there only equal in value to things produced in Hong Kong with as little labour as Ford cars cost to make in Detroit? If people whose labour is highly productive exchange things with people whose labour is not nearly so highly productive, it is obvious that things produced by the more productive people exchange for things produced by a greater amount of labour undergone by the less productive people. Where Ricardo went wrong here was in supposing that what he saw was true as between countries was not equally true as between different inhabitants of the same country. It is quite true, as he says, that it is conceivable that cloth made in England by 100 men might exchange for wine made in Portugal by 80 men, in which case "England would give the produce of the labour of 100 men for the produce of the labour of 80." It is also true, as he says, that the exchange might be advantageous to both countries even if the Portuguese could make the cloth themselves with the labour of 90 men. But it is quite wrong to assert, as he does, "Such an exchange could not take place between the individuals of the same country. The labour of 100 Englishmen cannot be given for that of 80 Englishmen."

"The difference," he explains, "between a single country and many is easily accounted for by considering the difficulty with which capital moves from one country to another to seek a more profitable employment, and the activity with which it invariably passes from one province to another in the same country." (We should expect him to mention the mobility of labour as well as that of capital, but the fact is that he always supposes that capital moves labour, so that the omission is of no significance.)

Here he appends a foot-note which both shows that the real example which he had in his mind was the importation of corn into England and gives away the case for the alleged difference "between a single country and many."

The note says:

> "It will appear then that a country possessing very considerable advantages in machinery and skill, and which may therefore be enabled to manufacture commodities with much less labour than her neighbours, may, in return for such commodities, import a portion of the corn required for its consumption, even if its land were more fertile and corn could be grown with less labour than in the country from which it was imported. Two men can both make shoes and hats, and one is superior to the other in both employments; but in making hats he can only exceed his competitor by one-fifth, or 20 per cent., and in making shoes he can excel him by one-third, or 33 per cent.; will it not be for the interest of both that the superior man should employ himself exclusively in making shoes, and the inferior man in making hats?" (1st ed., p. 160; 3rd, p. 142; chap. vii, middle).

That is, England being able to manufacture, say, cloth, with much less labour than Poland, may with advantage import corn from Poland though this corn could be grown with less labour in England: just as an individual in England being able to make boots with 33 per cent. less labour than a second individual, may with advantage make more boots than he wants and exchange the surplus for hats, although he can himself make hats with 20 per cent. less labour than the second individual. The international and the domestic cases are precisely similar, and the doctrine that "the labour of 100 Englishmen cannot be given for that of 80 Englishmen" is implicitly denied, since the first individual, "the superior man," will certainly not give the produce of an hour of his labour for the produce of an hour's labour of the second individual; if he had to do that, it would evidently pay him better to make his own hats, as he would make in 48 minutes as much hat as he could buy with an hour's labour in making boots.

In our own age, when we are accustomed to compare the productive power of different peoples, it seems remarkable that Ricardo should not have thought of the possibility of the people of one country being "superior," and getting more in consequence. If we found that the labour of 80 Portuguese was worth as much as the labour of 100 Englishmen, we should ask ourselves anxiously whether, and if so why, the Portuguese were "superior men." Ricardo thinks of them merely as average men like ourselves, but able to produce more because their soil or climate is superior. If asked why, in that case, we do not emigrate to Portugal, he replies that capitalists fear to send their capital into countries in which they are not resident, and dislike to go and settle in foreign countries themselves. These feelings, which he, though himself a Jewish immigrant into England, "would be sorry to see weakened," check the emigration of capital, and labour only goes where capital leads the way. (*Principles*, 1st ed., pp. 160–2; 3rd, p. 143; chap. vii, middle.)

§ 6. *Breakdown of the Pure Labour Theory.*

Ricardo's immediate followers, James Mill and McCulloch, were loth to agree to his unwilling admission of the influence of interest on capital as a modification of the pure labour-cost theory of value. They tried to get over the difficulty by the somewhat naïve device of asserting that capital was hoarded or accumulated labour and its interest the wages of that labour. But this absurdity was never widely accepted,[1] and the pure labour-cost theory was soon superseded by a cost of production theory in which quantity of labour appears as only one of the determinants of value instead of as the sole determinant.

This is not at all surprising. Looking back at this interval of time upon the pure labour-cost theory of value, we can see plainly enough that the only truth in it is that the amount of labour required to produce a commodity is often *one* of the many

[1] Ricardo himself expressed dissent (*Letters to McCulloch*, p. 153). Even if interest is put out of sight, there is a difficulty about spreading the labour required to produce an instrument over the things produced with the aid of the instrument. If a factory is to last 100 years and then fall down suddenly, it is specious to say, "Add one-hundredth of the labour of building the factory to the immediate labour required for each year's output"; but what if the instrument is not, as Ricardo rashly alleged all instruments were, "perishable"? (*Principles*, 1st ed., p. 22). Over how many years' use are we to spread the initial labour of building the Suez Canal or the Great Western Railway? If an instrument is kept by repairs in a condition as good as new, it is infinitely "durable"; the labour of so keeping it is part of the labour required for the annual output, and there is no difficulty about including it, but how is the initial labour to be brought in? See below, pp. 280–83.

things which affect the supply, and therefore the value, of that commodity. *Other things remaining equal,* if a thing currently produced by labour comes to require more labour to produce it, its value will rise, and *vice versa :* and *given equality of wages and absence or sameness of other expenses,* things which require equal amounts of labour to produce them will be equal in value because they will be supplied in the degree required to make them equal in value. But this equality of other things does not occur in actual life, and there is no good reason for taking out one of many of the causes of variation in supply and saying value depends upon that cause alone provided all the other causes are put out of action; the same thing might be said of any of the other causes.

Probably the pure labour-cost theory owed some of such popularity as it enjoyed to the popular confusion between the creation of value and the creation of useful and valuable things. If it is believed that labour actually creates value, the doctrine that the value of a thing depends on the quantity of labour required for its production and on nothing else is very attractive, since no claim that anything else actually creates value is likely to be put forward, at any rate by the unsophisticated. But in fact labour, far from creating value, destroys it: it enlarges supply and relieves rather than causes scarcity. It is not the presence and the labour of bricklayers which makes houses scarce and dear; it is when the bricklayers are absent or lay few bricks that we feel the pinch. It is the absence, not the presence of labour which forms one of the numerous causes of that limitation of supply which is essential to value.

Two at least of the brighter intellects of the eighteen-thirties saw this. Richard Whately, while holding the Drummond professorship of political economy at Oxford in 1831, said:

"It is true, it so happens by the appointment of Providence that valuable articles are in almost all instances obtained by Labour, but still this is an accidental, not an essential circumstance. If the aerolites which occasionally fall were diamonds and pearls, and if these articles could be obtained in no other way, but were casually picked up, to the same amount as is now obtained by digging and diving, they would be of precisely the same value as now. In this, as in many other points in Political Economy, men are prone to confound cause and effect. It is not that pearls fetch a high price because men have dived for them; but, on the contrary, men dive for them because they fetch a high price." (*Introductory Lectures on Political Economy*, 3rd ed., 1847, p. 235. The lecture in which the passage occurs was not printed in the 1st ed.)

Senior wrote in 1836:

" Economists who consider labour, using that word in its popular sense, as a necessary constituent of wealth, appear to have been led to that opinion by observing, first, that some quality besides mere utility is necessary to value; secondly, that all those things which are useful and are acquired by labour are valuable; and thirdly, that almost everything which is valuable *has* required some labour for its acquisition. . . . It is true that wherever there is utility, the addition of labour as necessary to production constitutes value, because, the supply of labour being limited, it follows that the object, to the supply of which it is necessary, is by that very necessity limited in supply. But any other cause limiting supply is just as efficient a cause of value in an article as the necessity of labour to its production. And, in fact, if all the commodities used by man were supplied by nature without any intervention whatever of human labour, but were supplied in precisely the same quantities as they now are, there is no reason to suppose either that they would cease to be valuable, or would exchange in any other than their present proportions." (*Political Economy*, 8vo ed., pp. 23–4.)

§ 7. *The Labour-and-other-Sacrifices Theory.*

Endeavouring to amend the labour-cost theory, Senior hit on the idea that there is an " agent distinct from labour and the agency of nature, the concurrence of which is necessary to the existence of capital, and which stands in the same relation to profit as labour does to wages" (*Political Economy*, 8vo ed., p. 59). He called this " Abstinence " for want of a better name, and regarded it as a " sacrifice " (*ib.*, p. 59, and, in italics, p. 100). This enables him to arrive at the proposition, " By cost of Production, then, we mean the sum of the labour and abstinence necessary to production." Where commodities " are the subjects of equal competition," and " may be produced by all persons with equal advantages," they will exchange in proportion to their costs of production as thus defined, because all the persons will try to do the best they can for themselves with their labour and their abstinence and this will arrange supplies so that equality of remuneration will result (p. 101).

If we overlook the difficulty of making a "sum" of—adding together—labour and abstinence, and the fact that in the world as hitherto known to mankind all people have not equal "advantages," this theory is not unattractive, and it is certainly more plausible than the pure labour-cost theory.

But more admissions followed. J. S. Mill not only accepted the view that interest was "according to Mr. Senior's well-chosen expression, the remuneration of abstinence" (*Principles*, Ashley's ed., p. 405), so that abstinence had to be reckoned as part of the cost of production, but added as another element, "risk" to the capitalist, and, as a disturbing force if not exactly an element, permanent inequalities of remuneration of labour as between different occupations.

The admission of "risk" played no great part in the history of the theory. Risk seems at least as disagreeable as "labour and abstinence," and no one who is satisfied that he can add together labour and abstinence will make much difficulty about throwing in risk as well. But the introduction of differences of earnings shook the whole edifice, which was based on the proposition that if any persons did not get the uniform standard price for the "sacrifice" which they made in labouring, abstaining, or risking, some of them would remove their labour or capital from the business in which this happened, and the movement would go on until the remuneration in that business was brought up to the general level. Now Mill, without realising in the least the effect of what he was doing, abandoned the assumption of equality of advantages expressly required by Senior and took things as he found them in the actual world:

"When the wages of an employment," he says, "permanently exceed the average rate, the value of the thing produced will, in the same degree, exceed the standard determined by mere quantity of labour. Things, for example, which are made by skilled labour exchange for the produce of a much greater quantity of unskilled labour; for no reason but because the labour is more highly paid. If, through the extension of education, the labourers competent to skilled employments were so increased in number as to diminish the difference between their wages and those of common labour, all things produced by labour of the superior kind would fall in value, compared with things produced by common labour, and these might be said, therefore, to rise in value. . . . Wages do enter into value. The relative *wages* of the labour necessary for producing different commodities affect their value just as much as the relative *quantities* of labour. . . . In strictness, therefore, wages have as much to do with value as quantity of labour. . . ." (*Principles*, Ashley's ed., pp. 460–1.)

In Mill's seventeen propositions summarising his theory of value (*ib.*, p. 480), the fourteenth gives permanent differences of wages as a cause of different values alongside differences in quantity of labour, and the fifteenth, while saying differences of wages are not so important as differences in quantity of labour, admits that they are not "insignificant."

It is true that some part of the higher wages enjoyed by skilled labour may be, so to speak, struck off as repayment of greater initial cost in training and postponement of earnings, but what is beyond this cannot possibly be added to the "sacrifices" supposed to be incurred by the labourers in labouring and the capitalists in abstaining or risking. Cairnes, in *Some Leading Principles of Political Economy*, 1874 (Pt. I, chap. iii), exposed the weakness of Mill's position and argued that we ought to recognise the existence of "non-competing groups" of labour within any country and treat the values of things produced by them in the same way as Ricardo treated the values of the things exchanged in international trade, that is, as determined by what Cairnes calls "reciprocal demand," and which might better have been called "relative supplies."

At this stage the labour-and-other-costs theory should have been recognised as moribund, but Marshall, with that exaggerated "youthful loyalty"[1] from which age never released him, gave it a new lease of a sort of life by creating a "money-cost of production" or "expenses of production" theory, the relation of which to the "real cost" or "efforts and sacrifices" theory remained throughout very obscure. In an article published in the *Fortnightly Review* for April 1876, and apparently intended as a counterblast to Cairnes' criticism of Mill, he said, "a point of view was conquered for us by Adam Smith, from which a commodity is regarded as the embodiment of measurable efforts and sacrifices."

[1] See below, p. 204.

"Proceeding from its new point of view, Political Economy has analysed the efforts and sacrifices that are required for the production of a commodity for a given market at a given time; she has found a measure for them in their *cost to the person who will purchase them*, and then enunciated her central truth. This central truth is that producers, each governed under the sway of free competition by calculations of his own interest, will endeavour so to regulate the amount of any commodity which is produced for a given market during a given period, that this amount shall just be capable on the average of finding purchasers during this period at a remunerative price: a remunerative price being defined to be a price which shall just be equal to the sum of the exchange measures of those efforts and sacrifices which are required for the production of the commodity when this particular amount is produced, *i.e.* to the sum of the expenses which must be incurred by a person who would purchase the performance of those efforts and sacrifices." (*Memorials*, pp. 126–7.)

Marshall thought that Mill would have done well to invent "some new term, say 'expenses of production,'" for this sum, and to use "cost of production" only for "efforts and sacrifices as they affected those who underwent them," and he added that for his part he intended in future to say that "the exchange-values of two commodities tend to bear to one another the same ratio as their *expenses of production*."

By this plan he evaded rather than met the criticism to which Mill had laid himself open. Expenses or money-cost of production vary with two things, the number of units of the various requisites paid for and the value of each unit. Mill had got into trouble by professing to teach the old theory that the value of the product depended (only) on the number of units (or, shortly, the amount) of labour and capital, and at the same time admitting that it was influenced by the value of the unit of labour. Marshall tried to get out of the difficulty by replacing the old statement that the value of a product depended (only) on its cost of production (in the sense of the amount or number of units of requisites necessary) by a statement that it depended on the money-cost or expenses of production (in the sense of the number of units of requisites necessary multiplied by the value per unit).

He thus really abandoned the old theory that the value of the product depends (only) on the amount of the "efforts and sacrifices" involved in its production; he admitted that it depends also on the value per unit of these efforts and sacrifices. But if he grasped the effect of what he was doing, he was singularly unsuccessful in making it plain. In the *Fortnightly Review* article he only obscures it by the curious doctrine that the money-cost is a " measure " of the " efforts and sacrifices " required for the production. What does this mean? A little light is thrown on the question by two sentences at the top of p. 126 in the reprint in the *Memorials :*

> " Mill was aware, though some of his critics forget, that one aggregate of diverse efforts and abstinences does not bear a ratio to another. When we speak of ratio between an effort and an abstinence, or even between two diverse efforts, we assume, *ipso facto*, an artificial mode of measuring them in terms of some common unit, and refer to the ratio between their measures."

This seems to suggest that we are not to think, as we naturally should, of comparing the *amount* of effort involved in making a watch with the amount involved in making a wheel-barrow and saying it is double or treble or tenfold, but that we may say it is *measured by* twice as much, three times as much, or ten times as much money. The early *Economics of Industry* is perhaps plainer :

> " It may happen that an hour's work by a business manager or two days' work by a watchmaker or three days' work by a carpenter or ten days' work by an agricultural labourer may all have the same exchange measure, say a guinea. A guinea may also be the exchange measure of the abstinence or sacrifice involved in the loan of 20 guineas for a year. These various efforts and abstinences, these elements of Cost of production, are certainly not equal to one another. But they would all exert an equal influence upon value; because their Economic measures, the expenses which would have to be incurred by anyone who would purchase them, are all equal " (p. 97).

If there is no way of measuring except by money-cost, the statement that these various efforts and abstinences " are certainly not equal " is rash; they may be, for all Marshall knows; he is only entitled to say that he does not know that they are equal. Later (on p. 147) we are told :

> " The Normal wages of skilled labour of any given degree of difficulty may vary slowly. But at any time and place they are

determined by the social and economic condition of the people, and they may be said to *measure* the efforts involved in the work."

This certainly implies the existence in Marshall's mind of a measure other than money-cost, since the skilled labour is supposed to remain the same in amount while its money-cost changes; if the money-cost were the only measure, when the wages rise or fall, we should be obliged to decide that the labour was greater or less than before in exactly the same proportion. The truth of this cannot be obliterated, though it is somewhat obscured by the rather hesitating assertion in the second of the two sentences, that the wages "*may be said* to measure the efforts involved in the work." Even if it were true that three days' carpentering efforts and two days' watchmaking always "measured" the same at the same time and place, that would not prove that a rise of carpenters' wages relatively to those of watchmakers such that two and a half days' carpentering became worth as much as two days' watchmaking would necessarily indicate that the "efforts" of carpenters in a day's labour had risen in proportion to those of watchmakers.

The fact is that wages cannot "be said" in any ordinary use of the words to "measure efforts." What they measure is the value of the work done, not the effort involved. Still less can the return received by the owner of capital "be said" to "measure" his "abstinence" or "sacrifice." What it measures is the *value* of the aid to production afforded by the employment of the capital. The statement that "the exchange-values of two commodities bear to one another the same ratio as their expenses of production" is a banal truism; the prices of things must obviously be equal to or rather be the same thing as their expenses of production, if all that is got by the producers (including, of course, the profit-taker) and nothing else is included. Even if some employers or other profit-takers are making not a profit but a loss, it is still true that the price equals the expense of production, since the loss is merely a negative profit which reduces expenses as defined, just as a subsidy from the state or a free gift from an individual would do.

But Marshall did not say "the exchange-values of two commodities bear to one another the same ratio as their expenses of production," but only that they "*tend to bear*" that proportion, and these three words are of immense importance, as they allow the introduction of a discussion which occupies a large part of Marshall's *Principles* and furnishes a sort of cloak under which both the old doctrine of values being in proportion to efforts and sacrifices (Marshall's "real cost of production" as opposed to his "money-cost" or expenses of production) and the new doctrine of efforts and sacrifices being measured by expenses of production quietly melt away into nothingness.

The words indicate, as is made quite plain in the 1879 *Economics of Industry*, that "exchange-values" and "expenses of production" are not to be understood as actual values and expenses (including profits), but are to be interpreted in such a way as to allow the actual value or price of a commodity (and consequently its actual expenses of production in the sense defined) to be either above or below its "expenses of production" in the sense intended.

The "exchange-values" are to be "normal values" and the "expenses of production" are to be "normal expenses of production"; as both are not actual phenomena like actual values and actual expenses, it is easy to make them agree—it is merely a matter of definition.

"The Law," we are told, "which regulates Normal value follows at once from the Law of Normal Supply. Whenever the [actual] price is above the [normal] Expenses of production there are forces at work tending to bring it down; whenever the [actual] price is below the [normal] Expenses of production, there are forces at work tending to raise it. Just as when a weight is suspended by a string, if the weight is disturbed towards the left from its position of equilibrium or rest, the force of gravity at once tends to make it swing back. Soon it does swing back to its position of rest; but it does not stop there; it moves on to the right, and then the force of gravity makes it swing back to the left, and so on. If frequently disturbed, it will hardly ever remain in its position of equilibrium, but will always oscillate about it.

"The Normal price, or as Adam Smith says, 'the natural price, is as it were the central price to which the [actual] price of every commodity is [1] continually gravitating. Different accidents may sometimes keep them suspended a good deal above it, and sometimes force them down even somewhat below it. But whatever may be

[1] Misquoted: Smith wrote, as required by "they" in the next sentence, "the prices of all commodities are"; *W. of N.*, Vol. I. p. 60.

the obstacles which hinder them from settling in this centre of repose and continuance, they are constantly tending towards it.' And the Law of Normal Value is :

> The Normal value of a thing in any market, or, that value which would on the average be brought about by the undisturbed action of free competition among its producers, is equal to its [normal] Expenses of production there. Whenever the value is below this level, forces are brought into play which tend to raise it; whenever it is above this level, forces are brought into play which tend to lower it. The value of a commodity is in equilibrium and has no tendency either to rise or to fall when the amount produced can just be sold at a price equal to its [normal] Expenses of production " (pp. 77–8).

For clearness I have inserted in square brackets " actual " and " normal " where required. The *Economics of Industry* itself has already said (p. 76) that the expenses are normal expenses, and about fourteen pages later (p. 92) it begins to use the term " normal expenses " instead of the simple and misleading " expenses " in similar situations.

The doctrine is little more than what it professes to be, a réchauffé of Smith's doctrine of natural price and natural rates of remuneration for the producers, with just one important variation in the fact that rent of land is thrown out of its position alongside wages and profits by the Ricardian device of treating it as a surplus over expenses instead of a part of expenses. It tells us nothing, and its only good use is to serve as a peg on which Marshall hung many suggestive reflections on the real causes of changes in actual values. Unfortunately the very amplitude of these reflections obscures the fact that Marshall abandoned as time went on his early hopes of rehabilitating the " real " cost of production theory by the substitution of a " money-cost " or " expenses of production " theory.

The *Principles* repeats the distinction between real and money-cost or expenses of production, but says very little about the relation between the two.

In the first edition there was one passage in which it is implied distinctly that the " normal Money Cost of equipping a good boat with an efficient crew " will vary with the " normal Real Cost " provided the general purchasing power of money remains stationary (p. 412), but the passage disappeared when the paragraph was remodelled in the fourth edition, and when the text of the first edition was mostly restored in the fifth edition the reference to real cost was significantly omitted (p. 371).

In another place in the *Principles* Marshall speaks of the real-cost of production theory in a detached way, as if it was held by others rather than by himself. In the first edition the passage, which follows a statement that estimates have to be made a long time beforehand and are therefore liable to great error, runs thus:

> "This then points to a limitation of the doctrine that the price at which a thing can be produced represents its Real Cost of production, that is, the efforts and sacrifices which have been directly and indirectly devoted to its production. That doctrine might indeed represent facts accurately enough in a stationary society in which people's habits of life and the methods and volume of production remained unchanged from one generation to another; provided that people were tolerably free to choose those occupations for their capital and labour which seemed most advantageous. But in an age of change such as this the equilibrium of normal demand and supply does not thus correspond to any precise relation between an aggregate of pleasures got from the consumption of the commodity and an aggregate of efforts and sacrifices involved in producing them (*sic*); and it would not do so even if normal earnings and interest were exact measures of the efforts and sacrifices for which they are severally the money payments" (1st ed., pp. 503–4).

It is surely a fairly drastic condemnation of the doctrine to say that it is not true of our age because that is an age of change (like all others known to us), and would not be true of that age even if earnings and interest exactly measured efforts and sacrifices; and further, that it would not be true even of an imaginary stationary state unless a freedom to choose occupations such as has never yet been known were present. But as time went on the condemnation becomes stronger still. In the second edition the words "This then points to a limitation" are replaced by "We shall gradually discover a great many different limitations of the doctrine," and we are told that "the remainder of the present volume will be chiefly occupied with interpreting and limiting this doctrine, that the value of a thing tends in the long run to measure its cost of production" (pp. 408–9). In the sixth edition the whole of the second sentence, which asserts the truth of the doctrine under certain conditions in a stationary state, is omitted (the next sentence being made to begin with "For, in an age of rapid change," instead of "But in an age of change," eds. 6 and 8, p. 347). All editions (p. 515 in ed. 1 and p. 352 in ed. 8) speak of "the way in which the efforts and sacrifices which are the real cost of production of a thing underlie the expenses which are its money cost," but the sixth edition fails to say, as the previous editions do two pages earlier, that the expenses of production "more or less closely correspond" with the efforts and sacrifices which constitute the real cost of production (p. 513 in ed. 1).

The doctrine of real-cost of production had indeed fallen low when nothing remained of it except the proposition that it "underlies" the money-cost and consequently the money-value of a commodity. But at this point we must go back some considerable distance in time in order to pick up the history of theory with regard to the influence of utility upon value.

§ 8. *Utility.*

It isusual to say th at the labour-cost theory, however modified by the admission of other costs of production, was defective or one-sided in that it did not allow for the influence of demand. In one sense of "demand" this reproach only means that insufficient recognition was given to the fact that when we talk of the influence of the supply of an article on its value, we must think of the magnitude of that supply in relation to the supply of other things rather than measure the magnitude of the supply by the absolute number, weight, or size of the articles in question. It is not absolute but relative plentifulness which makes any article cheap. There is indeed no such thing as absolute plentifulness or scarcity. When we say bread or diamonds are scarce or plentiful, we are comparing the supply of the moment with the supply of some other period or the supply of bread or diamonds with the supply of other things at the same period.

Consequently, when we mean by greater or less demand for a thing merely that other things are supplied in larger quantities and think of this as raising the value of the thing, we have not really "got away from the side of supply." To say that values are settled "by supply and demand," with "demand" taken in this sense, is only a clumsy and confusing way of saying that values are settled by the relative supplies of things. Things which are supplied are offered in exchange for other things which are supplied, and the supply of the one is the "demand" for the other in that sense of "demand."

But "demand" constantly conveys to our mind a totally different idea, the idea of something in the minds of some of the persons concerned in the transactions which are under review. The demanders are supposed to demand a thing or service which they want to get, and their demand is supposed to be greater or more insistent when they want it more. Rather curiously, the demand in this sense has been treated as if it was created by a quality possessed by the thing or service itself, called by Adam Smith "value in use" and by most later writers "utility."

This term has given trouble because when used in ordinary language it is generally thought of as a quality of being "useful," and the word "useful" is applied to things which serve the coarser and more elementary needs of life and is denied to those which supply the ornamental and artistic needs, and also to everything regarded by the speaker as "no good" or pernicious, however much others may like it. "Ophelimity," or in English "desiredness," has been suggested as a substitute.

Still more trouble has been given by the fact that the ascription of the quality of being desired to the commodity or service is apt to make us fall into the mistake of regarding this quality as something inherent in the commodity or service instead of something which waxes and wanes in the minds of human beings according to the circumstances of the moment. If we talk of the utility of rain, we are apt to forget that the Prayer Book contains a prayer for the cessation of rain as well as one for rain. Water is the stock example of a thing which has high utility and little value, but we may be sure that Noah in his more desponding moments thought it had high disutility.

To the general neglect of "utility" or, in other words, of the relative desire for different commodities and services there was one prominent and early exception in Jean-Baptiste Say. But he could do no better than merely allege that the value of a thing open to free competition measured its utility. In order to measure production, he says, we want a "precise measure of the degree of utility of each thing."

"But how," he continues, "is the utility to be measured? What seems necessary to one person seems quite superfluous to another. Nevertheless, whatever variety be found among the tastes and needs of men, people make a common estimate (*une estimation générale*) of the utility of each particular object, an estimate of which we can get an idea from the quantity of other objects which they will give in exchange for the thing. I can, for example, judge that the utility of a coat is three times as great as that of a hat, if I find that people will in general give three hats in exchange for one coat." (*Traité*, 1st ed., Vol. I. pp. 24–5; 2nd ed., Vol. I. p. 4.)

Nowadays very few readers will be inclined to accept that. They will begin to consider whether they would not rather walk down the Strand thirty times without a hat than once without a coat, or whether they would not think a hat more useful than a coat under a blazing sun in the Sahara, and whether the comparative advantage of accepting a gift of three hats or of one coat would not be affected by the number of hats and coats already in their possession.

But we are of a later age, and have somehow absorbed the teaching of the economists of the last thirty or forty years. More primitive men seem always to have tried to think of the utility of any kind of thing as a whole, and without regard to special circumstances. They saw that value was dependent on abundance, but not that abundance has also something to do with utility. They did not notice that in contrasting utility and value in the way they did they were contrasting the utility of the whole supply or stock of a commodity with the value of something different, namely, a unit of the supply or stock.

When Adam Smith said, "Nothing is more useful than water. . . . A diamond, on the contrary, has scarce any value in use" (above, p. 164), he must have been thinking of water as a whole and diamonds as a whole. If he had asked, "Which is the most useful, a drop of water or a diamond the same size?" who would not have answered, "Under ordinary circumstances the diamond, of course"? Ricardo followed in the same line:

"When I give 2000 times more cloth for a pound of gold than I give for a pound of iron, does it prove that I attach 2000 times more utility to gold than I do to iron? Certainly not; it proves only, as admitted by M. Say, that the cost of production of gold is 2000 times greater than the cost of production of iron. If the cost of production of the two metals were the same, I should give the same price for them; but if utility were the measure of value, it is probable I should give more for the iron." (*Principles*, 3rd ed., p. 332, chap. xx, end.)

He only thinks it probable, evidently being at sea as to what would actually happen. Now with the aid of modern theory let us ask what would happen if the cost of production were as low for gold as for iron. Ricardo is doubtless right in thinking he would then pay the same price, but he overlooks the fact that he would then use ever so much more gold than he does now. Not to go beyond his library, he would have gold instead of silver candlesticks, gold tops to his inkpots, gold handles to his fire-irons, gold handles to his doors, and solid gold or gold-leaf picture frames instead of troublesome gilt things. Outside he would have gold on the roof of his house instead of slates and lead. He would then begin to think that gold was a much more useful metal than he had any idea of. There is no standard of utility which can be appealed to regardless of quantity. The supposition, "if utility were the measure of value," implies the possibility of our being able to say, for example, "1 oz. of iron is as useful as 2 of gold." Ricardo hesitates to say that: hence his "probably." It would be absurd to say that. I could do very easily with a silver watch instead of a gold one, but I could do more easily without the iron fire-grate in my lumber-room where I have never yet had a fire, and that fire-grate weighs more than 2000 times as much as the gold in my watch. The truth is that we can only compare the utilities of two different things by estimating how much we would give of the one for the other, and that is valuation. The fact that at the present moment I am refusing to buy both another sixpenn'orth of gold and another sixpenn'orth of iron, and that not long ago I did buy each, shows that I as a matter of fact did find more gold 2000 times as useful as more iron. The last sixpenn'orth of gold and the last sixpenn'orth of iron that I bought, or the next sixpenn'orth which I do not buy, must be of equal utility to me, and that means that a bit of iron is of equal utility with a bit of gold weighing 1/2000 as much.

That people want still more of any particular thing less and less as they get more, or, in the language commonly used in economic works, that the utility or "desiredness" of additional quantities of any particular thing declines as it becomes more abundant, was occasionally noticed. Jevons, in his preface to the second edition of his *Theory*, collected a number of examples from nineteenth-century writers. But these were all "anticipations"; that is to say, they had no influence over the general development of thought. It is to Jevons himself in England and to Karl Menger in Austria that the credit is due of pushing the discussion of value into a new and fruitful field.

In his *Theory of Political Economy*, 1871, Jevons announced that attention to the "exact nature and conditions of utility" would give "the true key to the problem of economy." [1]

"In the first place," he says, "utility, though a quality of things, is *no inherent quality*. It might be more accurately described, perhaps, as a *circumstance of things* arising out of their relation to man's requirements. As Mr. Senior most accurately says, 'Utility denotes no intrinsic quality in the things which we call useful; it merely expresses their relations to the pains and pleasures of mankind.' We can never, therefore, say absolutely that some objects have utility and others have not. The ore lying in the mine, the diamond escaping the eye of the searcher, the wheat lying unreaped, the fruit ungathered for want of consumers, have not utility at all. The most wholesome and necessary kinds of food are useless unless there are hands to collect and mouths to eat them.[2] Nor, when we consider the matter closely, can we say that all portions of the same commodity possess equal utility. Water, for instance, may be roughly described as the most useful of all substances. A quart of water per day has the high utility of saving a person from dying in the most distressing manner. Several gallons a day may possess much utility for such purposes as cooking and washing; but after an adequate supply is secured for these uses, any additional quantity is a matter of comparative indifference. All that we can say, then, is that water, up to a certain quantity, is indispensable; that further quantities will have various degrees of utility; but that beyond a certain point the utility appears to cease.[3]

[1] The 2nd ed. reads "Economics."
[2] The 2nd ed. adds "sooner or later."
[3] Instead of "beyond a certain point the utility appears to cease," the 2nd ed. reads "beyond a certain quantity the utility sinks gradually to zero; it may even become negative, that is to say, further supplies of the same substance may become inconvenient and hurtful" (p. 48).

" Exactly the same considerations apply more or less clearly to every other article. A pound of bread per day supplied to a person saves him from starvation, and has the highest conceivable utility. A second pound per day has also no slight utility : it keeps him in a state of comparative plenty, though it be not altogether indispensable. A third pound would begin to be superfluous. It is clear, then, that *utility is not proportional to commodity* : the very same articles vary in utility according as we already possess more or less of the same article." (*Theory*, 1st ed., pp. 51–3.)

Jevons next asks us to distinguish carefully between

" the *total utility* arising from any commodity and the utility attaching to any particular portion of it. Thus the total utility of the food we eat consists in maintaining life, and may be considered as infinitely great ; but if we were to subtract a tenth part from what we eat daily, our loss would be but slight." [1]

We must not accept this idea of total utility too readily, but we may let it stand for the moment.[2]

" We shall seldom," Jevons says, " need to consider the degree of utility except as regards the last increment which is consumed, and I shall therefore commonly use the expression *final degree of utility*, meaning the degree of utility of the last addition, or the next possible addition of a very small or infinitely small quantity to the existing stock." [3]

That this " final degree of utility," usually shortened into " final utility," has some close connection with the value of things is pretty obvious. We buy just as many pounds of tea or anything else as we think are worth the price which we have to pay, and then we stop : if the price were higher we should buy fewer, and if it were lower we should buy more, just because of this variation of utility which Jevons has been pointing out. So the utility of our final purchase goes along with the price, and if we are perfectly well-balanced people, the utility purchased with the final shilling in each class of expenditure will be equal.

[1] *Theory*, 1st ed., p. 54. The 2nd ed. adds, " We certainly should not lose a tenth part of the whole utility of food to us," p. 49.

[2] The " total utility " of anything such as water or gold seems to be only measurable by comparing the loss which we should suffer by the total disappearance of the thing with the loss which we should suffer by the total disappearance of something else, and this kind of comparison is indistinguishable from valuation of the totals. Cp. below, pp. 203–4.

[3] *Ib.*, 1st ed., p. 61 ; the 2nd ed., p. 55, in place of " which is consumed," reads " which has been consumed, or, which comes to the same thing, the next increment which is about to be consumed."

If anyone is surprised at this and inclined to doubt it, he should be asked, " But if it is not so with you, why don't you redistribute your expenditure? If you don't think that the final shilling's-worth of tobacco brings you as much good as the last shilling's-worth of sugar or haircutting, why don't you cut down your expenditure on tobacco and spend the difference on these other things? "

When we have to deal with several or many persons with different means and tastes, the connection between final utility and value is not quite so clear, since the rich will be able to buy more of all things taken together than the poor, so that the last shilling's-worth spent by the millionaire on any commodity is very likely to be much less important to him than the last shilling's-worth spent on the same commodity by a person of small means. But still it remains the fact that greater supply will tend to reduce the value because at least some of the consumers have to be induced to buy an additional quantity which is of less utility to them: the final utility of the article must fall.

Jevons' exposition and many others founded on it are a little apt to suggest to the reader that he can pick out particular gallons of water or pounds of bread and say, " This gallon or pound has more utility than the others because it is earlier or comes first." Care must be taken to avoid any such notion. What is earlier and what later simply depends on when we choose to make our period begin. If we hold that the day begins at midnight, our first drink will be at breakfast, except when we come home late, and then it may be at supper. If we go to the theatre several times a week, which is the first and which the last performance? Do we get more from Monday's performance than from Saturday's?

What ought to be suggested is not that any one part of the supply has actually more utility, ophelimity, or desiredness than another, but merely that the greater the supply is, the less is an additional unit wanted compared with an additional unit of other things. The more water or bread we are already supplied with per day or per annum, the less shall we want any additional gallon or pound as compared with some addition to other things which we want. If we go to the theatre three times every week, we must not expect to find Thursday's performance less enjoyable than Tuesday's, and Saturday's less enjoyable than Thursday's, although we are certain that another day's attendance would not be worth the price charged—that we could spend the money better in some other way.

The theory is not, as Jevons claimed, the true key to the whole doctrine of value, but it is really the key to a large part of it, since it explains what had never been properly understood before, why increasing the supply of anything tends to lower the value of that thing, and decreasing the supply tends to raise it.

Karl Menger expounded the same theory in his *Grundsätze der Volkswirthschaftlehre*, published at Vienna in the same year, 1871, as Jevons' *Theory*. Neither he nor Jevons found much immediate acceptance. The old school could not see anything in the new theory. Fawcett, in the most popular manual of the time, continued to serve up J. S. Mill unaltered and unadorned. Cairnes, perhaps the most respected economist of the time in England, was "wholly unable to conceive how anything amounting to a real explanation can be extracted" from the new doctrine (*Some Leading Principles*, Pt. I. chap. i, near end).

"Manifestly," he says, "by utility Adam Smith and Ricardo, and those who have followed their doctrine on this point, have understood the quality of being suitable to human purposes—this quality purely and simply, and irrespective of extraneous considerations; while they would doubtless have regarded the degree of utility as measured by the importance of the purposes to which the useful commodity ministered. In this sense it is true beyond controversy that water is useful, even though it fetched nothing in the market, and more useful than many articles—*e.g.* alcohol—that sell for more. The world could manifestly get on better without alcohol than without water. Similarly, it is true to say that a diamond is less useful than, *e.g.* coal, and that gold is less useful than iron; or at all events that the degree of utility of these several products—the importance of the services which they render in the economy of human society—is not represented by the proportions in which they exchange for each other."

This hopelessly confounds the importance of the *whole* of a commodity with the ordinary subject of valuation, the *unit* of the commodity taken separately and sold separately. The purposes to which the useful commodity ministers are conceived as all the purposes, taking them all together. Let alcohol pass, as we have there the case of an article as to which it is alleged most of mankind make a mistake, and let us take the next example but one, gold and iron. The world, says Cairnes, could get on better without gold than without iron, that is, better without *any* gold than without *any* iron. But if we take the utility thus so to speak in a lump, surely we must take the value of the things in the same way. If we do that, the supposed opposition between utility and value promptly vanishes, since if the world, as a whole, had to buy all the iron in one lot or have none at all, and to buy all the gold or have none at all, it would doubtless (if the presence of bidders from the Moon or Saturn made it necessary) bid more for the iron than for the gold, and then the value of (all) the iron would be greater than that of (all) the gold.

The confusion in Cairnes' mind between the commodity as a whole and the unit of the commodity bought and sold is most manifest in his comparison of "*a* diamond" with "*coal*." Like should be compared with like: coal as a whole is not only more useful but more valuable than diamonds as a whole; and who would say that a quarter-ounce of diamond was less useful than a quarter-ounce of coal?

Even Marshall, nearly twenty years younger than Cairnes, and only twenty-nine years old when Jevons' *Theory* appeared, failed at first to appreciate the importance of the book. Long afterwards he said that Ricardo was one of his "heroes" and that his "youthful loyalty to him boiled over" when he read Jevons' *Theory*.[1] Certainly the review of it which he wrote for the *Academy* of April 1, 1872, reprinted in *Memorials of Alfred Marshall* (pp. 93–99), in no way brings out the importance of Jevons' exposition of the "diminishing utility of successive increments."

But by the time the early *Economics of Industry* was published seven years later, Marshall was ready to give diminishing utility an important place in his explanation of what he called the law of demand. "It is a matter of common experience" that the price of a commodity varies with the quantity offered

[1] *Memorials*, p. 100, top.

for sale, and this shows how "the utility of anything to a man, its power of satisfying his wants, depends partly upon the quantity of things of the same kind that he has already. The more he has of it the less will be the utility of more of it to him." If he is buying flannel, and the price is a shilling a yard, and he buys twenty yards and no more, "this shows that the utility to him of the twentieth yard is not less than the satisfaction he could get by spending the shilling in other ways, but that the utility of a twenty-first yard would be less than this satisfaction. In other words, a shilling just *measures* the utility of the twentieth yard, the final yard which he buys. To use Mr. Jevons' happy phrase, the *Final Utility* of a yard of flannel to him is measured by one shilling" (pp. 68–9). The "Law of Demand" is given as—

> "The amount of a commodity which finds purchasers in a market in a given time depends on the price at which it is offered for sale; and varies so that the amount demanded is increased by a fall in price and diminished by a rise in price. Its price measures its Final Utility to each purchaser, that is, the value in use to him of that portion of it which it is only just worth his while to buy" (p. 71).

In a later chapter (Book II. chap. v.) we are told that "there is one exceptional case in which value is determined entirely by demand." This is where "the supply is fixed"; then "the price is determined solely by the utility of the thing; Demand is the sole regulator of value" (pp. 92–3)—a somewhat surprising proposition excused rather than defended in the *Principles*.[1] We should naturally believe that the largeness or smallness of the supply, although it is "fixed," would have something to do with determining the value. "Raphael's pictures" are the example adduced by Marshall, but would not their value be greater if still fewer of them existed and smaller if more of them existed? Ricardo, it is true, had said at the end of the fourth paragraph of his *Principles* that the value of such things "varies with the varying wealth and inclination of those who are desirous to purchase them," but if Marshall was impressed by this authority, he might also have noticed that Ricardo begins that

[1] In *Principles*, ed. 8, pp. 348–9, "if a person chooses to take the stock for granted and say that the price is governed by demand, his brevity may perhaps be excused so long as he does not claim strict accuracy."

very paragraph with the very different statement that their value "is determined by their scarcity alone."

§ 9. *Elasticity of Demand and Increasing and Diminishing Returns.*

Marshall, having accepted the final, or, as he prefers to call it (following, he says, von Thünen[1]), "marginal" utility explanation of the fall in value of an article when more is to be sold, and having, as we have seen above (pp. 195–6), reduced the theory of value depending on real cost (alone) to nothingness, was able to elaborate a supply and demand theory of value in a way which had been impossible to economists hampered by ignorance of *why* greater supply tended to reduce value and by belief that, while market fluctuations or "market prices" were governed by supply and demand, natural or normal prices were governed in the case of all commodities currently produced and not monopolised, by real-cost of production. It is true that he constantly opposes the influence of demand rather to "cost of production" than to "supply," but as supply is supposed to depend on this normal money-cost of production, that wording makes no more difference than the parallel interchange between "demand" and "utility." Book V in editions 1 to 4 is entitled "The Theory of the Equilibrium of Demand and Supply," and in later editions "General Relations of Demand, Supply, and Value." By far the greater part of it is devoted to Normal supply and demand, and in this the characteristic note is the consideration of how the value of the commodity is affected by changes of supply and changes of demand.

The effect of changes of supply will, it is explained with great skill, depend on what Marshall christens "elasticity of demand" (*Principles*, ed. 1, p. 162; ed. 8, p. 102).

Uninstructed men in search of arguments against the justice of a change in price which hurts their interest have always been apt to complain that it is out of all proportion to the change in the magnitude of the supply, so that we may safely suppose that comparisons between the magnitude of the change in price and the change in supply must have been made from a very remote antiquity. In the seventeenth century Davenant pub-

[1] Preface to 1st ed. of Marshall's *Principles*, p. x, note.

lished an estimate made by himself or Gregory King, and usually called "Gregory King's estimate," that a deficiency of 10 per cent. in the harvest raised the price of corn 30 per cent.; a deficiency of 20 per cent. raised it 80 per cent.; a deficiency of 30 per cent. raised it 160; 40 per cent. raised it 280, and 50 per cent. no less than 450 per cent. (Davenant, *Balance of Trade*, Sect. iii).

I cannot quote anything in support of my recollection, but my impression is that I remember Chancellors of the Exchequer and others in my youth, when remissions of taxation were more common than they are now, speaking of the national revenue being "elastic" or "showing elasticity" when a reduction of customs or excise duty on an article was followed by an increase of consumption which largely reduced or altogether wiped out the loss which would be expected on the assumption that the smaller tax would be levied only on the original amount. Probably taking the hint from this, Marshall adopted the plan of calling the demand for a commodity highly elastic when it stretched itself out largely in response to any given fall of price, and less elastic when it stretched itself out only a little. Corn in England in the seventeenth century was a thing for which the demand, in this way of speaking, had little elasticity. People found it did them very little good to have very much more than the normal harvest, and that it was very unpleasant indeed to have very much less. Cherries, no doubt, had a much more elastic demand; the harvest of cherries might easily have been either double or only half of the normal without any enormous shifting of price occurring in consequence.

Marshall's exposition of elasticity of demand, perhaps owing to the origin of the phrase suggested above, is a little apt to make readers think too exclusively of how much of a given commodity can be sold at different prices, and thus forget that this is only another way of putting the question how much different alterations in the amount of the commodity put on the market will move the price. It is all very well for a publisher with copyright to estimate how many copies of a book he can sell at 15*s*. and how many at 10*s*., but the problem presents itself to most producers in the form of the question, what the price will be when they and their competitors together produce various amounts. Of course the answer to the question how much can be sold at different prices gives the answer to the question how much will the sale of different amounts affect the price, but this is apt to be overlooked unless it is explicitly insisted upon.

But this defect is easily remedied, and the discussion is eminently helpful in enabling people to understand the effect of changes in supply upon prices. With regard to the effect of changes in demand Marshall is also helpful, though his touch is here not quite so sure.

In thinking of the sale of a certain amount of some commodity at once and not troubling ourselves about possible future augmentations or diminutions of this supply we are content to suppose that the demand acts just like the supply, only inversely: that is, just as increase of supply tends to reduce value, so increase of demand tends to raise it. This no doubt is quite correct. But is it correct if we are thinking of the sale of a commodity which is being continuously produced and the production of which is liable to increase or diminution? Or is the dealer right who tells us of one thing that it is dear because there is such a big demand for it, and of another that it is dear because there is so little demand for it?

Marshall decides quite justly in favour of the dealer. If by increase of demand we meant "increase in proportion to the supply," the case would be different; but as we mean increase in absolute demand, so that absolutely more of the commodity can now be sold at the old price, we have to take account of the fact that larger quantities are often likely to be produced at less "real cost" per unit than smaller quantities. Rejection of the doctrine that values are in proportion to real costs involves no denial of the fact that a diminution of "real costs" will tend to diminish the value of a currently produced and unmonopolised article.

Wherever it happens that larger quantities are in fact produced at less cost per unit[1] and competition is effective, the

[1] Of course it is not true that larger quantities will always be produced at less cost even when it is true that they could be. An increase in the demand for boots might be met, and often has been met, simply by an increase in the number of small bootmaking shops, enterprise being insufficient to set up bigger establishments which could produce cheaper.

fact that more of the commodity can be sold at the old price than before owing to the increase of the demand will eventually cause the price to fall. Suppose the demand to begin with is for 100 type-writers at £40 each, and then rises to 10,000 at that price; some of the producers, if not all of them, are likely to find their sales rising so much that they are able to produce each unit at much less cost. The enormous profit will tempt them to try to sell still more even if they have to lower the price to do it: if they are too conservative to take advantage of the increase of demand, it is likely that new men will see profit in coming into the trade and setting up large establishments in it.

It is, of course, one of the commonest of all economic experiences that enormous numbers of commodities have become cheaper because increase of population or increased means or desire of the same population to buy them has made it possible to produce them "on a larger scale." The phenomenon is much too big to be airily dismissed as "an exception to the general rule that increase of demand tends to raise value." Marshall does not try to treat it as such, but he does not seem quite happy in endeavouring to find it a place in his general theory of supply and demand and value.

He and, following him, H. D. Henderson in *Supply and Demand*, 1922, like to think of the increase of demand causing a fall of price as if it generally happened only after an interval in which the increase of demand caused the price to be higher than before.[1] They suppose it to work by in the first place causing a rise of price which increases profits, which increased profits encourage expansion of production, which in turn cheapens the product. But it is clear that though a temporary rise of price may sometimes occur, in the great majority of cases it does not. Ordinarily the producers go on selling at the same price, but sell more, and it is not higher price but greater gain at the same price which encourages production and eventually brings about a fall of price. Thus the endeavour to confine the operation of the principle to "long-period" changes of price, and so to preserve the apparent symmetry of the theory of demand and supply in the case at least of "market values," fails.

[1] Marshall, *Principles*, ed. 8, p. 455; Henderson more uncompromisingly, *Supply and Demand*, p. 29.

In regard to "long-period" prices, Marshall is obliged to follow the example set by Ricardo of dividing commodities into classes with different laws. Increase of demand will raise value in case of commodities "obeying the law of diminishing return," leave it unchanged in case of commodities "obeying the law of constant return," and lower it in case of those "obeying the law of increasing return." It must surely be admitted that this very much destroys what he calls "the fundamental symmetry of the general relations in which demand and supply stand to value" (*Principles*, ed. 8, p. 820).

"We might," he tells us, "as reasonably dispute whether it is the upper or the under blade of a pair of scissors that cuts a piece of paper, as whether value is governed by utility or cost of production. It is true that when one blade is held still and the cutting effected by moving the other, we may say with careless brevity that the cutting is done by the second; but the statement is not strictly accurate and is to be excused only so long as it claims to be merely a popular and not a strictly scientific account of what happens" (*ib.*, p. 348).

The simile is striking and effective when applied, as Marshall applies it, to fish already on the slabs in a market unprovided with refrigerating appliances on a hot Saturday, and to some commodities the cost of which is not affected by whether much or little is produced, but it is very puzzling when applied to a commodity which will fall in value when more of it is demanded. The two blades of the scissors then seem to be required to move in the same direction, which is contrary to the nature of scissors.

§ 10. *Conclusion*

It is a commonplace that value is and must be a matter of comparison between things valued. We cannot say that all things have risen or fallen in value, because there is nothing outside all things with which they can be compared in value. Whenever we say that any one thing has risen or fallen in value without adding "compared with" some other thing or things, we really have in our minds some other thing or things. The uninstructed person ordinarily has money in his mind, and his statement that a thing has risen in value means that a unit of it exchanges for more money, and he does not ask himself whether it would be more true to say that money had fallen in value. But the period of great emissions of money which followed the war of 1914–18 familiarised large numbers of persons with the idea that money can change in value, and should be regarded as rising in value when it will buy more of everything and even when it will buy more of "most things." Consequently it has become a very common practice to decide first whether a commodity or service has risen in value compared with money, and then to correct the result by allowing for any change which may have taken place in the value of money. If money has risen or fallen equally in comparison with every other commodity or service, this method presents no difficulty. Then, if, say, the commodity or service in question has risen from sixpence to a shilling, while at the same time all other commodities and services have gone up in the same proportion, we can say with certainty that the value of the commodity or service has not altered.

But of course economic phenomena are not so neat as that. Something like it occurred during the worst period of the worst inflations of currency, but in more moderate changes in the value of money we find nothing nearly approaching an equal percentage rise or fall of prices: some prices will have moved, owing to special causes, in the opposite direction to the more general trend; and even if they have all moved in the same direction, they will not have moved by the same percentage. To collect the percentages on all commodities and services is obviously impossible, and if it were possible, there would still be the difficulty of deciding how much weight to allow for each and how to avoid double reckonings when one thing is used in the production of another. Should we reckon wheat as equal to or as 200 times as important as pepper? Should we leave rubber out of account because its price comes into that of tyres and other things?

The makers of index-numbers of prices wrestle with these and other difficulties, and produce general percentages which are accepted by those who are familiar with them as by no means perfect, but as giving estimates at least a good deal better than what they themselves could make by the kind of *coup d'œil* known as general observation.

If we think with the aid of one of these index-numbers, we mean by the value of a thing or service the basketful (so to speak) of the commodities which its money-value would buy, the commodities in the basket being selected and the quantities of them decided by the constructor of the index-number. For the moment and the purpose in hand we accept the basketful as representative of the "other things" with which we want to compare the value of our commodity or service.

Having thus obtained a certain definiteness in our conception of what constitutes more or less value, we can proceed with more likelihood of success to try to generalise about the reasons why things and services have the values they have, and why from time to time these values change.

The champions of "utility" seem to have been right in starting, so to speak, from human wants. To have value a thing or action must be believed by somebody or other to serve some purpose which he wishes to see fulfilled, and this belief appears to set in motion the negotiation which leads up to the exchange in which the value of the thing or action emerges. The champions of "cost of production" were right in thinking something else besides "utility" was necessary, but confused the whole discussion by declaring that this other thing was "cost of production" instead of something like "sufficient limitation of available quantity." The quantity of every thing and every action on this finite globe of ours is limited, so that if we merely say "limitation of quantity," that is not enough for our purpose; the sand-dunes formed by sand blown from the face of the cliff at Southbourne-on-Sea were limited to some millions of tons, but this was more than what was required for building purposes there, and so boards used to be put up, "Sand may be taken from here," on building plots which were encumbered with drifts.

"Sufficient limitation of available quantity" is better than "sufficient limitation of supply," because "supply" suggests to the mind a stream of production measured by the amount produced in a period of time, whereas we want to include things like land, houses, and coin and other currency where the quantity available is only slowly affected by the weekly or annual production, and where, therefore, we require to think of the stock in existence; nay, more, we want to include also the things of which the production is no longer possible. It is not using language in its ordinary and therefore convenient sense to talk of the "supply" of land or houses or Raphael's pictures.

Granted that the thing or action is wanted and therefore entitled to be called a commodity or service, and that it is sufficiently limited in available quantity to have value, the degree of limitation of quantity then becomes important in conjunction with the "elasticity of demand." The higher the degree of limitation the higher will be the value, but how much higher each per cent. of limitation will drive the value will depend on the elasticity of demand.

Production, of course, reduces the degree of limitation, and therefore the value of any commodity or service which is produced. Consequently production as a whole tends to support the value of commodities never or no longer producible as compared with that of producible commodities; and the proportions in which production is distributed between different producible commodities and services is of great importance in determining their relative values.

The real-cost of production theorists assumed that it was at any rate approximately true that production involved painful effort and sacrifice, and that competition arranged production, and consequently the values of products, so that people were equally "rewarded" for equal efforts and sacrifices. The labourer gave painful effort, the capitalist underwent painful sacrifice in not selling all that he had and trying to spend the proceeds in "immediate consumption" although the landlord received his rents without any sacrifice at all. How the painful effort of the labourer and the painful sacrifice of the capitalist are to be measured so as to make us sure that £5 worth of interest is the reward of a sacrifice equal in real cost to the effort of which £5 worth of wages is the reward was never satisfactorily explained; apparently the fact that the two things are each worth £5 was accepted as proof of their equality in "real cost."

We have to reject altogether the view that competition does or could so arrange production. We see that labour, though it may often have painful incidents, and may always be described as "effort," is not essentially painful, but is on the whole distinctly a "good," not an evil, and we notice that it is admitted that highly-paid kinds of labour are often the most enjoyable; so that we fail to see any validity in the doctrine that value is in part (and chiefly) compensation for real cost in labour. As for the doctrine that the rest of value is compensation for the sacrifice which the capitalist undergoes when he "abstains from" or "waits for" consumption of his capital (or what he can buy with it), this seems merely an ingenious attempt to make the capitalist's using or lending his capital appear to be a "sacrifice," and therefore as proper a subject of "reward" or "remuneration" as the "effort" of labour was supposed erroneously to be. It is sufficiently condemned by the fact that nobody thought of the landlord as undergoing exactly the same "sacrifice" in using or letting his land, though he has just the same opportunity as the capitalist of selling his property and spending the proceeds in "immediate consumption."

To admit that in the real world production is not so distributed as to make values such that equal efforts-and-sacrifices are equally "rewarded" in the value of the products, and yet to construct a wholly imaginary and impossible "stationary state" or other condition of things where "economic forces have had time to work out their effects," is a bad way of approaching the task of explaining values and their changes. It provides, it is true, a basis from which to start: the actual may be explained by showing how it deviates from the ideal imagined, and Marshall has made the best of this possibility. But this ideal is necessarily vague and shadowy, and arguments founded on what would happen in it cannot be corrected by experience, so that error is extremely probable.

It is far better to take the actual past and present conditions of the world as our basis from which to start. History tells us how certain values have changed; let theory tell us why such changes took place and may be expected to take place again in similar circumstances in the future. So in dealing with the influence of production upon values we shall do well not to create an imaginary state of things in which production was so regulated that values came out in such a way as to reward efforts and sacrifices in proportion to their amount and then modify this scheme by "limitations" to make it agree with the actual world. It will be far better to accept the values known to exist or to have existed at some point of time as the result of the physical conditions of the universe and the past history of mankind, and to conceive the theory of the influence of production upon values as an orderly discussion of the causes of actual and possible changes (from one actual state of things to another state of things actual or supposed).

I am inclined to put first among such changes something which, perhaps owing to its very obviousness, has scarcely received sufficient attention—that part of the progress of human knowledge which we class as discovery and invention. Examples are scarcely necessary; we all know the effect of discoveries of new and prolific sources of diamonds, gold, and other minerals in diminishing the value of those commodities. At the initial values, the prolificness of the new sources makes working them so attractive that a great increase of supply takes place, which, in accordance with the principle of diminishing utility of increased supplies, brings about a fall in the value of the minerals in comparison with other things in general.

The fall in the value of the object discovered measured in other things in general is, of course, the same thing as a rise in the value of other things in general measured in the object discovered. But in addition to an alteration in the ratio of exchange between the object discovered and other things in general, we must not forget that the discovery may cause special changes in the values of some particular things other than the object discovered. Something may serve the same purpose as the object discovered and will fall in value along with it and for the same reason: for example, a discovery of oil will tend to reduce the value of coal, because it increases the supply not indeed of coal, but of fuel. And, on the other hand, something may be required for getting or utilising the object discovered, and the value of this may be affected, rising or falling in accordance with Marshall's explanation of the effect of changes in demand. For example, a discovery of iron ore of good quality may raise the value of coal lying near, and the discovery of gold may diminish the value of jack-hammers by causing their production to be larger and therefore cheaper.

Invention is at least as important as discovery, and its effects are perhaps even more complex and widespread. It reduces the value of the products to which it is applied, as the invention of printing, for example, has reduced the value of books and the invention of jack-hammers has reduced the value of gold. Things which serve the same purpose as the product to which the invention is applied are very seriously affected; if they serve no other purpose, they will certainly be reduced in value along with that product, and probably will be reduced so much that it is no longer anyone's interest to produce them, in which case they disappear, as hansom cabs have done from our streets; if they also serve some other purpose, whether they are reduced or increased in value will depend on whether the fact that a smaller quantity will now be produced means greater or less ease of production per unit.

Changes in population, unlike discovery and invention, have had almost more than justice done them in regard to their effect on values. They certainly are important. Increase in the number of mankind, while the magnitude of the stores of material and power provided by Nature remains stationary, must of itself tend to raise the value of unmanipulated materials and power as against that of all kinds of products in the production of which the co-operation of large numbers of persons is useful. So we expect, for example, increase of population to raise the value of land compared with that of watches and type-writers. But this effect has not been so overwhelming as we might expect, the reason being that it is counteracted by the discovery of new sources of scarce materials and by the inventions which have made transport easier and thereby made the known sources of scarce materials more available. Moreover, raw or unmanipulated materials play a smaller part in production than is usually assumed. Agricultural products have been quite erroneously classed with raw materials, and treated consequently as if they could not be obtained more easily in consequence of the increased specialisation and co-operation made possible by increase of population. In fact the superior food and raiment of modern times is due in great part to the greater population which has been a necessary condition of utilising different parts of the earth's surface for the production of different things. Without the transport machinery and facilities which only a large population can provide, there could be little movement of wheat, cotton, wool, bananas, coffee, and tea. Without the interchange of ideas and methods which a large population facilitates, there would have been little of the enormous improvement in vegetable and animal stocks which has actually taken place.

CHAPTER VIII

THE THEORY OF THE VALUE OF LAND

§ 1. *Early Theory; Rent an Index of Prosperity.*

It is only late in history that land becomes private property dealt with and thought of in the same way as movable things. Hence it is not surprising that it is late in the history of economics before the value of land is considered to be covered by the general theory of value. Till then land is supposed to be something exceptional, *sui generis*, and its value is supposed to require a separate theory of its own. And in a country where most of the land was occupied by tenants rather than owners, the annual or rental value of land is certain to attract more attention than the capital value. Hence the evolution in England of the theory of Rent.

So far as I know the earliest theory of rent is Sir William Petty's. He says:

"But before we talk too much of Rents, we should endeavour to explain the mysterious nature of them, with reference as well to Money, the rent of which we call usury; as to that of Lands and Houses, afore-mentioned.

"Suppose a man could with his own hands plant a certain scope of land with corn, that is, could dig, or plough, harrow, weed, reap, carry home, thresh and winnow so much as the husbandry of this land requires; and had withal seed wherewith to sow the same. I say, that when this man hath subducted his seed out of the proceed of his harvest, and also what himself hath both eaten and given to others in exchange for clothes and other natural necessaries; that the remainder of corn is the natural and true rent of the land for that year; and the *medium* of seven years, or rather of so many years as makes up the cycle within which dearths and plenties make their revolution, doth give the ordinary rent of the land in corn.

"But a further, though collateral question may be, how much English money this corn or rent is worth? I answer, so much as the money which another single man can save within the same time over and above his expense if he employed himself wholly to produce and make it; *viz.* let another man go travel into a country where is silver, there dig it, refine it, bring it to the same place where the other man planted his corn; coin it, &c., the same person all the while of his working for silver, gathering also food for his necessary livelihood and procuring himself covering, &c. I say the silver of the one must be esteemed of equal value with the corn of the other: the one being perhaps twenty ounces, and the other twenty bushels. From whence it follows that the price of a bushel of this corn to be an ounce of silver." (*Treatise of Taxes and Contributions*, 1662, in *Econ. Writings*, ed. Hull, p. 42.)

This is very unsatisfactory as an explanation of rent, for why should the annual value of *any* piece of land which a man can cultivate be equal to the surplus over necessaries which an average silver miner can make? If this were true, every cultivator who has to pay rent would do well to give up his holding and go to silver mining. Moreover, it implies that the values of all pieces of land cultivable by one man are equal, and Petty himself elsewhere admits that this is not so. Land "near populous places," he thinks, will yield more rent than land "intrinsically alike" at some distance (*Econ. Writings*, p. 49), and in different countries rents will vary in proportion to the density of population:

"If there were but one man living in England, then the benefit of the whole territory could be but the livelihood of that one man: but if another man were added, the rent or benefit of the same would be double, if two, triple; and so forward until so many men were planted in it as the whole territory could afford food unto. For if a man would know what any land is worth, the true and natural question must be, How many men will it feed? How many men are there to be fed? But to speak more practically, land of the same quantity and quality in England is generally worth four or five times as much as in Ireland; and but one quarter or third of what it is worth in Holland; because England is four or five times better peopled than Ireland, and but a quarter so well as Holland." (*Political Arithmetic*, 1690, p. 67, in *Econ. Writings*, p. 286.)

To anyone inclined to be despondent about the progress of economics, these opinions of the greatest economic genius of the seventeenth century should be very comforting. Whatever doubts and difficulties may still remain, we certainly have made some advance.

Davenant, in his *Essay upon the probable methods of making a people gainers in the Balance of Trade*, 1699, estimated the proportion of rent to net produce, by which he means all the produce except seed. The rent of corn land he makes £2,200,000, and the net produce "above £9,000,000," which is "full four rents," while the rent of "pasture and meadows, woods, coppices, forests, parks, commons, heaths, moors, mountains, and barren land" he puts at £7,000,000, and the produce at only £12,000,000, which "does not make fully two rents," there being little charge either in cultivating the land or gathering the product thereof, comparatively to what there is in the arable land" (pp. 72–3; in *Works*, ed. Whitworth, Vol. II. pp. 216–17).

This calculation of the produce as a certain number of rents was probably suggested to Davenant by what seems to have been the usual rough generalisation, "three rents, one for the landlord, one for the farmer, and one for the labourers,"[1] which I think I remember Lord Beaconsfield quoting to his tenants at the annual dinner at Hughenden, and which seems to have been an old English rural commonplace. Cantillon says "the landlord usually has one-third of the produce of his land" (*Essai*, p. 57), and "the farmer who directs the work usually receives two-thirds of the produce, of which one-third pays his expenses and maintenance, and the other is left to him as the profit of his undertaking" (*ib.*, p. 266).

Unless we dignify with the name of theory the very obvious truism that if the produce is divided between the labourers, the farmer, and the landlord, and we choose to regard two of the shares as coming first, we can speak of the third as the surplus over and above the other two, these estimates do not involve any theory of the value of land. I know of no seventeenth-century or early eighteenth-century suggestion of reasons for alteration in the proportion of produce falling to the landlord. The probability is that it was taken to be about one-third, and no one troubled his mind with the question whether it might or might not increase or diminish in the course of time.

Now, if with or without reason, the proportion of rent to

[1] I have tried in vain to find some connection between this and the nursery rhyme—

"Ba, ba, black sheep, have you any wool?
Yes, sir; yes, sir; three bags full."

produce is regarded as fixed, it is clear that the only possible theory about the rise and fall of rent is that it must rise and fall with the aggregate value of the produce, and so long as there is no noticeable change in the value of the unit of produce, this aggregate value will be taken to depend on the magnitude of the produce. To have a large produce is obviously a good thing, and therefore a rise in the value of the land of a country was looked upon, not askance, as it has been in England since the beginning of the nineteenth century, but as one of the greatest signs of national prosperity. This is, I think, the most natural view. A rise in the value of land in any particular locality within a " country " is always taken to show that the locality is prosperous, and there is no very obvious reason for supposing that the case of a whole " country " is different.

The Physiocrats were only giving form and exactness to the general opinion when they depicted rent as a surplus over the maintenance of the labourer given by the bounty of Nature. As Turgot put their doctrine in his *Réflexions*, § 7, they thought that " the position of the cultivator is very different " from that of the artisan :

> " The land, without the intervention of any other man or any institution, pays him directly the price of his labour. Nature does not bargain with him to make him put up with receiving no more than the absolute necessaries of life. What she gives is proportionate neither to his needs nor to a conventional valuation of his day's work; it is the physical result of the fertility of the soil and the correctness rather than the difficulty of the means which he has used for rendering it fruitful. Since the labour of the cultivator produces more than enough for his needs, he can, with this surplus which Nature gives him as a pure gift over and above the wages of his toil, buy the labour of other members of the society. These in selling it to him get no more than their living; but the cultivator reaps, besides his subsistence, independent and disposable goods which he is able to sell without having bought. He is therefore the single source of the goods which by their circulation animate all the labours of society, because he is the only person whose labour produces more than the wages of the labour."

Going a little beyond popular opinion, the Physiocrats even claimed that rise of rent was a sign of prosperity when it was caused not by an increase of produce but by a rise in the price of produce. Du Pont de Nemours says that things may be bought and sold several times, but what is important is their quantity and the prices at which they are sold first-hand :

" The more completely these prices are subject to the natural order, and the more continuously they are high, the more profitable they are in the trade done with the foreigner, the more they animate agriculture, the more they keep up the value of the different products of the territory, the more they increase the revenue of the sovereign and the owners of land, the more they augment the money of the nation and the amount of wages paid for the remuneration due for the labour or employment of those who are not primary owners of products."

And in a note to this even more precisely :

" The interest of the cultivator is the original motive power (*le premier ressort*) for all economic operations and for all success in agriculture : the more continuously products are high-priced, the better are farmers assured of the annual return of their outlay, the more does cultivation increase, and the more income does land bring in, both in consequence of the good price of products and by the increase of the annual reproduction ; the more the annual reproduction increases, the more the riches of the nation are multiplied and the power of the state augmented." (*Physiocratie*, 1767, p. 83).

It is to be noticed that the possibility of selling to the foreigner is here kept in view. Whether high or low prices of any particular kind of produce are regarded with favour in a country will clearly depend largely on whether the people of that country are most interested as producers or consumers of the kinds of produce in question. If they export much of it, they will regard a high price with favour ; if they import much of it, they will prefer a low price. In Adam Smith's time Great Britain was in a neutral position so far as agricultural products were concerned, there being no considerable balance either way, and this is perhaps in part at least the cause of the very ambiguous position occupied by Smith in regard to the value of land.

§ 2. *Neutrality of Adam Smith.*

On the one hand, the " conclusion " of his " very long chapter " on the Rent of Land is an emphatic assertion of the absolute coincidence of the interest of the landlords with that of the society of which they form a part :

" I shall conclude this very long chapter with observing that every improvement in the circumstances of the society tends either directly or indirectly to raise the real rent of land, to increase the real wealth of the landlord, his power of purchasing the labour, or the produce of the labour of other people.

" The extension of improvement and cultivation tends to raise it directly. The landlord's share of the produce necessarily increases with the increase of the produce.

" That rise in the real price of those parts of the rude produce of land, which is first the effect of extended improvement and cultivation, and afterwards the cause of their being still further extended, the rise in the price of cattle, for example, tends too to raise the rent of land directly, and in a still greater proportion. The real value of the landlord's share, his real command of the labour of other people, not only rises with the real value of the produce, but the proportion of his share to the whole produce rises with it. That produce, after the rise in its real price, requires no more labour to collect it than before. A smaller proportion of it will, therefore, be sufficient to replace, with the ordinary profit, the stock which employs that labour. A greater proportion of it must, consequently, belong to the landlord.[1]

" All those improvements in the productive powers of labour, which tend directly to reduce the real price of manufactures, tend indirectly to raise the real rent of land. The landlord exchanges that part of his rude produce which is over and above his own consumption, or, what comes to the same thing, the price of that part of it, for manufactured produce. Whatever reduces the real price of the latter, raises that of the former. An equal quantity of the former becomes thereby equivalent to a greater quantity of the latter; and the landlord is enabled to purchase a greater quantity of the conveniencies, ornaments, or luxuries which he has occasion for.

" Every increase in the real wealth of the society, every increase in the quantity of useful labour employed within it, tends indirectly to raise the real rent of land. A certain proportion of this labour naturally goes to the land. A greater number of men and cattle are employed in its cultivation, the produce increases with the increase of the stock which is thus employed in raising it, and the rent increases with the produce." (*W. of N.*, Vol. I, p. 247.)

The interest of the landlords is consequently, he says, " strictly and inseparably connected with the general interest of the society," and they would never mislead the public with a view to

[1] But later on (Vol. I. p. 317) Smith says just the contrary; " In the progress of improvement, rent, though it increases in proportion to the extent, diminishes in proportion to the produce of the land."

promote their own interest if they really understood that interest (which, he adds, they " too often " fail to do).

On the other hand, Adam Smith's account of the manner in which rent first emerges into the economic system and his explanation of its nature give his readers a much less pleasant impression of the value of land.

In the chapter on the component parts of the price of commodities in a passage already quoted (above, pp. 166–7) he tells us that in the early and rude state of society the whole produce of labour belongs to the labourer, but that later the labourer has part of his produce taken away from him by the owners of stock and part by the landlords, who love to reap where they never sowed.

The chapter on Wages tells the same story in a shorter and less picturesque form, with the difference that rent appears as the first additional component of price instead of the second. In the " original state of things . . . the whole produce of labour belongs to the labourer," but " as soon as land becomes private property, the landlord demands a share of almost all the produce which the labourer can either raise or collect from it. His rent makes the first deduction from the produce of the labour which is employed upon the land " (Vol. I. pp. 66–7). In the chapter on Rent it is explained that some part of the rent may be " no more than reasonable profit or interest for the stock laid out by the landlord on its improvement," but it can " scarce ever " be the case that the whole of the rent is so, for—

" The landlord demands a rent even for unimproved land, and the supposed interest or profit upon the expence of improvement is generally an addition to this original rent. Those improvements, besides, are not always made by the stock of the landlord, but sometimes by that of the tenant. When the lease comes to be renewed, however, the landlord commonly demands the same augmentation of rent as if they had been all made by his own.

He sometimes demands rent for what is altogether incapable of human improvement. Kelp is a species of sea-weed, which, when burnt, yields an alkaline salt, useful for making glass, soap, and for several other purposes. It grows in several parts of Great Britain, particularly in Scotland, upon such rocks only as lie within the high-water mark, which are twice every day covered with the sea, and of which the produce, therefore, was never augmented by human industry. The landlord, however, whose estate is bounded by a kelp shore of this kind, demands a rent for it as much as for his corn-fields.

"The sea in the neighbourhood of the islands of Shetland is more than commonly abundant in fish, which make a great part of the subsistence of their inhabitants. But in order to profit by the produce of the water, they must have a habitation upon the neighbouring land. The rent of the landlord is in proportion, not to what the farmer can make by the land, but to what he can make both by the land and by the water. It is partly paid in sea-fish; and one of the very few instances in which rent makes a part of the price of that commodity is to be found in that country.

"The rent of land, therefore, considered as the price paid for the use of the land, is naturally a monopoly price. It is not at all proportioned to what the landlord may have laid out upon the improvement of the land, or to what he can afford to take; but to what the farmer can afford to give" (Vol. I. pp. 145–6).

The unpleasant impression of the nature of rent which this gives is only slightly modified by the subsequent semi-apologetic statement that it "enters into the composition of the price of commodities in a different way from wages and profit.

"High or low wages and profit are the causes of high or low price; high or low rent is the effect of it. It is because high or low wages and profit must be paid in order to bring a particular commodity to market that its price is high or low. But it is because its price is high or low, a great deal more, or very little more, or no more than what is sufficient to pay those wages and profit, that it affords a high rent, or a low rent, or no rent at all" (Vol. I. p. 147).

Smith seems to have been strangely forgetful of the meaning of "monopoly" when he declared that the rent of land was "naturally a monopoly price." By derivation and in ordinary usage a person who has a monopoly of anything is one who is the only person who has the power of selling it. Landlords taken all together, it is true, are the only persons who have the power of selling land or the use of it, but they are very numerous, and do not act in concert as one person. The fact that the area of land in the world is limited in quantity is sometimes brought up in defence of the term monopoly as applied to landownership, but there are many other things which are more precisely limited in quantity than land, and no one thinks of calling the owners of these things monopolists so long as they sell in competition with each other. Smith himself does not seem to rely on the limita-

Q

tion of land, but (as is very obscurely suggested by his explanatory sentence beginning "it is not proportioned") on the fact that the price is not governed by the cost of production—which is surely quite insufficient to justify the term "monopoly."

The apologetic passage about rent being not the cause but only the effect of the price of produce is plausible but subtly misleading. It is quite true that certain land is valuable because it is useful for producing certain valuable things and its quantity is sufficiently limited, but this is equally true of labour and capital: people are paid for certain work and for the use of certain instruments made by man because their work and their instruments are useful for producing certain valuable things and are sufficiently limited in quantity. Wages and "profit" are effects of the price of products in exactly the same sense as rent is. And if we find it not unreasonable to say that the high wages of the workers in a particular trade are the cause of the high price of its product, we must find it equally reasonable to say that the high value of some particular land is the cause of the high price of its products. In both cases we are really putting a symptom of the cause in place of the cause itself; we know very well that the high value of the particular work and land would fall if there were more of that kind of work and that kind of land or if there were less demand for the particular products.

The details of Smith's theory of rent are not worth much examination. He had a curious belief that "land in almost any situation produces a greater quantity of food than what is sufficient to maintain all the labour necessary for bringing it to market, in the most liberal way in which that labour is ever maintained," and "to replace the stock which employed that labour together with its profits," so that "something, therefore, always remains for a rent to the landlord" when food is produced (Vol. I. p. 147); but when other things are produced, it depends on circumstances whether the land is worth anything or not. This doctrine never obtained any vogue, and plays no part in the history of economic theory: it is an academic curiosity and nothing more.

But rent was getting into politics, and when economic questions get into politics, though they are often somewhat roughly handled, they are really thought about, and often more progress is made towards answering them than would have been made if they had been left to the traditional arm-chair economist or even to his modern successor who sits on a stool in front of a type-writer. And so it was with rent.

§ 3. *The Corn Bounty: "No-rent Land."*

The story begins with discussions about the corn bounty, which had been given since 1688 on each quarter of corn exported from England when the home price was below a certain figure.

A bounty on export means that the taxpayers of the country giving it provide a sum of money to be paid to anyone who exports a given quantity of a particular article. The corn bounty of 1688, so far as wheat was concerned, meant that whenever the home price was below a certain level, anyone who exported a quarter of wheat from England could get 5*s*. from the taxes levied in England in addition to whatever he could get from the foreigner to whom he sold the wheat.

If in the absence of a bounty the price of wheat is 32*s*. in Harwich and 30*s*. in Rotterdam, obviously no wheat will be exported: if the cost of transport from Harwich to Rotterdam is 2*s*., there would be a loss of 4*s*. But if a bounty of 5*s*. on export is now given, there will be a gain of 1*s*., provided that the exportation makes no change in the price on either side. The Dutch will give 30*s*., and the English taxpayer will give 5*s*., total 35*s*., out of which transport has to be paid, leaving 33*s*. net, against the 32*s*. which can be got in Harwich. But of course the prices will be affected. Europe indeed is a big area which will not be much affected by all the import which can come from England, so that we need not trouble about the trifling fall which will occur in the Rotterdam price. Much more important is what will happen in Harwich; wheat cannot be sold there at two prices—in one way or another the wheat for home consumption and the wheat for export will come to bear the same price.

But what price? Most readers will say without much hesitation that the price in Harwich will be the Rotterdam price less the cost of transport, that is, 33*s*. This, they will say, will enable some to be sold for consumption in Harwich and some to be sold to the Dutch. No doubt this is correct, but why has the bounty thus caused the Harwich price to rise from 32*s*. to 33*s*.?

Nowadays people think this would happen because they have, probably without knowing it, been brought up on the Ricardian theory of rent. Before that was invented, most people seem to have argued that as the bounty widened the market for English corn, and so "encouraged tillage" and made corn more plentiful, it must tend to reduce the price of corn, since plenty always makes things cheap. They observed, too, that the price of corn had, in fact, fallen since the imposition of the bounty, and for the greater part of mankind *post hoc ergo propter hoc* is a good argument.

Adam Smith hated the bounty because it was part of the mercantile system of encouraging exports and discouraging imports, but he had no convenient theoretic weapon with which to attack it. He shifted his ground a good deal as time went on, and is very far from convincing. But the vigour with which he asserted his view that the bounty tended to raise rather than to lower the price of corn, though not backed by successful argument, put supporters of the bounty on their mettle, and caused one of them, James Anderson, to anticipate a portion of the Ricardian theory of rent.

The beauty of the bounty, Anderson contended, was that, as it was only given when the home price was below a certain figure, it prevented violent changes in the price of corn, and so acted as a sort of insurance to the farmer, which made agriculture less hazardous, and therefore tended to make production greater on the whole by causing the occupation to be more attractive. In considering how big the bounty should be, he was led to think of lands being of different grades of fertility and therefore bearing different rents. He said:

"In every country there are various soils, which are endued with different degrees of fertility; and hence it must happen that the farmer who cultivates the most fertile of these can afford to bring his corn to market at a much lower price than others who cultivate poorer fields. But if the corn that grows on these fertile spots is not sufficient fully to supply the market alone, the price will naturally be raised in that market to such a height as to indemnify others for the expense of cultivating poorer soils. The farmer, however, who cultivates the rich spots will be able to sell his corn at the same rate in the market with those who occupy poorer fields; he will, therefore, receive much more than the *intrinsic* value for the corn he rears. Many persons will, therefore, be desirous of obtaining possession of these fertile fields, and will be content to give a certain premium for an exclusive privilege to cultivate them; which will be greater or smaller according to the more or less fertility of the soil. It is this premium which constitutes what we now call *rent*, a medium by means of which the expense of cultivating soils of very different degrees of fertility may be reduced to a perfect equality." (*Observations on the Means of exciting a Spirit of National Industry*, 1777, p. 376.)

The price of corn, he thinks, must be kept up to a level which will " enable the farmer to cultivate so much of those unfertile fields as will be sufficient to furnish grain to supply the whole inhabitants with food in the scarcest years."

In his *Inquiry into the Nature of the Corn-laws with a view to the new Corn Bill proposed for Scotland*, 1777 (p. 45, note), he divides all the soils of the country into classes A, B, C, etc., and explains that as the produce of each must be sold at the same price, while the cost of production increases as you go down in the scale, " it must at length happen that the expense of cultivating some of the inferior classes will equal the value of the whole produce." If class D is the one which it just pays to cultivate without paying any rent, farmers taking the higher classes of land will be able to give something out of each bushel to the landlord.

This is the " static " or " differential " part of later rent theory, the part which insists on the differences of rents. Adam Smith had taken it for granted that everyone knew that better land was worth more than worse, and did not dwell on the fact at all. At the time nobody, not even Adam Smith himself, though he is known to have read Anderson,[1] seems to have taken any notice of the explanation. It could not get attention until it was linked up with the Ricardian dynamic theory based on the conception of diminishing returns. That conception was only just glimmering in Smith's mind, and Anderson himself was one of those agricultural enthusiasts who believe, or at any rate try to believe, in something which is nearly the opposite of diminishing returns. He says that with proper management productiveness may be made to keep pace with population, whatever that may be.[2]

Even Malthus had not yet realised diminishing returns when

[1] See Anderson's *Calm Investigation of the Circumstances which have led to the present Scarcity of Grain*, 1801, p. 18.

[2] *Recreations in Agriculture*, etc., Vol. IV. (1801), p. 374.

he published the second edition of the *Essay on the Principle of Population* in 1803. From what he says about the bounty we can gather not only that the theory of diminishing returns was not present to his mind, but also, which is more remarkable, that he then supposed high rent to be a cause of high price (p. 455, bottom; 460, top). Diminution of returns is distinctly contradicted when he says, " if it be admitted that the cultivation of corn is capable of being encouraged by a bounty like other commodities, it will scarcely fail to follow that the greater plenty occasioned by this encouragement will in the long run lower the price " (p. 462).

He had read some of Anderson's rhapsodies about the indefinite productiveness of land, and makes no general objection, though he does in one place suggest anticipation of the theory of diminishing returns (in the converse) by saying that when population has been accidentally reduced, the remaining people will be better able to feed themselves than before, since it will no longer be necessary to cultivate the worse lands (p. 472).

§ 4. *Rent Unpopular ; " Diminishing Returns."*

The hard times towards the end of the war made a difference. People began to look on rents with less favour than their ancestors had done. Long before, in 1776, a Newcastle schoolmaster, Thomas Spence, had tried to start a movement, not for nationalising, but for parochialising the land of England. Living in a county where the parishes are very large, he did not see the absurdity of parochialisation as students at the School of Economics in the parish of St. Clement Danes can see it. He proposed to dispossess the landlords and give the land to the parish, which would let it for a rent which was, after national and local taxes had been paid out of it, to be divided equally between all the inhabitants of the parish. About 1812 his plan began to be popular, and the " Spencean Philanthropists," as his followers called themselves, created some alarm. It was said that " the cry of ' No landlords ! ' stood rubric on the walls." [1]

This, coupled with the agriculturists' demand for more protection, made people think about rents. Thomas Buchanan, in his edition of the *Wealth of Nations*, 1814, was struck by the

[1] Anonymous pamphlet quoted in *Production and Distribution*, p. 223.

fact that Smith said that landlords like other men love to reap where they never sowed, without giving any reason for their being unlike other men in their success in doing it. He seized on Smith's own term "monopoly" and said it was because they have a monopoly which causes the supply of agricultural produce to be stinted till it "rises above the level of wages and profit." The Physiocrats he declared to be quite wrong in thinking rent the only possible source of taxation, since it is itself simply taken out of the pockets of other people; it arises "from the high price of the produce of land, which, though it be advantageous to those who receive it, must be proportionally injurious to those who pay it" (Vols. I. pp. 80, 99; III. p. 272).

Here was a terrible change from the old view of rent as a sign of prosperity, and from Adam Smith's glorification of the landlord's position as identical in interest with that of the community! But the most serious attack was based not on this misuse of the word "monopoly," but on the invention of the theory of "Diminishing Returns to Agriculture." The first suggestion of this theory in relation to the Corn Law controversy was made by Malthus—imprudently, as he was on the "landlord" side. In his *Observations on the Effects of the Corn Laws*, 1814 (pp. 40–41), he said that a part, and he should think no inconsiderable part, of the greater expense of raising corn in England as compared with the continental corn countries was "occasioned by the necessity of yearly cultivating and improving more poor land to provide for the demands of an increasing population; which land must, of course, require more labour and dressing and expense of all kinds in its cultivation." This idea was strongly confirmed by the evidence collected by the committees on agriculture appointed by the House of Commons and the House of Lords; the agriculturists imagined they were strengthening their case for protection by insisting on the greater cost of growing wheat on the additional land which had recently been turned to that purpose.

On reading the reports of these committees Edward West was moved to publish "a principle in political economy which occurred to" him "some years" before.

"The principle is simply this, that in the progress of the improvement of cultivation, the raising of rude produce becomes progressively more expensive, or, in other words, the ratio of the net produce of land to its gross produce is continually diminishing." (*Essay on the Application of Capital to Land; with observations showing the impolicy of any great restriction on the importation of corn, and that the bounty of* 1688 *did not lower the price of it*, pp. 1, 2.)

"Each equal additional quantity of work bestowed on agriculture," he says, "yields an actually diminished return," from which it follows that "the whole of the work bestowed on agriculture in the progress of improvement yields an actually diminished proportionate return" (p. 6). In every country there are innumerable grades of land, and those that are best in quality and situation combined will be taken into cultivation first, and cultivation will gradually spread to poorer and poorer land. Division of labour and application of machinery *tend* to make agriculture more productive, but "the necessity of having recourse to land inferior to that already in tillage, or of cultivating the same land more expensively, *tends* to make labour in agriculture less productive in the progress of improvement. And the latter cause more than counteracts" the former (pp. 9, 25).

Hence the existence of rent. "It is," says West, "the diminishing rate of return upon additional portions" of expenditure on land which "regulates, and almost solely causes, rent" (p. 49). If returns did not diminish, the produce of any piece of land would be unlimited, "and this would have the same effect as an unlimited quantity of land convenient for cultivation," but the necessity of having recourse to poorer land and to more expensive cultivation of the old land increases rent; when the demand for corn increases, "the growing price of the additional quantity," and therefore "the actual price of that quantity," must be increased, but all corn is sold at the same price, and the farmer gets only ordinary profit, "which is afforded even on that corn which is raised at the greatest expense," so that "all the additional profit on that part of the produce which is raised at a less expense goes to the landlord in the shape of rent" (pp. 49–51).

It seems clear that West can claim whatever credit is due for the introduction of the practice of talking of "diminishing returns" in agriculture and the use of the theory or "law" of diminishing returns as an argument against agricultural protection.

If properly used, the theory was quite a good weapon. The agricultural protectionists were saying, as James Anderson had done long before, that more corn could be raised in Great Britain at no greater or even at less growing cost than the existing cost. Sir Henry Parnell, Chairman of the House of Commons Committee referred to by West, had said, in presenting its Report, that the object of its proposal for greater protection was to " secure a greater production of grain at the same time with diminished expenses in producing it and at reduced prices to the consumer." Everyone knew, he argued, how increased capital cheapened manufactures, and the same thing was true of agriculture.[1]

Now against the belief that indefinitely more corn could be grown in Great Britain without increase, but rather with a decrease of cost, it was a perfectly sound argument to point out that it is obviously impossible to grow an unlimited amount of corn on any given area, and that the highest possible amount never is actually raised from any area for the very good reason that to raise so much is so difficult that it is not worth while to attempt it; and further, that every cultivator, whether producing for sale or for his own consumption, stops far short of the possible maximum because beyond some point the difficulty of raising more rises in larger ratio than the increase of produce—to use an example, he knows that adding 10 per cent. to his labour and expense would add only something under 10 per cent. to the produce, and this something is too little to be worth while. So, just as the holder of a quarter of an acre would be a fool if he tried to grow everything he wanted on his own holding, so any large population on a small area, whether called a " country " or not, would be foolish to try to grow all it wanted on that area.

But West encumbered the argument by embodying it in an explanation of the historical rise of rent and fall of the return on capital, which was completely wrong. The actual rise of rent and fall of the return on capital could not possibly have been due, as he alleged, to a diminution of the returns to agriculture, since no such diminution had actually taken place. Obviously in the course of history both the average and the marginal return to agricultural work had increased enormously. He was misled

[1] June 15, 1813. The speech is quoted more fully in Cannan, *Production and Distribution*, p. 152.

into overlooking this by the abnormal circumstances of his own time and country: it could be plausibly, though probably not correctly, contended that there had been some diminution of agricultural returns in England during the Napoleonic period.

Unfortunately a more eminent economist, misled by the same circumstances, followed exactly the same line. Immediately after West's pamphlet was published, and before he had seen it,[1] Ricardo brought out his *Essay on the influence of a Low Price of Corn upon the Profits of Stock, showing the inexpediency of restrictions on importation: with remarks on Mr. Malthus's last two publications, " An Inquiry into the Nature and Progress of Rent " and " The Grounds of an Opinion on the Policy of Restricting the Importation of Foreign Corn."* As this suggests, it was inspired by disagreement with Malthus rather than, like West's pamphlet, by consideration of the Committee's investigations. Malthus in these two pamphlets, published almost at the same time as West's, had opposed the doctrine of rent being due to " monopoly," and had tried to reinstate the older theory of its being a pure gift for which all ought to be thankful. Rent exists, he said, because land can produce more than enough to pay its cultivators—which of course is a fortunate circumstance—and because population grows when food is present—which does not seem unfortunate—so that he is able to speak of rent in highly eulogistic terms. But he admits that it is also due to the comparative scarcity of fertile land, never realising how fatal this would be to his apology for rent.

Ricardo fastened on the admission. He begins the *Essay* with imaginary history. " In the first settling of a country rich in fertile land " there will be no rent, and the whole of the surplus over what the farmer pays out in cost of cultivation will be farmer's profits. Holding, as all his contemporaries did, a subsistence-modified-by-custom theory of wages, and having most confused views about the nature of capital and the relation between the rate of profit and the proportion of income obtained by the profit-maker, Ricardo imagined that in this early stage the farmer would get a very high rate of profit, say, for example, 50 per cent. Then—

[1] This may be safely inferred from *Letters of Ricardo to Malthus*, p. 63, text, and note 2, and from the fact that West makes no complaint against the *Essay* in his preface to his *Price of Corn and Wages of Labour*, 1826.

"After all the land in the immediate neighbourhood of the first settlers were cultivated, if capital and population increased, more food would be required, and it could only be obtained from land not so advantageously situated."

And when all the more fertile land was in cultivation and more food was required, less fertile land would have to be taken into cultivation. The produce from the less well-situated and less fertile land would cost more in cultivation and transport to the market; and so also would any additional produce forced from the better land first cultivated. So the rate of profit on these portions of the produce would be less than it had been on what may be called the earlier portions. The competition of farmers for the best land would cause rents to be offered for them, and the payment of these rents would bring all profits in agriculture down to the lower level. (Profits in trade and manufactures, which are in competition for capital with agriculture, would also fall to that level.)

In this way, Ricardo contends, rent emerges and progresses wholly at the expense of profits. Rent is, he thinks, the consequence of Nature not having provided a sufficiency of fertile well-situated land. In place of Malthus' panegyrics on rent we have—

"The interest of the landlord is always opposed to the interest of every other class in the community. His situation is never so prosperous as when food is scarce and dear; whereas all other persons are greatly benefited by procuring food cheap." (In *Works*, p. 378, in *Econ. Essays*, ed. Gonner, p. 235.)

Belief in that proposition should, we might think, have been sufficient to make Ricardo into a "Spencean philanthropist," but in fact he seems to have made some division in his mind which enabled him to think of the landlord's interest as opposed to that of the rest of the community when promoted by Protection, and coincident with that of the rest of the community when promoted by the "natural course of things." For he immediately continues:

"High rent and low profits, for they invariably accompany each other, ought never to be the subject of complaint if they are the effect of the natural course of things. They are the most unequivocal proofs of wealth and prosperity and of an abundant population compared with the fertility of the soil."

The "natural course of things" which raises rent and lowers profit appears to be the increase of capital and population: if this raises rent, it only means that the country is rich in the aggregate and populous. But if rent is raised and profit lowered by Protection, the country is poorer in the aggregate and less populous than it need be. In the long run, however, according to the subsistence-modified-by-custom theory of wages, neither the natural course of things nor Protection will make any difference to the individual wage-earner, so that it is difficult, on Ricardo's own principles, to justify his statement that the landlord's interest is opposed to that of every other class, unless we take him to be thinking only of the short run, during which he believed that the wage-earners benefit somewhat from the increasing demand for labour.

He was certainly thinking of the short run when he contended that all "improvements" in agriculture, by which he means not investments of capital in improving land but improved methods of agriculture, reduce rent. He did not expound this doctrine at any length in the *Essay*, but evidently already regarded it as of some importance, as the peroration of the *Essay* is as follows:

> "If the interests of the landlord be of sufficient consequence to determine us not to avail ourselves of all the benefits which would follow from importing corn at a cheap price, they should also influence us in rejecting all improvements in agriculture and in the implements of husbandry; for it is as certain that corn is rendered cheap, rents are lowered, and the ability of the landlord to pay taxes is, for a time at least, as much impaired by such improvements as by the importation of corn. To be consistent, therefore, let us by the same act arrest improvement and prohibit importation."

In the chapter on Rent in his *Principles* Ricardo developed this doctrine much more elaborately, endeavouring to prove it by a series of arithmetical examples which are quite inconclusive even of the short run in which demand is supposed to remain unenlarged. I have shown this in some very arid pages of *Production and Distribution*,[1] and will not repeat the demonstration here. It is unimportant compared with the fact that in a foot-note which he appended near the end of the chapter on Rent in the third edition (p. 72) Ricardo admitted, not only

[1] Pp. 321–35 in which, however, the following corrigenda should be noted: p. 330, l. 17, for $\frac{3}{7}$ read $\frac{4}{7}$; p. 335, ll. 17 and 31, for $\frac{7}{8}$ read $\frac{14}{8}$.

as in the *Essay*, that the fall of rent caused by improvements would after a time be followed by a recovery to the old level, but that it would at last result in a rise of rent *above* that level:

> "I hope I am not understood as undervaluing the importance of all sorts of improvements in agriculture to landlords—their immediate effect is to lower rent; but as they give a great stimulus to population, and at the same time enable us to cultivate poorer lands with less labour, they are ultimately of immense advantage to landlords. A period, however, must elapse during which they are positively injurious to him."

As Richard Jones pointed out in 1831 (*Essay on the Distribution of Wealth*, pp. 211–12), it was quite wrong to suppose that improvements are introduced so suddenly and completely as to cause the temporary drop of price imagined by Ricardo. They will be introduced and the population and demand for food will increase nearly *pari passu*, so that no period of "injury" to the landlord will occur. And whether this is so or not, the admission that improvements are ultimately beneficial to landlords is sufficient to destroy the contention of the *Essay* that the interest of the landlords is "always" opposed to that of the rest of the community.

In short, the attempt to hang round the landlords' necks a badge bearing the legend, "We feed on diminishing returns," fails utterly in face of the admitted fact that in the course of civilisation they have been enormously benefited by improvements which resulted in increased returns.

§ 5. *Differences of Rent.*

It is sometimes supposed that while the explanation of the "progress of rent" given by West and Ricardo must be abandoned, the scheme put forward by them and before them by James Anderson, in which the land in use is divided into various grades of productiveness of which the most productive yields the highest rent and the lowest yields no rent at all, is by itself, without the "dynamic" theory, sufficient to show that the principle of diminishing returns plays a part in the determination of the value of land which it does not play with regard to other things, and thus places the value of land in a category by itself.

"If," it is said, "there were no tendency to diminishing returns, it would be unnecessary to use more than a little of the highest grade: there would be as much of this as could possibly be wanted, so that even it, as well as all other land, would be valueless. Therefore the value of land is dependent on diminishing returns." But if this is true of land, it is equally true of any other materials or instruments. Coals, houses, horses, and automobiles may be divided into grades, and if we suppose such plenty of the highest grade that anyone can have as much as he likes, even that grade will have no value. We arrive at this conclusion directly, but we might, if we pleased, go through the hollow form of saying, "If an ounce of coal could be made to give as much heat as an unlimited number of tons, if the best house could be made to accommodate comfortably the population of the world, and if the best locomotive could pull an unlimited number of trains in all required directions at once, there would be no need of using more coal, houses, or locomotives beyond the units which would do all the work required: so until the existing stock of these things wasted away, they would have no value."

If it is said that the existence of a grade of land which is used but bears no rent places land in a category by itself, the simple answer is that when any kind of thing is arranged in grades from the best to the worst, we come down to one which is only just usable and therefore brings in no income to its owner whether he lends it or uses it himself. There are always thousands of such houses actually in use, and the only reason that we find few such locomotives is because the scrap-iron value of the locomotive causes its owner to break it up a little before it reaches the "no-rent" stage of its existence. Even in this respect, the locomotive is not unlike land; just as the use of the locomotive *as a locomotive* will be abandoned before it reaches the absolute "no-rent" stage, so the use of arable land *as arable land* will generally be abandoned before it reaches the stage of yielding absolutely no rent when applied to that purpose, because it will usually yield a little more if scrapped for arable purposes and devoted to some other purpose.

An even lower depth is reached by those blind leaders of the blind, teachers and writers of elementary text-books, who have made generations of students fall into the blunder of supposing that the scheme of land arranged in grades gives a useful "formula" for the rents of different pieces of land. "The normal rent of any land," says a text-book published in 1888, "is got by deducting the produce of land on the margin of cultivation," that is, the no-rent land, "from the produce of the land in question" (J. E. Symes, *A Short Text-book of Political Economy*, p. 29). If this were true, the value of land would indeed be very unlike the value of everything else; no one imagines that the rent or annual lettable value of a cotton mill, a locomotive, or a spade is the excess of its produce over that of a cotton mill, a locomotive, or a spade which is just on the margin of use.

The explanation of this, at first sight amazing, blunder is that we ordinarily compare the rents of different lands by the amount of rent *per acre*, while West and Ricardo were led by circumstances to compare them by the amounts *per* £100 *of what they called "capital"* laid out by the farmer per annum. The grades of land in West and Ricardo are not arranged in order of the magnitude of rent per acre, but in order of the magnitude of the surplus over and above the normal profits of the farmer. Consequently the difference between the rents of any two grades is always, in Ricardo's own words, "the difference between the produce which they yield with a given quantity of capital and labour" (*Principles*, 1st ed., p. 54; 3rd ed., p. 57). He does not say, and there is no reason to suppose that he imagined, that the quantity of capital and labour which it is profitable to expend is the same per acre on all lands however cultivated. Obviously it is not; even in the same neighbourhood it may easily pay to expend ten times as much per acre on the fat land in the valley near the town as on the stony pasture far up the hillside. And the rent per acre will obviously depend not only on the ratio of the whole return to the expenditure, but on the amount of that expenditure. For example, if on equal areas the valley farmer spends £100 and gets a total return of £150, while the hill farmer spends £10 and gets a total return of £17, when farming profits are 20 per cent., the rents of the equal areas will be £30 for the valley and £5 for the hill, whereas Ricardo's "rents" on equal "capitals" will be not as 30 to 5, but as 30 to 50, the hill land being actually in a higher grade than the valley!

J. S. Mill, who, as a faithful disciple of Ricardo, should have made his master's meaning clearer, obscured it in a section of which he gives the misleading summary (in the Contents) of " The rent of land consists of the excess of its return above the return to the worst land in cultivation." Every reader would take this by itself to mean that the rent of any acre of land will be the excess of its produce over the produce of the worst acre in cultivation. In the body of the section Mill just saves himself by inserting "to the same capital." "The rent, therefore, which any land will yield is the excess of its produce beyond what would be returned to the same capital if employed on the worst land in cultivation." But he never points out that in fact the same capital would *not* be employed on an equal area of the worst land in cultivation, so that his formula gives no information about the rents of different equal areas. Fawcett, Mill's interpreter to the populace, is no better. In a " statement and proof " of Ricardo's theory of rent, he says, " the rent of land represents the pecuniary value of the advantages which such land possesses over the worst land in cultivation, the rent which this land yields being merely nominal in amount." Banality could not go further than this; how could the rent be anything but the difference between what it is and *nil?* But two pages further on he says, " the rent of any land may be estimated as the difference between the amount which it produces and the amount of produce raised from the worst land in cultivation." It is true that he adds that " net produce, not gross produce," is meant, but the explanation of the meaning of gross and net which he proceeds to give does not appear to be directed towards clearing up the question of the differing rents of equal areas. His " net produce " is simply what is left over after everyone except the landlord has been paid —which, of course, is the rent (*Manual*, 6th ed., pp. 114–16).

More cautious modern writers, including Marshall and Taussig, avoid the attempt to give any " formula " for the rents of different areas. Chapman has endeavoured (*Outlines of Political Economy*, 1911, p. 291, 3rd ed., p. 295) to improve the usual diagrammatic illustration of rent in such a way as to allow for the fact that different equal areas are cultivated profitably with widely different amounts of farmer's capital, but in so doing has destroyed the only merit the old diagram possessed—simplicity—

and diagrams which are not simple are seldom real aids to exposition.

§ 6. *The Distinction between Land and Capital.*

Adam Smith's remark that rent was the effect while wages and profit were the cause of prices, and Ricardo's whole system, required a sharp distinction to be made between "rent" and "profits." As rent was taken to come from land and profits from capital, this carried along with it a necessity for a sharp distinction between land and capital. In ordinary English "rent" was what was paid by the farmer to the landlord, and the "land" for the use of which this rent was paid included the farmhouse and its outbuildings and everything else affixed to the land and let to the farmer. But when Adam Smith introduced "capital" into English economics, he defined it in such a way that it included these fixtures. In his chapter on the Division of Stock he included in the "fixed capital of the society" both "farmhouses with their necessary buildings, stables, granaries, etc.," and "improvements of land" (*W. of N.*, Vol. I. p. 264). Unless "land" may be partly "capital," this evidently required him to omit from the "rent of land" all that is paid for agricultural buildings and land improvements, but in fact he did not do so, and constantly speaks of the landlord getting a "greater rent" in consequence of his providing these things (*e.g. W. of N.*, Vol. I. p. 153). When endeavouring to explain rent of land he resembles the notorious preacher who "looked the difficulty in the face and passed it by." He imagines a somewhat perverse reader contending that the *whole* of the rent of land is payment for improvements made by landlords, and then merely disposes of this contention—easily enough, of course—by showing that only a part of rent as commonly understood can be thus accounted for (*W. of N.*, Vol. I. pp. 145–6).

In the *Essay* Ricardo seems to have been just as little awake as Smith to the importance of the question. He begins by quoting with approval Malthus' definition of the rent of land as what remains "after all the outgoings belonging to its cultivation . . . have been paid, including the profits of the capital employed estimated according to the usual and ordinary rate of the profits of agricultural stock at the time being," without apparently

R

noticing that Malthus evidently meant by "the capital employed," the capital of the farmer only, so that the rent, in accordance with common usage, included all that the landlord receives from the farmer, and not merely that amount less what he receives in consequence of his investments of capital in farm buildings and improvements. It was only several pages later that it occurred to Ricardo to try to clear up the matter, and then he thought it worth no more than a foot-note to the word "rent" in the passage, "Rent, then, is in all cases a portion of the profits previously obtained on the land. It is never a new creation of revenue, but always part of a revenue already created" (in *Works*, p. 375; *Econ. Essays*, p. 231). The foot-note is:

"By rent I always mean the remuneration given to the landlord for the use of the original and inherent power of the land. If either the landlord expends capital on his own land or the capital of a preceding tenant is left upon it at the expiration of his lease, he may obtain what is indeed called a larger rent, but a portion of this is evidently paid for the use of capital. The other portion only is paid for the use of the original power of the land."

In the chapter on Rent in the *Principles*, Ricardo mixes up the question of return on landlord's capital very awkwardly with the question whether payments for timber, stone, and minerals removed from the land, and leaving the property depreciated thereby, are rent. In order to exclude these latter payments he substitutes "indestructible" for the rather unnecessary "inherent" of the *Essay*, so that his definition becomes, "Rent is that portion of the produce of the earth which is paid to the landlord for the use of the original and indestructible powers of the soil." He puts forward no argument in favour of this definition, but simply speaks of the "strict sense" to which he is "desirous of confining" the term rent, as opposed to "the popular sense in which the word is usually employed." Having assumed that the sense which he wishes the word to have is the proper one, he follows a bad example set by Adam Smith (below, p. 305) and accuses "popular language" of "confounding" rent with income from capital because in the English language as ordinarily spoken it means the periodical payments made by a tenant for the use of land and other immovables. Immediately after posing this definition, he says rent

" is often, however, confounded with the interest and profit of capital, and in popular language the term is applied to whatever is annually paid by a farmer to his landlord. If of two adjoining farms of the same extent and of the same natural fertility, one had all the conveniences of farming buildings and besides were properly drained and manured, and advantageously divided by hedges, fences, and walls, while the other had none of these advantages, more remuneration would naturally be paid for the use of one than for the use of the other; yet in both cases this remuneration would be called rent. But it is evident that a portion only of the money annually to be paid for the improved farm would be given for the original and indestructible powers of the soil; the other portion would be paid for the use of the capital which had been employed in ameliorating the quality of the land and in erecting such buildings as were necessary to secure and preserve the produce " (1st ed., pp. 49–50; 3rd, pp. 53–4).

The distinction, he says, between rent in his " strict " sense and the return to capital commonly included in " rent " is very important, because the " laws which regulate the progress of rent in the strict sense are " widely different from those which regulate the progress of profits, and seldom operate in the same direction," so that a tendency of rent in the strict sense to increase may be counteracted wholly, or less or more than wholly, by a tendency of the other part of rent in the popular sense to decrease.

He concludes the discussion by saying that in the future pages of the work, whenever he speaks of the rent of land he wishes to be " understood as speaking of that compensation which is paid to the owner of the land for the use of its original and indestructible powers." In fact, he very often forgets this wish, and leaves his readers to gather from the context as best they may, which " rent " he means.

In the chapter on Taxes on Rent in the *Principles* (the second " Chapter VIII " in the text and " VIII " with an asterisk in the Contents of the first edition, and therefore perhaps an afterthought) he contrasts the effect of taxing rent in the strict sense with that of taxing rent in the popular sense. A tax on " strict " rent, which near the end of the chapter he calls " the real rent of land," will fall " wholly on the landlords," but a tax on rent in the popular sense (" rent as now constituted ") and making no distinction between its two parts, will " discourage cultivation " and so raise the price of raw produce by checking landlords' investment of capital in land-improvements. In the sketchy, vague way in which he generally talks of taxes he says:

"There can be little doubt but that if a tax were laid on rent, landlords would soon find a way to discriminate between that which is paid to them for the use of the land and that which is paid to them for the use of the buildings and the improvements which are made by the landlord's stock. The latter would either be called the rent of house and buildings, or on all new land taken into cultivation such buildings would be erected and improvements would be made by the tenant and not by the landlord. The landlord's capital might indeed be really employed for that purpose; it might be nominally expended by the tenant, the landlord furnishing him with the means, either in the shape of a loan or in the purchase of an annuity for the duration of the lease" (1st ed., pp. 222–3; 3rd, p. 193).

Does he here contemplate the Legislature passing an Act to tax rent as defined in Chapter II of Mr. David Ricardo's *Principles of Political Economy and Taxation*, and leaving it to the landlords and tenants to make this as little as they please by "calling" as much as they like of the rent in the popular sense "rent of house, buildings, and landlords' improvements"? Or is the Legislature supposed to enact that the "rent of land" without further definition is to be taxed, and then allow the landlords and tenants to arrange for as many other quarterly payments from the tenant to the landlord during the tenancy as they like? In either case the suggestion is childish in the extreme. At this stage Ricardo seems to have completely overlooked two important considerations:

(1) Little can now be certainly known about the "original properties of the soil" of a farm which has been centuries in occupation and cultivation, and accounts have seldom been preserved showing what capital has from time to time been invested in improving and equipping it, and if such accounts exist, it is not easy to say how much of the capital was prudently invested nor what rate or rates of interest should be allowed.

(2) Supposing that in some way or other estimates of the annual value of the original powers and of the capital expended were arrived at independently, the sum of the two would sometimes be greatly above and sometimes greatly below the total annual present value of the farm. The capital actually expended

would often differ widely from the capital which would now be necessary to obtain the same result.

But when he came to write the later chapter on Poor Rates, he was led to consider the possibility of withdrawals of capital from agriculture by the landlords not renewing perishable things like farm buildings, and this caused him to abandon—characteristically again in a foot-note—the distinction between rent and profits (and therefore between land and capital), upon which his doctrine about taxation of rent and nearly everything else that he had taught about rent is based :

> " In a former part of this work I have noticed the difference between rent, properly so called, and the remuneration paid to the landlord under that name for the advantages which the expenditure of his capital has procured to his tenant; but I did not perhaps sufficiently distinguish the difference which would arise from the different modes in which this capital might be applied. As a part of this capital, when once expended in the improvement of a farm, is inseparably amalgamated with the land, and tends to increase its productive powers, the remuneration paid to the landlord for its use is strictly of the nature of rent, and is subject to all the laws of rent. Whether the improvement be made at the expense of the landlord or the tenant, it will not be undertaken in the first instance unless there is a strong probability that the return will at least be equal to the profit that can be made by the disposition of any other equal capital; but when once made, the return obtained will ever after be wholly of the nature of rent, and will be subject to all the variations of rent. Some of these expenses, however, only give advantages to the land for a limited period and do not add permanently to its productive powers : being bestowed on buildings and other perishable improvements, they require to be constantly renewed, and therefore do not obtain for the landlord any permanent addition to his real rent " (1st ed., p. 362; 3rd, p. 306; chap. xviii, end).

This note appeared in the first edition. It was evidently added after the chapters on Rent and on Taxes on Rent had been written, and very probably after they were set up in type. But both the second and third editions were brought out during Ricardo's lifetime, and in neither did he make any attempt to revise those chapters by adopting into them his new definition of rent in the " strict sense." It is indeed difficult to see how he could have done so. The whole " Ricardian theory " of the rise and fall of rent is built up on the assumption that " land " in the "strict sense" (*i.e.* the object for which "rent of land" in the "strict sense" is paid) is given by Nature in certain quantities of certain qualities. The note gives up this assumption by admitting that strict rent is paid for qualities which have been conferred on parts of the earth's surface by improvements in it made by man. In other words, it admits that valuable land yielding rent in the "strict sense" or "real rent" can be, and constantly is being, made by man in just the same sense as steam-engines are made by man. No doubt the earth's surface cannot be increased, but this is a fact of the same nature as the fact that the different kinds of matter provided by Nature cannot be increased. It has exactly the same relevance to the value of land that the fact that there is only a certain amount of iron ore in the world has to the value of steam-engines. We do not think of steam-engines as being increased when their weight rises, but when their horse-power is augmented; the augmentation of the productive power of an acre of land is exactly analogous to the augmentation of the horse-power of a ton of iron ore fashioned into a steam-engine.

§ 7. *Ricardo on the Value of Forests, Mines, and Quarries.*

Having abandoned "original" in his definition of rent as what is paid for "the original and indestructible powers of the soil," Ricardo is left with "indestructible." As I have already remarked, he inserted this adjective in order to exclude payments to the landowner for timber, stone, and minerals removed from the property and not replaced. Stone and minerals are, of course, never replaced on the property, and when he places timber along with these things, he is thinking not of continuous forestry in which the average age of the trees is kept nearly stationary by new planting, but of an owner who denudes his land by selling all his timber at once.

His purpose was excellent, but it could not be fulfilled by the insertion of the word "indestructible." Area is indestructible, but original fertility can be and often is destroyed by exhausting cultivation, while advantages of situation can be and often are destroyed by the opening of new routes and the removal of populations from the vicinity. What was wanted was to explain that rent (in the ordinary sense) which the landlord gets for agricultural land is got from tenants who are bound by the terms of their tenure, explicit or implicit, to carry on " good cultivation " —not to let the farm " run down " or deteriorate—so that the rent or " annual value " to which it is regarded as equivalent is not a wasting thing but something which may be expected to continue without diminution in the absence of external changes like a fall in prices. If a landlord is in any year getting more than this by denuding his estate of timber, or by letting people carry away gravel or stone or minerals from it, he is in the same position as if he sold portions of the surface out and out to purchasers; he is " realising " (*i.e.* exchanging for money) some of the capital value of his estate rather than receiving " income " from it.

Nobody accustomed to converse in ordinary English calls the money arising from such realisations " rent."

Trouble in this matter seems to have been started by the fact that Adam Smith speaks of the rent of forests (without excluding what I have called denudation), the rent of quarries, and the rent of mines. He may possibly have known some quarries or mines which owing to the regularity and smallness of the local demand seemed likely to yield about the same amount annually into an indefinite future, and which were therefore let for fixed annual sums called rents. But in the concrete cases which he mentions the payments are not fixed annual sums but percentages of produce extracted. The probability is that he was led into calling such payments " rent " by the fact that he had rashly analysed all prices into only three component parts—wages, profit, and rent: if not taken by the sovereign (such as the King of Spain and the Duke of Cornwall), such payments went to the landlords like rent proper, and they certainly were neither wages nor profits, so that he was compelled to call them " rent "—or give up his classification, an alternative which, no doubt, never crossed his mind.

At the beginning of the chapter on Rent in his *Principles*, Ricardo confusedly complains of Adam Smith here using rent in its " popular sense " (1st ed., p. 50; 3rd ed., p. 54) which is just what Smith is not doing, but soon, much more reasonably, says that when forest land is denuded, " the compensation " is " paid for the liberty of removing and selling the timber, and not for the liberty of growing it," and in case of mines and quarries, it " is paid for the value of the coal or stone which can be removed from them and has no connection with the original and indestructible powers of the soil." The mention of "liberty of growing it" and "indestructible powers" both rightly, though very obscurely, suggest that what is paid for liberty of deteriorating the property is not rent.

But after having said all this in the chapter on Rent, and concluding that in the future pages of his work he wished rent to be understood as in the sense in which he defines it, he proceeded, with an inconsistency astonishing even in him, to entitle his very next chapter, "On the Rent of Mines," and said in it, "Mines as well as land generally pay a rent to their owner." The explanation of the inconsistency seems to be that at the beginning of the chapter on Rent he was thinking chiefly of his doctrine that rise of land rent is caused by diminishing returns. Now there is no reason to believe that he thought that there was any rise of mine rent, and there is some reason to believe that he thought there was an increase of returns at any rate in gold and silver mining, since he remarks that if any fall in the value of gold and silver has taken place in recent times, "it is to be attributed to improvements in the mode of working the mines" (1st ed., p. 80; 3rd p. 78). It would thus appear to him desirable to differentiate between land value and mine value. But by the time he came to write the first pages of the next chapter he had been struck by the fact that mines resemble land, (1) because their value is "the effect and never the cause of the high value of their produce," (2) because "if there were abundance of equally fertile mines, which anyone might appropriate, they could yield no rent," and (3) because where mines of various qualities exist, "the return for capital from the poorest mine paying no rent would regulate the rent of all the other more fertile mines." The objection to this (taking the points in the reverse order) is that neither the poorest mine nor the poorest surface land "regulate" the value of the better, that sufficient abundance will prevent any instrument of production—not only mines and surface land—from having any value, and that all instruments bear the same relation to the value of their products as land does to its products.

§ 8. *Decay of the Ricardian Theories of Rent.*

From the foregoing account it will be seen that by the time Ricardo had done with the Ricardian theories of rent very little of them was left. The history of the remains is scarcely worth studying in detail. The political inducement to represent the landlords as fattening on diminishing returns disappeared when the Corn Laws were repealed in 1846, and the academic desire to explain how the doctrine that the values of products depended solely on labour cost or labour-modified-by-capital-cost could be reconciled with the payment of rent for unimproved land necessarily waned gradually as that doctrine lost its hold. Twentieth-century text-books either say nothing about the Ricardian theories or adopt a very apologetic tone in describing such parts and versions of them as they think most plausible.

It is generally, though perhaps not very clearly, realised that if anything is both desired and sufficiently limited in quantity, the laws of its value are unaffected by its origin, whether that be ascribable to Nature or to man. Land, therefore, is coming to be regarded merely as one of the numerous things which are desired as instruments or materials for the production of desired things. A certain fogginess still prevails about the limitation of its quantity. Marshall, for example, insists that land differs from other instruments because the stock of land "at any time is the stock for *all* time."[1] But it is only the area of the surface of the globe which can be thus spoken of, and that is of as little importance as the definite limitation of every kind of matter, on or in the globe. What is desired in land is not mere area but productive powers. Nature provides each piece of land with these in different degrees, but the amount of them on any particular piece can be and constantly is being varied, generally in the direction of increase, by man. Consequently land, considered as a desirable object, is no more absolutely fixed in quantity by the fact that the area of the globe is fixed than metal tools and machinery are fixed in quantity by the fact that there is only a certain amount of these metals on and in the earth.

[1] *Principles*, ed. 8, p. 536, and much the same on p. 431. In both places Marshall inserts "in an old country," and p. 431 seems to indicate that by an old country he means one in which no cultivable land remains uncultivated. But if a country is not isolated from the rest of the world, what possible difference can it make whether the uncultivated but cultivable land is inside or outside it?

CHAPTER IX

THE THEORY OF THE COMPARATIVE VALUE OF CAPITAL AND INCOME

§ 1. *Early Theory about the Rise and Fall of Interest.*

I HAVE given this chapter, which deals with questions commonly placed under the heading, "The Rate of Interest," its present long title in order to emphasise the fact that the rate of interest and the number of years' purchase for which an annuity or a piece of rent-bearing land will sell are merely different ways of expressing the value-relationship of capital and income. To say that an annuity of £1 will sell for £20, or that a net rental of £1 will sell for £20, is obviously the same thing as to say that £20 invested in the purchase of an annuity or land will yield 5 per cent. per annum. Both statements mean that capital is worth or is valued at twenty times the annual income derivable from it, or, to put the same thing in other words, that one year's income is worth one-twentieth or 5 per cent. of the capital from which it is derived.

Early thinkers were too much occupied with discussing the legitimacy of interest from a moral or religious point of view to think about the causes which make interest high or low; and the cognate or identical problem, what makes the number of years' purchase given for land or an annuity less or more does not seem to have attracted any attention. In the seventeenth century, when the religious and moral objections to usury had worn out, English thought on the causes of high and low interest was stimulated by argument about the expediency of reductions of the legal limit. A strong opinion prevailed among all who had no money to lend that low interest was a good thing. The preamble of the Act of 1623, which reduced the legal maximum from 10 to 8 per cent., alleged that the fall of prices made so high a rate as 10 per cent. prejudicial to agriculture and commerce; the Commonwealth Act of 1651 further reducing the maximum to 6 per cent. gives the same reason, and that of 1660, which re-enacted this reduction, says the previous reductions had been " beneficial to the advancement of trade and improvement of lands by good husbandry," and advantageous because they reduced the rate " to a nearer proportion with foreign states with whom we traffic."

Sir Josiah Child, being not a member of the well-known banking firm but a great East India merchant, wrote in 1668 very wildly in favour of still further reduction.[1] His insistence on the lowness of the rate of interest in Holland as compared with that prevailing in England caused an opponent to produce a pamphlet[2] which contended that a low rate of interest was not the cause, as Child alleged, but the effect of national riches, and Child in his reply[3] admitted that it might be an effect of riches, though he persisted in saying it was also a cause.

But then and for a long time afterwards it was more usual to ascribe lowness of interest to plenty of money, rather than to plenty of all kinds of accumulated riches. John Locke, writing about 1671 (though the work was not published till 1691), said that the rate of interest depended " upon the whole quantity of the then passing money of the kingdom in proportion to the whole trade of the kingdom, *i.e.* the general vent of all the commodities." [4]

The philosopher here was only adopting, as philosophers generally do, the popular opinion of the time. John Law, a business man, though somewhat a speculative one, writes as if everyone knew that a greater quantity of money would cause interest to fall (*Money and Trade Considered*, 2nd ed., 1720, p. 17). Montesquieu believed that the importation of the

[1] *Brief Observations concerning Trade and Interest of Money*, a 4to pamphlet of 38 pp.

[2] *Interest of Money Mistaken: or a Treatise showing that the abatement of interest is the effect and not the cause of the riches of a nation and that 6 per cent. is proportionable interest to the present condition of this kingdom.* Anon. 1668.

[3] *Trade and Interest of Money considered*, which bound up with *Brief Observations* became *A Discourse of Trade* in 1690, and *A New Discourse of Trade* in 1694.

[4] *Some Considerations of the Consequences of the Lowering of Interest and Raising the Value of Money*, 1691, 2nd ed., 1696, p. 72.

precious metals from the New World diminished the rate of interest in Spain from 10 to 5 per cent. :

"That," he says, "was inevitable. A great quantity of silver was suddenly brought into Europe: soon fewer persons were in need of silver; the price of everything went up, and that of silver went down; the continuity of values was broken, all old debts were extinguished. It reminds us of the time of the Mississippi scheme, when everything had enormous value except silver. After the conquest of America those who had money were obliged to lower the price or the hire of their merchandise, that is to say, they had to lower the rate of interest they charged. Since then the rate has never been able to get back to its old height because the quantity of money in Europe has increased every year." (*Esprit des Lois*, 1748, xxii. 6.)

It is true that he gives as additional reasons for the general fall, the reduction of interest on state loans and the greater ease of transporting silver from one country to another, but these are even less plausible than the first, and he attaches much less importance to them.

The acuteness of David Hume enabled him to see that the fact that increase of money lowered the value of money did not prove that it lowered interest rates (*Political Discourses*, 1752, "Of Interest"). He points out that as the principal and the interest are both reckoned in money, any given sum of interest falls in purchasing power exactly in the same proportion as the principal sum: if £100 will only buy what £50 bought before, £5 paid in interest on it will only buy what £2 10*s*. bought before, so that there is no ground for Montesquieu's idea that the man who has £100 to lend must lend it at a lower *rate* than before because his merchandise is depreciated—when he lends it at the same rate as before he is lending it for less in commodities and services.

Hume himself regarded the level of interest as being settled by demand and supply. The rate is high when society consists almost entirely of landlords and peasants, for then there are many borrowers and few lenders. The rise of a "moneyed interest" composed of men who have got rich by trade tends to reduce the rate of interest by increasing the number of lenders and their power to lend. The increase of the moneyed interest causes a "rivalship" among its members which tends to reduce profits, and profits and interest being alternative ways of getting income, this makes people willing to lend at lower rates.[1]

Cantillon, writing a little before Hume, though what he wrote was not published till 1755, also rejects what he calls the "commonly accepted idea of all who have written about commerce," that increase in the quantity of money reduces interest: abundance and scarcity of money, he holds, raise and lower the price of all things without having any necessary connection with the rate of interest, which is often high where things are dear and low where they are cheap. He is rather more definite than Hume about the connection between trade and interest, beginning his chapter on "Interest of Money and its Causes" thus:

> "Just as the price of things is fixed in the higgling of the markets by the quantity of things exposed for sale in proportion to the quantity of money offered for them, or, which is the same thing, by the proportion of the number of sellers to that of buyers; so the interest of money in a country is fixed by the proportion between the number of lenders and that of borrowers" (p. 264).

Interest, he says, began with loans to necessitous persons, and its height was then regulated by the necessities of the borrowers and the fear and avarice of the lenders. ("Fear," because one who lends faces the risk of incurring expenses, law-suits, losses, and the hatred of the borrower.) But in more civilised times most borrowing is by undertakers of business risks, and the demand for loans comes to depend upon the prevalence of such undertaking, so that, for instance, in China interest is very high because the number of undertakers there is very great, even the provision of meals to people working in the fields being undertaken for profit. Extravagance of nobles

[1] Böhm-Bawerk says that Hume's essay on interest showed that the rate of interest in a country does not depend on the quantity of its money, "but on the amount of its riches or stocks." This, I think, is a misreading of Hume's statement, "High interest arises from three circumstances: a great demand for borrowing; little riches to supply that demand; and great profits arising from commerce." In this "little riches" goes closely with "to supply that demand." Two pages further on Hume explains that in order to have many lenders in a country it is not necessary that there should be a large stock of money, but "only requisite that the property or command of that quantity, which is in the state, whether great or small, should be collected in particular hands so as to form considerable sums or compose a great monied interest." He is always thinking of the concentration of lending power, not of the magnitude of accumulated stocks.

and landlords tends to raise interest, not only because such persons want to borrow directly, but because their conduct induces undertakers to borrow for the businesses which their extravagant demands cause to flourish. War also raises interest for this same reason as well as by causing greater risk: demand for munitions causes undertakers to borrow in order to supply this demand.

Cantillon is thus on the main subject scarcely further advanced than Hume, but he has some very good suggestions about the different rates charged to different classes.

Turgot and Adam Smith make a great step forward by definitely introducing increase of accumulated riches as a factor in the determination of interest. The heading of Section 80 (79) in Turgot's *Réflexions* is:

"The price of interest depends immediately on the relation between the demands of the borrowers and the offers of the lenders; and this relation depends chiefly on the quantity of movable riches accumulated by savings made from incomes and annual produce to be converted into capital, whether this capital is in the form of money or in any other sort of goods which have a value in commerce."

The text of the section says it is not the quantity of money which causes rises or falls of the rate of interest,

"but only the total of capital existing in commerce, that is to say, the actual total of valuable movables of all kinds which have been accumulated, saved gradually from incomes and profits to be employed in bringing in to their owner fresh income and profit. It is these accumulated savings which are offered to the borrowers, and the more numerous they are, the lower is the interest of money, provided that the number of borrowers is not correspondingly increased."

The next two sections attribute the historical fall of interest to the fact that the spirit of economy has generally prevailed over the spirit of luxury.

Adam Smith in his lectures taught very plainly that the rate of interest did not depend on the amount of money but "on the quantity of stock." He attributed the fall of the rate since the discovery of America not to the influx of gold and silver into Europe, but to the fact that down to that time the disorder of the Middle Ages prevented much accumulation of stock; in the more favourable modern period stock was accumulated much more rapidly.

"We may further observe," he is reported to have said, "that what one trade lends to another is not so much to be considered as money as commodities. No doubt it is generally money which one man delivers to another in loan, but then it is immediately turned into stock, and thus the quantity of stock enables you to make a greater number of loans. The price of interest is entirely regulated by this circumstance. If there be few who have it in their power to lend money, and a great number of people who want to borrow it, the price of interest must be high, but if the quantity of stock on hand be so great as to enable a great number to lend, it must fall proportionably." (*Lectures*, p. 220.)

§ 2. *The "Rate of Profit."*

By the time he sat down to write the *Wealth of Nations*, Smith had discovered that the rate at which lenders are willing to lend, and the rate at which borrowers are willing to borrow, are affected by the rate of return on capital which can be obtained by the lenders if they do not lend, and by the borrowers if they do borrow and employ the capital. Interest on loans becomes "a derivative revenue" derived from and depending for its magnitude on the "profit" which can be got by the actual employer of capital whether that capital is his own or only borrowed.

This was a step forward; it carried the inquiry further by asking why people were willing or compelled to pay more for loans when less was offered on loan, and why people were willing or compelled to take less for the money they lent when more was on offer. But it certainly introduced difficulties which were absent from the inquiry into the causes of high and low loan-interest.

In the first place, unlike loan-interest, or perhaps it would be safer to say in a much higher degree than loan-interest, the rates of profit obtained by different persons and by the average person in different trades differ in consequence of the different quantities and qualities of the labour undergone by the employers of the capital; in other words, "profits" often include what is sometimes a small and sometimes a large element of remuneration of labour. The profits of a railway company all go in dividends to shareholders who do no work in connection with the railway, and so such profits include no remuneration of labour; the profits of an itinerant fruit or vegetable seller are nearly all remuneration of labour, and between these extremes there are an infinite number of gradations. Consequently the rate of profit as commonly understood, except in the case of such companies as include all remuneration of labour in working expenses, does not give the ratio between capital value and annual value anything like so well as the rate of loan-interest does.

Adam Smith was at times perfectly aware of this. He explains, for example, that the high profits of apothecaries and small grocers are mostly remuneration for their labour (*W. of N.*, Vol. I. pp. 113–14). Yet when dealing with profits in general, he deliberately shuts his eyes and alleges that profits "are regulated altogether by the value of the stock employed and are greater or smaller in proportion to the extent of this stock" (Vol. I. p. 50). But as he considers that the rate of loan-interest gives the only reliable information about the rise and fall of profits, and assumes that the rate of profit rises and falls *pari passu* with the rate of loan-interest (Vol. I. p. 90), he may be taken to have eliminated remuneration of labour, so that his rate of profit becomes the same thing as the ratio of the annual value of capital to the value of the capital. Later writers usually followed his lead, and in quite recent times it has become a common practice to substitute "rate of interest" for "rate of profit" as the name of the ratio of annual to capital value. This practice has the inconvenience of compelling us to say "loan-interest" when we mean interest in the ordinary sense of the word and not in this artificial sense given to the word in the economists' dialect of the English language.

Secondly, a rate or ratio is necessarily "on" something, and there is no doubt or difficulty in saying what any rate of loan-interest is "on." Obviously it is on the principal, the sum lent, and is reckoned by some period of time, usually (nowadays) a year. The rate of profit, on the other hand, has long had two different meanings. In one, which has been gradually gaining ground, it is, like the rate of loan-interest, "on" a capital sum which is, or is assumed to have been, invested, and it is invariably reckoned by the year. In the other, and much older sense, it is "on" the amount expended in connection with a particular transaction, and is not limited as to time, but simply covers the period elapsing between the beginning and the end of the transaction. A secondhand bookseller may say quite truly that he is making only 10 per cent. while his customers prefer to say, equally truly, that he makes cent. per cent. He means that he is only getting yearly 10 per cent. on the capital which he has invested in the business; they mean that when he buys a book he only gives half the price at which he sells it—this year, next year, or ten years hence.

This ambiguity gave rise to endless confusion in economic arguments from Adam Smith's time down to near the end of the nineteenth century, and it must be borne constantly in mind by readers of what was written during that period.

In the chapter on Profits of Stock in the *Wealth of Nations*, Smith began by bringing to bear on profit the doctrine which he had taught about loan-interest in his lectures. Increase of stock, he says, "tends to lower profit." Competition caused by increase of stock employed in any trade lowers profit in that trade, "and when there is a like increase of stock in all the different trades carried on in the same society, the same competition must produce the same effect in them all." Here he gives no explanation of the manner in which competition acts, but in dealing with the converse case of "a diminution of the capital stock of the society," he argues that this diminution raises the rate of profit by lowering wages and at the same time raising prices:

> "By the wages of labour being lowered, the owners of what stock remains in the society can bring their goods at less expence to market than before, and less stock being employed in supplying the market than before, they can sell them dearer. Their goods cost them less, and they get more for them" (Vol. I. p. 95).

This is very unsatisfying, not only because the connection of wages with a diminution of capital and the connection of lower wages with a higher rate of profit on capital are difficult matters to unravel, but also because, as West pointed out in 1815,[1] it is fallacious to assume that because reduced production in a

[1] *Essay on the Application of Capital to Land*, pp. 20–23.

single trade will cause the products of that trade to rise in value, reduced production in all trades will cause the value of the products of all trades to rise in value. The value of each is reckoned in the others, and each cannot rise against all the others.

But in addition to this very unsatisfactory theory, Smith had a glimpse of something better. In trying to explain why "new colonies" have both high profits and high wages, though his general theory puts wages and profits in opposition to each other, he thinks of the investments of capital possible at any time being arranged in a scale of profitableness, and of the most profitable being naturally taken first, so that the larger the capital is, the lower down in the scale investment has to go, while competition reduces profit in the other investments to the same lower level (Vol. I. p. 94). But he had no clear idea of what constitutes profitableness in the sense of capacity to yield a high rate of profit on capital, and supposed it to depend on high fertility of soil and comparatively low wages.

§ 3. *The West–Ricardian Theory of the Rise and Fall of Profit.*

With the West–Ricardian theory of the causes of variation in the ratio between capital-value and annual value I dealt at considerable length in my *Theories of Production and Distribution.* Here I may pass much more lightly over it. Its great characteristic was its insistence on what West (in the preface to his *Price of Corn and Wages of Labour,* 1826) called the principle "that the diminution of the net reproduction or the profits of stock which is observed to take place in the progress of wealth and improvement must necessarily be caused by a diminution of the productive powers of labour in agriculture."

A ludicrously incorrect picture of primitive society was drawn. It was pictured as consisting of labourers absolutely without property on the one side and capitalist-employers on the other: the labourers were supposed to be granted a bare subsistence by the capitalist-employers, who were able to retain a very large profit because in that primitive state cultivation was not pushed very far, and so was extraordinarily productive and yielded a very large surplus over and above the subsistence of the workers.

It is easy, someone may object, to talk about " large " profits and surpluses, but largeness is relative, and what we want to know here is whether the surplus imagined was large in proportion to the capital employed. There was nothing on the face of the exposition to show that it was supposed to be so, but the belief that the workers only got a bare subsistence, coupled with the more absurd belief that early agriculture was very productive, involves the result that the capitalist-employers must have received an amount large in proportion to what they had spent in wages. And this, owing to the prevalent confusion of capital with a year's working expenses and the equally prevalent practice of ignoring all working expenses except wages, was taken to be practically, if not exactly, the same thing as an amount large in proportion to the capital employed.

The large profits of the primitive capitalist-employers were supposed to be diminished by the " progress of wealth and population " in this way: increase of population increased the demand for food and so raised the price of agricultural products: this increase of price would have made it possible to cultivate poorer land and to cultivate the old land more expensively without any reduction of profits if it were not for the fact that higher (money) wages must now be paid in order to enable the labourers to buy as much food as before, since the produce per head is smaller, which is equivalent to saying that the labourers get a larger proportion of the produce and a smaller proportion is left for the capitalists. That this smaller proportion meant a lower rate of profit on capital seemed fairly obvious when it was generally assumed that wages for a year sufficiently represented capital; if the amount required to pay the wages became a larger proportion of the whole produce than before, the profits left to the capitalist would necessarily be smaller in proportion to the wage-bill. Farmers using the better land could not escape the fall of profit by refusing to cultivate more expensively and so avoiding the decline of produce per head; they too would have to pay the higher wages and they would also have to pay higher rent.

Profits elsewhere than in agriculture were supposed to be simply regulated by the competition of agriculture. Ricardo rejected almost with contumely the common opinion " that profits on agriculture no more regulate the profits of commerce than the profits of commerce regulate the profits on agriculture," and "that they alternately take the lead."[1]

This grotesque theory became and remained what may be called the orthodox English doctrine for more than a generation. J. S. Mill made a pitiful attempt to restate and prove it, and long after his time it was taught to unfortunate youth, rather weakly in Fawcett's *Manual* and more uncompromisingly in Mrs. Fawcett's *Political Economy for Beginners*.

Hodgskin, in his *Popular Political Economy*, 1827 (pp. 226, 267), Chalmers, in his *Political Economy in connection with the moral state and moral prospects of Society*, 1832 (chap. i. §§ 2–7), and, more effectively, H. C. Carey, *Principles of Political Economy*, Pt. I., 1837 (p. 58), all pointed out the very obvious fact that the returns to agricultural labour had actually not diminished but had greatly increased in the course of "the progress of civilisation." This, of course, knocked the bottom out of the theory that the historical fall of the rate of profit was due to diminution of agricultural returns. But the believers in that theory took no notice, and the public clings to a discredited economic theory, as it does to a discredited religion, until a better is provided.

§ 4. *The Quantity and Utility Theory.*

Eventually a better theory was found in the doctrine that interest depends on the quantity and the utility of accumulated material equipment. Lord Lauderdale in his *Inquiry into the Nature and Origin of Public Wealth*, 1804, Mountifort Longfield in his *Lectures*, 1834, and von Thünen in *Der Isolirte Staat*, 1st ed., 1826, 2nd ed., 1842, all conceived the return on capital as arising from the fact that suitable instruments enable labour to produce more than it can without them in spite of the fact that the instruments may require repair and renewal, and that the labour necessary for this has to be added to the labour of working the instruments.

[1] *Essay*, in *Works*, p. 379; in *Econ. Essays*, p. 237. See also *Principles*, 1st ed., pp. 147–51; 3rd, pp. 132–5; and Cannan, *Production and Distribution*, pp. 282–4. Ricardo even alleged that the invention of machinery could never increase profits unless it was applied to cheapen the "food and necessaries of the labourer" (*Principles*, 1st ed., pp. 154–5; 3rd, 137–8; chap. vii, beginning).

Longfield and von Thünen carried the matter even further by explaining that the owners of the instruments could not expect to get the whole of the difference between what labour could produce with the instruments and what it could produce without them, because the competition of capitalists caused all the instruments to be supplied on terms which were no better than those which could be obtained where the advantage of employing them was least. As Longfield put it, a spade might make a man's labour twenty times more productive than it would be if he worked with his finger-nails, but the owner of the spade could not expect to get nineteen-twentieths of the resulting produce, since such-like instrumental equipment was abundant enough to enable and cause it to be used "in cases where it is not so capable of multiplying the efficiency of the labourer," and "the profits of this portion must regulate the profits of the rest."[1] As von Thünen put it, "the use of the last-applied increment of capital" fixes the height of the rate of interest.[2]

This at any rate should have given economists the cue for explaining the working of one great factor in the determination of the rate of interest, namely, variations in the amount of material equipment in the world. It is a well-established commonplace of commercial life that increase of capital tends to lower, and decrease of capital to raise, the rate of interest, and increase and decrease of "capital" in this context involves increase and decrease of houses and other buildings, fixed and movable machinery, improvements of land, convenient stocks of consumable goods and everything else which may be summed up under the head of material equipment. Under the play of motives provided by private property and competition, additions to this mass of material equipment will be made at the points considered most likely to give the best return; and if any casual destruction of part of the mass is effected, as, for instance, by earthquake, warlike operations, fire or flood, this part is likely to be restored in preference to adding new things elsewhere, because the restoration will give a better return. It follows that

[1] *Lectures on Political Economy*, p. 195, quoted more fully in Cannan, *Production and Distribution*, pp. 309–10.

[2] *Isolirte Staat*, quoted in Böhm-Bawerk, *Kapital und Kapitalzins*, 1884, p. 195, and in Marshall, *Principles*, 1st ed., 1890, p. 545 n., 8th ed., p. 522 n. Longfield also refers to "the last portion of capital brought into operation," *Lectures*, p. 193.

at any one time a tolerably uniform margin or frontier of investment is reached, and that increase of material equipment in this sense tends to reduce the rate of interest by compelling an advance of the frontier. If all the investments yielding, say, 5 per cent. and over are filled up and new savings come forward, investments which offer a prospect of somewhat less than 5 per cent. (and which were not made before because better returns could be found elsewhere) will be made.

Before 1890 Marshall, as references in the first edition of his *Principles* show, had become acquainted with von Thünen's work and thought highly of it. But there is no sign of such acquaintance in his 1879 *Economics of Industry*. The chapter on Interest (Book II. chap. x.) is very obscure, and treats the rate of interest too much as the result of a bargain between lenders and borrowers, regardless of the fact that most capital is not lent, and that when capital is lent, the rate which the borrowers will agree to pay depends on what return they can get. The "Law of the Normal Rate of Interest," we are told, is

> "When the economic conditions of a country have been nearly uniform for a long period of time, the supply of capital is such that the rate of interest which can be obtained for it is that which has been required to cause this supply to be forthcoming; and the rate thus determined is the Normal rate" (p. 126).

It would be difficult to beat this as an example of an "economic law" which gives no real information. The only redeeming feature in the exposition is that it does introduce invention as a thing which affects the rate of interest, taking the example of the invention of steam locomotion having "given room" for the employment of a great deal of capital, and thus "enabled capital to increase much faster than population without causing any fall in the rate of interest" (p. 126, bottom).

Sidgwick, in *Principles of Political Economy*, 1883, shows a great advance, and subsequent writers would have done well to have read and followed him instead of ignoring him. He says the rate of interest tends to correspond with the average additional produce expected from the "last increment of floating capital," and therefore varies with the "recognised opportunities of profitably using capital to aid labour" (Contents, p. xiii). He observes the fact, seldom if ever noticed before his time, and often ignored even now, that Invention may diminish as well as increase these recognised opportunities:

"Even if we could predict roughly the amount of improvement which the industry of the future may be expected to receive from invention, it would still be quite uncertain how far this improvement will involve the enlargement of the field of employment for capital. Hitherto inventions have generally had the effect of complicating and prolonging the processes of industry while at the same time increasing the ultimate productiveness of labour. But this has not always been the case; and so far as I know, there is no reason why the inventions of the future should not be chiefly in the direction of simplifying and abbreviating industrial processes; so that at each step of improvement the demand for capital will be restricted instead of being enlarged." [1]

Unfortunately at this stage the progress of theory as to the rise and fall of the rate of interest was interrupted by the publication of Böhm-Bawerk's *Kapital und Kapitalzins* in two parts, *Geschichte und Kritik der Kapitalzinstheorien*, 1884, and *Positive Theorie des Kapitales*, 1888, which were translated into English by Smart as *Capital and Interest*, and *The Positive Theory of Capital* in 1890 and 1891. These books, especially the first, diverted attention from the substantial question of the causes of the rise and fall of the rate of interest to the more difficult and much less useful question of the reason why there is any rate of interest at all. Böhm-Bawerk classified Thünen's theory of interest among the "indirect (*motivirte*) productivity theories," and he would have put Longfield's and Sidgwick's theories in the same class if he had been acquainted with them. While admitting that labour could produce more with the assistance of capital than without, he rejected productivity theories on the ground that the writers who put them forward never showed why the value of the capital and the value of the product should not be such, the first so great and the second so small, as to prevent any interest being obtainable. This very feeble argument—we will discuss it later on—apparently made economists somewhat afraid of adhering to any productivity theory and consequently weakened their explanations of the rise and fall of interest. Böhm-Bawerk's own explanation was perfectly useless. It did indeed ascribe the variations of the rate to altera-

[1] P. 158; cp. p. 289; in 2nd ed. pp. 152, 272, 383.

tions in the relative magnitude of population and capital and in the recognised opportunities of employing capital, but it was encumbered by a preposterous reversion to the conception of capital as a fund for the support of labourers during a "production period," and it shows nothing like Sidgwick's clear conception of the different effects of different kinds of invention.

In his *Principles* Marshall seems to have been still dominated by the idea that what is wanted is not comprehensive generalisations about the causes of rise and fall, but a statement confined to the effect of alterations in the rate on the amount of savings, and through this on the future of the rate itself. He therefore provides a formula resembling that already quoted from the early *Economics of Industry* :

"Thus then interest, being the price paid for the use of capital in any market, tends, like other values, towards an equilibrium level; and that equilibrium position is such that the aggregate demand for capital in that market, at that rate of interest, is equal to the aggregate stock forthcoming there at that rate" (1st ed., p. 625, 8th p. 534, omitting the words "like other values" and "and that equilibrium position is").

We may, however, gather from his brief references to the history of the rate that he believed the three great influences to be accumulation, which tends to reduce the rate, increase of population and invention, both of which, he holds, tend to raise the rate; I doubt if he anywhere shows appreciation of the effect of invention in lowering the rate (see esp. 1st ed., p. 723; 8th, pp. 680–1).

Irving Fisher in *The Rate of Interest*, 1907, endeavoured to improve upon Böhm-Bawerk, and made some important contributions to portions of the subject, but his doctrine is the same as Marshall's belief just quoted. "The thrift, foresight, self-control, and love of offspring which exist in a community" tend to lower the rate of interest, and "the progress of inventions" tends to raise it (p. 334). Invention is again conceived as only of the kind which requires elaborate material machinery.

Taussig, whose chapters on interest in *Principles of Economics*, 1911, are well worth attentive study, says (Vol. II. p. 14) "there seems to be substantial agreement among modern economists" that "at any given period the rate of return on capital depends on the gain in productiveness from the least effective part of the capital," which is true if a certain latitude in the interpretation of "least effective" be allowed. "The rate of interest for long periods—decades at a time—depends on the demand for capital with reference to a supply which is constantly and quasi-automatically increasing. It depends on a race between accumulation and improvement" (p. 27). We miss in this the usual inclusion of increase of population as a cause tending to raise the rate, but Taussig is doubtless here taking increase of capital as meaning increase of capital per head, which renders reference to population unnecessary. He does bring in population at the top of the next page. Though he makes "improvement" (the full phrase is "invention and improvement in the arts," p. 25) tend to increase the rate without qualification, it appears that he does not wish to deny that some kinds of "improvement" may tend to reduce the rate, but only to assert that such kinds are in fact more than counterbalanced by those which tend to raise the rate.[1] This may be true, but there is no possible way of proving it, and whether it is or not, it seems desirable to follow Sidgwick in insisting, as I did in *Wealth*, 1914 (pp. 135–6; 3rd ed., pp. 138–9), on the high importance of inventions which do away with the necessity of elaborate material machinery.

§ 5. *Application of the Theory.*

If the theory that the rate of interest tends to be raised by increase of population and a particular kind of invention, and to be reduced by increase of material equipment and a different kind of invention, is tried by the usual method of application to particular cases, both suppositious and real, it seems to stand the test well.

Let us begin by supposing the rate to be established at some figure, say 5 or 6 per cent., and ask what would be the effect of an enormous increase of population without any corresponding increase in the material equipment. The answer is that in the

[1] I infer this from the statement near the bottom of p. 25: "the progress of invention and of improvement in the arts . . . has never shifted the line to the left." A shifting of the line referred to towards the left would mean a fall of the rate of interest, and the proposition that improvement has never caused a fall seems to imply that it might have done so.

first place the annual value of the existing material equipment would rise. More houses will be urgently wanted, and though the people will be individually poorer, their greater number will enable them to pay more in the aggregate for the existing house-room. Railways and ships will bring in more to their owners per annum because there are more people to use them and to produce goods to be transported by them. Factories, commercial buildings, and plant of all kinds will also bring in more per annum because there are more people wanting their products. This, of course, would produce no rise of interest if the capital-value of all these things and of other material equipment rose *pari passu* with their annual value. But their capital-value will not be raised like their annual value by the increase of population. In time, of course, the increased population will save more, but for the moment there is by hypothesis no more capital for investment than there was before. The cost of new houses, buildings, and plant and machinery of all kinds will be less than before because labour will be plentiful and cheap. The conclusion is irresistible that annual value will rise in proportion to capital-value, or in other words the rate of interest will rise.

If anyone doubts, let him take the converse and more possible case of a large decrease of population—say in consequence of a new Black Death—and ask what the effect of that would be. Would not the effect quite obviously be to destroy altogether the return on a great deal of existing means of production, transport and distribution, and to lower the return on the rest? This would not affect the rate of interest if the capital-value of such as continued to bring in some income fell correspondingly. But it would not do so. The decrease of population would affect the new investments as well as the old; it would clearly become much more difficult to find any new 5 or 6 per cent. investments: owners of any additional capital coming forward would have the choice between new and old investments, and their reluctance to accept the poor return of the new would tend to maintain the capital-value of the old.

Next let us take changes in the material equipment in the shape of improved land, buildings, machinery, and convenient stocks of all kinds of things. It is true that change here is only the reverse aspect of change in population, since the one thing has to be thought of in relation to the other. Nevertheless it may be well to look directly at this aspect also.

Suppose first an increase of material equipment while the population remains stationary. We have already certain houses, factories, railways, ships, and other material equipment bringing in a certain revenue per annum. Add largely to them without any addition to the population, and how can we expect to get as good a return on the new capital invested as on what was invested before? The annual value of an additional house, factory, or line of railway will be less than before, and nothing has happened to suggest that it will cost any less to provide such items. If the new investor, confronted by the smaller return offered by available additions to the material equipment, turns to the old investments and attempts to buy up existing houses, factories, etc., he raises their capital-value and lowers the rate of interest there also.

If anyone doubts, let him do the same as he did with the change in population—turn the question the other way about and ask what would happen if the material equipment diminished while the population remained the same. Supposing the diminution takes place by way of indiscriminate destruction, as by earthquake or warlike operations, some of the parts destroyed may be so important that it will be decided to restore them at the expense of less important parts. For example, if a portion of the main L.M.S. line between London and Rugby were destroyed, it would be worth while to tear up the rails of the Aylesbury branch in order to restore it if there were no unemployed rails to be had. Supposing, on the other hand, the process of diminution was gradual and understood, arising from the fact that the people as a whole were not maintaining their material equipment unimpaired, the least important parts—those which would reduce income least by their disappearance—would be selected for non-renewal. If the L.M.S. shareholders are to "live on their capital" by "starving the line," the management must let the line deteriorate, and when the deterioration becomes extreme enough to force abandonment of some of it, the Aylesbury branch will be allowed to go before the main line. Thus, whether the diminution of material equipment be the result of indiscriminate destruction or of deliberate and calculated neglect, it will result in the withdrawal of capital from the less profitable employments and tend to confine it to those in which the return is higher.

As to invention, everyone can see that inventions like that of the steam locomotive pulling vehicles on rails tend to raise the rate of interest. That invention made transport much easier, but it required not only a road-bed and rails but heavy cuttings, embankments, and tunnels to avoid steep gradients, so that its exploitation absorbed an enormous amount of the world's savings for many years, and thus prevented the necessity of investing in less profitable ways.

Nor, when the fact is once pointed out, is it difficult to see that there are inventions which work in the opposite direction, by showing us how to do things more easily with less elaborate material equipment, or, which comes to the same thing, enable us to get more service out of the same material equipment. Examples of this kind of invention are not so obvious as those of the other kind, because when a machine is improved by greater elaboration there is something to show—an elaborate machine to admire; but when a machine is improved by simplification or when an improved method does away with a machine altogether, the superseded machine is broken up and disappears, so that there is no opportunity of saying, "Look at this great clumsy machine costing thousands of pounds which we do not now require." For examples of this kind of invention we may point to the discoveries which have made it possible to transmit many more messages on one line of telegraph, and which have made it possible by methods of control to put much more traffic on a single or double line of rails.

When we think of these various factors together, it does not seem surprising that interest was enormous in early times when material equipment was extremely scarce, that it fell rapidly in the seventeenth century when accumulation was rapid and the increase of population slow, and that it has fluctuated rather than moved steadily in either direction during the subsequent period in which the growth of population and elaborating invention have fought on one side with varying success against the growth of capital and simplificatory invention on the other.

§ 6. "*Spendthrift Demand for Capital.*"

Some readers are sure to complain that I have made no mention of what is often called the "spendthrift demand for capital," the demand of those who borrow not in order that they may procure and use some instrument which they expect to yield a money-income like a factory, but in order that they may be able to spend more money on themselves, their families, and perhaps their friends. The old common example of this kind of borrower was the roystering "landlord" who mortgaged his land in order to have money to spend on his horses, his dogs, and his drunken friends; the modern example is the government which carries on a war with borrowed money, especially if it is unsuccessful. "Does not such conduct," it will be asked, "quite obviously tend to raise the rate of interest?"

The answer is that spending of this kind undoubtedly tends to raise the rate of interest, but that I have already taken account of the fact in making accumulation tend to reduce the rate of interest. The important thing is not that the roystering landlord borrows, but that he spends. The borrowing enables him to spend more than his income, but he could spend just as much (and a little more) by selling his land or parts of it and living on the proceeds. If he sold instead of borrowing, no one would think of saying he was "demanding capital" and raising the rate of interest by selling; but so far as the whole community is concerned, his selling and his borrowing come to the same thing. In both cases he is simply negativing the savings of others and making the accumulation of the whole community less than it would be if he spent less. When we talk of accumulation tending to reduce the rate of interest, we mean the net accumulation of the whole community, not the gross accumulation of private property by individuals, which is partly counterbalanced by the decumulation effected by the spendthrifts.

The borrowing of the spendthrift government should be looked on in just the same light as that of the spendthrift landlord. The only difference is that while the landlord cannot borrow more than the value of his property, since no lender will trust his promise to earn enough to pay the interest, the government can raise much more by borrowing than the selling value of such property as it has. It can do so because the lenders trust it to be able and willing to collect the interest by levying taxes from people unable or unwilling to remove their property and their persons from the area subject to its jurisdiction. But this does not in the least alter the essential fact that the spendthrift government is negativing the savings of private persons and thereby preventing the accumulation of the community from being as great as it otherwise would be.

The question may perhaps be represented as one of mere phraseology. Suppose that the cost of the war of 1914–18 had all been borrowed by the governments concerned, and that this borrowing had just used up all the savings made by private persons during the period, and that the equipment of the world was left just the same at the end of the war as it was at the beginning. I should say then that no accumulation had taken place, and if the population had remained unaltered and no inventions had been made, I should expect the rate of interest to be unaltered. Those who think of "spendthrift demand" as tending to raise the rate of interest would also say it would be unaltered, but would explain the fact by saying that the supply of capital had just balanced the demand (industrial plus "spendthrift"), and would regard the national debts as additions to the capital. This will be reasonable enough if we identify "capital" with the private property of individuals, and the meaning we ascribe to a word is only a question of nomenclature.

That there was, however, some real confusion of mind about the effect of government borrowing is shown by the discussion which took place during the war of 1914–18 between persons who thought that borrowing compelled posterity to pay for the war, and those who thought that whether the money was raised by taxes or loans made no difference to posterity, since the cost of the war, in fact, had to be paid day by day at the time. Here neither party was quite right. It was true that the war had to be paid for day by day at the time, but there were two sources from which the cost could be met: first, diminution of unnecessary expenditure on other things, and second, diminution of additions to equipment. Now taxes no doubt do to some extent tend to diminish additions to equipment by making people able to save less, but, unless quite extraordinarily bad, they do not tend to diminish them so much as government borrowing: the money borrowed comes entirely from savers and is looked on by them as an investment, whereas the money raised by taxes comes partly from persons who are not saving at all and are therefore obliged to cut down their consumption, unless they have property and pay out of capital, which rarely happens. Moreover, the portion of the tax-receipts which comes from savers will not be wholly taken from savings, but will be found in part by reduction of the savers' consumption. Consequently, raising the cost by borrowing was less favourable to the maintenance and increase of the equipment than raising it by taxes, and the greater the proportion raised by borrowing, therefore, the smaller the equipment left to "posterity" in the sense intended of persons surviving the war.

§ 7. *Meaning of "The Rate of Interest."*

At this point it is probable some obstructive objector will ask, "But what right have you to talk as if there were only one ratio of value between capital and income—only one rate of interest? Look at this stockbroker's list of investments and you will see that dividends differ enormously, many being *nil* and some over 100 per cent. per annum."

The answer to this is, firstly, that the differences of dividends are not always real differences in the return on the original investment; since—

(*a*) In a few (and diminishing number of) cases dividends are "declared free of tax," while in most cases they are subject to tax. When the income-tax is 4*s*. in the pound or one-fifth, and a profit of 5 per cent. made by a company is to be divided among the shareholders, the company may declare a dividend of 5 per cent. and deduct one-fifth from each dividend-warrant or declare a dividend "tax-free" of 4 per cent. and pay this in full, but in both cases the shareholders and the national revenue get the same amounts.[1]

(*b*) Very often the existing capital sum on which the dividends are reckoned does not accurately represent the original sum

[1] A shareholder who is exempt from income-tax recovers from the tax-collecting agency the same sum (one-fifth of the £5, one-fourth of the £4) whether the dividend is "free" or "subject."

invested. A "hundred pounds" of $2\frac{1}{2}$ p. c. Consols may have been originally taken up in Pitt's time at about 60—that is to say, the original investment was not £100 but only £60, on which the £2 10*s*. now paid is $4\frac{1}{6}$ per cent. On the other hand, a "hundred pounds" of Great Western Railway stock may have been part of an issue made at 150 in the eighteen-nineties, so that a dividend of 6 per cent. on it would be only 4 per cent. on the amount invested. Many very high dividends are explainable by accumulations made long ago out of undivided profits; in the past the company did not distribute the whole of the actual profits, but put part into the business, so that the dividends of the present are calculated on a capital smaller than the amount actually invested.

(*c*) The dividends in the stockbroker's list are only for the one year immediately past, which may have been abnormal. To find the real return on the original investment we should have before us the whole of the dividends from the beginning and into an indefinite future. If *nil* was paid for a hundred years, 50 per cent. per annum for ever afterwards would not be as good as 3 per cent. from the beginning would have been.

All this, and the explanation of many other differences which are only apparent, is easy enough. But when all such apparent differences are explained away, there still remains enormous diversity of returns.

Part of this, however, obviously arises from the fact that the original investments were made at different times. The fact of investments made at different times having different returns would be, of course, perfectly compatible with the most absolute uniformity of the rate of interest at any one time. We should expect to find investments made in the eighteen-nineties when the rate was low to be now yielding less than those made lately when the rate has been higher.

But there is, in fact, great diversity of return even among investments made at the same time. Investments are made in the hope of future return without any certain knowledge of what the future will bring. Some fall short of even modest expectations, others exceed the wildest anticipations.

It is really impossible to hold the doctrine that the rate of interest is uniform at any one time and place if the rate is understood to be the return actually obtained. But the most extreme diversity does not preclude the existence of an average, and I think it is really the average that we are thinking of and should think of, when we discuss the causes of variations in the rate.

To this it may be objected that what exactly the average for each period is will not be known before the Day of Judgment, since investments do not as a rule work themselves out in a short period of time like those of Böhm-Bawerk's supposititious fishermen. This is true, but fortunately for purposes of general economic theory we do not require to know exactly what the rate is at any time. It is sufficient for us to know that whatever it is, certain things will tend to raise it and others to lower it.

When we must refer to the actual rate, as when we try to check our theory by reference to history, we can for modern times take the opinion of "the market"—the persons who buy and sell stock-exchange securities—as an indicator. These persons show what they think by varying the prices of securities which give a definite and certain income. If the prospects of high returns in new enterprises are considered good, the price of securities yielding fixed and certain incomes naturally falls, because it seems more relatively advantageous to invest in the new enterprises than to take up, buy, or continue to hold (at the old prices) the securities yielding a given fixed income.

Of course this market is not infallible; it is sometimes too optimistic and sometimes too pessimistic, and possibly on the whole inclines too much one way or the other, we do not know which. But any permanent bias it may have is probably slight, and we can smooth out its temporary fluctuations by taking averages over a year or two instead of being content with the prices of a particular moment. It would be rash to assume that because very safe securities yielding £4 per annum are valued on an average in some year at £100, exactly 4 per cent. is the return which will actually be obtained on an average by all the investments made in that year, but we may be pretty sure that in the absence of quite extraordinary events it will not be as much as 6 per cent. nor as little as 3 per cent.; and we may be quite sure that if in some subsequent year the same or similar securities are priced at only £80, the rate will have risen.

For earlier periods, during which there was no market dealing in securities, we can do little more than try to deduce what the actual return on investments must have been from our knowledge of the rates of interest charged for short-term loans, and this is fragmentary and likely to be misleading.

To conceive "the rate of interest" at any time as the average obtained, or at any rate reasonably expected to be obtained, by investments made at that time, appears to be much more convenient than to conceive it as the rate which can be obtained without "risk." Marshall gives us the example of a mediæval prince who borrowed a thousand ounces of silver, promising to repay it at the end of a year with five hundred ounces in addition:

"There was, however, no perfect security that he would fulfil the promise; and perhaps the lender would have been willing to exchange that promise for an absolute certainty of receiving thirteen hundred at the end of the year. In that case, while the nominal rate at which the loan was made was fifty per cent., the real rate was thirty.

"The necessity for making this allowance for insurance against risk is so obvious that it is not often overlooked." (*Principles*, 8th ed., p. 588.)

Now if the lender had in fact got a third party of undoubted solvency to guarantee principal and interest on condition of the lender undertaking to pay him two hundred pounds at the end of the year, the lender would get at the end of the year 1500 less 200, that is, 1300, and therefore might quite truly be said to have "really" only got 30 per cent. instead of the full 50 paid by the borrower, and the borrower might perhaps be said to have promised to pay 30 per cent. interest and 20 per cent. "insurance against risk." But there is not the faintest suggestion that any such guarantee was secured or that insurance of any kind was effected. It is vastly improbable that the borrower paid 1300 and no more. Probably he paid the whole 1500 as promised: if not, he most likely paid neither interest nor principal at all. If he paid in full there is no reason for saying he only paid 30 per cent. interest; and if he did not pay at all, he certainly paid neither interest nor "insurance."

It would, of course, be more reasonable to say that the lender only got 30 per cent. on the whole if he lent out, say, 100 sums of £1000 at 50 per cent. per annum to 100 persons, only 60 of whom paid and continued to pay, while the other 40 defaulted, since he would then get £30,000 a year from his original capital; but this simply means a reversion to the conception of "the rate of interest" as an average of all the rates obtained. The suggestion that the lenders get something for taking "risk" and the borrowers pay it disappears. What is above the average only compensates for what is below.

A refinement on the doctrine that something is received and paid for risk is that something is received and paid for "uncertainty-bearing." It seems to be supposed that the risky investments on the whole, the bad being taken with the good, yield rather more return than the safe ones, which is true if the term "risky" is taken in the sense of involving risks of the kind which tend to deter owners of capital from investing. Then the extra yield is said to be payment for "uncertainty-bearing," and is thus something[1] over and above interest, which is supposed to be payment for abstinence or "waiting." This too makes "the rate of interest" somewhat less than the average rate of interest as commonly conceived by ordinary persons, and is obviously inconvenient. It may be regarded as the last dying kick of the doctrine that value depends on "real costs" in "efforts and sacrifices."

§ 8. *The Rate of interest on Short-term Loans.*

Doctrine such as we have been discussing about the rate of interest obtained on investments seems at first sight to have very little relation to the rate charged and obtained on loans for short periods and loans repayable on demand. Rates here seem at first sight bewilderingly different to different classes of borrowers and on different classes of loans. To take only the most prominent examples, we have in this country the Bank of England publishing a rate at which it professes to be willing to discount approved bills of exchange, while the other banks offer a rate 1½ or even sometimes 2 per cent. below that "bank rate" on "deposit accounts," which means money lent to them repayable at a week's notice, and either less than this or nothing at all on "current accounts," which means money lent to them repayable

[1] But not much; see Pigou, *Economics of Welfare*, 1920, p. 920, n. 1.

immediately without notice; at the same time these banks will be lending money under individual agreements with each customer, some of it repayable at any time at the option of the borrower, and some repayable on fixed dates at rates not uniform, but all appreciably higher than the bank rate. Neither the bank rate nor any of the other rates correspond at all closely in their variations with the investment rate.

The most remarkable discrepancy appears in the fact that while the average investment rate may be 5 per cent., a large number of the banks' customers lend the banks hundreds of millions in the aggregate by keeping credit balances on which they get either interest well below the investment rate or nothing at all. Why do they not invest the money and get the investment rate? The answer is easy; for the same reason as they keep a certain amount of cash in their pockets or tills without investing it. It is extremely inconvenient to have all your property "locked up," as the phrase is, in the form of lands, houses, goods, and other such things, and not to have a shilling wherewith to purchase a frugal lunch. It is only a little less inconvenient to have it so locked up that you have not got twenty or fifty pounds wherewith to pay your quarter's rent or your child's school bill. You cannot arrange your income so that it comes in just at the moment when it is wanted for expenses and in blocks of exactly the right size. You might, of course, keep the same reserve in cash in the house, but that is either risky or productive of trouble and expense in precautions against fire and thieves: moreover, if the bank pays no interest, it very probably performs some services gratis, such as giving you cheque forms (which are so much more convenient than cash for making payments that you are ready to pay *2d.* stamp duty on them rather than forgo their use), and perhaps receiving dividends for you.

But while this may explain the customers' willingness to let the banks have their money for nothing or at a very low rate, why, it may be asked, does not competition between banks and the desire of each bank to get more business compel or induce them to offer better terms? The answer is firstly, and chiefly, that the services already mentioned which are furnished by the banks to their customers cost the banks large amounts in premises and salaries, and secondly, that the banks do not actually get the free use of the whole of the money entrusted to them. To be solvent in the long run and on the whole is no use to a bank. Each of its branches must be able at all business hours to meet all demands that will in fact be made upon it, and in practice, though these can be foretold with considerable accuracy, the caution of managers will lead to considerably more being kept than eventually turns out to have been necessary.

Other differences of rates can be explained on the same or similar principles. For example, a loan which is repayable, and will certainly be repaid, on a fixed and early date is obviously more convenient to the lender than one which, even if nominally repayable at short notice from the lender, may in practice be irrecoverable for a considerable period.

That the rates charged by the banks and the rates allowed by them to their customers are not very unreasonable is shown by the fact that a small diminution of the difference between the rates at which they borrow and the rates at which they lend would sweep away the whole of their profit.

§ 9. *The Rate of Interest when Money is Appreciating or Depreciating.*

We have so far assumed that the purchasing power of money remains stable. When it does not, some complications are introduced. The best way of approaching them is to begin by thinking of interest reckoned in something other than money. In practice interest is never now bargained for in anything but money, but it clearly might be. The Jewish law forbade "usury of victuals." There is nothing to prevent anyone making a loan of a hundred bushels of wheat at an interest of 5 bushels of the same quality of wheat per annum; this would be a 5 per cent. per annum loan just as much as a loan of £100 at £5 per annum. No one will find any difficulty in seeing that if a loan were contracted on these terms, the lender would gain by any appreciation of wheat during the continuance of the loan, and lose by any depreciation. And it is not much more difficult, though it may require slightly more thought, to see that the borrower would lose by the appreciation and gain by the depreciation of wheat; his object in borrowing cannot be merely to hold the wheat—if he did that he would simply lose the cost of storage and the 5 bushels of interest. He must intend to part with the wheat in exchange for some other commodities or services, and expect to get in consequence enough of some kind of product to make him able to pay the 5 bushels per annum and (if required) the 100 bushels of principal lent. If the 105 bushels are gradually growing to be worth more of other things at the end of the year it will obviously be more difficult for him to find them than if they continue with the same purchasing power, or, still better, if they decline in purchasing power.

Consequently, if, while wheat was appreciating, lenders insisted on lending nothing but wheat, and that for wheat-interest only, borrowers would hold out, and hold out successfully, for a lower rate of interest; and if borrowers insisted on borrowing wheat at wheat-interest when wheat was depreciating, lenders would hold out, and hold out successfully, for a higher rate of interest.

And if it were the practice to make loans and pay interest upon them in a dozen different commodities, and these commodities were all known to be varying in value at different rates, there would be a dozen different rates of interest at the same time and place.

In fact, as I have already remarked, loans are never now made on terms of interest being paid in commodities other than money. But it has sometimes happened that two kinds of money, one of which was known to be depreciating in value rapidly while the other was regarded as approximately stable, have been used in loan transactions at the same time, and then two widely different rates of interest have appeared side by side. In Austria, for example, during the great inflation which followed the war of 1914–18, the rate of interest in Austrian crowns, which were known to be depreciating rapidly, was vastly greater than the rate in Swiss francs, which were regarded as approximately stable.

The principle works, though not so obviously, when there is only one money in use and all transactions are effected in it. When a money which has been stable begins to depreciate, at first all that happens is that lenders lose and borrowers gain, but this does not go on very long before the effort to borrow more and more in order to participate in the gain, combined with the growing reluctance of lenders to lend (instead of buying commodities and services for themselves), drives up the rate of interest, which in case of extreme depreciation of money such as that of the German mark in 1923 will go to almost incredible heights. In the converse case, where money which has been stable begins to appreciate, at first all that happens is that lenders gain and borrowers lose, but soon the borrowers become more reluctant to borrow and the lenders more anxious to lend, so that the rate of interest is driven down. But the effect of appreciation is never so spectacular as that of depreciation, since appreciation is never in practice carried to such lengths as depreciation.

The capital-value (in the depreciating or appreciating money) of fixed annuities of money of course varies inversely with the rate of interest; if money depreciates and the rate of interest rises, the capital-value of all fixed annuities falls in proportion.

But there is nothing in all this to suggest that depreciation of money raises the rate of the real return on capital, or that appreciation lowers it. When the rate of interest is raised by depreciation, the lender keeps his money-capital intact, and gets more money annually for his loan, but both the capital sum and the income sum are declining in value, so that he is no better off than with lower interest paid in stable money. When the rate of interest is reduced by appreciation, the lender keeps his money-capital intact and gets less money annually for his loan, but both the capital-sum and the income-sum are rising in value, so that he is no worse off than with higher interest paid in stable money. To put it in another way, if the capital were lent and the interest paid in a stable medium, the ratio of the one to the other would be unchanged.

We may be tempted to follow Marshall (*Principles*, 8th ed., p. 594) in applying the term "nominal" to the rate in the appreciating or depreciating money, and thinking of the rate which might be paid in a stable medium as the "real rate." But to call something which occurs, and is well known to ordinary persons, "nominal," and something else which is only imagined, "real," is generally likely to cause confusion. It is especially undesirable when the so-called "real" thing is dependent on a necessarily makeshift measurement of general purchasing power such as is provided by index-numbers of prices.[1] It seems

[1] See Irving Fisher, *The Rate of Interest*, 1907, pp. 84–5, and chap. xi.

much better to be content with saying that when money is appreciating or depreciating, the rate of interest, as commonly understood, is not to be accepted without correction as indicating the real return obtained on the investment of capital; the reason being that the units in which the capital is reckoned at the time of lending are larger or smaller in value than the units in which both it and the interest on it are reckoned as the loan grows older.

§ 10. *Why is there a Rate of Interest?*

If the question, Why is there a rate of interest? is put in the form "Why is there a ratio between capital-value and income-value?" it looks rather silly, but a vast amount of learning and ingenuity has been spent upon it by Böhm-Bawerk and others. I have kept it to the end of the chapter not as a *bonne bouche*, but because I think the answer to it is a mere corollary to the answer to the question, What makes the rate rise and fall? If we know what causes the rate to fall, we ought to be able to say easily enough why, in fact, in the world we know, it is more than zero per cent.

We have seen that increase of knowledge, if it took the direction of showing how our desires might be easily satisfied without instruments of enjoyment and production—without land, houses and beds, ploughs and power-looms and all other things of which convenient stocks exist in civilised life—would tend to reduce the rate of interest. If this went far enough, it would mean that we could get everything we wanted without any instruments or stocks of things at least as easily, if not more easily, than when we were provided with such things.

There would be still some demand for loans in the sense that A would desire B to work for him in the present in exchange for A's promise to work for B at some future time, but it seems unlikely that this demand would not be more than balanced by the desire of B and others like-minded to secure provision for old age by working for A in the present in exchange for A's promise to work for them in the future, so that on the whole this would be more likely to produce a negative than a positive rate of interest.

Thus one of the reasons for the existence of a rate of interest is the fact that our present state of knowledge makes a stock of instruments and other things desirable. If it did not, the rate would probably be negative.

Next we must have regard to the fact that accumulation tends to reduce the rate. If accumulation proceeded far and fast enough, and was not counteracted by more demand caused by increase of population and changes in knowledge of the appropriate character, it would increase the fertility and other good qualities of land and make such liberal provision of stocks of tools and other things that all would be present in such quantities that nobody would work a single minute in order to have the use of more of them, coupled, as usual, with the obligation of maintaining them.

So we can say—if we think it worth saying—that another of the causes of the existence of a rate of interest is the limited quantity of accumulated material equipment.

If we are asked the rather childish question, "But why are these tools and other things so limited in quantity? Why aren't there enough of them to reduce the annual value to *nil?*" the answer is that the world could not have produced enough even if it had denied itself everything except the barest necessaries of life and efficiency from the earliest times down to the present moment, and of course it has not so denied itself, and would have been very foolish if it had.

Thirdly, we must remember that diminution of population tends to reduce the rate of interest. If the population disappeared entirely, interest would, of course, disappear with it, so that we may say—again if we think it worth saying—that one of the conditions required for the existence of the rate of interest is the existence of people who live, work, and produce.

In conclusion we may remark that those who find something mysterious in the existence of a rate of interest should consider what a strange universe that would be in which there was no rate of interest, although people existed and maintained the institution of property. Can we even imagine a state of things in which no instruments either of production or direct enjoyment (including land) were desirable? Can we imagine a state of things in which such instruments were desirable but were so plentiful that everyone could have as much of them (in quantity and quality) as he wished for? The supposition, be it remembered, involves land and houses and machines of all kinds being absolutely worthless, since limitation of available quantity is necessary for the emergence of value.

When we are invited to wonder why we can purchase a perpetual annuity of £100 a year or a piece of land yielding a clear income of £100 a year for twenty or thirty years' purchase, and it is suggested that we should naturally expect to be asked to pay the sum of £100 + £100 + £100 . . . and so on into an infinite future, let us reply that a world in which the value of every annuity, whatever its amount, and every piece of rent-bearing land, whatever the annual rent, was infinite, appears to us a very much odder one than that in which we live and in which people's capacity to buy future income is limited by their means.

Böhm-Bawerk seems inclined to shirk this infinity issue. In his criticism of "Turgot's fructification theory" he says, "Accidents apart, a piece of land will yield its rent for a practically (*praktisch*) infinite series of years. The possession of it assures the owner and his heirs the amount of the yearly use, not for twenty or forty times only, but for many hundred times—almost (*fast*) for an infinite number of times" (*Capital and Interest*, p. 67; in the original p. 77). Why "practically" and "almost"? So too in dealing with Land Rent in the *Positive Theory*, p. 355, after speaking of a quarry exhausted in a hundred years, he says, "the case of all other lands is different from that of the quarry, but only in degree. If a field is considered capable of producing crops for 1000 years—or 2000 years if one should prefer it, for literal infinity in human affairs is out of court—and if the future crops are to be valued as highly as the present ones, the valuation will reach an exorbitant height, viz. £100,000 or £200,000, and the yearly rent of £100 will present the character of a breaking-off of the parent stem of wealth—a very gradual destruction of the stem, but still a destruction, not a net income. Landowners would be lords of a giant stem or stock of wealth, but they would have no net income." This cutting down of infinity to 2000 years' purchase serves to put out of sight the impossibility of the price of the land being equal to £100 + £100 + £100 . . . continued indefinitely.

Similarly, in dealing with income derived from possession of instruments other than land, Böhm-Bawerk likes to hide away the permanence of the improvement in man's position arising from their possession. In the fisherman example which he adopted from Roscher (*Capital and Interest*, pp. 112–14; and see above, Chap. VI. § 2) the fisherman is supposed able to catch 3 fish per day when he has no boat nor net, and 30 when he has a boat and net; it takes him 50 days to make the boat and net, and being apparently very short-lived and subject to sudden dissolution, these articles last quite well for 100 days' actual fishing, and then are completely worn out. On these suppositions Böhm-Bawerk says, "the surplus of products due to the employment of capital is represented for the whole period by $3000 - (150 \times 3) = 3000 - 450 = 2550$ fish, and for each single day by $\frac{3000}{150} - 3 = 17$ fish. In this surplus of products is manifested the physical productivity of capital."

There would be no objection to this if it had been confined to the statement that the advantage of having and using the "capital" could be reckoned at 17 fish *per day*, but the inclusion of the statement that "for the whole period" it amounts to 2550 is quite misleading. Of course the advantage only begins when the fisherman has completed the construction of the boat and net. But from that time onward the surplus of 17 fish per day continues indefinitely, "barring accidents" as with land. Once equipped with boat and net—"provided with capital"—the fisherman catches 30 instead of 3 fish per full fishing day and gives one-third of his working time to repair and renewal of the boat and net, so that on the average for each working day (work including repairing and renewing the boat and net) he catches 20 fish, which is 17 more than the 3 he would have caught without the boat and net. Then, by the time he has worn out the first boat and net by 100 days' actual fishing, he will have given 50 days' work to the construction of new ones, and thus will be as well equipped as before, and be able to enjoy the 20 fish per day not only for those 150 days but for all time, so long as he pursues the same line of conduct.

CHAPTER X

THE CLASSIFICATION AND "DISTRIBUTION" OF INCOME

§ 1. *Anticipations of the Classification into Wages, Profit and Rent.*

THE traditional classification of incomes into rent, profits and wages or into four shares obtained by a slight modification of that classification has become so firmly implanted in the minds of most economic students that it seems almost shocking to suggest that it did not fall down from heaven as an inspired revelation but was evolved from circumstances with no claim to universality. Yet, in fact, without going further away in place or time, we may probably quite safely conjecture that no ancient Greek, Roman or Hebrew, nor even any mediæval thinker, ever classified all income under these three heads. Aristotle, it may be said, had some idea of profit from trade and money-lending and of wages for labour, but these he regarded as unnatural methods of acquisition arising in a not very reputable way from exchange. Rent he does not think of at all, and we may be sure that it would not be thought of anywhere or at any time except in a small corner of the world for a small period of its history.

The first beginnings of the classification may be detected in the seventeenth century in England when the "land lord" found himself a "land owner" (as we say), the possessor of a valuable object which he could let for money rather than a feudal superior enjoying certain dues from his semi-servile men. Petty speculated about the determination of rent, and both he and Davenant estimated its amount in England. Moreover, Petty's estimate of the national aggregate income, making the land yield £8,000,000, the "other estate" £7,000,000 and "the labour of the people" furnish the remaining £25,000,000 of the total of £40,000,000 (*Verbum Sapienti*, 1691, in *Econ. Writings*, ed. Hull, p. 108), certainly anticipates the classification into wages, profit and rent. But this anticipation is a statistical accident rather than a contribution to economic theory. The income from property other than land is described as yielded by houses, ships, cattle, coin and "wares, merchandises and utensils of plate and furniture"; it is not called "profit" nor spoken of as belonging to a distinct class of persons. To give this class of income the place which it won in later economics it was necessary that the modern evolution of economic organisation should be somewhat further advanced.

By the time that Cantillon wrote his essay—about 1730—the prominent feature in the agricultural organisation of England and important parts of France had come to be the letting of land to farmers and the employment of labourers by those farmers. It was natural for those who were familiar with this organisation to think of the persons engaged in agriculture as consisting of the landlords, the farmers and the labourers. Other industries were obviously coming to be very largely organised by persons who worked a business and employed wage-earners in the same way as the farmers, and with the same motive, the acquisition of profit. It is not surprising that the farmers and the other employers came to be classed together. In his chapter on the Par between the value of land and labour Cantillon says: "The farmers in Europe seem to correspond with the overseers of slave agricultural labourers in other countries, and the master-craftsmen who employ several journeymen seem to correspond with the overseers of slave craftsmen" (p. 51), and at the beginning of chap. xii in Part I he merges the agricultural and manufacturing employers in a larger class of "entrepreneurs," who, with the King and landlords and the wage-earners, make up the whole society.

The word "undertaker" had already in his time been long used in ordinary English of a person who has engaged in or undertaken some business or other "on his own account," which means in such a way that the profit, if any, will go to him, and the loss, if any, will be borne by him. In the English of everyday life it has since become specialised in the narrower sense of the person who undertakes the business of disposing of corpses in the conventional manner, though many such persons now prefer to call themselves by some other name, such as "funeral furnisher." But it is still used in the old sense by the draftsmen of Acts of Parliament and provisional orders relating to such businesses as the providing of water, gas and electricity. Cantillon must have been familiar with it, and if he wrote his Essay in English, no one can doubt that "undertaker" must have appeared in it wherever "*entrepreneur*" occurs in the French version which has come down to us. And if that version was composed by him in French, we cannot doubt that he chose the word "*entrepreneur*" as the proper French equivalent of the English "undertaker." His *Essai*, therefore, when it describes the nature and function of the "*entrepreneur*," may safely be taken to be giving his view of the nature and function of the "undertaker," and in quoting it I re-translate "*entrepreneur*" back again into the original "undertaker."

Chapter xiii of Part I of the Essay is headed "The circulation and exchange of raw produce and merchandize, as well as their production, is carried on in Europe by undertakers and on speculation (*au hazard*)." It begins by saying:

> "The farmer is an undertaker who promises to pay the landlord for his farm or land a fixed sum of money without knowing for certain how much he will get out of the undertaking (*entreprise*)."

He cannot foresee all the events which may affect the quantity and the price of his output, "and consequently he manages the undertaking of his farm in uncertainty (*avec incertitude*)." Persons set up as undertakers (*s'érigent en entrepreneurs*) of the carriage of his produce to the nearest town. They bind themselves to pay him a certain price (*un prix certain*), the market price of the day, with the intention of themselves realising in the town an uncertain price which must meet their expenses "and leave them a profit on their undertaking (*un profit pour leur entreprise*)," while the variation of prices in the town makes this profit uncertain. Other persons set up as merchants (*marchands*) or undertakers and buy the raw produce, giving a certain price for it with the view of selling it again either wholesale or retail at an uncertain price.

> "These undertakers can never know the amount of consumption in their town nor even how long their customers (*chalans*) will buy from them, seeing that their competitors (*rivaux*) will try in all

sorts of ways to attract customers (*les pratiques*) from them; all this causes so much uncertainty for all these undertakers that bankruptcies occur among them daily" (p. 66).

The manufacturer who buys wool cannot tell what profit he will get from his undertaking when he sells his cloth to the draper; change of fashion may ruin his sales. The draper is an undertaker who buys at a certain price from the manufacturer in order to sell at an uncertain price, since he cannot foresee the amount of the consumption:

"It is true that he can fix a price and resolve not to sell unless he gets it, but if his customers (*ses pratiques*) leave him in order to buy cheaper from someone else, he will be eaten up (*il se consumera*) by expenses while waiting to sell at the price he fixes, and this will ruin him as much as or more than if he sells without profit.

"Shopkeepers and all kinds of retail dealers are undertakers who buy at a certain price and sell in their shops or in public places at an uncertain price" (pp. 67, 68).

The number of these undertakers suits itself to the number and the consumption of their customers (*chalans*). If there are too many hatters in a town, those that get the least custom (*les plus mal achalandés*) go bankrupt. If there are too few, the profitableness of the undertaking will encourage new hatters to open shops, "and it is thus that undertakers of all kinds become proportioned to the speculative prospects (*se proportionnent au hazard*) in a country."

"All the other undertakers, such as those who take charge of mines, of entertainments (*spectacles*), of buildings, etc., merchants in domestic and foreign trade, sellers of cooked food, pastrycooks, public-house keepers, as well as those who are undertakers in their own labour and have no need for stock (*fonds*) to set up with, such as jobbing workmen, tinkers, menders of clothes, chimney-sweeps, water-carriers, live in uncertainty, and are proportioned in numbers to their customers. Master workmen, such as shoemakers, tailors, upholsterers, hairdressers, etc., who employ journeymen in proportion to the work which they have, live in the same uncertainty, since their customers may leave them any day; undertakers in their own labour in the arts and sciences, such as painters, physicians, lawyers, etc., live in the same uncertainty. If one attorney or lawyer makes £5000 a year by serving his clients or customers (*cliens ou pratiques*), and another makes only £500, we may consider them as having those sums in uncertain wages (*gages incertains*) from those who employ them" (pp. 69, 70).

All the inhabitants of a country excepting the King and landlords

> "can be divided into two classes, to wit, undertakers and wage-earners (*gens à gages*); and these undertakers are, so to speak, on uncertain wages, and all the others on certain wages for the time during which they enjoy them, although their functions and rank are very unequal. The general who has his pay, the courtier who has his allowance, and the domestic who has his wages all fall into this class. All the rest are undertakers, whether they set up with a stock (*un fond*) to carry on their undertaking, or are undertakers in their own labour without any stock, and they can be considered as living in uncertainty (*comme vivant à l'incertain*). Even beggars and thieves are undertakers belonging to this class" (pp. 71–2).

Whatever may have been the actual usage of the words "undertaker" and "entrepreneur" in his time, it is clear that Cantillon desired to divide the active members of society (other than king and landlords) into two classes: firstly, the persons engaged under wage-contracts, and, secondly, undertakers, working not for a definite employer but on their own account; it is also perfectly clear that neither the employment of other persons nor the possession and control of capital, nor even the control without the ownership of capital was necessary to make a person an undertaker in his conception of the term.

He does not expressly attempt any classification of incomes, but his discussion implies that the gross gains of the landlords, the undertakers, and the wage-earners are often subject to a deduction for interest paid by them on their debts. A farmer, he tells us, who owns the capital necessary for working his farm will get, after paying his rent, two-thirds of the produce. One of these thirds will pay all his expenses, including his own maintenance, and he will have the other third for himself (*pour lui*). If a wideawake labourer (*un laboureur entendu*) can find someone who will lend him the necessary stock or money wherewith to buy it,

> "he will be in a position to pay this lender all the third rent or one-third of the produce of a farm, of which he will become the farmer or undertaker. Nevertheless he will regard his position as better than before, considering that he will find his living in the second rent and will be master instead of servant as he used to be, and that if by his great economy and by cheating himself a little on the

necessaries of life (*en se fraudant quelque chose du nécessaire*) he can by degrees accumulate some little stock, he will be able to reduce his debt each year and will eventually manage to get for himself the whole of the third rent" (pp. 266–7).

In the same way a wideawake journeyman hatter may set up as an undertaker by borrowing the necessary capital and abandoning to the lender the "profit" until gradually by depriving himself of some small amount of what passes as necessaries (*en se frustant un peu de son nécessaire*) he can amass the stock for himself, and then "the item of profit (*l'article du profit*) will all remain with him" (p. 270).

So perhaps we may say that Cantillon thought of landlords receiving rents, undertakers receiving profits and other gains, wage-earners as receiving wages, and then having to give up part of their rents, profits and wages to lenders if they happened to have borrowed at interest. It is difficult to imagine what he would have replied to an objector who asked him why rent of land should not be similarly regarded as part of the profit of the farmer which he has to surrender to the landlord; general belief in the natural productivity of land prevented such a question being asked, and would probably have furnished him with some kind of answer.

It is more important to notice that his classification does not rest on the same basis throughout. The distinction between his rent and his other two kinds of income is based on their origin or destination. Rent is derived from land and goes to king and landlords; the gains of undertakers and the wages of wage-earners are derived from their industrial activity and go to the active producers. But the gains of undertakers are distinguished from wages, not by the nature of the source or the different character of the recipients—a water-carrier "on his own" gets his gain from carrying water just like a water-carrier who is paid by wages—but by the nature of the arrangement under which they get their pay.

The Physiocrats agreed with Cantillon in making a special sort of income for king and landlords, but adopted an entirely different classification of workers by dividing them not into undertakers and wage-earners but into "productive" and "sterile" classes. Here the distinction is founded not on the source or the destination of the income, but on the nature, or perhaps we should say the amount, of the services performed—the Physiocrats would not allow us to say the nature or amount of the product, since they held that the sterile class did not produce. But this classification never gained wide acceptance, and naturally disappeared altogether when the fundamental likeness of the productive and sterile classes was finally admitted.

Such importance as the Physiocrats had in the matter of classification is rather to be found in their insistence on the importance of "advances" and "capitals." That doubtless has something to do with the fact that Turgot, in reviving the entrepreneur forty years after Cantillon's death, makes him far more of a capitalist than Cantillon had done. He begins by saying that in each trade "the workers or the entrepreneurs who set them to work" must have "a certain stock of movable goods accumulated in advance (*un certain fonds de richesses mobiliaires amassées d'avance*" (*Réflexions*, § li; in Daire's *Œuvres de Turgot*, § liii). But he then lets the alternative of the workers having this stock drop out of sight, so that the "capitalist entrepreneur" (*entrepreneur capitaliste* in heading of § lxi; in Daire, lxii) becomes a necessity. He shows no sign whatever of inclination to follow Cantillon by including among entrepreneurs all persons working on their own account even if they have no capital, and by a rather subtle confusion between the actual state of things and the physiocratic ideal of large enterprises, he manages to push the entrepreneurs who have only small capitals so much into the background that his readers are induced to think of the producers in a properly developed society as consisting on the one hand of "simple craftsmen who own nothing but their hands, advance nothing but their daily labour, and have no profit beyond their wages," and on the other of entrepreneurs who "are all in possession of large capitals which they turn to account by setting men to work by means of their advances" (§ lxi; in Daire, lxii).

In considering capital employed in commerce, Turgot has no hesitation in speaking of a merchant's business as an "undertaking" which he would not "undertake" without the expectation of profit, but it is only after several pages, in which merchants are sometimes distinguished from entrepreneurs in agriculture and manufacture, that he brings himself to include merchants among entrepreneurs. Thus his entrepreneur may be said to be a capitalist who engages actively in the conduct of his business, and more especially one who employs labour and has a large capital. He ignores the non-capitalist who "works on his own account."

He does not, however, believe that the whole income of the capitalist-entrepreneur is derived from his possession of capital. Only a part of his income is so derived, and its amount may be estimated by what he would get if he used his capital to buy land. The rest consists of "the wages due to his labours, his cares, his risks, and even his skill, since doubtless, if the profit were equal, he would have preferred to live on the income which he could have acquired with the same capital" (§ lx; in Daire, lxi). Here we have the principle of distinguishing incomes according to their source or destination, which Cantillon had applied only to the distinction between rent and other income, applied to the distinction between profit and wages, which Cantillon had distinguished in the ordinary way, that is, by the kind of arrangement or contract under which they are received. What people habitually call profit because that is the ordinary name for gains made in a particular way is, according to Turgot, partly "wages," although none of it is agreed for and paid in the way wages in the ordinary sense are agreed for and paid, because part can be said to be derived from labour and to go to a person who has laboured.

§ 2. *The Idea of "Distribution."*

In his lectures Adam Smith does not seem to have made use of the classification of incomes into rent, profits and wages. In the *Wealth of Nations*, however, it plays a great part, being used firstly for the explanation of prices, and secondly, apparently as an afterthought, for the explanation of Distribution.

In regard to prices Smith was in search of "sources of value" [1] and thought he had found them in the rents, profits and wages necessary for the production of commodities, or at any rate

[1] In the first ed. of *Wealth of Nations* he says, "profits of stock are a source of value"; in later eds., "profits of stock are a component part" (of the price of commodities), and the same change is made in reference to rent (Vol. i. p. 51, notes 3 and 7).

that he could safely allege that wages, profit and rent were the "component parts of price."

Nearly nine-tenths of Book I of the *Wealth of Nations* are concerned, not with the subjects mentioned in its title but with prices. About one-tenth is occupied by "the causes of improvement in the productive powers of labour" if "the origin and use of money" is included under that head. Chapters v, vi and vii are intended to show, as Smith himself says, "wherein consists the price of all commodities," "what are the different parts of which this real price is composed," and "what are the causes which sometimes hinder the market price, that is, the actual price of commodities, from coinciding exactly with what may be called their natural price" (Vol. I. p. 30). And the remaining chapters, on wages, profit and rent, are introduced by the statement, "The natural price itself varies with the natural rate of each of its component parts, of wages, profit and rent; and in every society this rate varies according to their circumstances. . . . I shall, in the four following chapters, endeavour to explain, as fully and distinctly as I can, the causes of those different variations" (Vol. I. p. 65).

Wages, profit and rent are discussed not because they are shares in distribution, but because they are the "component parts of price"—"In every society the price of every commodity finally resolves itself into some one or other or all of those three parts." How little Smith when writing the body of these chapters was really thinking of the "order according to which" the produce was "distributed among the different ranks of the people" (heading of Book I) is shown by the fact that he makes the horses and oxen employed in cultivation earn "wages or maintenance" along with the labourers because the cost of keeping them is part of the price of the products. "In the price of corn, for example," he says, "one part pays the rent of the landlord, another pays the wages or maintenance of the labourers and labouring cattle employed in producing it, and the third pays the profit of the farmer" (Vol. I. p. 52).

But before he wrote his "Introduction and Plan of the Work" and affixed a heading to Book I, he hit—unfortunately, I think—on the idea that his discussion of prices would serve as a theory of Distribution.

This term " distribution " was, when he wrote, a neologism so far as economics was concerned. It is true that at the end of the seventeenth century the statisticians, Gregory King, Petty and Davenant, made estimates of the income of different classes of English society which suggest to our minds a study of actual distribution. Gregory King in an attempt to estimate the " income and expense of the several families of England for 1688 begins by giving the 160 " temporal lords " 40 heads per family with an average income per family of £2800, making £448,000 in all. The 26 spiritual lords follow with 20 heads per family and an average income of £1300, making a total of £33,800. Then come baronets, knights, esquires, gentlemen, persons in offices, merchants, persons in the law, clergymen, freeholders, farmers, persons in sciences and liberal arts, shopkeepers and tradesmen, artisans and handicrafts, naval officers, military officers, common seamen, labouring people and outservants, cottagers and paupers, common soldiers, vagrants, each with similar estimates of numbers, and average and total incomes.[1] But the interest of such statisticians was in the total of the product, not in its distribution, and they did not discuss the distribution of the total under that or any other name.

Both the word " distribution " itself and the verb " distribute," from which it is derived, were introduced into economic theory, or at any rate first given any considerable prominence in economic theory by Quesnay, of course in their French forms. The Economic Table itself gives as one of the " things to consider " the distribution of its " three kinds of expenditure." Quesnay's own *Analysis of the Table* says, " it is by the order of the distribution of expenditure that the effects of good and bad national policy can be estimated." [2] Mirabeau in his Explanation of the Table describes " *l'ordre distributif de la consommation des productions de crû entre toutes les classes de citoyens* " (p. 39), which is very suggestive of the words in the title of Book I of the

[1] *Natural and Political Observations and Conclusions upon the State and Condition of England*, written in 1696, but not published till 1802, as an appendix to George Chalmers' *Estimate of the Comparative Strength of Great Britain*. But the table referred to in the text and a great deal more of King's work was published by Davenant in his *Balance of Trade*, 1699. See above, pp. 17, 18.

[2] *Œuvres de Quesnay*, ed. Oncken, p. 320.

Wealth of Nations, "of the order according to which its produce is naturally distributed among the different ranks of the people."

But "the three kinds of expenditure" in the Table were not the categories of wages, profit and rent: they were productive expenditure from rent and taxes, and sterile expenditure. The classes or ranks of the people were not the labourers, the owners of stock or capital, and the landlords: they were the productive class, the King and landlords, and the sterile class. Consideration of distribution did not mean consideration of the amounts of income obtained by different ranks of the people: it meant consideration of the effects of variations of the different kinds of expenditure—policy could be judged good or bad "according as expenditure comes back to or is withdrawn from the productive class." Mirabeau thinks nothing of inequality of income; if there were fewer landlords, he says, the greater the surplus over personal consumption each of them would have. But then they would give away more, or collect others to help them to consume their income, and thus their "expenses would be found to be distributed nearly in the same way as if there had been a greater number of landlords, each with a smaller expenditure."

"We should regard in the same light," he proceeds, "the inequality of the gains or profits of members of the other classes, within which the advances, the interest and the profit of the undertakers (*entrepreneurs*) of agriculture, commerce, manufactures, etc. are transmitted to the workers. These things, by successive and reciprocal distribution, furnish by gradation in their turn profits (*gains*) or wages (*salaires*) to all who follow gainful occupations. From which it results that even the expenditure of the rich is no more than a distributive transmission of expenses which is extended to all other citizens in proportion to their earnings (*salaire*)" (pp. 49–50).

Turgot emphasised the importance of the term distribution by introducing it into the title of his *Réflexions sur la formation et la distribution des richesses*, and strengthened the habit of applying it to the annual produce by treating even the *distribution des richesses* as distribution of the annual produce, although *richesses*, like our own "riches," would have suggested to the older schools of thought capital rather than income. But he applied the term distribution to the process by which, rather than to the proportions in which, the produce is divided, telling his readers about the different methods of making an income and not about the greater or less amounts of income obtained by the different parties in distribution.[1]

Mirabeau's account of the Economic Table was translated into English (very badly) in 1766,[2] but no English or Scotch economist seems to have made any technical use of the term distribution before Adam Smith produced the *Wealth of Nations.* He himself is not reported to have introduced the term or the verb "distribute" in his lectures, and in the *Wealth of Nations* it is only the verb which appears, and that very seldom. In Book I. chap. vi., after saying that the price of every commodity must finally resolve itself into wages, profit and rent, or into two or one of these three parts, Smith adds:

> "As the price or exchangeable value of every particular commodity, taken separately, resolves itself into some one or other, or all of those three parts; so that of all the commodities which compose the whole annual produce of the labour of every country, taken complexly, must resolve itself into the same three parts, and be parcelled out among different inhabitants of the country, either as the wages of their labour, the profits of their stock, or the rent of their land. The whole of what is annually either collected or produced by the labour of every society, or what comes to the same thing, the whole price of it, is in this manner originally distributed among some of its different members. Wages, profit and rent are the three original sources of all revenue as well as of all exchangeable value. All other revenue is ultimately derived from some one or other of these" (Vol. I. p. 54).

The passage looks like an afterthought inserted when the dissertation on prices which forms the bulk of Book I was already far advanced, if not quite completed. Without the title of Book I, "Of the Causes of Improvement in the productive Powers of Labour and of the Order according to which its Produce is naturally distributed among the different Ranks of the People," the passage might very probably have passed unnoticed. But with it and the title of the Book also before them it was inevitable that readers would suppose Smith to have written the two-thirds of Book I comprising the four chapters on Wages, Profit and Rent, as a theory of distribution. This happened,

[1] Compare § xxix (Daire xxx) with the sections which it summarises.
[2] See note on p. 30 above.

and it settled the contents of Distribution in books about economic theory for a century and a half at least.

Distribution has, of course, in ordinary language a great many different meanings and shades of meaning in different contexts. The distribution of small-pox between the vaccinated and the unvaccinated is not quite the same thing as the distribution of coal by the railways, and the distribution of prizes at an agricultural show by her Grace the Duchess is not quite the same thing as the distribution made by the judges. But when the distribution of sums of money or of property measured in money is spoken of, there is seldom any doubt that the speaker is thinking of the division of the money, and if he talks of inequalities in the distribution or of persons faring better or worse in the distribution, he is thinking of the proportions in which the total is divided—it is not the process of handing the money or the property over to the recipients that he has in mind, but the comparative magnitude of the recipients' shares.

Consequently, if the last four chapters of Book I of the *Wealth of Nations* had been, as the passage about distribution into wages, profit and rent would naturally lead any reader to expect, chapters on the aggregate income derived from labour, from stock and from land respectively, the distribution of produce would have been taken to mean the division of the total produce between those three categories of income. Discussion of distribution might have started from the old generalisation of three equal parts, one to the labourers, one to the farmer and one to the landlord (see above, p. 220), and then taken the line of inquiry whether this was ever true, whether it applied to manufactures as well as agriculture, and how, if at all, it had been modified by modern developments. At any rate it would have been clearly seen that a larger proportion of the whole going to any one of the three shares would mean a smaller proportion left for the other two taken together: a statement about an increase or decrease of income derived from any one of the three sources would have been taken to be a statement about the aggregate amount of that kind of income, and the theory of distribution would have taught something about the relative magnitude of the three aggregate amounts.

But Adam Smith, approaching wages, profit and rent, as he

actually did, with the intention of explaining his theory of prices, had little occasion to consider the relative magnitude of the aggregate shares of the total income obtained from labour, capital and land. He never once makes any statement about the aggregate derived from labour or the aggregate derived from stock. The proportion of the whole produce which is received by the owners of land he does sometimes mention, but as he says towards the end of Book I (Vol. I. p. 247) that " the extension of improvement and cultivation " gives the landlord " a greater proportion " of the produce, and in Book II that " in the progress of improvement, rent, though it increases in proportion to the extent, diminishes in proportion to the produce, of the land " (p. 317), we may safely conjecture that he had given little thought to the subject, and that consideration of it was unessential in the exposition of his theory. His variations of wages, profit and rent were not variations in the proportions of the total produce or income taken by these three categories of income, but variations in the absolute amounts of wages per wage-earner, and of rent per acre, and variations of profits per cent. of capital, *i.e.* variations of the ratio between capital and the income derived from it.

Thus any reader who simply accepted what appeared on the face of it to be Adam Smith's interpretation of Distribution was bound to understand it as a theory of the causes of the rise and fall of wages per wage-earner, rent per acre and profit per cent. of capital, and some readers were likely to become confused between Distribution in this highly artificial and peculiar sense and the same word in the sense of division of the produce.

Jean-Baptiste Say, Smith's first " populariser," who influenced the English economists almost as much as the French, led the way towards confusion in this matter. In the first edition of his *Traité d'économie politique* in 1803 he says at the beginning of Book II, " Of Money," that the next thing to do is to " show how and in what proportions the distribution of the thing produced, that is, the value of the products, is distributed among the members of the society (*montrer comment et dans quelles proportions s'opère entre les membres de la société la distribution de la chose produite, c'est-à-dire de la valeur des produits*) " (Vol. I.

pp. 413–14). Book III of the *Traité* is "Of the Value of Things," Book IV is "Of Incomes (*Revenus*)," and begins with words which suggest that its principal subject will be an examination "of the different ways in which values produced are diffused (*se répandent*) throughout the society, and the proportions in which they are distributed (*les proportions suivant lesquelles elles se distribuent*)." Chapter iv of this book undertakes to explain "By what machinery the value of products is distributed (*Par quel mécanisme la valeur des produits se distribue*) amongst the producers," and chapter v is to tell us "According to what proportions the value of products is distributed (*Suivant quelles proportions la valeur des produits se distribue*) between the three sources of production," but in reality it never approaches the question, unless we are to suppose that the proposition "as a society grows richer, wages increase and the profits of capital diminish" (Vol. II. p. 183) is intended as an answer. The bulk of the rest of Book IV deals with categories of income quite in Adam Smith's manner, and the second edition of the *Traité*, published in 1814, confirmed the application of the term Distribution to that kind of discussion of income by throwing the former Books on Values and Incomes together into one Book entitled "The Distribution of Riches." The former chapter professing to tell in what proportions the value of products is distributed disappeared, but a note in the Analytical Table asserts that the chapters on the different kinds of income "treat of the proportions according to which the gains of which incomes consist are distributed between the producers" (Vol. II. p. 398). They do nothing of the kind, and it is clear that Say attached no exact sense to "proportions."

Ricardo is apparently more definite, but in reality much more confusing than Say. In the Preface to his *Principles* he says, "In different stages of society the proportions of the whole produce of the earth which will be allotted" to wages, profit and rent "will be essentially different," and "to determine the laws which regulate this distribution is the principal problem in Political Economy." If this stood alone we might suppose him to be using the word "proportions" as loosely as Say, but in chapter i he gives an example which leaves no doubt whatever of his meaning. "By improvements in machinery and agriculture," he says, "the whole produce may be doubled; but if wages, rent and profit be also doubled, these three will bear the same proportions to one another and neither could be said to have relatively varied." But if the doubling were made up by wages only increasing 50 per cent. and rent 75 per cent., while profits increased 175 per cent., it would be "correct" to say that "rent and wages had fallen, while profits had risen." Similarly, if "of every hundred hats, coats and quarters of corn produced the labourers had 25, the landlords 25 and the capitalists 50," and, when the produce was doubled, the labourers and landlords had 44 each, and the capitalists 112, he would "say that wages and rent had fallen and profits risen; though in consequence of the abundance of commodities the quantity paid to the labourer and the landlord would have increased" (1st ed., pp. 44–5; 3rd, pp. 49–50, § 7).

This is perfectly clear. But Ricardo's performance falls considerably short of his promise. He produces no theory about the proportion of the whole produce taken by rent, and his theory of the causes which settle the proportions in which the remainder of the produce after deduction of rent is divided is so obscured by his method of expounding it that few of his contemporaries and scarcely any of the next generation cared to grapple with it. The essential parts of it seem to consist in the first place of the truism that if a total is divided into two parts, one called wages and the other profits, the proportion of the whole allotted to wages cannot rise without diminishing the proportion allotted to profits; secondly, of the theory that the wage-earners must have a certain subsistence and will not get more, and thirdly, of the obvious deduction from this that the smaller the produce per head, the greater the proportion of it which must be allotted to wages and the smaller the proportion left for profits. Ricardo and his immediate disciples, the two Mills and McCulloch, failed, in spite of some effort on the part of McCulloch at least, to keep the question of the proportion allotted to profits clear, as it, of course, ought to have been kept clear, from the perfectly different question of the ratio between profits and capital, and the confusion was fatal to any lucid treatment of the subject.

Such interest as was felt in the subject was due to the belief that the produce per head or productiveness of industry was actually declining and thereby reducing the rate of profit. As this belief gradually waned away with the growing prosperity of the nineteenth century, Ricardo's abortive attempt to "determine the laws which regulate the distribution" of income between wages, profit and rent gradually ceased to be discussed. Economists fell back on the conception of the theory of distribution evolved by an accident from Smith's arrangement of the *Wealth of Nations*, that is, they considered the staple of the theory to consist of theories about the variation of wages per wage-earner, profits per cent. of capital, and rent per acre of land. It did not occur to any of them to try to make the three theories co-ordinate. If the theory of rent concerned the value of a unit of land, could not the theories of wages and profits be made to concern, not wages per worker and profits per cent. of the value of instruments of production and enjoyment, but the value of some unit of labour and some unit of actual instruments? If the theory of profits concerned the income derived from the investment of £100 in instruments, could not the theories of rent and wages be made to concern not rent per acre and wages per worker but the income derived from £100 invested in land or in the training of a worker? Or if both these suggestions were, as no doubt they would be, unacceptable, and if the theory of wages concerned wages per worker, why should not the theories of profits and rent be made to concern profits per capitalist and rent per landlord?

In 1888, I, or the author who has subsequently developed or degenerated into me, being then in the heyday of youth, aspired to alter the treatment of a large part of economic theory by bringing out a little book entitled *Elementary Political Economy*—why not "Elementary Economics," especially as the immediate model was Thomas Raleigh's *Elementary Politics*, I cannot now remember, though I think I preferred "economics," but was overruled by the publishers.[1] In this book Distribution is only mentioned as a name commonly given by economists to a consideration of "the causes on which the relative or comparative

[1] The publishers were the Oxford University Press, and the University of Oxford still shows its proverbial attachment to lost causes by occasionally reviving the old term, abandoned elsewhere.

size of individuals' incomes depend, so far as private property and exchange are concerned" (p. 65). The comparative size of incomes is then said to depend on values, so that a discussion of value precedes three sections dealing with the causes which determine the comparative size of (1) the incomes individuals derive from labour, (2) the incomes individuals derive from property, and (3) the aggregate income derived from property and the aggregate income derived from labour. It is clearly explained that as each of the two classes of proprietors and labourers may vary in number in relation to the aggregate incomes enjoyed, the comparison of the two aggregates tells us nothing about the comparative size of the income of the average individual proprietor compared with that of the average labourer.

Little notice was taken of this ambitious attempt to reconstruct economic theory by making it in the first place explain the causes of greater or less productiveness of industry, and then the causes why different individuals and classes received, some much, and others little, of the whole produce.[1] I concluded that destruction of the old edifice must precede construction of the new, and after five years' work produced in 1893 a *History of the Theories of Production and Distribution in English Political Economy from* 1776 *to* 1848, containing a vigorous and detailed attack on the slovenly way in which distribution had so far been treated. I even went so far as to entitle the inquiry into wages per wage-earner, profits per cent., and rent per acre, "Pseudo-distribution," in contradistinction to "Distribution Proper," which I took to be theory about the proportions in which aggregate income is divided between classes and persons.

But that book for many years only excited some little annoyance in the minds of persons wedded to the traditional treatment of economic theory, and its sale was so small that it had to change its publisher when the first edition of only 502 copies was at last sold out in 1902. Encouraged by the greater success of the second edition (1903), I made a third effort to get

[1] The reviewers on the whole were favourable, but in those days they were mostly amateurs whose knowledge of the orthodox treatment was not very thorough. The only reviewer who was really moved was "D" in the *National Reformer*, which was, I think, Bradlaugh's organ. He said the book "may be regarded as the outcome of the academic reaction against economics. It wipes out the main features of sound economic classification" (January 6, 1889).

the theory of distribution put on a logical basis by appealing to the New World in an article on "The Division of Income" published in the Harvard *Quarterly Journal of Economics* for May 1905. This began by ridiculing current academic treatment of rent, interest and wages as not in the least helping to give an answer to the questions which people rightly think important, and then revived the plan of *Elementary Political Economy* with regard to the division of aggregate income between property and labour and between individual proprietors and individual labourers. This article was reprinted without alteration in my *Economic Outlook* in 1912, and the constructive part of it is re-stated in *Wealth, a Brief Explanation of the Causes of Economic Welfare,* which was first published in January 1914.

The old conception, however, was deeply rooted and difficult to shake. Marshall during this period seemed to move, if at all, rather backwards than forwards in this particular matter. In the earlier *Economics of Industry*, 1879, he had shown some signs of breaking away from tradition by giving Distribution a mere chapter instead of the usual "Book" or "Part," making it chapter vii in Book II: "Normal Value." It does not appear until after Rent has been disposed of, and it says, "the problem of *Distribution* with which we shall be chiefly occupied during the rest of the present volume consists of an inquiry into the way in which" what remains after deducting rent and taxes from the annual income of the country "is divided up" (p. 95). In the first edition of the *Principles*, 1890, Marshall reinstated Rent as a share in Distribution, but still showed signs of distrust of the traditional treatment by giving the last Book, which is for the most part a discussion of wages, profit and rent, the title "Value, or Distribution and Exchange." In 1907, however, in the fifth edition, he abandoned this title and substituted "The Distribution of the National Income."

Taussig, in his *Principles of Economics*, 1912, at the beginning of Book V: "The Distribution of Wealth," formally adheres to the old conception, but he shows some appreciation of the need for change by including a substantial chapter on "Inequality and its Causes."

§ 3. *Confusion initiated by Adam Smith about the Basis of Classification.*

The slowness displayed by economists in realising the faulty character of their traditional treatment of distribution was largely due to the confusion introduced by Adam Smith's attempt to give new meanings to the well-established and useful words, wages, profit and rent. The want of sound literary education and knowledge which was characteristic of many of the best known exponents of economics prevented them from seeing that when a word is commonly used to indicate one thing, it is always either futile or mischievous to define it arbitrarily as something else.

Cantillon had been content to leave the words rent, wages and profit pretty much as he found them. Rent he did not meddle with at all. Wages he slightly extended by including under the term what we usually call salaries; this was not a very serious addition, since both wages and salaries are paid under contract of service for work done by a "servant," as would have been said in Cantillon's time, or, to put it in a more modern way, are paid by an employer to a person employed according to an agreement under which the employed person is to work more or less under the direction of the employer for a sum agreed on, the only difference between wages and salaries being that salaries are usually bigger and paid at longer intervals than wages. Profit Cantillon did modify rather more by making the "undertakers" who get it include all producers who are not wage-earners, whereas in the ordinary language of his time and of ours, profit is only got where some expense or risk of expense in actual money outlay is incurred. To Cantillon an itinerant watercress-seller who manages to make himself a basket and to collect cress without paying anything to anyone is an undertaker making profit, whereas ordinary people in Cantillon's time and ours would not say he made a profit unless he had to pay out money for the basket or for leave to pick the cress; we might say such a person got "earnings," but we certainly should not say that he received "wages," if we were speaking ordinary English—if we said he got wages, our hearers would imagine him to be employed by a greengrocer and selling on his behalf—so that Cantillon's extension of the term seems inevitable if it is desired to include all incomes under the three heads, and not very confusing, as it does not involve a transfer from one head to another.

Turgot, probably writing about the same time as Smith, though his work was published a few years earlier, suggested, without actually attempting to make, a rather more confusing departure from ordinary French when, after saying that only a part of the income of the capitalist-entrepreneur was derived from his capital, he added that the rest consists of "the wages (*salaire*) due to his labours, his cares, his risks, and even his skill," since this, if taken literally, involves the transference of an immense amount of what is commonly called profit to the head of wages (*salaire*). But there is little reason to suppose that Turgot had any idea of recommending an actual change of terminology. He would have doubtless been content if someone had said merely, "though the second part of the capitalist-entrepreneur's income is not wages, it is, like wages, received by him because he labours."

Adam Smith went much further on the downward path. He begins with a statement which can be construed in a sense which makes it true, but is very misleading:

> "Whoever derives his revenue from a fund which is his own, must draw it either from his labour, from his stock, or from his land. The revenue derived from labour is called wages. That derived from stock by the person who manages or employs it is called profit. . . . The revenue which proceeds altogether from land is called rent, and belongs to the landlord" (Vol. i. p. 54).

Now it is quite true that *some* of the income derived from labour (*i.e.* drawn by a person who gets it because he labours) was called wages in Smith's time and is still so called, but there is also a great deal of such income which is not called wages. It is quite true that the income derived from stock or capital (*i.e.* drawn from stock by a person because he owns it) by the person who both owns and manages it was and still is called profit, but a great deal of income besides this is also called profit. It is quite true that *some* of the income "which proceeds altogether from land" (*i.e.* presumably, which is got by a person because he owns land) was called and still is called rent, but a great deal of income which proceeds altogether from land was not and is not called rent, and a great deal of what was and is called rent does not " proceed altogether " or at all from land.

Smith himself admits that this statement of what " is called " wages, profit and rent is not borne out by " common language." He says, " a gentleman who farms a part of his own estate . . . *is apt to denominate*, however, his whole gain profit," and " we *seldom hear of* the rent of a plantation, but frequently of its profit." Though common farmers oversee the work of their men and work a good deal with their own hands, whatever remains to them after they have paid their rent and kept up their stock " *is called profit*." All the gains of a workman who works with his own capital " *are commonly called* " profit.

When, therefore, he says that all income is " derived from " labour, stock or land, and that the parts derived from each of the three sources " *are called* " respectively wages, profit and rent, we must understand him to mean that they are properly so called, or so called in a language which he favours as being superior to English as " commonly " spoken. He imagines it superior because, he thinks, it does not " confound " income derived from one source with that derived from other sources. The landowner who farms, in his opinion, " confounds rent with profit "; the " wages " of the farmer and of the independent workman " are confounded with profit "; and the " rent " and " profit " of a working gardener, owning his garden, are both " confounded with wages." [1]

Of course in none of these four cases is there really the least confusion or confounding of different things either in common language or in the minds of those who prefer to use it rather than the artificial jargon invented by economists. The farmer who owns his farm knows quite well that as he does not pay rent for his farm, his profit—what is left to him after paying the expenses of the business—should be greater than the profits of farmers with similar farms who have to pay rent. The farmer who oversees his men and lends a hand in the work knows quite

[1] Not, however, by being *called* wages, but by being ignored (no doubt as trifling) when the whole gains of such a person " are commonly considered as the earnings of his labour."

well that if he did not, he would have to pay out more wages, and his profits would be less. The workman who works on his own account is not in the least likely to forget that he works, nor likely to be content with the much smaller profit he might make if he had to pay ordinary wages before reckoning it. The man who cultivates his own valuable land with his own hands, using his own capital, knows quite well that he should get more income than if he had to pay rent for the land and hire or interest for the capital. Confusion was really introduced by Adam Smith's unconscious attempt to construct a new language better than the ordinary English which is well understood by the people who speak it. Henceforward Smith himself and most of his successors down to the present day fell into constant confusions owing to failure to decide whether they were to think and speak of wages, profit and rent in the old well-established "common" sense of the words or in the new and artificial senses which Smith tried to give them in the sixth chapter of the *Wealth of Nations.*

In dealing with differences of profit in Book I, chapter x, Smith remembers that he has defined wages as the income derived from labour. "The apparent difference," he tells us, "in the profits of different trades is generally a deception arising from our not always distinguishing what ought to be considered as wages from what ought to be considered as profit." An apothecary, he says in illustration of this, may sell his drugs for ten times what he gives for them, but "the greater part of the apparent profit is real wages disguised in the garb of profit," *i.e.* the greater part of what is called his profit in ordinary language is called wages in the new nomenclature, because it is derived from labour. In another illustration Smith says that a small grocer may make 30 per cent. on his capital of £100, while a "considerable wholesale merchant" in the same place is only making 8 or 10 per cent. on a capital of £10,000, and this is explained by the fact that £20 out of the small grocer's "profit" (in the ordinary sense) is "wages" (in the new sense).

But in chapter vi a little before the passage which lays down the new definitions and says that the farmer gets wages for his work as overseer directing the general operations of the farm, Smith gives examples of profits obtained by two manufacturers in which he treats the "supposed labour of inspection and direction" as of no account whatever in the determination of the gains of business (pp. 50–51). The chapter "Of the Profits of Stock" shows no trace of any appreciation of the fact that much of what is profit in ordinary language is wages in the new language. The chapter "Of the Wages of Labour" begins with a description of a supposed primitive state in which the labourer had "neither landlord nor master to share with him," and then tries to say what would have happened to "the wages of labour" if this state had continued, "wages" here being clearly wages in the new sense of income derived from labour rather than the sense in which the word is used in ordinary language. But almost at once we are told that landlords appeared and would not let the labourer use the land without paying for it, and "masters" somehow became necessary in order to advance the labourer his maintenance, and demanded profit for the service, so that the labourer came to be paid by wages in the ordinary sense of the word. There is, of course, Smith proceeds to admit, even in modern times such a person as the "independent workman" who does not get wages in the ordinary sense.

> "Such cases, however, are not very frequent, and in every part of Europe, twenty workmen serve under a master for one that is independent; and the wages of labour are everywhere understood to be what they usually are, when the labourer is one person and the owner of the stock which employs him another" (p. 68).

This, Adam Smith seems to suppose, completely absolves him from giving any further attention to his own definition. Henceforward throughout the chapter wages are wages in the ordinary sense; they depend, in fact, "everywhere upon the contract usually made" between masters and men (p. 68), and we hear nothing whatever about the kinds of income from labour—wages under the definition of chapter vi—which are obtained either by the independent workman or by the undertaker who manages a business. In short, so far as the distinction between wages and profits is concerned, Smith simply abandoned his new language and reverted to the old and well-understood meanings of the words.

As to the distinction between profit and rent, the fact that

Adam Smith proposed to call all income from land by the name of rent, though ordinary language only applies that term to payments made by tenants to landlords for land let to them by landlords, does not seem to have given rise to any difficulty. The English people have been long accustomed to rate and tax owners of land who occupy their own land by means of an estimate of the "annual value" in the sense of what it would let for to an hypothetical tenant, and it required no great intellectual exertion to suppose this annual value to be included when rent was discussed. But much trouble was given by the ambiguity of "land." This has already been considered above, in the chapter on the value of land (pp. 241–6).

§ 4. *Attempts to Re-define "Profit."*

J.-B. Say observed that "Smith involved himself in great difficulty by not separating the profits of the undertaker of industry (*entrepreneur d'industrie*) from the profits of his capital" (*Traité*, 1st ed., Vol. II. p. 221, note), and made a praiseworthy effort to clear the matter up. He says that such part of the profits of the capitalist-entrepreneur as he gets because he performs labour and not because he possesses capital "must be regarded as the wages of his labour (*doivent être regardés comme le salaire de son travail*)," and this is not to be taken as an early example of the pernicious practice followed by many later economists of saying that part of one class "must be regarded" as belonging to another class without being removed into it, when all that is meant is that it would have belonged to that class if a different basis of classification had been adopted. For Say used the word "profits" as equivalent to income, speaking of the "profits" of the labourer and the landlord as well as of the capitalist-entrepreneur. In his later editions he charitably attributes the confusions of the English economists to the poverty of the English language and the idiosyncrasy of English law. Ignorant or forgetful of the word "undertaker," he says in one place that the English "have no name for the *entrepreneur d'industrie*, though the Italians have four, "*imprenditore, impresario, intraprenditore, intraprensore* (6th ed., impression of 1876, p. 84, note); and in another place he says the confusion is explained by the fact that in English law anyone who shares in the gains and losses of an undertaking (*entreprise*) is regarded as an active partner (*associé gérant*, Book II. chap. vii. § 3; in 1876 impression, p. 393, note).

Tooke, as Say (*ib.*, p. 375) recorded with satisfaction, thought English economists would do well to accept his classification, and long afterwards J. S. Mill, probably with Say's criticism in his mind, declared that "French economists enjoy a great advantage in being able to speak currently of *les profits de l'entrepreneur*" (*Principles*, ed. Ashley, p. 406). But the heart of the matter was not touched by all this. The truth is that the English economists of the first three-quarters of the nineteenth century were quite willing to accept Smith's teaching about the apothecary and the little grocer in preference to his teaching about the two manufacturers, and therefore to throw out of "profits of capital" all that the undertaker gets in consequence of his personal activity rather than his possession of capital, but they threw it into the air instead of finding a place for it in their treatment of income derived from labour. It was, in fact, impossible for them to find a place for it there because they had not really substituted the second Smithian conception of "wages" as income derived from labour for the first and ordinary conception of it as income received under a contract of service. Their whole theory of wages was based on the idea of wages being advanced from the capital of employers, and could not possibly be made to include income received by undertakers not by way of advance but as a consequence of the success of their undertakings.

When at last the wage-fund theory of wages expired, the way was open for the classification of the earnings of undertakers' labour along with that of other kinds of labour. In this matter Marshall seems to have been a pioneer in the earlier *Economics of Industry*. As the little book is now not readily accessible to many readers, I will quote at length from pp. 95–6:

"The term 'labourer' has been used by economists to include all kinds of workers, and not merely unskilled labourers, to whom the term is confined in trade usage. And the term 'wages' has been used to include the earnings of all kinds of work except that of business management.

"The Earnings of Management are generally classed with interest by economists as well as by men of business. And this is doubtless the best classification in many social and some economic inquiries; because those who get the Earnings of Management are to some extent a separate class from those who get earnings of other kinds. Account will be taken of this fact when we come to discuss Market values, but in the theory of Normal values we are seeking for fundamental economic laws. And it is a universal rule of science that in seeking these fundamental laws, we should class together things that are similar in nature and may be expected to obey similar laws.[1] And therefore we shall find it best to class Earnings of Management with the earnings of other kinds of work; because they are similar in nature to other earnings and are in the long run governed by the same laws. The earnings of a business man are uncertain, but so are those of a fisherman; they are got by mental work, but so are those of the barrister and the physician, whose incomes have been classed by all economists with the wages of skilled labour. And if, instead of classing Earnings of Management with other earnings, we were to class them with interest under the head of profits, we should be classing together two things entirely different in nature and governed by wholly dissimilar laws. For though in the passing vicissitudes of trade it is sometimes difficult to draw a clear line between the interest on a business man's capital and his Earnings of Management, yet we shall find that there is little in common between those fundamental laws which determine in the long run the Normal rate of interest and those which determine the Normal Earnings of Management. It seems, therefore, best to class Earnings of Management with wages under the head of *Earnings*; to regard the net income of the country, after deducting rent and taxes, as divided not into wages and profits, but into interest and earnings" (pp. 95–6).

Here Marshall begins the practice, which he subsequently followed without much wavering,[2] of using both of two classifications of income. In one, income is classed as (1) rent, (2) profits consisting of (*a*) interest and (*b*) earnings of management, and (3) wages and salaries; in the other, the classification is (1) rent,

[1] This shows a strange forgetfulness of the fact that things may be similar in some respects and dissimilar in others. We may class coal in the cellar and wood in the shed together as fuel, but not as minerals.

[2] He does sometimes waver, e.g. *Principles*, 8th ed., pp. 611–12, where the "corrected" rate of profit is made to exclude earnings of management, which, he says, "ought to be classed under another head" than profit; here "profit" (when "corrected") takes the place of "interest" in the second of the two classifications above. Moreover, his invention of "quasi-rent" involved yet another classification (below, § 6).

(2) interest, (3) earnings, consisting of (*a*) earnings of management and (*b*) wages and salaries.

The plan (apart from all that concerns the division between the first and the other shares) is open to two objections. In the first place readers become confused between the two classifications. There is no harm in different classifications for different purposes, but these two were intended for the same purpose. In the second place, the nomenclature was unfortunate, both as regards " interest " and " earnings of management." " Interest " in ordinary language does not cover all income received in consequence of the ownership of capital, but only what is received by lenders of money: to try to extend the meaning of the term so as to make it cover the income of persons or companies using their own capital was certain to lead to great confusion. " Earnings of Management " was an unsatisfactory name for income estimated to be received by undertakers or entrepreneurs in consequence of their labour, because much labour of management is paid for by wages and salaries, whereas " Earnings of Management " in Marshall's classification was intended to cover only that part which is paid for by profits. Moreover, Marshall's " Earnings of Management " was really intended by him to cover a good deal more than what the words convey in any ordinary sense. Adam Smith's apothecary, for example, not employing a single assistant, did a good deal more for his apparently exorbitant profit than merely " manage " his business.

The kind of confusion likely to result is illustrated in Marshall's own exposition just quoted. In it he says, " The earnings of a business man are uncertain, but so are those of a fisherman." The contrast suggested here is between managing a business and working a net or line with one's own hands, whereas what is required is a contrast between wage-paid and profit-paid labour; the typical " fisherman " (who has, in fact, often been treated as a capitalist by economists) is profit-paid and not wage-paid. If he happens to be wage-paid, his earnings cease to be " uncertain " in the sense of depending on the success of the operations. Uncertainty in this sense, as Cantillon so well explained, is essential to " profits," and certainty in the inverse sense is essential to wages.

Many recent writers, especially Americans, have made a further inroad on the old terminology by giving the name of "profit" to the gains which the undertaker is supposed to make apart from any return on capital, so that income becomes divided into four, as follows: (1) rent, (2) interest, (3) profit and (4) wages and salaries. This conflicts with the ordinary meanings of both interest and profit, and is rather more confusing than Marshall's plan, in which profit retained its ordinary sense when used in one of his classifications and was dropped out altogether from the other.

More recently still, some writers have tried to throw out of "profit" in this new classification all that Marshall meant by his "earnings of management" and include it in the fourth class. Then, forgetting the metaphysicians who searched in a dark room for a black hat which was not there, they have exhausted themselves in efforts to discover what is left in "profit."

The only wise course in this matter seems to be to leave the words commonly employed to bear their usual and well-understood meanings and to use other expressions when something else is meant. The classification of income into wages, profit, interest and rent in the ordinary sense of those words is a useful one when the object is to distinguish incomes according to the kind of arrangement under which they are received. When the desire is to classify incomes according to their different sources, such as land, capital and labour, other terms should be used; the resources of the English and other Western tongues are not unequal to the strain—it is no great hardship to have to use three short words instead of one, as in "income from capital" instead of either "profits" or "interest."

§ 5. *The Attempt to re-define "Rent."*

We have already seen in the chapter on the Value of Land how both Adam Smith and Ricardo contradicted themselves about the meaning of land and thus left it in doubt whether the rent of land was to be understood as covering payments for at any rate a great deal of "improvements" made by man in or upon the earth's surface and upper crust, or was to be confined to what was paid for some obscurely conceived entity consisting of the land as given by Nature; there is no need to add anything on that matter except that no answer to the question "What is land?" has yet been agreed upon by those who wish to make a sharp distinction between land and other valuable property. But in § 7 of that chapter we found that Ricardo, after at first very reasonably holding that royalties on minerals taken away from a mine were not rent of land in the sense of income derived from the possession of land, but should be classed with money derived from selling once and for all the timber in a forest, proceeded to call such royalties "rent of mines," because he thought their relation to the value of the product of the mine was the same as that of the rent of agricultural land to the value of the product of agriculture. This was nearly the first of many attempts to extend the term rent in such a way as to make it cover much beyond what could be included in the rent of land even on a wide interpretation of "land"—attempts which were founded on the doctrine that every part of income which could be held not to "enter into the cost of production" ought to be called rent.

The first of these attempts known to me was made surprisingly early, two years before the publication of Ricardo's *Principles*, by Storch, a Russian who instructed the Grand Dukes Nicholas and Michael during the Napoleonic War, and published his Course of Instruction in French in 1815. In this he not only calls income derived from capital "*rente*," in which there is nothing very remarkable, as the French have always applied that term to the income of property-owners who are not entrepreneurs, but also has a chapter, "*De la rente des talents et des qualités morales*," in which he says that the natural qualities of a worker, when he possesses them "in an eminent degree," often secure for him an income over and above the wages which are necessary to cover the pains (*peines*) and sacrifices (*sacrifices*) incurred by him and by persons of ordinary natural ability who are in the same occupation as he is. His exceptional faculties are a prerogative which he owes simply to the bounty of Nature:

> "It is," he says, "this analogy with the rent of land which has led me to call this kind of income by the name of rent, a name which is applicable to an income which does not come from labour and is

drawn from a source belonging exclusively to him who enjoys it. There is, however, a great difference between this rent and that of land and capital. The rent of land or capital can be obtained by the labour of some person other than the proprietor, while the rent of talent must be obtained by him who owns the source of it. So, although this rent does not come from labour, it nevertheless is not independent income; it is inseparable from the labour of him who enjoys it, and consequently must be included in his wages. The name of rent is only appropriate to it in this one respect—that with the same labour and the same sacrifices, he who possesses the sources of it obtains more than he who does not possess them" (*Cours d'économie politique,* Vol. i. p. 369).

The interest of this passage lies in the fact that it shows perhaps more clearly than any of the later expositions, that what was at the bottom of attempts to extend the meaning of rent was desire to bolster up the doctrine of value being dependent on pains and sacrifices. The value of the land used in production having been pronounced the effect and not (like the pains and sacrifices of contributing labour and capital) the cause of the value of things produced on it, it was thought desirable to huddle under the cloak of rent every case in which it did not seem plausible to attribute value to pains and sacrifices incurred. Storch saw clearly enough that whatever a man got by exercising his natural talents, however eminent they might be, was remuneration of his labour, and therefore even the extra remuneration of extraordinary talents should be included in his wages (*salaire*), but at the same time he wanted to call the extra remuneration "rent" because it came to the recipient, as land rent was supposed to come to the landlord, from the bounty of nature, and not because he had incurred any pains and sacrifices.

Senior, eleven years later, going a little further in the few pages on economic terms which Whately placed at the end of the Appendix on ambiguous terms in his own *Elements of Logic,* 1826, was evidently inspired by the same motive as Storch. Quoting first some of the definitions of rent, wages and profits given by economists, he complains that they omitted from Rent the income arising from "the exclusive right to some instrument of production," other than land, "enabling the employment of a given amount of labour or capital to be more than usually productive." He says, "all extraordinary powers of body and mind—all processes in manufacture which are protected by secrecy or by law—all peculiar advantages from situation or connection—in short, every instrument of production which is not universally accessible, affords a revenue distinct in its origin from Wages or Profits, and of which the Rent of land is only a species."

This calmly assumes that rent ought to be defined not in the sense in which it was commonly understood by ordinary people, nor even in the sense in which it was commonly understood by the economists, but in a quite different sense, the superior convenience of which Senior made no attempt to prove. In his first lecture as Drummond Professor at Oxford, he recommended his auditors to read this Appendix, and said, "I almost regret now that I did not suggest in each place the definition which appeared to me the most convenient,"[1] but it is clear enough that the definition of rent which he then thought most convenient was the same as that which he expressly adopted later in his *Political Economy*, "all" revenue "that is obtained without any sacrifice; or, which is the same thing, beyond the remuneration for that sacrifice." If, he says,

"all that is produced is to be divided into rent, profit and wages—and certainly that appears to be the most convenient classification—and if wages and profit are to be considered as the rewards of peculiar sacrifices, the former the remuneration for labour, and the latter for abstinence from immediate enjoyment, it is clear that under the term 'rent' must be included all that is obtained without any sacrifice; or, which is the same thing, beyond the remuneration for that sacrifice; all that nature or fortune bestows either without any exertion on the part of the recipient, or in addition to the average remuneration for the exercise of industry or the employment of capital" (8vo ed., pp. 91–2).

This makes the convenience of the new definition depend on the validity of two propositions: (1) that all income should be classified as rent, profit and wages, and (2) that wages and profit are to be regarded as the rewards of peculiar sacrifices. The first of these propositions Senior dismisses curtly with the remark that the classification "appears to be the most convenient." To the second he does not even give this very trifling measure of

[1] *Introductory Lecture on Political Economy* (6th Dec., 1826), p. 32.

support, but leaves it in the air as if it were something which never had been questioned and never would be.

When he comes to consider the "Relative Proportions of Rent, Profit and Wages" he asks:

"Is then the extraordinary remuneration of the labourer which is assisted by extraordinary talents to be termed Rent or Wages? It originates in the bounty of nature; so far it seems to be rent. It is obtained only on the condition of undergoing labour; so far it seems to be wages. It might be termed with equal correctness, rent which can be received only by a labourer, or wages which can be received only by the proprietor of natural agent. But as it is clearly a surplus, the labour having been previously paid for by average wages, and that surplus the spontaneous gift of nature, we have thought it most convenient to term it rent. And for the same reason we term *rent* what might with equal correctness be called fortuitous profit. We mean the surplus advantages which are sometimes derived from the employment of capital after making full compensation for all the risk that has been encountered, and all the sacrifices which have been made, by the capitalist. Such are the fortuitous profits of the holders of warlike stores on the breaking out of unexpected hostilities; or of the holders of black cloth on the sudden death of one of the royal family. Such would be the additional revenue of an Anglesea miner if, instead of copper, he should come on an equally fertile vein of silver. The silver would without doubt be obtained by means of labour and abstinence; but *they* would have been repaid by an equal amount of copper. The extra value of the silver would be the gift of nature and therefore rent" (pp. 129–30).

And, further, Senior holds, all the income derived from the possession of man-made things ceases to be profit as soon as they pass away by gift or inheritance from the person to whose abstinence and exertions they owed their creation.

"The revenue arising from a dock, a wharf, or a canal is profit in the hands of the *original constructor*. It is the reward of *his* abstinence in having employed capital for the purposes of production instead of for those of enjoyment. But in the hands of his heir it has all the attributes of rent. It is to him the gift of fortune, not the result of a sacrifice" (*ib.* 129).

Few, if any, economists went as far as this, and Senior himself made no use of his own classification, but the suggestion of a part of earnings of labour being somehow to be classed as rent became widespread. Marshall dallied with the idea in the earlier

Economics of Industry, saying rather half-heartedly, not that the remuneration of "exceptional natural qualities" either is or ought to be called rent, but only that "it may be regarded as a kind of rent." To explain what this means, however, he adds, "that is, it is the income derived from an agent of production the supply of which is determined by natural causes, and not by the deliberate outlay of human effort for the sake of future advantage" (p. 110). But this definition of rent is put forward in forgetfulness of the fact that the chapter on Rent deals only with land rent, and defines it as "that payment for the use of land which the owner can obtain by free competition for lending out the use of it to others" (p. 81). The new idea makes a fleeting reappearance in the proposition, "*Rent* of rare natural abilities is a specially important element in the incomes of business men" (p. 144), and I think that is all.[1]

In the *Principles* Marshall is less rather than more positive in asserting the "rent" character of the "high" (1st ed., p. 608) or "extra" (8th ed., p. 577) incomes "earned by extraordinary natural abilities." There is, he thinks, "a strong *primâ facie* case for regarding them" as rent or "producer's surplus resulting from the possession of a differential advantage for production freely given by nature." So far as the individual income of an individual is concerned the analogy is useful:

> "There is," he says, "some interest in the inquiry how much of the income of successful men is due to chance, to opportunity, to the conjuncture, how much to the good start that they have had in life; how much is profits on the capital invested in their special training, how much is the reward of exceptionally hard work; and how much remains as a producer's surplus or rent resulting from the possession of rare natural gifts" (8th ed., p. 577; cp. 1st ed., p. 609).

We may grant that such a "discussion" might be "interesting" to an auditor if it took place between disputants armed with illustrations from real life, such as,

"Look at Sir A. B. He started from nothing and was really

[1] Francis Walker, in propounding his peculiar theory of employer's profit (see below, p. 358), quotes this remark of Marshall's with approval, and says that he will follow the line taken with regard to rent in Whately's Appendix (attributing it erroneously to Whately himself). But he does not, in fact, reclassify in that way. He allows employer's profit to continue to be called profit, only alleging that it is a "species of the same genus as rent" and is "governed by the same law as rent" (*Political Economy*, 1883, pp. 247–8).

pretty stupid, but he died a millionaire just because he was so hardworking; he used to be at his office at seven every morning."

"Stuff! All his friends, and his enemies too, always told me that the real secret of his success was that he had extraordinary natural ability for persuading the other party in a bargain that it was desirable to agree to his terms."

But we may well question whether any definite conclusion would ever be arrived at such as that of Sir A. B.'s income of £50,000 a year, approximately £10,000 might be due to the happy chance which gave him C. D. as partner, £20,000 to the War, £6000 to his having had well-to-do sensible parents, £200 to the capital invested in his special training, £800 to his "exceptionally hard work," so that £13,000 "remains" for the "earnings" of his rare natural abilities.

Supposing that such a result *were* obtained, the only reason for "regarding" £13,000 a year as a rent or producer's surplus would be that it did not "enter into the cost of production" of the things Sir A. B. produced. But Marshall shrinks from alleging this. When, he says, we pass from the individual case to that of the whole body of persons in an occupation, "we are not at liberty to treat the exceptionally high earnings of successful men as rent without making allowances for the low earnings of those who fail" (1st ed., p. 610; 8th ed., p. 578). This is because the high incomes of the successful men in the trade attract potential entrants into that trade:

> "These fortunes are therefore part of the price that is paid in the long run for the supply of labour and ability that seeks the occupation: they enter into the true or 'long period' normal price of labour in it. They are not, as some writers have urged, a Rent which does not enter into that price and which is rather determined by that price" (1st ed., p. 609; 8th ed., p. 578, omits the last sentence).

§ 6. "*Quasi-rent*" *of Ordinary Transferable Property.*

While "earnings" of labour or even "earnings" by itself serves fairly well as a name for the income derived from all kinds of "labour" in the wide sense, ordinary English lacks any such short term for the whole of the income derived from the possession of property. For the part derived from agricultural land, houses and a few other things when they are let to tenants, the word "rent," understood, as it often is, as "net rent," or total paid by the tenants less landlords' necessary outgoings, does very well, and the economists' artifice in extending the sense of the term so as to make it include the net annual value of land in the hands of its owners as well as that received from tenants in the form of rent was quite legitimate and convenient.

Rent in this sense clearly does not "shade gradually" into "interest" as "interest" is commonly understood. We might as well say that "woman" shades gradually into "sister." The income—so many pounds or dollars per annum—derived from the property is "rent," but if we want to think and speak of it in relation to the investment of capital which someone has made in the property we call it "interest." We say, for example, that a certain property cost £1000 and yields a rent of £60 per annum, "which is 6 per cent. interest." The rent we regard as high or low according as it is greater or smaller than it was in the past, or according as it is greater or smaller than that of similar or neighbouring properties: the interest we regard as high or low according as the percentage which the income bears to the capital invested is greater or less. When, using ordinary language, we apply the term interest to any income, we have in our minds the relationship between that income and some capital sum, just as when we apply the term "sister" to any woman we have in our minds the relationship between that woman and some other person or persons.

This suggests the question why the economists did not extend the term rent to cover the whole of the income derived from property of all kinds whenever that income was to be thought of as an amount without reference to its magnitude in relation to any capital sum. The answer is that they were prevented from doing so by the fact that Adam Smith and his immediate followers were led by the social and political circumstances of their time to wish to treat "land"—an entity of the contents of which they had most hazy conceptions—as something very different from other kinds of property. They therefore jealously reserved the term "rent" to the income derived from "land"—and whatever this "land" was, it was certainly something much less than all the property which is or can be let for a rent in ordinary language.

Being precluded from extending "rent" so as to make it cover the income from all kinds of property, and having divided property into "land" and "capital" and failed to notice that the rent of land, even in the narrowest sense which any of them attributed to it, is interest on the money given for it by a purchaser, they caught hastily at the fact that capital yields interest, and used "interest" as the name of the income derived from property other than land, just in the same sense as that in which they used rent for the income derived from land. An unfortunate ambiguity was thus introduced into the meaning of interest; variation of interest, which before had meant only variation of the rate of interest on capital, that is, a high or low ratio of the value of the income to that of the capital, could now be understood also in the sense of variations of absolute income from property, irrespective of the capital invested.

If Marshall had introduced the term "quasi-rent" in order to clear up the difficulties caused by this ambiguity, and had succeeded in getting the term adopted for all the income derived from property other than land, he would have rendered a great service to the exposition of general economic theory in his time. His contemporaries were scarcely ready to abandon altogether the old attempt to distinguish sharply between land and other forms of property; adoption of the term quasi-rent—"a sort of rent"—would have helped them over the transition. "Rent and quasi-rent" is very little shorter than "income from property" and is less informative on its face, but it would have found more easy acceptance.

But Marshall's principal aim was always the explanation not of distribution but of values. In pursuing it he was encumbered by misplaced loyalty to the traditional doctrine that land and rent occupy different positions in regard to the value of products from those occupied by property other than land and the income derived from such property—the doctrine put by Adam Smith in the form rent is the effect, and wages and profit the cause of price, and by the Ricardians in the form, "rent does not (like labour) enter into the cost of production." Possessed by the belief that some ground must be found for this doctrine, Marshall thought he had found it in the fact that "the 'inherent properties' of land and other gifts from the bounty of Nature are incapable of increase by man's effort in any period of time, however long,"[1] whereas man-made things can be increased. But he also saw that a stock of man-made things cannot be increased instantaneously, and very often cannot be increased for many months or even years, during which, so far as its relation to values is concerned, it might just as well be an unincreasable gift of Nature. Then, he reflected, the longer the interval, the more like the gifts of Nature—"land" in the "purest" sense—is that stock of man-made things, and possibly he also thought, the greater the divergence of the income from what would be derived if the stock could be increased instantaneously, the greater the resemblance between the income derived from it and the income derived from land.

It was easy for him then to think of the distinction between rent of pure "land" and income derived from possession of a stock of man-made things as being a matter of degree, depending on the length of time it takes to alter the stock. That the income derived from these stocks was a sort of rent during the interval, a quasi-rent, very naturally suggested itself to him, and that apparently without causing him to notice that if the term were applied to incomes above, below, *and at* the level which they might be supposed to attain if the stocks could be instantaneously altered in magnitude to fit existing conditions of their production, all necessity for using "interest" in the sense of absolute income derived from the stocks irrespective of their capital value would be done away with. So in the Preface to the first edition he says, after speaking of the way in which long periods shade into short periods:

"Thus, for instance, the greater part, though not the whole, of the distinction between Rent and Interest on capital turns on the length of the period which we have in view. That which is rightly regarded as interest on 'free' or 'floating' capital, or on new investments of capital, is more properly treated as a sort of rent—a *Quasi-rent* it is called below—on old investments of capital. And there is no sharp line of division between floating capital and that which has been 'sunk' for a special branch of production, nor between new and old investments of capital; each group shades into each other gradually. And thus even the rent of land is seen, not as a thing by

[1] *Principles*, 1st ed., p. 493, with which cp. p. 196 and 8th ed., p. 147, where it is admitted that inherent properties *below* the surface have been "largely modified; partly impoverished and partly enriched" by human action, while "it is different with that which is above the surface."

itself, but as the leading species of a large genus; though indeed it has peculiarities of its own which are of vital importance from the point of view of theory as well as of practice" (p. viii).

In the first two sentences of this paragraph Marshall is evidently misled by the ambiguity mentioned above of "interest" as used by the economists. In the first sentence, "Interest on capital" is quite clearly not the Rate of interest, or income from capital considered in relation to the capital itself, but simply the absolute income derived from capital in the same sense as that in which "Rent" is the absolute income derived from land without any reference to its relation to the capital value of the land. "The distinction" seems to be short for "the difference in regard to their relations with value," and we may paraphrase the whole as, "the greater part, though not the whole, of the difference between income derived from land and income derived from man-made things in regard to the value of products turns on the length of the period which we have in view." But in the next sentence we cannot substitute "income derived from" for "interest on," since it would be nonsense to say "that which is rightly regarded as income derived from 'free' or 'floating' capital, or from new investments of capital, is more properly treated as a sort of rent on old investments of capital." Evidently in this second sentence Marshall has reverted to the ordinary use of the word interest, and is thinking of it as a "return," to use the old phrase, on the capital, measured by its magnitude in relation to that capital, so that the sentence may be paraphrased, "That which is rightly thought of as a return (reckoned at so much per cent.) on 'free' or 'floating' capital, or on new investments of capital, is more properly thought of as a sort of rent from the things obtained by the investment when the investment has once taken place."

After all, what authors say in their prefaces is much less important than what they say in their text. How did Marshall use the term quasi-rent in the body of his book? If the index is to be trusted, and I think it is in this particular case, he did not use it at all in the first 492 pages of the first edition. Book II is on "Some Fundamental Notions," and chapter vi of this is on "Income," but quasi-rent is not mentioned there. Instead, we are told that

"The benefits which the owner of wealth derives from it may be called the USANCE OF WEALTH.[1] They include as a special case the money income which is derived from capital and is called INTEREST; and this is most easily measured when it takes the form of a payment made by a borrower for the use of a loan, for, say, a year; it is then expressed as the ratio which that payment bears to the loan" (p. 142).

Then, after saying profits are interest on capital plus earnings of management, Marshall continues:

"The income derived from the ownership of land is commonly called RENT, and the term is stretched so as to include that derived from letting houses and even such things as boats, pianos and sewing-machines. In a much narrower use the term has been applied specially to the annual income derived from those free gifts of nature which have been appropriated. But this use again has been gradually extended until it includes the income derived from things of all kinds of which the supply is limited and cannot be increased by man's action. This we may take to be now established as the scientific use of the term, though it is not free from difficulties, as we shall see hereafter; and we cannot dispense entirely with the use of the term in its broader popular sense" (pp. 142–3).

It is difficult not to suppose this must have been written before Marshall thought of introducing the term quasi-rent.

When at last the term does make its appearance in the text, in Book VI, chapter iii, it seems at first to be treated as applicable in greater or less degree to income derived from an improvement of land or a machine according to the closeness of the relation between that income and the expenses of making the improvement or the machine (p. 493). This, of course, implies abandonment of classification according to source. A valuable machine is called a source of income to its possessor because if he did not possess it he would not have the income; it is now to be "regarded" as more or less "affording a Quasi-rent" (and less or more affording a profit) according to the length of time which it takes to add to the stock of such machines or to diminish the stock by wear and tear, or, which comes to much the same thing, according to the readiness of the supply of such machines to respond to alterations of demand for them.

[1] In spite of the capitals and of the fact that in the next three editions he describes it as a "convenient term" Marshall hardly ever uses this phrase, though the index is defective (as usual) in suggesting that he never does so (see pp. 612, 613, 723, notes 1 and 2).

Whether classification on this basis can be made useful in the explanation of values is arguable, but it would certainly be useless in the explanation of distribution. No one could say approximately how much quasi-rent he had and how much profit.

But as Marshall proceeds he soon, but apparently unconsciously, reverts to classification by source. In all his examples quasi-rent appears not as the name of a characteristic which a particular income may possess in greater or less degree, but as the name of the whole of the income derived from some possession, material or immaterial. In his examples it is put forward as ousting "profit" (less earnings of management) only when the income from the possession is either above or below an amount which would give normal profit on investment in producing such possessions. If "an exceptional demand for a certain kind of textile fabric" causes "the special machinery required" to "yield for the time an income" which is above what would be a normal return on the cost of making such machinery, this income —the whole of it, not the excess over normal—is "a high Quasi-rent." If, on the other hand, an unexpected fall of demand causes the machinery to yield for the time an income which is below what would be a normal return on the cost of making such machinery, the whole of this income is a low quasi-rent—"In this case the Quasi-rent will be not more but less than normal profits on the original investment" (1st ed., pp. 499–500). I know of no example in which Marshall applies the term to an income which is neither above nor below but coincident with normal profits, but there is nothing surprising in this: in such a case he regards the conception of quasi-rents as of no importance. And the case seems amply covered by the very definite statement which almost immediately follows the examples just quoted:—"In every case the Net income derived from the investment of capital, when once that investment has been made, is a Quasi-rent."

If any doubt remained as to Marshall's intention even in his first edition to include in quasi-rent all incomes derived from property other than land it should have been removed by the opening sentence of note 2 on p. 723:

"Attention has already been called to the fact that when the term 'capital' is used broadly so as to include all accumulated wealth, the aggregate 'interest' on capital (or more strictly its Quasi-rent, see the last note) must be used with corresponding breadth so as to include the 'usance' of all accumulated wealth."

Finally, in the fifth edition, 1907, quasi-rent found its way into the chapter headed "Income. Capital" (Book II., chap. iv), and is there described in a way which should leave no possible doubt whatever about the meaning Marshall intended it to bear:

"When any particular thing, as a house, a piano, or a sewing-machine is lent out, the payment for it is often called *Rent.* And economists may follow this practice without inconvenience when they are regarding the income from the point of view of the individual trader. But, as will be argued presently, the balance of advantage seems to lie in favour of reserving the term Rent for the income derived from the free gifts of Nature, whenever the discussion of business affairs passes from the point of view of the individual to that of society at large. And for that reason the term *Quasi-rent* will be used in the present volume for the income derived from such things as machines. That is to say, any particular machine may yield an income which is of the nature of a rent, and which is sometimes called a Rent; though on the whole there seems to be some advantage in calling it a Quasi-rent. But we cannot properly speak of the interest yielded by a machine.[1] If we use the term 'interest' at all, it must be in relation not to the machine itself, but to its money *value.* For instance, if the work done by a machine which cost £100 is worth £4 a year net, that machine is yielding a quasi-rent of £4 which is equivalent to interest at 4 per cent. on its original cost; but if the machine is worth only £80 now, it is yielding 5 per cent. on its present value" (p. 74, repeated on the same page in ed. 8, with the substitution of "machines and other appliances for production made by man" for "such things as machines").

Thus, whatever Marshall began with, he ended with the conception of quasi-rent as including the whole of the income derived from "machines and other appliances for production made by man," which we must, having regard to other parts of his exposi-

[1] We must understand here, "without reference, express or implied, to the capital invested in the machine." We "can properly" (*i.e.* we can intelligibly) say, and Marshall himself says five lines lower down, that the machine yields 5 per cent. on the capital reckoned to be invested in it.

In the 4th ed. of the *Principles*, chaps. viii. and ix. of Book V. are headed, respectively, "Rent or income from an appliance for production not made by man, in relation to the value of its produce," and "Quasi-rent, or income from an appliance for production already made by man, in relation to the value of its produce." The "already," which is otiose, but suggests the progress of Marshall's thought, is absent in the phrase as repeated in the first paragraph of chap. ix.

tion, take to include improvements of land and all other man-made things which are lucrative private property: it is the name of the income derived from these things in the same way as "rent" is the name of the income derived from land, and bears the same relation to interest as the rent of land bears to it—which may be best explained by saying that the quasi-rent of any property yields, provides, or, if the reader will, *is*, interest at some rate per cent. on the capital-cost or the capital-value of the property, just as rent provides or is interest at some rate on the capital-cost or capital-value of the land.

The only passage which I can discover in all the editions of the *Principles* definitely—in appearance, at any rate—inconsistent with this interpretation of quasi-rent is one which says that in a stationary state there would be "no such things as Quasi-rents; for the incomes earned by every appliance for production being truly anticipated beforehand, would represent the normal measure of the efforts and appliances required to call it into existence" (2nd ed., p. 482; 3rd ed., p. 502). This would seem to imply that the income is not a quasi-rent when it provides only normal interest on the investment. But I think the statement only occurs in the second and third editions: it appears to be distinctly withdrawn in the fourth edition, 1898, p. 520, where, without anything being said about quasi-rents, we are simply told that "In a stationary state the income earned by every appliance for production being truly anticipated beforehand, would represent the normal measure of the efforts and appliances required to call it into existence" (in ed. 8, p. 810).

The withdrawal in 1898 may perhaps be connected with the fact that Nicholson in Vol. II. of his *Principles* (pp. 80–81), published in 1897, had supposed that quasi-rent was not intended by Marshall to cover cases of normal return. Marshall said very brusquely that Nicholson had "failed to discover the drift" of the doctrine, but did not attempt to explain what was wrong with his interpretation (4th ed., p. 496 n.).

Many of Marshall's disciples have fallen into a different and worse heresy, by believing that their master taught that quasi-rent is not the whole of the income derived from the property, but only so much of it as is in excess of a normal return on the investment: they either ignore altogether incomes which furnish less than a normal return or treat the deficiencies between them and a normal return as "negative quasi-rents." [1] I cannot discover the least justification for this in any of the editions of the *Principles*, and I can only suppose that it has arisen from careless reading of some of the examples, an excess over cost not including interest on capital having been erroneously understood as cost including interest.

The existence of this heresy has hitherto prevented and will probably continue to prevent the adoption of the term quasi-rent as the name of income derived from property other than "pure" land. It has deprived Marshall of the credit he ought to have had for introducing a term which was very much required in the economics of his day.

§ 7. "*Quasi-rent*" *of Acquired Personal Qualities.*

Marshall's conception of the quasi-rent of personal qualities was exactly analogous to his conception of the quasi-rent of ordinary transferable property. A person is supposed to have a certain capital invested in training or accustoming him to some lucrative occupation, and the income which he derives from the qualities he thus acquires is interest at so much per cent. on the capital invested, but is to be called quasi-rent when thought of not in relation to the capital invested but as a certain amount, in the same way that rent is thought of: it differs from what Marshall calls the rent of "extraordinary natural abilities," because these are given by Nature like "pure" land (see especially pp. 577–9 in ed. 8).

But the idea does not seem to have the same usefulness here that it has or might have had in regard to ordinary transferable property. Such property is frequently, and apparently in an increasing degree, held by persons who do no work in connection with their own particular holding, and even when it is held by persons who work in connection with it, separation of the work

[1] *E.g.* A. W. Flux in *Economic Principles*, 1904, makes an excess over normal return a positive quasi-rent and a deficiency below normal return a negative quasi-rent (pp. 125–7), whereas Marshall seems to think of a negative quasi-rent as what is usually called a loss on working some equipment, since he speaks of the quasi-rent obtained from the capital in a business fluctuating "from a considerable negative to a large positive quantity" (*Principles*, 3rd ed., p. 702; 4th ed., p. 704); but in the fifth edition he changed "quasi-rent" into "income" in this passage (pp. 621–2; 8th ed., p. 622).

and the ownership may take place in consequence of the owner retiring from active management while continuing to hold the property, or in consequence of his selling or letting it, or in consequence of his death. Personal qualities, on the other hand, can only be used by the person in whom they are vested. He who possesses them cannot employ a manager and go off to golf, cannot sell them and invest the proceeds in war loan nor let them and receive the rent; and when he dies, they die with him.

The result of these differences is that we cannot estimate or form any definite idea of the supposed two parts of income, the part derived from the "source" of current labour and the part derived from the source of personal qualities, whether these are natural or acquired.

We could do so if the completest chattel slavery existed so that the workers occupied the same position towards owners that horses occupy at present. The workers would then have an income from their human slave point of view just like that which horses have at present from their equine point of view. It would amount (except in the case of a few kept as pets) to a subsistence or maintenance just sufficient for efficiency, and would cease when they became not worth keeping and were sold to the man-slaughterer to be turned into leather and glue or sausages. This would be the income which the labourers would derive from their labour, and if it were necessary to give a Frederick Leighton or Sarah Bernhardt rather more than the common herd, no one would think of calling the "extra income" by the name of rent. The owners of the slaves would get the rents and quasi-rents derived from the possession of property—the lucky owners of Leightons and Bernhardts would get large "rents" from "the rare natural abilities" which had been "freely given by Nature" to their slaves in the same way as owners of sites in the City get large rents from their land, and, as some economists less cautious than Marshall would say, in the same way as the lucky owners of Derby winners get large rents from the "rare natural abilities" of their horses.[1] The owners of ordinary slaves would get quasi-

[1] I cannot find that Marshall anywhere classes horses or superior horses along with pure land as yielding rent. But if the exceptional natural ability of a free man brings him a rent, it is not easy to see why the exceptional natural ability of a horse should not bring rent to its owner. Whether it is classed as rent or quasi-rent will, however, make no difference to the argument of the text above.

rents like the owners of ordinary horses at present. The income derived from property in slaves, *alias* the rents and quasi-rents yielded by them, would be separable from the income derived from labour.

But this would be so only because by the hypothesis free labourers had been turned into property of other persons; and this would make the whole situation completely different from the present. As things are, we have no ground whatever for supposing that of the income of workers, two portions, one, equal to the bare cost of maintaining them in efficiency, is remuneration of their labour, and the other, or remainder, is the rent and quasi-rent of their natural and acquired abilities. As Marshall himself says, " human beings are not brought up to their work on the same principles as a machine, a horse, or a slave " (*Principles*, 4th ed., p. 571; 8th ed., p. 504).

If any reader doubts, let him make the converse hypothesis by asking himself what would happen if horses were emancipated and given human powers of reasoning and bargaining, human family affections, and freedom to breed or not to breed as they pleased. Is there the smallest ground for supposing that their numbers and consequently the value of their work would be the same as it is at present? And if their numbers were different, could it still be alleged that their current labour was worth just as much as the cost of maintaining them in efficiency, and the remainder was rent and quasi-rent of their natural and acquired abilities?

If it be said that we need not suppose the pure labour portion of the income to be equal to the cost of requisites for efficiency, then the question presents itself, by what other criterion is the division to be made? No reasonable answer suggests itself to me.

My conclusion is that the traditional classification in which the income derived from labour is treated as a whole, differences of wages or earnings being taken as including differences explainable by the distribution of natural and acquired talents, is to be preferred to the entirely fanciful classification of labour incomes into income from pure labour and income from the labourers' property in their natural and acquired talents.

§ 8. *Conclusion.*

The vogue enjoyed for a century by the disjointed discussion of the causes of high and low wages (per head), profit (per cent.) and rent (per acre) to which Adam Smith had managed almost accidentally to give the name of Distribution is probably to be explained chiefly by the fact that two at least of the three very different questions discussed did seem to bear on the interests of groups of persons who at the beginning of the period regarded themselves and were regarded by others as separate social "classes." Both wage-earners and landlords were in 1776 much more homogeneous classes than they are now, and the wage-earners' prosperity obviously depends on wages per head and the landlords' equally obviously on rent per acre. The profit-makers were certainly much less homogeneous than the "landlords" or the "labourers," and the fact is reflected in the diversity of names given to them. "Monied interest," "undertakers," "manufacturers, merchants, and farmers," "owners of stock," "capitalists," "employers," "business men" were all used at one time or another, but none of them really filled the bill. Some of the persons were borrowers and others lenders, and these naturally did not regard the rate of interest with the same feelings, whatever the economists might say; the farmers, producing raw materials and food and selling them to persons employed in manufacturing, did not feel their interest the same as that of the manufacturers who were producing clothes and other things and selling them to the agricultural population. The class of profit-makers was, in fact, from Cantillon's time downwards, little more than a miscellaneous remainder after the other two classes had been taken out of the mass. No wonder the economists were more uneasy about this class than about the others and kept on trying to alter its contents.

Eventually they split or subdivided the income of the class into two shares, income from property other than land and income from business activity. On the one side, though they themselves did not perceive it till recently, this fell in well with the obliteration of the social distinction between landlords and owners of other kinds of property which was going on during the period, and helped towards a new economic classification in which the perfectly futile attempt to distinguish land given by Nature from other forms of property created by man has been abandoned. On the other side, the economists' recognition of a "labour" class among the profit-makers has not yet been seconded by an obliteration of social distinction between employers and employed as complete as that which has occurred between landlords and owners of other property, and consequently the wage-earners still largely delude themselves into pursuing the ideal of high wages rather than of high remuneration of labour, of which wages are only a form.

In the following chapters I propose to consider what has been and may be said about the incomes obtained in consequence of the performance of labour and the ownership of property respectively. Before doing so, however, it may be well to ask whether it is desirable to maintain any longer the fiction of Distribution, that is, the assumption, for purposes of exposition, that all products are first thrown into a common heap or thrown into a common pool and subsequently divided out among income-receivers.

I am inclined to answer the question in the negative. The assumption has always been applied to political countries, and this is very misleading. The union of Great Britain with Ireland, and the later separation of southern Ireland from that union, the creation of Poland and Czecho-Slovakia into separate states must have considerably altered the percentages of the total incomes of their countries received by particular inhabitants without really altering their relative incomes. Moreover, the incomes of the inhabitants of one country often depend very largely on production or demand in other countries. An Englishman's income, for example, may easily depend on production in America and demand in China, and it is much more reasonable to think of something being divided between him and some American and Chinese persons than to talk as if he could only get a larger or smaller share of an English total.

To improve upon the old idea of Distribution by making the whole world (or even the whole of the commercial part of the world if that is any smaller) the unit instead of the political country is impracticable. It would make the assumption too cumbrous to be workable. We cannot undertake to suppose ourselves throwing produce into a common heap along with Central Africans merely because we send them buttons or bicycles in exchange for ivory or rubber.

On the whole, therefore, it seems better for the theorist to drop the assumption underlying the use of the term Distribution, and to do so certainly makes the task of the historian of theory much easier, since in point of fact those who professed to consider Distribution constantly allowed conditions of production to affect "shares in distribution" not through the medium of the magnitude of the common heap and its subsequent division, but directly.

I shall therefore discard Distribution and discuss the incomes of workers and of property-owners not as proportions of a common whole but as absolute amounts per head.

CHAPTER XI

INCOMES FROM LABOUR: THEIR GENERAL LEVEL

§ 1. *The Crude Subsistence Theory of Wages.*

In one of his rash moments Marshall declared that though such phrases as "the general rate of wages," or "the wages of labour in general," were "convenient in a broad view of distribution," yet "in fact there is no such thing in modern civilisation as a general rate of wages" (*Principles*, 8th ed., p. 533). His only reason seems to be that there are many kinds of labour and each of them is liable to its own special influences. But surely the fact that prices vary among themselves has long ceased to be regarded as an argument against the possibility of a general rise or fall of prices: or, to take Marshall's favourite analogy, there is no difficulty in saying that the trees in one wood are "generally higher" than those in another, although some of them may be shorter. No one really doubts that earnings are now generally higher than they were a thousand years ago. I do not think I need make any further defence of the inquiry undertaken in the present chapter into what has been said and may be said about the "general level" of labour incomes.

The general highness or lowness of the earnings of labour is a subject of wide interest which must have occurred to ordinary people before economics became a special branch of science, and must have been discussed before any theory of "distribution" was invented. Yet recorded discussions upon it do not go back to antiquity. If anyone wonders why not, let him ask himself why he never considers what regulates the earnings of horses. I suppose he would answer, "Because horses belong to the class of lower animals and therefore are not part of the human community. We don't let them bargain with us. They have got to take what we give them. If they go on strike we whip or spur them, and if that does not make them move in the required direction, we kill them, and make them into leather and glue."

That answer suggests why there were no theories of wages not only when slave labour was the predominant form of labour, but for a long time afterwards when the material condition of the free labourer was scarcely better than that of the slave had been. Thinkers and writers looked on both slave and freed worker much as we look on horses, simply assuming as an axiom that they get their subsistence and no more. As men, they scarcely counted; like horses, they were supposed to work for others who constituted the community. For the sake of that community they had to be maintained like horses in proper condition, and also, as the future supply of workers depended on their bringing up children, they must have enough to support families as well as themselves.

The amount required for this was a fixed quantity of the necessaries of life, so that there were no variations in real earnings to make a theory about. All that was required was a theory of money-wages, and this was very simple, namely, that " wages," *i.e.* money-wages, vary with the price of provisions so as to make the wage-earners always able to buy the same amount, no more and no less.

This doctrine comes out very clearly in the seventeenth and early-eighteenth century belief that taxes on commodities consumed by the poor simply raised money-wages by an amount sufficient to make the wage-earners able to buy as much as they could before the taxation was imposed, and therefore fell on the rich at home and damaged foreign trade by raising the cost of production of exportable goods. If the common people thought that they were, in fact, damaged by such taxes, the economic authorities of the time said they were wrong. Thomas Mun, for example, writing *England's Treasure by Forraign Trade* about 1630, says such taxes are not " so hurtfull to the happinesse of the people as they are commonly esteemed; for as the food and rayment of the poor is made dear by excise, so doth the price of their labour rise in proportion; whereby the burden (if any be) is still upon the rich, who are either idle or at least work not in this kind, yet have they the use and are the great consumers of the poors labour " (p. 85 in Ashley's reprint). Davenant, in his *Ballance of Trade*, takes it for granted that additional duties on beer will cause a rise in the money-wages of woollen workers, "the consequence of which will be that our woollen goods must come at a heavy and disadvantageous price into the foreign markets" (p. 145; Vol. II. p. 267 in *Works*). It does not occur to him to ask if the refusal of the foreigner to buy may not prevent the rise or reduce the price and wages again if they do rise. John Locke, in *Some Considerations of the Consequences of the Lowering of Interest and Raising the Value of Money*, written in 1671, says that if duties on commodities are imposed, the "poor labourer and handicraftsman cannot" pay them, "for he just lives from hand to mouth already," so that "either his wages must rise with the price of things, to make him live, or else, not being able to maintain himself and family by his labour, he comes to the parish" (p. 92).

To the facile assumption of the subsistence theory in the seventeenth century Sir William Petty is a brilliant exception. In his *Political Anatomy of Ireland*, which was written about 1672 and published in 1691, he has a crude anticipation of the modern "contribution" or "imputation" theory, regarding wages as to be discovered by deducting from the whole produce what might be supposed to be obtained from the land alone without any labour:

> "Suppose," he says, "two acres of pasture land inclosed, and put thereinto a weaned calf, which I suppose in twelve months will become 1 C. heavier in eatable flesh: then 1 C. of such flesh, which I suppose fifty days food, and the interest of the value of the calf, is the value or years rent of the land. But if a mans labour for a year can make the said land to yield more than sixty days food of the same or any other kind, then that overplus of days food is the wages of the man; both being expressed by the number of days food. That some men will eat more than others is not material, since by a days food we understand $\frac{1}{100}$ part of what 100 of all sorts and sizes will eat so as to live, labour, and generate. And that a days food of one sort may require more labour to produce than another sort is also not material, since we understand the easiest-gotten food of the respective countries of the world" (*Econ. Writings*, ed. Hull, p. 181).

Petty was much too clever for his time, and no one followed up the idea suggested. Fluctuations in real wages, which are incompatible with the rigid subsistence theory, began to be noticed, for Petty tells us that it was observed "by clothiers and others who employ great numbers of poor people that when corn is extremely plentiful, the labour of the poor is proportionably dear, and scarce to be had at all (so licentious are they who labour only to eat, or rather to drink)."[1] Complaints were frequent that people did not work so well in periods of high wages as in periods of low wages. But no one was stimulated to inquire why the variations took place, or to ask whether they were consistent with a rigid subsistence theory.

Sir Josiah Child in the preface to his *Discourse of Trade*, 1690, while endeavouring to confute an opponent who wanted to reduce wages in order to improve foreign trade, brings up the fact that "the Dutch, who are successful foreign traders, give generally more wages to all their manufacturers by at least two pence in the shilling than the English," and then says that this is evidence that Holland is richer than England. That makes wages depend on national riches rather than on subsistence, but Child does not explain how great riches cause high wages. Half a century later David Hume seems to hold the same view as Child, since he attributed the "high price of labour" in England to "the riches of the artisans and the plenty of money," but he too gives no explanation, though he was acute enough to see that there was something wrong with the doctrine that wages must be kept down for the sake of foreign trade :

> " 'Tis true the English feel some disadvantage in foreign trade by the high price of labour, which is in part the effect of the riches of their artisans as well as of the plenty of money : But as foreign trade is not the most material circumstance, 'tis not to be put in competition with the happiness of so many millions " (Discourse of Commerce, in *Political Discourses*, 1752).

A little before Hume, even the genius of Cantillon had failed to rise above the subsistence theory. Chapter xi of the First Part of the *Essai* tells us that a slave-owner will give his slaves a bare subsistence for themselves and something on which to bring up their children. "He will have to give their overseers advantages proportioned to the confidence and authority which they possess." He will also have to maintain young slaves while they are learning skilled trades and producing nothing, and he

[1] *Political Arithmetic*, 1690, in *Economic Writings*, p. 274.

must give the skilled workmen and their overseers a bigger subsistence than the labourers, because the loss of an artisan would be greater than that of a labourer, since it costs more to replace him by bringing up another youth in the same way.

If serfs or free peasants are employed, they will probably be a little better maintained than slaves would be, " and that according to the custom of the neighbourhood." But " it would always be more advantageous for a landlord to maintain slaves than to maintain free peasants, seeing that when he had brought up more than were wanted for his work he could sell the surplus like beasts, and get a price for them proportionate to the expense he had incurred in bringing them up."

Unlike his predecessors, Cantillon gives some thought to the question, " What is meant by enough to support a family? " Believing that half the children born die before seventeen and one-third under one year, he employs some very doubtful assumptions to prove that (the wife being just about able to support herself in addition to looking after the children) the man must have double what would be sufficient for himself alone. If, in fact, he is unmarried, he will either save up his second portion with a view to marriage, or more often will spend it in better living:

> " The married peasant will be content to live on bread, cheese, vegetables, etc., will rarely eat meat, will drink little wine or beer, will have scarcely any clothes which are not old and bad, and will wear them as long as he can: he will employ the surplus of his double portion in bringing up and maintaining his children: while the bachelor peasant will eat meat as often as he can, and will treat himself to new clothes, etc., and consequently will use his double portion for his maintenance."

Quesnay and the Physiocrats generally were so much interested in advancing their thesis that the agricultural worker supported the whole of society that they had no time for considering what he and the other workers got for themselves. Turgot is sometimes credited with having invented " the iron law of wages "—in French the *loi d'arain*, in German the *ehernes Gesetz*—because he states the subsistence theory with some emphasis: " In every kind of work the wages of the labourer must be, and in fact are, limited to what is necessary to provide him with his subsistence "

(*Réflexions*, § vi). But a careful study of the context will convince any reader that what Turgot was endeavouring to emphasise was not the limitation of the wage-earner's income to his subsistence, but the ability of the agricultural worker to produce more than his subsistence. He simply accepted the prevalent subsistence theory, adding nothing to it except perhaps his suggestion that the limitation is due to the competition of the labourers :

"The labourer as such,[1] who has nothing but his hands and his industry, only gets as much as he can sell his pains for to others. He gets a good or a bad price, but this good or bad price does not depend only on him : it results from the agreement which he makes with the man who pays for his work. That man pays him as little as he can; as he has the choice between a large number of labourers, he prefers the cheapest worker. The labourers are therefore obliged to lower their price, the one against the other."

And this attempt at explanation of the limitation of wages to subsistence is not very satisfying in the absence of any attempt, beyond the suggestion of the "large number" of labourers, to explain why the competition of employers should not counteract the competition of labourers.

§ 2. *Adam Smith's Supply and Demand Theory.*

In regard to Adam Smith's views on earnings, the report of his *Lectures* appears unusually defective, but so far as it goes it suggests that he taught in them much the same doctrine as appears in the *Wealth of Nations*, to which, therefore, we may turn at once.

There he starts with the proposition which became the foundation stone of the nineteenth-century socialism :

"The produce of labour constitutes the natural recompence or wages of labour.

[1] *Le simple ouvrier* seems best translated by "the labourer as such," taking "labourer" in the sense in which it was generally used by Adam Smith and his successors as covering skilled as well as unskilled wage-earners. "The mere Workman," as it is translated in the English version of the *Reflexions* in Ashley's edition (Macmillan's Economic Classics, 1898), is likely to suggest that the non-agricultural worker only is meant, since the next section begins with the statement that "the position of the cultivator is very different." But it seems clear from § 9 that "the cultivator" in § 7 is also the landowner, so that the contrast is not between workers doing different things, but between a mere wage-earner and a person who gets the *produit net* or rent as well as the earnings of his labour. In §§ iv, v, agricultural workers are distinctly included in *ouvriers*.

"In that original state of things, which precedes both the appropriation of land and the accumulation of stock, the whole produce of labour belongs to the labourer. He has neither landlord nor master to share with him" (Vol. I. p. 66).

Modern anthropologists may smile at this reconstruction of primitive society, but we must not be too hard on the speculative history of eighteenth-century writers. It was a method of exposition rather than a seriously believed account of what took place.

After some matter not relevant to our present purpose, Smith proceeds:

"But this original state of things, in which the labourer enjoyed the whole produce of his own labour, could not last beyond the first introduction of the appropriation of land and the accumulation of stock. It was at an end, therefore, long before the most considerable improvements were made in the productive powers of labour, and it would be to no purpose to trace further what might have been its effects upon the recompence or wages of labour.

"As soon as land becomes private property, the landlord demands a share of almost all the produce which the labourer can either raise or collect from it. His rent makes the first deduction from the produce of the labour which is employed upon land.

"It seldom happens that the person who tills the ground has wherewithal to maintain himself till he reaps the harvest. His maintenance is generally advanced to him from the stock of a master, the farmer who employs him, and who would have no interest to employ him, unless he was to share in the produce of his labour, or unless his stock was to be replaced to him with a profit. This profit makes a second deduction from the produce of the labour which is employed upon land.

"The produce of almost all other labour is liable to the like deduction of profit. In all arts and manufactures the greater part of the workmen stand in need of a master to advance them the materials of their work, and their wages and maintenance till it be compleated. He shares in the produce of their labour, or in the value which it adds to the materials upon which it is bestowed; and in this share consists his profit" (Vol. I. p. 67).

Since these deductions came into force, Smith holds, wages have depended on a bargain between "masters" and "workmen" in which, "upon all ordinary occasions," the masters "have the advantage" and are able "to force" the men "into a compliance with their terms." The advantage of the masters arises from their being able to combine more easily and without hindrance from the law, and from the fact that their need of workmen is not so urgent as the workmen's need of wages. To the reader's question, "Why do not the masters then reduce wages indefinitely?" Smith answers with the old subsistence theory, saying that there is

"a certain rate below which it seems impossible to reduce, for any considerable time, the ordinary wages even of the lowest species of labour.

"A man must always live by his work, and his wages must at least be sufficient to maintain him. They must even upon most occasions be somewhat more; otherwise it would be impossible for him to bring up a family, and the race of such workmen could not last beyond the first generation" (Vol. I. p. 69).

He does not inquire how the fact that the labourers would die out if they did not get sufficient to support a family prevents the masters from pressing their advantage in the bargain so far as to bring the wages below that level. It cannot be that the interest of the individual master prevents him from using his individual advantage to the utmost, since he does not rely on his own workmen's children, but can draw on supplies from elsewhere. Does the combination of masters take the future supply into account, and decide, "We must not press for too much, or where will our sons get their labour from?"

Another very important question is also left without any elucidation. If the masters are able in virtue of their advantage in bargaining to push the wages down from the whole produce to the level of subsistence, which is much lower, do they manage to retain the whole difference between produce and the subsistence of the labourers, so that every increase in "the productive powers of labour" goes to benefit them alone?

However, we need not pursue Smith's crude subsistence theory, as he himself, half-conscious probably of its difficulties, immediately proceeds to modify it out of all recognition. Living in Great Britain in the middle of the eighteenth century and being acquainted with France by personal visit and with other countries by voracious reading of history and travels, he could not fail to see that in fact wages are sometimes much above the subsistence level, and also that it is not in the least true that "the labourers must live"—they have often died of starvation, and failed to bring up sufficient children to maintain their numbers. He might well have scrapped what he had written about the masters' power to force wages down to a subsistence level, and, owing to the necessity of living, no further than that. But he preferred to emasculate it by defining the "ordinary occasions" on which it was true as occurring only in a country which has long been stationary in wealth, as, for example, he supposed China to be (Vol. I. pp. 73–4).

As amended and amplified, his theory is that the height of wages depends on the interaction of the demand for labour provided by certain funds and the supply of labour provided by the balance of births and deaths. Good wages diminish, and bad wages increase, mortality, especially infant mortality. When the funds which furnish the demand for labour increase rapidly, wages are high, because the increase of the supply cannot keep pace, and when the funds diminish, wages fall below the subsistence level: the subsistence level is reached and maintained when the funds have long been neither increasing nor decreasing, as would be the case in a country which had long been stationary.

With regard to the supply of labour, his doctrine is that it grows in response to the demand, and he seems quite satisfied with Cantillon's optimism on the subject. Cantillon had said, "the number of labourers, artisans and others who work in a State naturally proportions itself to the need for them" ("*se proportionne naturellement au besoin qu'on en a*" (*Essai*, Part I. chap. ix, title, but who is "*on*"?). Smith says that "the liberal reward of labour" increases the supply of labour "as nearly as possible in the proportion which the demand for labour requires" (Vol. I. p. 81).

But on the demand for labour he is far from clear, owing to the extraordinary vagueness of his conception of the funds which he supposes to provide that demand. He seems to find no difficulty in assuming that they increase and diminish with the "national wealth," which he identifies for the moment with two things which cannot in fact be added together, the revenue or income and the stock of the country; but we soon find that they actually consist only of two small portions of the revenue and stock, and we are given no reasons for believing that these portions are always the same fractions of the whole revenue and the stock, nor even that the portions and the whole always vary in the same direction.

The revenue portion is whatever surplus the rich have over and above what they judge sufficient to maintain their families, as appears from the following paragraph :

> "When the landlord, annuitant, or monied man has a greater revenue than what he judges sufficient to maintain his own family, he employs either the whole or a part of the surplus in maintaining one or more menial servants. Increase this surplus, and he will naturally increase the number of those servants."

"What he judges sufficient to maintain his own family" is doubtless just that part of his expenditure which goes to purchase commodities for the family consumption, and the portion of revenue which furnishes a demand for labour is simply that part of his expenditure which is spent on the direct purchase of labour. If the householder buys wood already cut up from a wood merchant who employs a man to cut it up, he demands no labour; but if he employs that man himself to cut up the same wood, he does demand labour. And if Smith had lived in this age of hotel life, he would have had to hold that the hotel inmate does not demand the labour of the hotel servants, but only maintains himself and his family when he pays the hotel-keeper's bill.

The stock, or capital, portion of the funds which furnish the demand for labour is an equally unsatisfactory conception :

> "When an independent workman, such as a weaver or shoemaker, has got more stock than what is sufficient to purchase the materials of his own work, and to maintain himself till he can dispose of it, he naturally employs one or more journeymen with the surplus, in order to make a profit by their work. Increase this surplus, and he will naturally increase the number of his journeymen" (Vol. I. p. 71).

Taken literally, this seems to imply that all increase of stock goes to the employment of more workmen, but Smith's theory of stock and capital as expounded in Book II does not suggest that the maintenance of labour requires more than a moderate proportion of the whole of the stock. There is nothing to prevent the weaver or shoemaker who finds that his capital is—rather mysteriously—increasing, from investing in machinery or even from stopping the increase by spending the surplus in better living.

The truth is that Adam Smith had here fallen into the popular habit of regarding the demand for labour as being provided by the rich and the capitalists. He was far from the sweet simplicity and correctness of his first chapter, in which " every workman " exchanges his goods for goods produced by other workmen, or, what comes to the same thing, for the price of such goods, so that the demand for labour comes for the most part from the incomes of the workmen themselves.

However confused its theory may be, the chapter on wages indicates a healthy change of sentiment in regard to wages, and change of sentiment is by no means to be disregarded in the history of economic theory. The patriotic economist now follows the philosopher Hume (above, p. 336) in looking on high wages with pleasure, instead of grudging them as making it harder for the " nation " to succeed in foreign trade. " The liberal reward of labour " is, Smith declares, " the natural symptom of increasing national wealth. The scanty maintenance of the labouring poor, on the other hand, is the natural symptom that things are at a stand, and their starving condition that they are going fast backwards " (Vol. I. p. 75).

Then after five pages devoted to showing that the condition of the workers in Great Britain is greatly improved, so that their wages must have risen above the subsistence level, he inquires whether the improvement is a good thing :

" Is this improvement in the circumstances of the lower ranks of the people to be regarded as an advantage or as an inconveniency to the society ? The answer seems at first sight abundantly plain. Servants, labourers and workmen of different kinds make up the far greater part of every great political society. But what improves the circumstances of the greater part can never be regarded as an inconveniency to the whole. No society can surely be flourishing and happy, of which the far greater part of the members are poor and miserable. It is but equity, besides, that they who feed, cloath and lodge the whole body of the people should have such a share of the produce of their own labour as to be themselves tolerably well fed, cloathed and lodged " (Vol. I. p. 80).

Moreover, he adds, the liberal reward of labour " is the cause of increasing population. To complain of it is to lament over the necessary effect and cause of the greatest public prosperity." And it also makes the existing population more industrious; "the wages of labour are the encouragement of industry, which, like every other human quality, improves in proportion to the encouragement it receives" (Vol. I. p. 83).

In the last paragraph of the chapter he replies to the objection that high wages are bad for trade. He admits that high wages make the price of the product high, but seems to mean only that they tend to make it high, as his argument is that the increase of stock which causes the increase of wages also causes labour to be more productive, so that less of the better-paid labour is required, and the diminution in the amount of labour to be paid for more than compensates for the increased value of each unit, so that the product can be sold even cheaper than before.

It is remarkable that Adam Smith should thus end the chapter on wages, as he began it, with a paragraph which certainly suggests the idea of the greater or less productiveness of industry having much to do with high and low wages, while giving up the whole inside of the chapter to a dissertation which seems never to rely at all on the very important fact that the produce per head furnishes at any rate the outside limit beyond which the earnings of labour cannot go for any appreciable time. Why, when writing this middle part of the chapter, did he never think of the eloquent passage at the end of his first chapter in which he represents "the accommodation of the most common artificer or day labourer in a civilised and thriving country" as immensely superior to that of an African king because the productiveness of his industry is so much increased by the division of labour?

Though he was prepared to rejoice over high wages when they came, Adam Smith did not consider it necessary to recommend any special scheme for raising them. This was quite natural, as he held that high wages were the result of prosperity. Let the country in general prosper and the labour of its inhabitants will be liberally rewarded. It did not occur to him that as his theory really made wages depend on the growth of population just as much as on the growth of the funds for the maintenance of labour, it might be worth while to consider whether it might ever be desirable to check the growth of population with the view of raising or maintaining wages.

§ 3. *Malthus on the Supply of Labour.*

In the main, Adam Smith's doctrine of wages was accepted for more than a century.

He himself had treated the funds for the maintenance of labour as the moving force in changes of wages, and had regarded the population or number of labourers as being governed by changes in wages rather than wages as being governed by changes in population. But growing interest in the condition of the working classes and the Malthusian discussions gave a new turn to the inquiry. As it appeared impossible, or at any rate very difficult, to quicken the growth of the funds for the maintenance of labour, why not improve matters by reducing the rate of growth of the numbers of labourers? Malthus in the second edition of his *Essay on the Principle of Population* preaches a new gospel to the labouring classes—a gospel of which the gist is, "To keep up your wages, keep down your numbers!" He says in Book IV. chap. iii:

"The object of those who really wish to better the condition of the lower classes of society must be to raise the relative proportion between the price of labour and the price of provisions, so as to enable the labourer to command a larger share of the necessaries and comforts of life. We have hitherto principally attempted to attain this end by encouraging the married poor, and consequently increasing the number of labourers and overstocking the market with a commodity which we still say that we wish to be dear" (pp. 508–9).

Experience has shown this to be quite futile, and "it is really time now to try something else." We ought to try the effect of a little withholding of the supply of labour:

"In an endeavour to raise the proportion of the quantity of provisions to the number of consumers in any country, our attention would naturally be first directed to the increasing of the absolute quantity of provisions; but finding that as fast as we did this, the number of consumers more than kept pace with it, and that with all our exertions we were still as far as ever behind, we should be convinced that our efforts, directed only in this way, would never succeed. It would appear to be setting the tortoise to catch the hare. Finding, therefore, that from the laws of nature we could not proportion the food to the population, our next attempt should naturally be to proportion the population to the food. If we can persuade the hare to go to sleep, the tortoise may have some hope of overtaking her " (p. 509).

We must, he thinks, show the poor " that the withholding of the supplies of labour is the only possible way of really raising its price; and that they themselves, being the possessors of this commodity, have alone the power to do this " (p. 510).

In a later chapter he puts forward a " Plan of a gradual abolition of the Poor Laws," of which the great feature is the making of a regulation that no child born from a marriage taking place after a certain fixed future date, and no illegitimate child born a year after that date, should receive poor-law relief:

" And to give a more general knowledge of this law, and to enforce it more strongly on the minds of the lower classes of people, the clergyman of each parish should, previously to the solemnisation of a marriage, read a short address to the parties, stating the strong obligation on every man to support his own children; the impropriety, and even immorality, of marrying without a fair prospect of being able to do this; the evils which had resulted to the poor themselves from the attempt which had been made to assist by publick institutions in a duty which ought to be exclusively appropriated to parents; and the absolute necessity which had at length appeared, of abandoning all such institutions, on account of their producing effects totally opposite to those which were intended " (p. 538).

It seems a little too much to expect the hypothetical M. and N. of the Prayer Book, and still more an actual John and Mary with their wedding-clothes on, to refuse to accept each other as wedded husband and wife at the very altar, so in a later edition Malthus puts the reading of the threatening address " after the publication of banns," in order, I suppose, that the prospective bridegroom would be able to forbid his own banns, or at any rate to prevent their being called more than once (in 5th ed., p. 179).

In a chapter " Of the modes of correcting the prevailing opinions on the subject of Population," he says that we must endeavour " to impress as strongly as possible on the public mind that it is not the duty of man simply to propagate his species, but to propagate virtue and happiness; and that if he has not a fair prospect of doing this, he is by no means called upon to leave descendants."

"The merits of the childless," he continues, "and of those who have brought up large families should be compared without prejudice, and their different influence on the happiness of society justly appreciated.

"The matron who has reared a family of ten or twelve children and whose sons, perhaps, may be fighting the battles of their country, is apt to think that society owes her much; and this imaginary debt society is in general fully inclined to acknowledge. But if the subject be fairly considered and the respected matron weighed in the scales of justice against the neglected old maid, it is possible that the matron might kick the beam. She will appear rather in the character of a monopolist than of a great benefactor to the State. If she had not married and had so many children, other members of the society might have enjoyed this satisfaction" (2nd ed., pp. 549–50).

The old maid, on the other hand, "like a truly benevolent man in an irremediable scarcity," has "diminished her own consumption" and has a better claim to gratitude than the matron.

Even the polite usages of society require altering:

"It is perfectly absurd as well as unjust that a giddy girl of sixteen should, because she is married, be considered by the forms of society as the protector of women of thirty, should come first into the room, should be assigned the highest place at table, and be the prominent figure to whom the attentions of the company are more particularly addressed. Those who believe that these distinctions, added to the very long confinement of single women to the parental roof, and their being compelled on all occasions to occupy the background of the picture, have not an influence in impelling many young women into the married state against their natural inclinations and without a proper degree of regard for their intended husbands, do not, as I conceive, reason with much knowledge of human nature. And till these customs are changed, as far as circumstances will admit, and the respect and liberty which women enjoy are made to depend more upon personal character and propriety of conduct than upon their situation as married or single, it must be acknowledged that among the higher ranks of life we encourage marriage by considerable premiums" (2nd ed., pp. 551–2).

But the difficulty is not considerable, he thinks, in the higher ranks of society. There the "preventive check" of prudence in regard to marriage already acts "to a considerable extent." The great need is to make the lower classes equally prudent, and here "the fairest chance" is to establish parochial education as suggested by Adam Smith, but with an important addition to Smith's curriculum :

" In addition to the usual subjects of instruction and those which he has mentioned, I should be disposed to lay considerable stress on the frequent explanation of the real state of the lower classes of society, as affected by the principle of population, and their consequent dependence on themselves for the chief part of their happiness or misery. If, in the course of time, a few of the simplest principles of political economy could be added to these instructions, the benefit to society would be almost incalculable " (p. 553).

His desire is to give the lower classes a higher " standard," though he does not use the modern term " standard *of life*."

" In most countries, among the lower classes of people, there appears to be something like a standard of wretchedness, a point below which they will not continue to marry and propagate their species. This standard is different in different countries, and is formed by various concurring circumstances of soil, climate, government, degree of knowledge, and civilisation, etc. The principal circumstances which contribute to raise it are, liberty, security of property, the spread of knowledge, and a taste for the conveniences and the comforts of life. Those which contribute principally to lower it are despotism and ignorance.

" In an attempt to better the condition of the lower classes of society, our object should be to raise this standard as high as possible, by cultivating a spirit of independence, a decent pride, and a taste for cleanliness and comfort among the poor."

Such a rise of standard would " be the most powerful means of preventing their marrying with the prospect of being obliged to forfeit such advantages, and would consequently raise them nearer to the middle classes of society " (2nd ed., p. 557).

§ 4. *Regulation of the Supply of Labour by the Standard of Life.*

This doctrine of the supply of labour and consequently wages depending not on a bare subsistence but on a movable standard of comfort or standard of life, as Malthus' " standard of wretchedness " came to be called, immediately won complete acceptance among economists. As the standard could be raised or lowered by the will of the working-classes themselves, it made them—usually personified in a somewhat misleading manner as " the labourer " in the singular number instead of the actual world-wide plural—appear to be the arbiters of their own fate. The doctrine was excellently put by David Buchanan in his edition of Smith's *Wealth of Nations*, 1814.

"Where the labourer is content, as in China, to propagate his race at the expense of every comfort, population will increase until poverty and wretchedness become the general condition of the labouring classes. But in a community of a different character, where the habits of the labourer are improved, he will not submit to marry and rear a supply of labour on such hard conditions; and in these circumstances population can never increase so far as to diminish the rate of wages below what is necessary to maintain him in comfort. The labourer may thus be said to have the fixing of his own wages, because when the supply of food is stationary it will depend on himself at what point to stop the supply of people" (Vol. IV. p. 47).

Philanthropists were advised to endeavour to raise the standard. Ricardo in the second edition (1819) of his *Principles* says, "The friends of humanity cannot but wish that in all countries the labouring classes should have a taste for comforts and enjoyments, and that they should be stimulated by all legal means in their exertions to procure them" (2nd ed. p. 95, chap. v, middle).

The lowness of Irish wages as compared with English was attributed to the alleged fact that the Irish labourer's standard made him content with potatoes and bare feet, while the English refused to propagate unless they could have wheaten bread and leather boots.[1]

No one seems to have thought that sound theory should discover some upper limit to the efficacy of restriction of the supply of labour in raising wages. James Mill, indeed, was so far carried away by enthusiasm for restriction that he says limitation of numbers may be carried so far as to raise the condition of the labourer "to any state of comfort and enjoyment which may be desired" (*Elements*, 1821, p. 53; 3rd ed., p. 67).

Any difference of opinion about the proper meaning to be attached to "natural wages," or, as we should say, normal wages,[2] seems to have been of no real importance. It did not in the least affect the unanimity of economists on the essentials of the

[1] Torrens, *Essay on the External Corn Trade*, 1815, pp. 57–8; McCulloch, *Principles*, 1825, pp. 349 ff.

[2] See Malthus, *Political Economy*, p. 247, and Cannan, *Production and Distribution*, p. 257.

doctrine of the regulation of the supply of labour by the "standard." And this doctrine remained unchanged throughout the whole long reign of the supply and demand theory of wages.

§ 5. *What Fund furnishes the Demand for Labour?*

About the other side of the picture, the demand for labour, there was less complete unanimity and also very much less clarity.

Of Adam Smith's two portions of the funds for the maintenance of labour, the first or revenue portion never took any real hold on the minds of subsequent economists. Most of them rejected the semi-physiocratic distinction between "productive" and "unproductive" labour on which it was based, and were therefore disinclined to divide the demand for labour between two funds, one of which was a part of income and the other a part of capital. All of them regarded Smith's "unproductive" labour as small in amount and importance compared with his "productive" labour. So, though the revenue portion occasionally made brief and transitory reappearances, as in John Stuart Mill's rather out-of-date *Principles* in 1848 (below, pp. 352–3), it became the general practice to speak as if "capital" alone furnished the funds which provided the demand for labour.

Malthus himself is very obscure on the subject, but the effect of his insistence on the welfare of the working classes being dependent on the growth of food was to suggest an identification of the "capital" which supports labourers with subsistence. Thus in the earliest economic school-book, Mrs. Marcet's *Conversations on Political Economy*, 1816, Caroline, the pupil, is made to ask, "What is it that determines the rate of wages?" Her teacher replies, "It depends upon the proportion which capital bears to the labouring part of the population of the country," and assents without criticism when Caroline paraphrases her answer into, "Or, in other words, to the proportion which subsistence bears to the number of people to be maintained by it" (pp. 117–18). In another place she says, "All the waste land in the country might be called work to be done, but there can be no demand for labourers to do that work until a sufficient quantity of subsistence has been raised to support such an additional number of labourers as would be required for that purpose" (p. 132).

We may suspect, too, a semi-conscious identification of this "capital" with subsistence in the minds of economists of this period when, as constantly happens, they give examples in which the labourers are, for simplicity, assumed to receive their wages in "corn." Corn is produced in annual harvests, so that a "stock" or capital of it exists at the beginning of the harvest year approximately equal to the consumption of the following twelve months.

That the "capital" which provided the demand for labour, or at any rate for most of the labour, was not the whole of the capital of society was always admitted. But there seems at first to have been some doubt whether or no the portion which furnished the demand for labour must always vary in the same proportion, or at least in the same direction, as the whole capital.

A Select Committee on the Poor Laws reported in 1817 that "What number of persons can be employed in labour must depend absolutely upon the amount of the funds which alone are applicable to the maintenance of labour," and that poor-rates therefore only maintained paupers instead of wage-earners employed by the ratepayers.[1] John Barton, in his *Observations on the Circumstances which influence the Condition of the Labouring Classes of Society*, 1817, was led by dislike of this proposition to champion the popular delusion that the investment of capital in machinery diminishes the total demand for labour. His pamphlet attracted the attention of Ricardo, Malthus and McCulloch.[2] They did not agree about the validity of his contention, but from this time forward it was generally admitted that the portion of capital providing the demand for labour might vary independently of variations of the total capital. Strictly speaking, it was admitted, wages depended not on "population and capital," but on population and a particular portion of capital, namely, that part which is "devoted to" or "appropriated to" the payment of wages. McCulloch expresses the idea perhaps more illuminatingly than any other writer:

"The capacity of a country to support and employ labourers," he asked his readers to believe, "is in no degree dependent on

[1] Parliamentary Papers, 1817, No. 462, Vol. VI. p. 17.

[2] Ricardo, *Principles*, 3rd ed., 1821, p. 479, note, chap. xxxi. end; Malthus, *Principles*, 1820, p. 261; McCulloch, *Principles*, 2nd ed., 1830, p. 541.

advantageousness of situation, richness of soil, or extent of territory. These, undoubtedly, are circumstances of very great importance, and must have a powerful influence in determining the rate at which a people *advances* in the career of wealth and civilisation. But it is obviously not on these circumstances, but on the actual amount of the accumulated produce of previous labour, or of capital, devoted to the payment of wages, in the possession a country at any given period, that its power of supporting and employing labourers must wholly depend. A fertile soil affords the means of rapidly increasing capital; but that is all. Before this soil can be cultivated, capital must be provided for the support of the labourers employed upon it, just as it must be provided for the support of those engaged in manufactures, or in any other department of industry.

"It is a necessary consequence of this principle that the amount of subsistence falling to each labourer, or the *rate* of wages, must depend on the proportion which the whole capital bears to the whole amount of the labouring population. . . .

"To illustrate this principle, let us suppose that the capital of a country appropriated to the payment of wages would, if reduced to the standard of wheat, form a mass of 10,000,000 of quarters: if the number of labourers in that country were *two* millions, it is evident that the wages of each, reducing them all to the same common standard, would be *five* quarters." (*Principles*, 1825, pp. 327–8; in the 3rd ed., 1843, "in no degree" in line 2 was altered to "not directly," p. 379.)

J. S. Mill, remembering Adam Smith's revenue portion of the funds for the maintenance of labour, and also that the capital portion was not supposed by anyone to be the whole of the capital of society, invented or popularised the term "wages-fund," which modern usage has amended into "wage-fund," for the fund which was supposed to furnish the demand for labour. He says wages are ordinarily determined by competition, and then proceeds:

"Wages, then, depend upon the demand and supply of labour; or, as it is often expressed, on the proportion between population and capital. By population is here meant the number only of the labouring class, or rather of those who work for hire; and by capital, only circulating capital, and not even the whole of that, but the part which is expended in the direct purchase of labour. To this, however, must be added all funds which, without forming a part of capital, are paid in exchange for labour, such as the wages of soldiers, domestic servants, and all other unproductive labourers. There is, unfortunately, no mode of expressing by one familiar term the aggregate of what may be called the wages-fund of a country : and as the wages of productive labour form nearly the whole of that fund, it is usual to overlook the smaller and less important part, and to say that wages depend on population and capital. It will be convenient to employ this expression, remembering, however, to consider it as elliptical, and not as a literal statement of the entire truth." [1]

But he very seldom shows any sign of remembering to follow his own advice. Like the rest, he usually forgets that some part of the fund is not capital and that the remuneration of some part of labour (in the wide sense of the economists) is not income of those who "work for hire," *i.e.* for wages and salaries, and his disciples followed his practice rather than his precept.

His populariser, Fawcett, who was Professor of Political Economy at Cambridge before he became a politician, said in his lectures on the *Economic Position of the British Labourer*, 1865 :

"I think that you are all sufficiently acquainted with the elementary principles of Political Economy to know that the circulating capital of a country is its wage-fund. Hence, if we desire to calculate the average money wages received by each labourer, we have simply to divide the amount of this capital by the number of the labouring population. It is therefore evident that the average money wages cannot be increased, unless either the circulating capital is augmented or the number of the labouring population is diminished" (p. 120).

The fact is that it was essential to the wage-fund theory that the wage-fund should consist entirely of capital, or at least so largely of capital that the part of it which was not capital could be safely neglected. The whole object of the theory was to make the demand for labour appear to come from a fund already in existence before the labour to be remunerated had been performed, and this object would have been completely defeated if it had been admitted that the wages, or any considerable portion of the wages, of a particular period (by which in practice was meant any particular year) was produce of *that* period. So long as the wage-fund was understood to consist entirely of capital, or at least to such an extent that the part which was not capital might

[1] *Principles*, Book II, chap. xi, § 1; the last ed. published in Mill's lifetime, followed by Ashley's ed., p. 344, reads, "has been called" instead of "may be called," which possibly, but not certainly, indicates that Mill disclaimed having invented the term himself. Eds. from the 3rd read "depend mainly" in line 1 : Ashley's ed. does not record either alteration. "Custom" is the other factor."

be safely neglected, the wage-fund theory was prevented from being merely equivalent to the true but fatuous statement that the aggregate of wages divided by the number of labourers gives the average wage. For it had been taught by all economists that capital was the result of saving or accumulation, and through all the expositions of the supply and demand theory of wages from Adam Smith downwards there ran the assumption that the "capital" devoted to the payment of wages is a fund which has to be accumulated, and which cannot be increased except by further accumulation or saving.

The point at issue may perhaps be made clearer by a simile taken from water-supply. If we have a really continuous supply of water from a waterworks, we have no use for a cistern, and how much water we can get depends simply on how much we can run through our service pipe and taps. But if the supply is cut off occasionally for periods of different lengths, it will be good for us to have a cistern which will carry us over the longest of such periods, and how much water we can use during any one of such periods will depend on the capacity of our cistern. And if the water were only turned on by the waterworks during the night, when we are not using any, the amount of water we could use in a day would be determined by the stock of water in the cistern at the beginning of the day.

The population-and-capital theory of wages pictured a situation like this. The cistern, or rather the barn, was filled once a year, and the earnings of the whole of the following twelve months had to be got out of it and could not be more than was in it when it was filled. It was never realised that the supply of finished goods and services which constituted "real wages" was "turned on" more or less every day throughout the year, including Sundays (for the Sunday dinner requires to be cooked and the church bells rung). Even at night there is a trickle, which gets stronger and stronger between five o'clock and ten, continues at full pressure till twelve, then drops considerably for a couple of hours, resuming nearly full pressure at two, dropping violently at five, and then falling off further gradually till it reaches the nightly minimum.

It was true that the raw material of *some* of the articles consumed by workers could only be produced in annual batches, so that the amount of such articles finished and consumed during the twelve months following the harvest corresponded fairly closely with the amount in stock at the end of the harvest, and it would not have been worse than rather inaccurate to say that the amount of wheaten bread, for example, which could be consumed in the months to elapse before the next harvest came in could not exceed what could be made out of the stock of wheat and flour in existence at the beginning of those months. But this is a rule which applies to all consumers of the articles in question, and not merely to wage-earners, and if the wage-fund theorists relied on it, they should have thought of a " profit-fund " and a " rent-fund " as well as a " wage-fund."

The fall of the wage-fund theory is sometimes attributed to the attacks made on it by Francis D. Longe in his *Refutation of the Wage-Fund Theory*, 1866, and W. T. Thornton in his book *On Labour, its Wrongful Claims and Rightful Dues*, 1869. But in fact Longe's criticism fell flat, and Thornton's was only important because it caused J. S. Mill to say he no longer believed in the existence of a wage-fund. Neither Longe nor Thornton was able to rise above the atmosphere in which they had been brought up, and they accepted so much of what was erroneous that J. E. Cairnes' defence of the wage-fund theory in *Some Leading Principles of Political Economy*, 1874, appeared a fairly effective answer to them.

They put nothing at all satisfactory in the place of the theory they condemned, and J. S. Mill, after announcing in an article in the *Fortnightly Review* for May and June 1869 (reprinted in his *Discussions and Dissertations*, Vol. IV.), that Thornton had convinced him that there was no wage-fund, declared in the preface to the seventh edition (1871) of his *Principles* that the results of the recent discussions on the matter were " not yet ripe for incorporation in a general treatise on Political Economy," and let his exposition of the wage-fund theory stand unaltered, though he slightly changed two passages in which the power of trade-unionism in regard to wages was dealt with (see Ashley's ed. of *Principles*, pp. xxxi, 934, 936). His too faithful disciple, Fawcett, continued to preach the wage-fund doctrine in his widely used *Manual* (6th ed., 1883, pp. 129 ff.).

" Nature," it used to be said, " abhors a vacuum." Certainly the human mind is very reluctant to part with one theory before something else is put in its place. The wage-fund theory did not disappear till replaced by the appearance, or perhaps we should say the resuscitation, of what may be called the Produce-less-deductions theory of the earnings of labour.

§ 6. *The Produce-less-deductions Theory of Wages.*

The theory which looks for the explanation of the general level of earnings in the amount of the produce per head and the proportion of that produce which is deducted for other shares than earnings is implied in Adam Smith's famous statement that in the "original state of things which precedes both the appropriation of land and the accumulation of stock, the whole produce of labour belongs to the labourer," but in the present state of society he has to give up a portion of the produce to other classes (above, p. 339). If that is the case, the height of his remuneration must evidently depend on the amount he produces and the proportion deducted from it.

It is difficult to see what objection can be made to this except that it is a truism. A truism is, I suppose, a truth which is so universally recognised that it is unnecessary and tiresome to mention it. But the proposition that general earnings depend on the amount of the produce per head and the proportion taken for other shares than earnings was certainly not a truism in this sense so long as it was generally taught that wages depended on population and capital or on the number of wage-earners and the amount of the wage-fund. Those doctrines denied that the produce had anything to do with the level of earnings except in so far as, conjoined with saving or accumulation, it affected the magnitude of the capital devoted to the payment of wages.

Writing in 1826, just fifty years after the publication of the *Wealth of Nations*, Sir Edward West could speak of the doctrine "that the demand for labour depends solely upon the amount or rate of increase of wealth or capital of a country" as "pervading almost every page of every book of note upon the subject of Political Economy" (*Price of Corn and Wages of Labour*, pp. 85–6). He thought it "an error of immense importance," and shows some appreciation of the influence of the magnitude of the labourer's produce. In the next fifty years many writers seem to have groped for the produce-less-deductions theory. Senior desired to make "the funds for the maintenance of labour" depend on the productiveness of labour employed in producing commodities consumed by the labourers and "the proportions in which the produce is shared between the capitalist and the labourer." Mountifort Longfield taught much the same doctrine in Dublin about the same time. Much later, Jevons and J. L. Shadwell came nearer still to a definite produce theory.[1] But all these writers marred their doctrine by compromising in some way with the capital-and-population theory or by some other fatal confusion. Neither they nor anyone else effected much towards replacing the reigning theory with a better one until exactly a century had passed since the *Wealth of Nations* was printed.

Then, in 1876, Francis Amasa Walker, the son of another American economist, Amasa Walker, having noticed that American agricultural wage-earners sometimes received the greater part of their wages no earlier than their employers received their profits, brought out his *Wages Question, a Treatise on Wages and the Wages Class,* in which he repeated the argument of an article which he had contributed to the *North American Review* for January 1875.

He says the wage-fund theory teaches that

> "There is, for any country, at any time, a sum of wealth set apart for the payment of wages. This fund is a portion of the aggregate capital of the country. The ratio between the aggregate capital and the portion devoted to the payment of wages is not necessarily the same. It may vary from time to time with the conditions of industry and the habits of the people; but at any given time the amount of the wage-fund under the conditions existing is determined by the amount of capital" (chap. ix, beginning).

Against this he holds that "There is no wage-fund irrespective of the number and industrial quality of labourers" (heading of chap. ix), the fact being that "The wages of the labourer are paid out of the product of his industry" (title of chap. viii). The wage-fund theory, he says, argues that "capital must

[1] See Senior, *Lectures on the Rate of Wages*, 1831, p. iv, and *Political Economy*, 1836, pp. 180–5 in 8vo ed.; Longfield, *Lectures*, 1834, pp. 209–12; Jevons, *Theory*, 1871, p. 259, 2nd ed. p. 292; Shadwell, *System of Political Economy*, 1877, pp. 133 ff.

furnish the measure of wages," but he holds that "wages are, in a philosophical view of the subject, paid out of the product of present industry, and hence that production furnishes the true measure of wages" (p. 128). "It is the value of the product, such as it is likely to prove, which determines the amount of wages which can be paid, not at all the amount of wealth which the employer has in possession or can command" (p. 130).

Walker taught the same doctrine in his more widely read *Political Economy*, 1883.

§ 7. *Earnings of Labour other than Wages.*

It is curious that Walker, who did such good service in finally burying the wage-fund theory of wages, should have failed entirely in dealing with such earnings of labour as are not received in the form of wages. His doctrine on this subject, known sometimes as "Walker's theory of profits," and at other times as Walker's "theory of rent of ability," is one of the wildest creations of nineteenth-century economic thought.

Observing that some employers get only a bare subsistence (and that partly at the expense of their creditors), while others get more than that *plus* the current rate of return on their capital, he first arbitrarily declared that this surplus over bare subsistence and current rate on capital was alone properly entitled to be called "profit," and then that it was the remuneration of the exceptional natural abilities of those who got it, and this led him to the conclusion that it was a surplus of the same nature as the rent of land, and consisted "wholly of wealth created by the individual employers themselves over and above the wealth which would have been produced in similar industrial enterprises by the same labour-force and capital-force under the control of employers of a lower grade of economical efficiency" (*Political Economy*, ed. of 1885, § 296; almost the same in ed. of 1892, § 325).

This very strange scheme of things in which the product of the exceptionally gifted employers is somehow supposed to be segregated from other produce, although the whole produce is produced by the wage-earners and the employers working in co-operation, never found much acceptance, but difficulty certainly was felt in regard to the position of the capitalist-entrepreneur's profit by the early exponents of the theory that the general level of wages depended on the productiveness of industry and the proportions in which its produce was divided.

That the old theories of crude subsistence and population-and-capital could not be applied to a labour portion of the income of either the "independent workman" or of the capitalist-entrepreneur was indeed fairly obvious.

The independent workman, as conceived by Adam Smith (*Wealth of Nations*, Vol. I. p. 67) and everyone else, was a man who worked on his own account, probably at some form of manual labour, selling his product direct to customers who in no way supervised his operations, employing no assistants, and possessing so little capital that he could remain a "workman" and not be regarded as an owner of stock or capital. He got, according to Adam Smith, two distinct revenues, profits of stock and wages of labour, and presumably he got the same amount of each as would have been forthcoming if these two revenues had belonged "to two distinct persons." So, according to the crude subsistence theory, the wages portion of his total revenue should have been a bare subsistence. But the wages of the wage-paid labourers were only pressed down to the subsistence level by the rapacity of the masters, who "have the advantage in the dispute" (*Wealth of Nations*, Vol. I. p. 68; above, p. 339), and we can scarcely imagine the rapacious master in the independent workman grinding down the labourer in him by means of an advantage in bargaining. If we do not do so, however, the master in him will not get the proper normal return on his capital.

The population-and-capital theory of wages served no better. According to it the remuneration of labourers is limited by the fund provided for their maintenance before they produce, and is independent of the amount of their produce. But if a number of "independent workmen" decide to work an extra hour a day, and this increases their output and its aggregate value, is it reasonable either to suppose that the increase in their remuneration comes to them entirely in their capacity of "masters," or to allege that the previously existing fund for their maintenance must have been enlarged before they could work the extra hour?

The capitalist-entrepreneur's income from labour could not be covered by the old theories of wages any better than that of the independent workman. It could not be contended, as the crude subsistence theory required, that the rapacity of the masters embodied in them brought down the remuneration of the labourers embodied in them to the subsistence level, nor that this particular part of their income was somehow, and unlike the rest of their income, limited by some part of their capital.

The new view of wages as coming simply out of the produce and being governed by the magnitude of the produce and the proportion in which that produce is divided between earnings and the remainder, made it seem easy to deal with the earnings of the independent workman. He was regarded as receiving the whole of his produce (and benefiting to the extent of its whole value), and, as the proportion falling to him in virtue of his being a capitalist was by hypothesis very small, the direct dependence of his labour-income on the magnitude of the produce could be modified only to a trifling extent by changes in that proportion. So no one troubled about that proportion, beyond, perhaps, assuming that the independent workman got the current rate of return on capital, and his labour-income was taken to depend exclusively on his produce.

But this facile solution could not be applied to the labour-income of an undertaker who has too much capital invested in his business or whose working expenses are too large to allow him to pass himself off as a "workman" who himself produces his output. It is easy to think of the produce of an independent workman making baskets on his own account as so many baskets, and of his labour-income as nearly all these baskets. But the labour-income of a manufacturer who owns a large well-equipped spinning factory and employs hundreds of operatives is, even at what he considers the best of times, very far from being equal to the value of nearly the whole output of the mill. In fact it is much more easy to think of the output of the mill as the produce of the operatives who give up a share of their produce to the manufacturer, than to think of it as the produce of the manufacturer who has to surrender a share of his produce to the operatives.

Moreover, the fact that the income of the independent workman had always been called "earnings," and reckoned as large or small according as they were large or small per man per day, made it much easier to include the determination of his earnings under the general theory of income from labour than it was to include earnings of labour performed by the capitalist-entrepreneur, whose income was called "profits" and was reckoned not per man per day, week, or year, but as a rate per cent. on his capital.

This reckoning by rate upon capital was, of course, the natural result of the income of the capitalist-entrepreneur being regarded —unlike that of the independent workman—as predominantly the income of a capitalist rather than of a workman. In comparing the gains or losses arising from different business transactions it is constantly more convenient to set side by side the ratios which the gains (or losses) bear to the expenses than to set side by side the absolute amounts of the gains or losses. And when book-keeping and ideas of accountancy have developed, it becomes convenient to institute comparisons between various businesses by looking at the ratios which the gains or losses of the different businesses bear to the capital employed. The success or ill-success of a business comes to be judged by the ratio which the income it brings in bears to the capital embarked in the business. Hence the capitalist-entrepreneur comes to be spoken of as "making" some percentage on his capital per annum, say 10 or 20 per cent. rather than, like a doctor or an architect (both "independent workmen"), as "making" a certain absolute sum, say, £500 or £1000 a year.

Occasionally even the older writers, when they happened to consider the element of "wages of management" included in profits, would emancipate themselves from ordinary practice and calculate the income per man. Adam Smith himself did it for his apothecary, who might, he says, quite reasonably get a thousand per cent. on his drugs, as they would only cost him £30 a year. Though he does not give the actual figure, he evidently has in his mind that the apothecary would then be making only £300 a year, which would be "no more than reasonable wages." In the case of his "little grocer" he puts the profits at "forty or fifty per cent. upon a stock of a single hundred pounds," and then, evidently deducting £10 for income from the capital (at 10 per cent.), he speaks of "thirty or forty pounds a year" as "not too great a recompense for the labour" (*Wealth of Nations*, Vol. I. pp. 113–15). So too Senior, sixty years later, says that the rates of profit obtained by active capitalists are supposed to run from an average of less than 10 per cent., got by those who have the biggest capitals, up to more than 7000 per cent. per annum got by stall fruit-sellers, and points out that even this 7000 per cent. must be an under-estimate, as it only means about a shilling a day, which is too little, as it "would scarcely pay the mere wages of the labour" (*Political Economy*, 8vo ed., pp. 203–4). But in general both Adam Smith and his followers were content to think of the whole of profits as high or low according as the ratio to the capital was high or low, and this militated against a clear conception of a part of profits being earnings of labour determined like other earnings.

And, lastly, the enormous variations of income obtained by capitalist-entrepreneurs starting with equal capitals as compared with the much slighter differences of wages, made it difficult to believe that the same influences governed both. Trouble here would be avoided if people could only succeed in bearing always in mind that the manner in which the incomes of individual capitalist-entrepreneurs are arrived at necessitates far wider divergences from the average than those that commonly occur among wages and salaries and rates of interest. A person contracts to receive a certain wage or a certain rate of interest and will not take anything much below what he supposes to be the market rate; and the payer of wages or interest contracts to pay the wages or interest and will not give much more than what he considers the market rate of either. Consequently, wages and interest in individual cases keep fairly close to normal or average rates. The profitmaker, on the other hand, expects to make his profit in consequence of the receipts exceeding the expenses of his business; the receipts and expenses are often enormous compared with the capital employed and the normal remuneration of the labour of any single man. In such cases a slight variation of the relation between receipts and expenses owing to a change in either or both may either run the profit up to a point far above the normal or run it down not only to zero, but much further, into the negative region known as "loss."

Now if the capitalist-entrepreneur happens to be getting a normal total, this seems easily decomposed into normal remuneration at the current rate on capital and normal remuneration for the kind of labour involved. But such cases are rare—the average usually is. Ordinarily the total will be either above or below the normal. If it is above, how is the excess to be apportioned between the capital and the labour? Are we to give all to capital or all to labour, or to apportion it *pro rata* between them? And if the total is below the normal, what are we to do about the deficiency? Is it to be charged to capital or to labour, and if, when it is charged to first one of the two, and when that is exhausted to the other, there is still a deficiency—in ordinary language when there is a loss on the business—is this negative return on capital or negative earnings?

Such questions cannot be answered, but they can quite properly be avoided by saying that the doctrine that the earnings of the labour of the capitalist-entrepreneurs come under the same rules as other earnings of labour does not require us to be able to apportion the total obtained by any individual capitalist-entrepreneur between his capital and his labour, but only to be able to say that the whole body of capitalist-entrepreneurs taken together gets approximately the current rate of interest on their capital, and in addition the remuneration for their labour settled in the same way as if it was paid for by way of wages and salaries.

We know that they get as much, or they, or enough of them to equalise matters, would give up undertaking and work for salaries and invest their capital in companies. We know that they do not get more, or the persons who work for salaries and have some capital of their own invested in companies, or enough of them to equalise matters, would sell their stocks and shares and give up their situations and become undertakers. Of course such interchange is constantly going on and does, in fact, keep things always nearly level.

So the earnings which workers receive otherwise than by way of wages and salaries come under the same rule of produce-less-deductions as wages and salaries themselves.

§ 8. *Ultimate Causes of Variation in the General Level of Earnings.*

To say that the general level of earnings varies with the produce per head and the deductions made from it does not by itself take us very far. We want to know something about the reasons for variation in the produce and in the deductions.

For the causes of variation in the produce per head it is clear that we should look to the theory of production. It is obviously unnecessary to repeat at this point the whole theory of production. But it is perhaps desirable to pause for a moment to dwell on the practical importance of variations in produce as compared with that of variations in the deductions. Of course, if the matter is looked at as mere abstract arithmetic, the deductions are as important as the total to be divided. If you are to have what is left of an apple after somebody else has deducted something from it, and nothing is said about the size of the apple, you cannot say the size of the apple is more important than the percentage of the deduction, since it is better to have half a small apple than to have a tenth of one twice the size. But the situation is different if the magnitude of the total is known to vary enormously and the percentage of the deduction is low and stable. If the deduction has been 30 per cent. and the size of the apple becomes four times as great, the deduction would have to rise to as much as 82½ per cent. to deprive you of all benefit from the increase of the total.

Now the measurement of produce is beset with difficulties, but none of us has any real doubt that the productive power of man has increased enormously in the course of history and that if he has at all reduced his exertions, he still exercises enough of this increased power to make his produce very many times greater than it was. The measurement of the percentage deducted from the total for shares other than earnings is also surrounded by difficulties, but it would be simply grotesque for anyone to suggest that changes in the percentage of deductions can, in fact, have had anything like as great an effect on the general level of earnings as the change in the productiveness has had. A not unlikely estimate of the percentage of deductions in modern times is 35 per cent., leaving 65 per cent. for earnings. So when the produce per head was only half what it is now, the earnings could not have been so great even if the deductions had been nothing at all; and if productiveness were now doubled, the percentage of deductions would have to rise to the enormous figure of 67½ per cent. to deprive earnings of all advantage from the change.

It is quite certain, therefore, that in practice variations in the produce per head have been of much greater importance in determining the level of earnings than variations in the percentage of the total deducted.

The causes of variation in the percentage of the deductions must not be too lightly dismissed by a reference to the theory of value. It is true that the percentage of deductions is settled by the value of all the work done compared with the net rental value of all the income-yielding property. It is all the same whether we say "one-third is deducted," or "the value of the work done in a period is double the net rental value of the property," since the net rental value of the property is the income derived from the property.

But that does not make the deductions a simple question of value. In simple cases of value we are thinking of the exchange relation between a definite unit, for example, a bushel—any one bushel—of corn, and commodities and services in general. The size and quality of the unit are fixed, and the aggregate amount of other commodities and services is also treated as fixed, or at any rate as not subject to appreciable alteration in the period considered. In dealing with the deductions, on the other hand, we have to think, not of the net rental value of a single definite unit of property, but of the aggregate value of a varying number of units: the analogy is not with the value of a single bushel of corn, but with the value of the whole harvest, consisting, as it does, of a larger number of bushels at one time than another. Moreover, on the other side of the comparison also, the work done, we have not to deal with something which may be taken as fixed in total amount, but with something which varies in amount like the property units.

Thus the percentage of the deductions made comes to depend on the relative quantities of service rendered by labour and property as well as on the values of each unit of service, and as a relative increase of quantity on either side tends directly to increase the aggregate value of that side (because there are relatively more units), but also at the same time tends indirectly to diminish the aggregate value of that side by reducing the relative value of each unit, the final result depends on the relative strength of those two opposing tendencies.

This probably looks somewhat unintelligible. What it means will become clearer if we ask ourselves, "Why has the percentage of deductions increased in the course of history?" No one would be likely to answer this by saying, "Because the worker has to give up a larger proportion of his time to paying for the use of any given instrument of production or enjoyment than he used to do in the earliest period of which we know anything." Workers of the present day would be very much astonished if they were offered the tools, machinery and houses which were used a thousand years ago. The paraphernalia for the use of which they give up about a third of their time is immensely better—more serviceable—than that for which their predecessors had to pay. Each unit of service is obtained by giving up a much smaller proportion of time, but the units are much more numerous, so that there has been a rise of relative aggregate value.

So far as man-made things are concerned, this is pretty generally admitted. No one supposes that the workers give more of their time to get the use of an instrument or a house or a piece of furniture of the old kind. It is recognised that these things are now of a different kind and better. But it is often supposed that land is an important exception. It is supposed to remain the same from age to age instead of "increasing" like other things. But this is making far too much of mere *area* of land; it is really much the same as if it were alleged that other things had not "increased" because in the aggregate they did not weigh any more. It is admitted that land can be improved in fertility, and it is really equally indisputable that it can be improved in situation. London, it may be said, was always situated on the Thames: true, but it was not always situated on the railways which now run into it, and the Thames is not the same Thames but a vastly improved one. The increase of the deductions has thus taken place in consequence of increase in the quantity of service obtained from the property paid for, and in spite of a fall in the amount paid for units of that service.

We must, however, take care not to forget that though the increase in the number and elaborateness of the instruments of production in any given state of science increases the quantity of service which can be got from them, science—knowledge—is constantly changing, generally increasing, and changes in knowledge very often affect the amount of service which can be got from instruments as compared with that which can be got from other and more or less elaborate instruments or without any instruments at all.

If some discovery in agriculture makes an acre of land as good as two were before, the unit of service afforded by land becomes less valuable. So too, if science discovers a method of weaving which requires less elaborate machinery than that before used, the more elaborate machinery, so long as it continues to exist, though just as capable of yielding service as before, will not bring in the old income, because the value of the unit of service will be reduced by the competition of the less elaborate machine. Such discoveries are very favourable to the general level of earnings, since they both increase the produce per head and diminish the relative value of the unit of service for which deduction has to be made, while they do not raise the number of units.

Other changes in knowledge, however, only show us how to get things easier provided we equip ourselves with more or more elaborate machinery than before. Such machinery cannot be got for nothing. The produce per head, allowing, of course, for the maintenance of the machinery, will be larger, but the good effect of this upon the general level of earnings will be counterbalanced to some extent by an increase in the percentage deducted, since the more numerous or more elaborate machines will not appear, unless more income is drawn from them.

This, again, may look rather unintelligible. It will seem plainer if we ask ourselves what would be the effect (*a*) of a discovery that everything now done with the help of land and instruments could be as easily done by bare hands, and (*b*) of a discovery that by doubling all our instruments we could increase the income of the community fourfold. It seems fairly obvious that the first of these kinds of improvement in knowledge would certainly raise the level of earnings, since it would at once increase produce per head and abolish deductions; and that the second kind of improvement, while tending to increase the accumulation and eventually bringing about an increase in produce per head, would also cause an increase in the percentage of deductions which might more than counterbalance the advantage of greater produce per head.

§ 9. *Conclusion.*

Before leaving the subject of general earnings, we may ask ourselves whether the modern view leaves any place for fragments of the old theories.

Subsistence earnings may well be supposed to be the rule in the lowest stages of human development when men are little above rabbits or apes. The people then may be supposed to be all on the same level, and to propagate to an extent which would make the returns to industry as small as was possible with a continuance of existence. But at all higher stages considerable inequality prevails. The lowest classes of earnings are at and below the subsistence level, but the others are much higher; the general level is well above subsistence.

The standard of wretchedness, standard of comfort, or standard of life theory, which taught that the labourer prevented his wages falling below the standard by cutting off supplies of labour when the level of earnings threatened to fall below that level, breaks down because it only explains why earnings do not fall, whereas, in fact, the history of civilisation is the history of gradual rise of earnings. It is no use to answer the objection by saying that the rise takes place because the standard rises, since the essence of the idea of a standard is something which the workers have become " accustomed to from habit."

The " population and capital " theory was wrong in representing every increase in population as tending to diminish earnings: increase of population is sometimes required in order that the greatest produce per head may be obtained; but the theory would have been right if it had only taught that increase of population *may* tend to reduce produce per head, and always tends to increase the proportion of the deductions. It was quite wrong in teaching that increases in capital or in some ill-defined portion of capital went straight into the workers' pockets in wages, but it would have been right if it had taught that every increase of capital was favourable to earnings in so far as it increased produce per head and cheapened the units of service rendered by capital, even if it increased the aggregate value of all the service taken as a whole.

CHAPTER XII

INCOMES FROM LABOUR: THEIR INEQUALITIES

§ 1. *Occupational Differences: Supplies of Labour.*

MEDIÆVAL thinkers appear to have accepted inequality of earnings between occupations in much the same unquestioning way as they accepted inequalities of political and social rank. There were high-class workers and low-class workers just as there were men and lords and kings. That the armourer should be paid more than the scullion was no more a subject for inquiry than that a squire should be a humble person compared with a belted earl or the Lord Bishop of Durham. Even Francis Hutcheson, Adam Smith's master, lecturing at Glasgow, had said that things were dearer if they were produced by persons who, "according to the custom of the country, are men in high account and live in a more splendid manner; for the expense of this must be defrayed by the higher profits of their labours, and few can be thus maintained" (*Introduction to Moral Philosophy*, p. 209).

When the more commercially-minded modern thinkers noticed occupational differences of earnings, they were inclined at first to attribute them merely to the different value of the work done, oblivious of what seems so plain to us, the fact that this was a mere restatement of the problem in other words. To say that certain work is ordinarily more highly paid than other work is simply the same thing as saying that it is ordinarily of greater value.

Cantillon gets a little beyond this. Part I. chap. vii of his *Essai* is headed, "The work of a labourer is worth less than that of an artisan," which is a mere statement of fact, but the chapter is really an attempt to explain why the labourer's work is worth less. It runs:

"The son of a labourer at seven or twelve years of age begins to help his father, either in watching cattle and sheep, or in tilling soil, or in other kinds of country work requiring neither art nor skill.

"If his father apprenticed him to a trade, he would lose by his absence during the whole of the time of his apprenticeship, and would also be obliged to pay for his maintenance and the expenses of his apprenticeship for several years: so we have a son chargeable to his father and bringing in nothing by his labour till after the lapse of a certain number of years. A man's expectation of life is not reckoned at more than ten or twelve years, and as some of these must be lost in learning a trade, and most trades in England require seven years of apprenticeship, a labourer would never be willing to have his son learn a trade if tradesmen did not get much more than labourers.

"Those, therefore, who employ artisans or tradesmen must necessarily pay their labour at a higher rate than that of a labourer or unskilled workman; and the work will necessarily be dear on account of and in proportion to the expense and risk necessary before anyone can perfect himself for the trade."

This suggests a reason for not trying to remove the inequality rather than a reason why the inequality actually exists. If the existing incentive to the parent to bring up his son to be a skilled worker were taken away, the parent would decline to incur the loss and expense involved. No doubt; but that does not explain why, in fact, the incentive exists. We cannot explain a phenomenon simply by saying that some awkward results would follow its disappearance: that fact may make us rejoice that the phenomenon exists, and may prevent us from making efforts to remove it, but does not in the least explain why it came into existence.

Adam Smith profited greatly in this matter from reading Cantillon, and made a considerable advance by definitely introducing variations in the supply of labour to the different occupations as the cause of differences of earnings. We may well suppose that when Cantillon said the labourer would not bring his son up to a trade unless it had advantages which compensated the disadvantages, he had at the back of his mind the idea that this fact would cause a reduction in the supply of labour to skilled occupations if their comparative attractiveness fell, and an increase of supply if it rose, so that the difference between the remuneration of skilled and unskilled labour would be kept approximately stationary. But he does not say so: nor does he say that the normal superiority of skilled earnings will be just sufficient to compensate the disadvantages of expense and risk.

Adam Smith says both these things, and says them not only of the difference between skilled and unskilled earnings, but of all differences between occupational earnings. "In a society where things were left to follow their natural course, where there was perfect liberty, and where every man was perfectly free both to choose what occupation he thought proper, and to change it as often as he thought proper," he holds that "if in the same neighbourhood there was any employment evidently either more or less advantageous than the rest, so many people would crowd into it in the one case, and so many would desert it in the other, that its advantages would soon return to the level of other employments." Thus occupational differences of wages wherever competition is allowed to work are all to be explained by the fact that there are "certain circumstances in the employments themselves which either really, or at least in the imagination of men make up for a small pecuniary gain in some, and counter-balance a great one in others" (*Wealth of Nations*, Vol. I. p. 101).

The principal of these circumstances so far as Smith was "able to observe" were five in number: (1) the agreeableness or disagreeableness of the trade, (2) the easiness and cheapness or difficulty and expense of learning it, (3) the constancy or inconstancy of employment in it, (4) the small or great trust which must be reposed in those who are employed in it, and (5) the probability or improbability of success in it.

Of these, the first, agreeableness, and the third, regularity of employment, will pass muster. In choosing between trades, persons certainly take into account not only the amount of money which can be earned by an average person in a year or whatever period is long enough to make fluctuations cancel each other, but also these other two "circumstances." Agreeableness obviously attracts and disagreeableness repels. Regularity of employment is highly prized, so that regular employment is more sought after than irregular employment bringing in the same earnings in the long run.

But the other three "circumstances" cannot be allowed to pass. In regard to certainty of success, what Adam Smith had in his mind was the indisputable fact that the mass of mankind does not form perfectly accurate estimates of chances of gain and risks of loss, and that the supply of labour to the different trades will be influenced by the miscalculation. But to call the overestimate which the budding curate forms of his chance of becoming Archbishop a circumstance which in the imagination of men tends to counterbalance the low average remuneration of the clergy is decidedly awkward. It would seem much better to say that such miscalculations prevent competition from having the effect of completely equalising the advantageousness of employments.

The second of the five " circumstances " is open to even more serious objection. Every *man* may be free to choose his occupation and change it as often as he thinks proper, but the choice of occupation is commonly made before manhood is reached, and the expense of training for it is seldom borne by the worker himself. The fact that somebody else has borne certain expenses in order to fit him for his work is no disadvantage to him, and cannot counterbalance the advantage to him of higher remuneration. The difficulty is at most only partially surmounted by the fiction involved in treating parents and children as one, so that a disadvantage to his parents may be reckoned as counterbalancing an advantage to the worker himself. More and more of the expense of education is met from other than parental resources—from endowments, State and local taxation.

Moreover, there is nothing whatever to show that the excess of earnings in the occupations requiring expensive training is an exact or even an approximate equivalent of the necessary or actual expense involved. As Marshall says (*Principles*, beginning of Book VI, 8th ed., p. 504), expenditure on education and training is not made quite on the same principles as investments in machinery or even in training horses. Experience suggests that down to our own time, at any rate, the occupations which require expensive training bring in on the whole a better return, after account is taken of expenses and all other advantages and disadvantages, than those which require no such expense; and there is nothing to prove that the opposite of this would not result if endowments and State assistance grew very considerably. Smith himself suggests that the remuneration of the clergy was poor compared with that of mechanics in consequence of the endowments devoted to the training of clergymen. In order to make this seem not to contradict his general principle, he had to treat these endowments as an interference which increased "the competition in some employments beyond what it naturally would be," but it is not possible to say that pious founders or even the State interfere with men's freedom to choose occupations when they make it easier to choose those which require expensive training.

It is surely better to regard the different expense of training as a thing which, under existing and probable circumstances, causes real inequality both of net advantageousness and of earnings taken alone.

Much more objectionable is Adam Smith's fourth "circumstance," the "small or great trust which must be reposed in the workman." Cantillon had said, "when capacity and trustworthiness are required, as from jewellers, account-keepers, cashiers, and others," the work is paid for at a higher rate (*Essai*, p. 27). Misled by this teaching, Adam Smith says, "The wages of goldsmiths and jewellers are everywhere superior to those of many other workmen, not only of equal but of much superior ingenuity, on account of the precious materials with which they are entrusted." He gives no reason for the implication that being in charge of precious materials is a "disadvantage," but proceeds:

> "We trust our health to the physician; our fortune and sometimes our life and reputation to the lawyer and attorney. Such confidence could not safely be reposed in people of a very mean or low condition. Their reward must be such, therefore, as may give them that rank in society which so important a trust requires" (Vol. I, p. 107).

Not only is there here no trace of any suggestion why the "confidence" should be treated as a disadvantage counterbalancing high remuneration, there is also a curious reversion to the mediæval idea of payment according to rank. The doctrine is not even as plausible as Hutcheson's since Hutcheson does at any rate suggest that if the consumer insists on the producers living splendidly, he cannot maintain many of them, which at any rate suggests that the number of workers is important.

Smith's exposition was accepted very uncritically by most of the next generation of economists, but Malthus saw more clearly that free competition does not secure exactly or approximately just that relative supply of labour to the different occupations which would bring about equality of advantageousness (see *Principles*, 1820, pp. 243–5), and J. S. Mill put the small or great trust " circumstance " in its proper place by suggesting a scarcity of persons of integrity (*Principles*, Ashley's ed., p. 391).

Clear progress was made, but it was obstructed by what remained of belief in the labour theory of value, which hindered frank acceptance of the doctrine that occupational differences of earnings arise from the supply of labour to the different occupations not being such as just to equalise them. Ricardo, as we have seen above in the chapter on value in general (p. 176), endeavoured to evade difficulty by saying that he was concerned with changes of values rather than with the reasons why one pound or one cubic foot of one thing is at any time worth two pounds or two cubic feet of another, and that the relative wages of different occupations did not change much. But Marx scorned any such weak subterfuge, and boldly maintained that the better-paid occupations involve *more* labour per hour of work than the less well-paid, which he chooses to call " unskilled " :

> " Skilled labour counts only as simple labour intensified, or, rather, as multiplied simple labour, a given quantity of skilled being considered equal to a greater quantity of simple labour. Experience shows that this reduction is constantly being made. A commodity may be the product of the most skilled labour, but its value, by equating it to the product of simple unskilled labour, represents a definite quantity of the latter labour alone. The different proportions in which different sorts of labour are reduced to unskilled labour as their standard are established by a social process which goes on behind the backs of the producers, and consequently appears to be fixed by custom. For simplicity's sake we shall henceforth account every kind of labour to be simple unskilled labour; by this we do no more than save ourselves the trouble of making the reduction " (*Capital*, Aveling's trans., Vol. I. pp. 11–12).

If this mystical view were correct, occupational differences of earnings would be non-existent, since if the worker in one occupation was paid twice as much as the worker in another, that would only show that his labour was twice as great.

The modern economist does not imagine, to take the example given by Cantillon, Adam Smith and Ricardo, that the "jeweller's" labour is greater than that of the less well-paid common labourer.

He recognises that the output of one class of labour is frequently of higher value than the output of an equal quantity of another class of labour. He ascribes the difference of value primarily to the causes which make one kind of labour more plentiful compared with others, pointing out in the first place that trades present other advantages and disadvantages besides high and low pecuniary earnings, and in the second place, that legal freedom of choice of occupation does not carry with it effective freedom of choice in the sense of enabling everyone who wishes to become equipped with the training necessary for any occupation that he happens to select. The fact that this effective freedom of choice is limited leads in practice to an inequality not only of earnings but of whole advantageousness, and does so even if expense of training, by whomsoever borne, is reckoned a disadvantage to the person carrying on the occupation.

We ought not to be puzzled, as people sometimes are, by advantages being treated as a set-off against low earnings and disadvantages as a set-off against high earnings, while at the same time we observe that in practice the better-paid trades seem the most agreeable and the worse-paid the less agreeable.

Firstly, we must remember that outside opinion has nothing to do with the matter—what has to be considered is the opinion of people who are in fact potential recruits to the industries. The idea of working underground is extremely repulsive to most people who are unused to it, but this will not maintain the earnings of miners if there are large numbers of people in the mining districts who do not share the feeling. When this is kept in mind, much of the difficulty disappears.

Secondly, we must remember that the people who, owing to the limitation of what may be called effective competition, are in a position to get high occupational earnings are for the same reason by that very fact able to pay, so to speak, for other advantages. If you have the choice between £2000 a year with only one week s holiday and £1750 with six weeks' holiday, you will probably prefer the second alternative, but if the choice open to you was between £200 a year with one week's holiday and £175 with six weeks, you would probably say you could not afford to give up the £25. So it is not at all surprising that the people in the favoured occupations have longer holidays and other advantages which can be obtained by a certain sacrifice of income. This makes no inroad on the principle that agreeableness is a set-off to low income and *vice versâ*, since if the agreeableness were not present, the earnings would be even higher than they are.

The absolute dependence of occupational differences of earnings upon the relative supply of labour to the different occupations is strongly illustrated by the very low earnings obtained in occupations which happen to be attractive to persons with other means of support, when such persons are numerous. Thousands of persons in this country are glad in districts where the work is not very heavy to serve as magistrates without any salary at all: so in those districts it is not necessary to pay salaries. Many kinds of work which can be done by women without much interfering with that care of their own families and homes which happens to be their principal employment are very poorly paid. It is often said that this happens because these persons "can afford" to take small earnings. It is true that if there were no persons who could afford it, the work could not be done at such low rates, but that is simply because the supply of labour would be smaller. People do not offer their work cheap because they can afford it, but because they have many competitors.

§ 2. *Occupational Differences: Demands for Labour.*

It may be asked, "Why so much insistence on the supply side of the problem? Why say that only the relative supply of labour to the different occupations determines their different earnings? Has demand for the products no influence?" The answer is twofold. In the first place, much that is conveyed by the term demand has been already brought in by the addition of the word "relative" to "supply." When an occupation increases its proportion of the whole of the labour force of society, by that very fact it diminishes the demand for its product in the sense of the amount of goods available to be offered in exchange for it. If all the world were bootmakers and nothing more, there would be no demand for boots in the sense of something offered in exchange for boots. Secondly, the remainder of what is meant by demand is of only temporary importance, whereas what we are trying to arrive at is an explanation of enduring differences. Changes in the desires of people for different products will often account for violent temporary disturbance of the usual scale in which occupations rank, but after a time the old scale will reassert itself. Increase the desire for boots, and for some years the bootmakers will benefit, but eventually, after not many years, the number of bootmakers will have increased enough to wipe out the advantage. Diminish the desire for boots and the bootmakers will suffer, but soon desertions from the trade, and still more the diminution of recruits to it, will restore it to its old place in the scale of occupations.

§ 3. *Occupational Differences: Efficiency.*

It may be asked also, "Is it not suspicious that the rule for occupational earnings should be so different from the rule for general earnings? General earnings were said to depend chiefly on output, and now we are told that the earnings of an occupation depend on the supply of labour to it. Has output no influence?" The answer to this is easy. General earnings depend chiefly on output because the greater part of the output is itself the earnings of the workers. But the earnings of a particular occupation are not to any large extent the output of *that* occupation: they are the product of *other* occupations, and how much of the product of other occupations can be got in exchange depends on the *value* of the output of the occupation, and that certainly is by no means the same thing as the magnitude of its output.

The question of the relation between the magnitude and the value of the output of a particular trade is involved in all discussions about the effect on earnings in a trade of variations in the efficiency of the workers employed. Such discussions arise when by one set of advisers the workers in a particular trade are told that in order to raise their earnings in that trade they should be more efficient, and by another set of advisers that they should ca' canny and be as inefficient as possible.

If we are to think only of immediate effects, we must not wholly accept or condemn either of these gospels. Everything depends on the elasticity of demand for the output. If the consumers of the output have what is called an elastic demand for it, that is, if they will buy a good deal more of it when the price is even only slightly reduced, then an increased number of units of output per worker will in the aggregate sell for more than the smaller number produced before, and the worker will benefit by increased efficiency. Suppose, for example, that the trade is basket-making and the workers turn out 5 baskets which sell for 8*s*. each: that then some preacher of efficiency persuades them to increase their efficiency so that they produce 10 baskets, and the doubling of the total only sends the price down to 7*s*. per basket, then the output per person will rise in value as well as in quantity and be worth 70 shillings instead of 40 shillings, so that the worker will benefit. But if the demand is much less elastic, so that the doubling of the output sends the price down to 3*s*. 6*d*., then the output per person, though doubled in quantity, will fall in value, and be worth only 35 shillings, so that the worker will lose. Conversely with ca' canny: if the output is reduced to 3 baskets and the price rises to 15*s*., the output, though diminished in quantity, will rise in value from 40*s*. to 45*s*. and the workers will benefit, but if the price only rises to 10*s*., the value of the output will fall from 40*s*. to 30*s*. and the workers will lose.

We may well suppose that cases of considerable elasticity predominate, but whether they do or not is unimportant, since the immediate effects of changes in efficiency must necessarily be of very short duration so long as the choice of occupations is free. A rise of the earnings of the basket-makers from 40*s*. to 70*s*. would bring in a crowd of recruits to the trade, and a fall from 40*s*. to 30*s*. would keep out recruits and encourage desertions from the trade, so that very soon the trade would be back at its old place in the scale of occupations. If the new standard of efficiency remained permanently, and the alteration meant that there was either more or less hardship in the work, this would be counterbalanced by some increase or reduction in the earnings, but the relative " net advantageousness " of the trade would be unaltered, though, of course, general earnings, the earnings of all trades taken together, would be slightly improved if the efficiency of the particular trade was increased and slightly damaged if it was decreased.

For ease of exposition I have deliberately chosen an example in which we can readily suppose the capitalist-employer to be absent, but his presence makes no important difference. If the basket-makers were employed by capitalists in expensive factories equipped with valuable machinery, the first brunt of the effects of any change in their efficiency would fall on the capitalists. If the output doubled and the price only fell to 7s., the employers would for the moment get all the gain, but this would encourage them and others to employ more basket-makers, with the effect of still further increasing the total output, and by that increase, bringing down the price to the level which would yield approximately the old amount to each worker. If, on the other hand, the output fell off to three-fifths, and the price only rose to 10s., the business would cease to be profitable so long as it was continued on the same scale with the old wages: lower wages or want of employment would keep out recruits and encourage desertions from the trade just as if there was no capitalist intermediary.

The conclusion is that for the immediate interests of the persons employed in a trade, the elasticity of demand for the products determines whether a policy of efficiency or of ca' canny is desirable, and the most we can say is that as elasticity predominates on the whole, efficiency will more often be the best policy. But for keeping a trade permanently in a good position as compared with others, it is no use to recommend either efficiency or inefficiency. If anyone has any lingering doubt about this, let him ask himself whether he really believes that superior efficiency has anything to do with the higher relative remuneration of those trades which are actually the best paid. Clearly we do not and cannot account for the differences which exist between the remuneration of trades which produce quite different things by referring to the different quantity of output per worker. It is not possible to say, for example, that a surgeon produces more than a bus-driver or even that a spinner produces more or less than a weaver. There is no common standard by which the efficiency of the different sorts of labour can be compared.

Rejection of the gospel of efficiency as a remedy for low earnings in a particular trade of course must not be supposed to involve any belief that the preaching of that gospel is to be condemned as heartily as the gospel of inefficiency. If efficiency does no good to that trade, it will at any rate benefit the rest of the community, whereas the ca' canny policy damages the rest of the community. Moreover, the rival gospels are not likely to be preached to only one trade, and the wider the circle in which the gospel of efficiency finds acceptance the better, whereas the wide acceptance of the gospel of ca' canny can only lead to universal ruin.

§ 4. *Occupational Differences: Men and Women.*

The principle that the relative earnings of the different occupations are determined in the long run by the relative supplies of labour solves many problems which without it seem very puzzling.

Among them is that of the inferiority of women's occupations as compared with men's. This inferiority has sometimes been ascribed to some mysterious action of Providence which it would be impious to inquire into, and at other times, especially by male thinkers, to the natural superiority of the male species. But if the general principle be properly grasped, there will be no difficulty in seeing that the real primary cause of the inferiority of these occupations is the greater relative supply of labour to them. There is not one of them which would not rise in the scale of occupations if the supply of labour to it were cut down.

There cannot be any dispute about the primary cause. But the answer to the further question, "Why does this greater relative supply of labour exist?" is more difficult, and we can scarcely hope for unanimity of opinion about it. There are, however, certain facts which may be taken as admitted. The first is that the number of women slightly exceeds that of men: the second is that men are industrially superior to women in some occupations and inferior in others: and the third is that some occupations are closed against one or the other sex by social custom or prejudice, reasonable or unreasonable.

It would be very surprising if these facts did not lead to an inequality between the sexes. Equality could only be expected in either of two very improbable circumstances: (1) if the industrial abilities of the two sexes exactly balanced when taken all together, or (2) if the general industrial superiority of one sex was exactly balanced by obstructions to its employment which caused it to be so confined to overstocked employments as to bring down the value of its work to the same level as that of the industrially inferior sex.

We may therefore take it that the actual lower advantageousness of women's employments is due either to women on the whole having smaller or fewer good industrial qualities than men, or to their being kept by social custom and prejudices in fields of employment too small for their number, or, thirdly, to a combination of these two possibilities.

I shall not expose myself to odium by trying to decide whether the first, second or third of these possibilities is the actual fact. I shall be satisfied if the reader admits that one or other must be the fact. If he has any doubt, let him ask himself whether the position of women's occupations would not be much worse than it is (*a*) if women had only one arm instead of two, or (*b*) if they were allowed in no occupations except nursing and typing, or (*c*) if both these hypotheses were the fact.

§ 5. *Occupational Differences: Combination.*

Another puzzle solved by attention to the principle that occupational earnings are regulated by the relative supplies of labour to the different occupations is the effect of combination on occupational earnings. There is a widespread impression that combination of persons employed in an occupation raises the level of earnings in that occupation as compared with others in which there is no combination or not so much. So long as the wage-fund theory reigned, economists denied that the impression was correct. But when the trade unions had won an established position, there was a tendency to cry "hats off to trade unions," and abandonment of the wage-fund theory was accompanied by a doctrine that combination among workers raised wages by diminishing an "inequality of bargaining power" supposed to exist between them and—not the consumers for whom they really work, but—their immediate employers.

This "inequality of bargaining power" is an old story, which goes back at least to Adam Smith, but it is extremely difficult to get hold of any substance in it either to accept or contradict. Smith himself practically abandoned the doctrine immediately after putting it forward (above, p. 340). Marshall is often credited with holding it, but, in fact, scarcely does so. He says, "labour is often sold under special disadvantages arising from the closely connected group of facts that labour power is 'perishable,' that the sellers of it are commonly poor and have no reserve fund, and that they cannot easily withhold it from the market" (*Principles*, 8th ed., p. 567).

The "often" in this passage is repeated in the marginal summary, which says "labour is perishable and the sellers of it are often at a disadvantage in bargaining," and on the next page it is expressly stated that the doctrine does not apply to all kinds of labour. It does not apply, Marshall says, to domestic service,[1] nor to the "highest grades of industry," which, "as a rule . . . have the advantage in bargaining over the purchaser of their labour." He adds that "the disadvantages of bargaining under which the vendor of labour commonly suffers depend on his own circumstances and qualities and not on the fact that the particular thing he has to sell is labour." All that he is really prepared to contend for is apparently that "manual labourers as a class are at a disadvantage in bargaining" (*Principles*, 8th ed., p. 569).

Now in ordinary life and language a seller is said to make a "bad bargain" when he sells below the market price, and it must be supposed that any circumstances which cause him to make such bad bargains place him at a "disadvantage in bargaining." This is fairly simple, but it is not at all easy to see how a whole class of sellers can habitually and as a rule make bad bargains and be at a disadvantage in selling. The price at which a whole class habitually sells must surely be the market price itself.

The claim that combination of workers in a trade removes their disadvantage in bargaining, then, cannot be distinguished from a claim that it raises the value of the work done.

The combination makes the workers into one body which is the only seller, or monopolist, of that kind of work so long as no one outside the body takes it up. All the usual rules or theory about the power of monopolists to raise prices apply to it. The engine for raising price is restriction of supply, and the degree in which price can be raised will depend on the elasticity of demand. The monopolist must be careful not to imperil the continuance of his monopoly by pressing his advantage so far that outside competitors spring up, and so on.

Applying this theory to the trade union, we can see that it is an extremely weak species of monopolist. Unless it has adventi-

[1] Because, apparently, domestic servants "are sometimes better able than their employers to act in concert"—a remarkably feeble argument.

tious aid from the legislature or the public administration of the country, it cannot prevent new competitors arising outside its own body except by the cultivation of a strong public sympathy, and this public sympathy will be withheld if the monopolistic advantage is pressed at all far. But in addition to this difficulty from outside competition, the union has always to contend with the much greater difficulty of keeping down the growth of its own body as soon as the work becomes appreciably more attractive. Trades are chiefly recruited from the children of persons employed in them and of neighbours of such persons, and the interests of these children are taken into account and weigh against the abstract interest of the "trade": if the children are kept out of the trade, the wages of the trade may be higher, but they will be obliged to put up with some less advantageous employment. Remembering this conflict of interest, we are not surprised that the historians of trade unionism tell us that in fact little has ever been accomplished by trade unionism in the direction of limitation of numbers (S. and B. Webb, *Industrial Democracy*, ed. of 1902, p. 713).

That purely temporary differences can sometimes be created in the comparative advantageousness of different trades not by the slow process of keeping out new-comers but by the threat of withdrawal of all the existing workers—*alias* a strike—is undeniable. Readers will probably be able to quote cases from their own knowledge where the position of some class of workers is higher at the moment in consequence of a strike or the possibility of a strike. But they should consider whether such a position is likely to be permanently maintained, and also whether the converse case of the workers in some trade being temporarily in a lower position owing to a strike does not occur. It certainly was very plausibly contended that the low position of the British coal-miners about 1928 was partly due to the effects of the combination policy of previous years.

If we want to draw lessons from history in this matter, we must not compare conditions at two probably abnormal moments, but take a view of, say, twenty or thirty years in each of several centuries. And if we do that, we shall find, I think, firstly that the scale of whole advantageousness in which occupations are arranged is very little altered, and secondly, that such alterations as have taken place can be explained easily and satisfactorily by causes other than the working of trade unionism.

It by no means follows that we must dismiss trade unions as pernicious or even useless in regard to the regulation of wages. We ought not to regard them as successful or unsuccessful according as they have raised or failed to raise wages, nor to regard employers' combinations as successful or unsuccessful according as they have lowered or failed to lower wages. To do so would be like judging a lawyer's skill by the proportion of cases he has won. The true function of combinations on both sides is to alter the conditions of the bargain when it requires altering, and to do that quicker and with less friction than it could be done by individual bargaining. In fact, of course, combinations are not always wisely managed, and the result is far from the ideal, but, paradoxical as it may sound to those who think all industrial trouble comes from combination of the side to which they are opposed, I am inclined to think that combination on both sides has been a useful and indeed necessary part of industrial organisation. I say "has been," because I do not wish to commit myself to the proposition that this will continue. It is quite possible, and as change is the rule, it is probable, that some other form of organisation will supersede both trade unions and employers' combinations.

§ 6. *Occupational Differences: Regulation.*

A rival is already in the field in the shape of legislative or administrative regulation of wages and hours. We think of it as a new rival, but regulation of wages is really very old; what is modern is merely that the regulation is now made in the interest of the wage-earners so that it lays down minimum rates, while the older practice was in the interest of the employers and laid down maximum rates. We need only concern ourselves with the modern form.

It is easy with the aid of modern police systems to enforce the kind of negative regulation involved in prescribing a minimum rate of wages for any one trade or for each of a few trades, even if the minimum fixed is much above what would otherwise be paid. The regulation does not, as is often very stupidly supposed, require anyone to pay these wages: it only requires everyone to abstain from paying less. It would not be contravened if no one employed anyone in the occupation. If the minimum were fixed very high, no wage-earners would be employed in the occupation, and the business would fall into the hands of independent workers selling the product direct to the consumers, or the work would be done by the consumers themselves or not at all. If, for example, legislation prescribed a minimum of £10 a day for wages of all persons employed in laundry work, nobody would be so employed. The work would be given out to single washerwomen who would not employ anyone, and if even this was stopped, we should wash our things at home in our basins and baths.

Actual regulation, of course, does not run to such an extreme; what it does is merely to secure that the number of persons employed at wages shall not exceed the number which can be employed without loss at the rate laid down. To take the same example as before, a strictly enforced regulation that no one employed in laundry work shall be paid less than 10*s*. a day will secure that the number of persons so employed is reduced or kept down to that which can be employed at that rate. The relation which prevails under free competition between the number of persons employed and the wages is reversed under regulation: under competition the numbers settle the wages, under regulation the wages settle the numbers.

The simplest result of a raising of the wages of an occupation by regulation would be the raising of the price to the consumer of the product till the price was sufficient to pay the increased wages. But this simple result seldom if ever occurs. There are various ways of modifying it.

(1) The regulation, if well enforced and severe, may create "places" in the old sense of employments so well paid that it is worth while to pay something to get into them. If the payment takes the form of a premium paid to the employer, the loss of the employer in higher wages is so far made up by gain from the premiums, and the tendency to rise of price so far defeated. If it takes the form of a bribe to foremen and managers, the loss of the employer in higher wages to the persons under regulation will be made up to some extent by his gain in having to pay less to these others who get the bribes.

(2) The cost to the employer of the higher wages may often be at least partially met by the withdrawal of other advantages of the employment, such as free coal, low rent for houses belonging to the employer, toleration of irregularity and slackness, and so on.

(3) The cost to the employer of the higher wages may be partially obviated by employing a superior class of persons. At one time it was common for local authorities to employ partially crippled and other decrepit men on road-sweeping; there arose an agitation against the low wages paid to these men, wages were raised, and soon none but able-bodied men were found in the employment. In an ordinary employment carried on for the usual motives, an increase of wages occasioned by regulation has just the same tendency to raise the quality of the persons employed. If you have to pay high wages you may as well get the best workers you can for the rate you have to pay.

An increase of efficiency arising from selection of workers from a superior class must not be confused with an increase of the efficiency of the same class. People often argue as if higher wages must always result in a proportionately increased efficiency of the persons already employed, but this is quite too optimistic. If it were true, it would open a royal road to wealth. Of course it is true that there is always some limit below which the wages of employment which form the sole income of the workers cannot profitably be reduced. Supposing the employer had the power of employing a person at a wage which would only just support life, it would be silly of him to do so: obviously it will be more profitable to give something more than that, so that the man may have strength to do some work. But it will not be profitable to give indefinitely more: the increase of efficiency got by each additional shilling or pound of wages per week will be less and less as the wage increases, so that a point must soon be reached beyond which it is not profitable to go. The point will be differently situated in different trades at the same time and place and in the same trade at different times and in different places. For example, it must be higher in England now for a coal-hewer than for an office lift-man: higher now for a shepherd in England than for a shepherd in the time of Elizabeth or William the Conqueror: higher for a textile mill-hand in Lancashire now than for one doing the same kind of work in Bombay.

Where exactly the point is situated in any particular occupation at some one time and place is difficult to decide with any certainty, but it seems very unlikely that the point is often above the wages actually paid. It is so easy to try the experiment of paying more, that it is difficult to believe that there would be no pioneers to do it and others to follow their example if it were really profitable.

These appear to be the general principles governing occupational earnings —the theory of the subject. We must not be too ready to abandon them merely because we often find cases in which the tendencies described have been defeated by counteracting incidents. For example, we may suppose that in some localised and not very large industry wages have been very low, and that a regulation raising them has been made after a public inquiry by an expert investigator armed with all the knowledge which can be obtained from the various departments of an efficient School of Economics. The trade, we will further suppose, survives the rise without any reduction in the number or of the non-pecuniary advantages of the persons employed and without any rise of price to the consumers. Such a case, if it occurs, need not disturb us. It is quite likely that this particular industry has been lagging behind the general march of progress and that its inertia has been overcome by the inquiry and the new light thrown on things by the expert from outside, so that the improvement would take place even if the regulation did not follow the inquiry, or if there was no penalty for disobeying it.

Nor must we imagine that the question is not one, as I have represented it, between persons employed in an industry and the consumers of the products of that industry, but between the persons employed and the persons who happen to be called their employers. In some important and large industries, of which medical service, the army, navy and domestic service are the most prominent types, the employers and the consumers are the same—there is nothing in the shape of middle-men employers-for-profit between the two bodies. In the other cases, the fact that the profits of the employers are placed between the wages and the price obtained for the product is seldom of more than very temporary and limited importance. Even the purest monopolist finds it profitable to raise his prices if he has to pay more for each unit of his output (Marshall, *Principles*, 8th ed., p. 482, top). He certainly will not bear the whole of the extra expense of raised wages.

Whether the profits go to an active organiser or to inactive shareholders makes little difference. Active organisation in any occupation is itself an occupation and is open to encouragement and discouragement which bring in recruits and throw out existing competitors. Investment of capital is attracted by high returns and repelled by low returns. It cannot, it is true, flow out of the trades in which it has taken on the form of specialised machinery, but such machinery can be reduced in time by non-renewal of the least profitable parts.

§ 7. *Individual Differences.*

Let us now think of inequalities of earnings as between one individual and another. Why does A manage to get good earnings while B only gets bad? Perhaps the most attractive manner to discuss the question is to ask, " What should a person do in order to get good earnings, without, of course, sacrificing more than he is willing of other advantages? "

(1) He must begin betimes by choosing suitable parents. They must be healthy in body and mind and possessed of all such ability as is transmissible by inheritance, so that he may inherit industrial ability so far as that is possible: they must be persons who will not spoil him by over-indulgence or by cruelty in his childhood: who are willing to sacrifice their own comfort and pleasure to some considerable extent for his sake: and who have a number of other virtues unnecessary to specify which will result in his being brought up "respectable." These are the most important requirements for his parents, but it is also extremely desirable that they should be accustomed to the best society, so that he will learn at an early age not to sniff, not to turn over leaves of a book with a licked finger, not to say " between you and I," and other niceties which differentiate the " upper classes " from the vulgar. And further it is desirable that his parents should be possessed of sufficient means to be able to pay a certain amount for his education and training as well as to do without getting him to supplement their income.

(2) He will do well to be born a boy rather than a girl.

(3) He must select his occupation, or have it selected for him, with good judgment, regard being had to his peculiar characteristics and also to the future prospects of the different trades; that is, he must select an occupation for which his talents are suitable, and prefer a trade which is going to grow to one which is going to decline.

(4) Once in his occupation, he must be industrious and as efficient as possible. The idlers, the fools, and other good-for-nothings will tell him that it is no use, that the standard wage will be paid him anyway, and that promotion goes entirely by seniority or favouritism, but he must treat them as the liars they are, and hold to the belief that though there are unlucky exceptions, yet as a rule the industrious and efficient do better than the lazy and inefficient. Even if held down by the rigidity of a standard wage, the industrious and efficient get more regular employment and can choose the best employers: however unsatisfactory the arrangements for promotion may be, the industrious and efficient have better chances, at any rate, than the others of obtaining it. We can often point out cases in which lazy and incompetent persons are making better earnings than industrious and efficient persons in the same occupation, but we know that this is not the rule but the exception.

Some authorities add to this list of requirements that it is desirable that the person should have some capital of his own, as this will, they think, enable him to enter what they consider the privileged occupation of being an "undertaker" or "entrepreneur." Now of course it is well for anyone to have capital of his own, because if he invests it wisely he will draw income from it. But those who hold that the occupation of being an entrepreneur is a privileged one mean more than that: they believe that, not as capitalist, owner of valuable property, but as worker the entrepreneur is favoured in comparison with salaried and wage-paid workers. They say that when work is done and property owned by the same person, more value is somehow generated than when the work is done by one person and the property owned by another.

But there is no such occupation as that of an entrepeneur in general. There are farmers, mine-owners, clothiers, carriers, hotel-keepers, newspaper-owners and thousands of other classes of entrepreneurs which require entirely different kinds of training. As a rule each trade trains and provides its own entrepreneurs or undertakers, so that if there were a scarcity of recruits to the undertaking of business because persons could not be found with both the training and the capital, the scarcity would be present inside the particular trades: the remuneration of farmers, for example, would be kept up by the rarity of persons with both knowledge of farming and farming capital, whereas, in fact, the capital is already there on the farms in the shape of farming stock, and the farmers have plenty of sons to replace themselves and their knowledge of farming.

It seems difficult to see any *primâ facie* case for the belief that the coincidence of training for the conduct of the different sorts of business with the possession of the property necessary for carrying them on is rare enough to have a value of its own in those businesses which are still carried on by single individual capitalists; and so far as I know nobody has ever tried to prove that this alleged rarity actually exists—its existence is simply assumed. In regard to the other businesses, those in which the training for the conduct of the business is not required by the owners of the property but by other persons whom they employ, the doctrine that the conjunction of the requisite training with the possession of the requisite capital has some value of its own falls between two stools: the value can only be got by relative scarcity of the product, which must be due either to deficiency of labour or deficiency of capital: it cannot be attributed to scarcity of the conjunction of any particular class of labour with capital. The belief that it can be so attributed is only supported by the very weak argument that Mr. Blank complains that capitalists will neither lend him money nor employ him as a director or manager: all that this means is that the capitalists prefer to lend and entrust management to other persons in whom they happen to have more confidence than they have in Mr. Blank.

The whole idea seems to have arisen from the difficulty felt, especially in America, in accounting for the very large incomes obtained by men like Carnegie, Vanderbilt and Ford. But surely the difficulty is imaginary. The work that these people do is important because it controls the work of so many other persons. If a man controls a business employing 100,000 men and makes some arrangement which makes each of these men's work worth 6*d.* a week more, he makes the net result of the business $\frac{100{,}000 \times 6d. \times 52}{240} =$ £130,000 a year better than before. If he is the entrepreneur he will get that amount. But is there anything surprising in that? It is merely because he is paid by the piece: his high earnings are analogous to the earnings of persons whose singing or writing is greatly admired by many people.

§ 8. *National Differences.*

So far we have taken no notice of "nations." We have discussed the general level of earnings, the relative earnings in different occupations, and the causes why the earnings of occupations and of individuals differ, without ever once suggesting that nationality is an important factor in the problem. This may seem startling in view of the facts that the mercantilists were almost solely concerned with the interests of "the nation"—their own particular nation—and that Adam Smith took an "inquiry into the nature and causes of the wealth of nations" to be a synonym for "political economy." But I do not think there is a more devastating error in the economic field than the belief that nations are water-tight or rather economic-tight compartments with permanently different levels of earnings due to the different natural resources of the national territories and the different policies pursued by the national governments.

If neither persons nor goods could be moved from one national territory to another, the belief would be defensible. Each national territory would be almost a separate world: the mere interchange of ideas which might take place by telegraph, telephone and wireless could only assimilate them in very small degree. But such a condition of things is grotesquely unlike the reality. The movement of men and goods over international boundaries (however "national" may be defined) has been and is enormous. Recently, it is true, there has been some increase in the usual efforts of governments to obstruct such movement, and it is conceivable that in some far future the apostles of separatist nationalism may realise their ideal of cutting up mankind into a few score or hundred economically independent units which will exchange nothing except perhaps shells and poison-gas. But if that is ever to be, it certainly is not yet, and it is not likely that the youngest of us will live to see it. For my own part I have sufficient faith in mankind to think that a gradual breaking down of national barriers is more probable.

The first thing to do in considering differences of national earnings is to make sure that we know what we mean when we say earnings are higher in one national territory than in another. Are we comparing the average earnings of all the earners, irrespective of their employment? Or are we comparing the earnings of occupations in the one territory with the earnings of the same occupations in the other territory? The comparisons are not identical unless the distribution of the earners between high and low grade occupations is the same in both territories. The working population of the one country, for example, may be much more employed in high-class commercial and manufacturing work than that of the other: in that case the remuneration of each occupation might be the same in the two countries, and yet the average remuneration per head would be higher in the first country than the second. To put it in another way, a higher average of earnings in one country than in another may be due either to the first country being more specialised in the better-paid employments, or to some or all of the employments taken separately being better paid than the same employment in the second country.

The question why national earnings differ may thus be resolved into two questions: (1) why the distribution of high-grade and low-grade employments between countries is what it is, and (2) why particular occupations have higher earnings in some countries than in others.

The first of these questions is usually treated under the head of localisation of industries, and it is not necessary here to say more than that it is not a matter of absolutely free-will choice, as the economic historians are apt to suggest when they talk, for example, of England having left off being an "agricultural country." It is a question chiefly of historical geography: a country with large deposits of accessible minerals has a high proportion of miners: one well situated for international commerce has a high proportion of merchants: one suitable for agriculture and little else has a large proportion of agriculturists; and so on. The suitability for many occupations need not be altogether "natural" in the sense of being dependent on the original physical characteristics of the country: it may be due to incidents of history, the occurrence of which can scarcely be attributed to causes called geographical. One of these incidents is good or bad policy on the part of the government of a territory in allowing the free movement of persons and goods in and out of the territory. Harassing restrictions may easily cause such well-paid occupations as work for the international market to shun a country in which they are imposed, and on the other hand a state may do a good deal to encourage the necessary science and technique so that the best exponents of both appear in and remain in its territory.

The second of the two questions, however, is more often the one which is in the mind of a person who asks why earnings are higher in one country than another. He will be thinking of certain figures giving the earnings of some particular trade or trades in one country alongside those of the same trade or trades in another country.

The favourite popular explanation is that the higher earnings are caused by the greater suitability of the country in which they occur for carrying on the trade or trades. It goes badly with another popular belief (or belief that once was popular), the belief that the people inhabiting countries with poor natural qualities are more likely to become rich in consequence of industry and frugality than those inhabiting the countries with great natural resources. And when we look at long-settled countries, we see little to support it. What is very obvious is that the unsuitability of a country for carrying on any occupation reduces not the earnings, but the number of those who are employed in the trade. Gross unsuitability keeps the number down to zero. Greenland is a very unsuitable country for elephant-hunting: Nigeria is a very unsuitable country for sleigh-makers. The consequence is not that elephant-drivers get starvation wages in Greenland and sleigh-makers starvation wages in Nigeria, but that there is not a single elephant-hunter in Greenland nor a single sleigh-maker in Nigeria. In less extreme cases comparative unsuitability for a trade is met by fewer persons being employed in the less suitable than in the more suitable countries rather than by less earnings being obtained by those who are employed. There is always a gradation in an employment because the fertility of the natural resources worked upon and the proximity of the producer to the consumers are both various and important. Take coal as an example: the fact that coal-fields or coal-mines in a country are of different richness and proximity to the consumers obviously makes it possible for the miners to have higher earnings in that country when there are few miners than when there are many. Consequently uniformity of miners' earnings in two countries can be attained by adjustment of numbers, each country using only its better mines, and the line at which use stops being the same in the two cases; for example, if there was nothing to consider except depth, each country would stop at x hundred feet, and as by hypothesis there is more coal above x hundred feet in country A than in country B, there would be more coal-miners in A than in B, but there is not the least necessity for their earnings to be different.

The theory of the subject is clear enough, and it is borne out by observation of the actual facts. If comparative suitability regulated earnings we should not find the very great similarity which exists between the scales in which occupations are placed in all the countries of the world. Such differences in the scale of earnings as we see are often counterbalanced by opposite differences in the other advantages. We find, for example, that domestic service wages are higher in the scale both in those countries where the servant is expected to work harder, and in those where the servant is regarded as low-class by other workers. In other cases the divergence from the usual scale is a temporary matter due to some change which necessitates movement of the workers. Gold-mining is a good example of this. Gold discoveries have usually been made rather suddenly in rather inaccessible places, so that the supply of labour was not readily forthcoming. If the Yukon gold-field had been discovered in England instead of in the inaccessible place where it was, those who worked it would only have got the same earnings as men employed on a new arterial road.

"In spite of all this," someone may say, "the fact remains

that the earnings of trades do obviously differ enormously from country to country. Look at the United States and China ! "

Some amount of difference is due to some of the countries being what is called " new," by which we mean only made easy of access to the rest of the world within the last few centuries. A good deal of North and South America is still attractive to immigrant workers, and one at least of the reasons clearly is the same as that which took workers to the Yukon, the fact that natural resources in those continents are still, in spite of the immigration and natural increase of population which has taken place since Columbus, somewhat more plentiful in relation to the number of people than they are in the outside world. The advantage to earnings tends to be wiped out in time by immigration and natural increase. Immigration can perhaps be kept in check, but there is probably more difficulty about the maintenance of a higher standard than that of other countries in regard to natural increase of population. But though it is rather improbable on the whole that the advantage will be maintained, it exists at present.

Whether enduring or fleeting, however, it is a small matter compared with differences of personal efficiency between the inhabitants of the different countries. All the really great differences are clearly due to this. What is the difference between earnings in England, an old, and the United States, a new, country, compared with the difference between, say, England and the Congo, both old countries? It is no use to talk of deficiency of capital or education, since these things could have been got by a more efficient people.

This leads us to the interesting and comforting reflection that though the gospel of efficiency cannot be preached with such confidence as is often assumed to the whole of any particular trade throughout the world, or even to any part of that trade which is absolutely protected from competition of the other parts, yet it may be preached with absolute confidence to the national divisions of a trade when they are in competition (either owing to imports or exports) with the outside world, just as it may be preached to each individual member of the occupation taken separately. It is, for instance, true that cotton operatives as a whole would not more than temporarily improve their relative position (except, of course, as consumers of cotton goods along with other such consumers) by improving their efficiency; but it is also true that if either the Indian or the Lancashire cotton operatives improve their efficiency as compared with each other or with the American and Japanese operatives, they will reap a benefit. The persons practising a trade do not cease to be individuals because they are a national group, and efficiency is certainly profitable to the individual. Each person, as we have seen, practising a trade benefits by an improvement in his own efficiency unaccompanied by a corresponding increase in the efficiency of his fellows in the trade; and the whole of the persons practising a trade in a particular country, if they are in the world-market, are in the same position.

If it is asked what are the causes of differences of national efficiency, a very long story is opened—the history of the world, and by no means only economic history, nor even that and political history: religious and every other sort of history has to be brought in. We cannot be sure that what we look on as permanent is really going to last. It is not certain that the peoples now most efficient will always be so; the others may improve faster and pass them in the race.

Much of the superiority of new countries is probably due to the admixture of peoples and the selection of the more adventurous persons from the old countries which was effected by voluntary migration. Whether the new countries can long preserve their advantage under the modern systems of restricted and officially selected immigration remains to be seen. In any case it can scarcely be more than a temporary matter, especially if the old countries continue to reduce their natality until they have no emigrants to send out.

CHAPTER XIII

INCOMES FROM PROPERTY

§ 1. *Their General Level.*

THE old scheme of Distribution or, as I called it,[1] Pseudo-distribution, discussing first wages or earnings per head, but then going on to two things, the rate of interest and the rent of given areas of land which were co-ordinate neither with wages per head nor with each other, gave rise to a very erroneous view of general economic tendencies. It suggested to the ordinary mind that the proportions of the total income falling to the three shares, those of labour, capital and land, must vary with the rise and fall of "wages," identified with wages per head; "profits," identified with the rate of return on capital; and "rent," identified with the annual value of a fixed area of land. And as the Ricardians taught, or seemed to teach, that unless population could be induced to stop increasing, which was supposed to be unlikely, rent must go on increasing and profit falling, while wages remained about the same, the outlook for what were considered the two meritorious classes, the labourers who toiled and the capitalists who abstained, was decidedly gloomy. No wonder the science of economics at the time won the sobriquet of "the dismal science." About the best that could be hoped for was an eventual "stationary state," which J. S. Mill thought might not be so very bad after all (*Principles*, ed. Ashley, pp. 746–51).

All this was, of course, mere nightmare. Wages per head, profit or interest per cent. and rent per acre are not proportions of the produce, and any one of them can be higher at one time than another without the "share" supposed to be indicated—the income derived from labour, capital or land as the case may be—having become a larger proportion of the whole produce.

[1] In *Production and Distribution*, chap. vii.

It does not follow that we ought to create a new Theory of Distribution in which we should attempt to lay down generalisations as to the division of the produce between three properly conceived shares of labour, capital and land. In the first place, capital and land are inextricably compounded together; the income derived from each cannot be discovered or estimated, and would be of no interest if it could be. Secondly, if this objection is met by lumping land and capital together as both "property," and discussing the division between property on the one hand and labour on the other, we run a very grave risk of preserving some of the old confusion, since it is highly probable that whatever the economist may say in deprecation, his readers or pupils will imagine that increases of the percentage of the total taken by earnings of labour mean, or at least indicate, increases of earnings per head.

Moreover, variation of earnings per head are much more interesting to the healthy mind than variations in the proportion of produce taken by labour, and are much greater. Therefore it has seemed advisable in this work to discuss earnings per head in chapters xi and xii, bringing in the division of produce only as one, and not the most practically important, of the things which affect them.

Now the question arises, Can property incomes be dealt with in the same way, so that the inquiry may continue on a logical basis? I think they can, although the idea of a general level of property incomes seems at first sight much stranger than that of a general level of earnings of labour.

In reality the two problems are very much alike. What we want to do in discussing earnings is to make clear the principal causes which determine how much people earn by labour, and what we want to do in discussing incomes derived from property is to make clear the principal causes which determine how much people receive in virtue of their possession of property. In regard to property incomes just as much as in regard to labour incomes, it is only reasonable to consider what makes the general level high or low before considering what makes the incomes of particular groups and individuals high or low in relation to each other at one and the same time.

The only real difficulty in conceiving the two problems as

parallel seems to arise from the fact that when we think of average earnings we usually confine our attention to the earnings of working adults and think of our average as the result of dividing the total of working adults' earnings by the number of such workers, while there is no such prominent class of property-owners whose property and number we can segregate from the rest. But this difficulty is surmounted when we reflect that what we were really in search of in regard to earnings was not particularly the factors determining the earnings of working adults, but the factors determining the general capacity of the people of all ages and qualities to earn, and that we merely take the earnings of the average working adult as an index of this. As there is no such index available in regard to what people receive in virtue of the possession of property, we are obliged—and the necessity is in no way a grievous one—to get at our general level of property incomes by conceiving an average obtained by dividing the total income from property by the number of persons in the whole population.

I proceed, therefore, to ask what the causes are which determine the general level of property incomes, or, in other words, the amount of income from property per head of population.

The answer must obviously be on the same lines as the answer to the corresponding question about the general level of earnings. Primarily the level will depend on the magnitude of the produce per head and the proportions in which that produce is shared; the average individual, conceived as one who gets the average income from labour plus the average income from property, receives a total equal to the produce per head (of the whole population) divided between the two kinds of income in the proportions in which the total is divided.

This absolves us from the necessity of saying much about the matter here, since the magnitude of the produce per head is a question belonging to or identical with the theory of production, and the division of the total between labour and property has been dealt with when we were considering the ultimate causes determining the general level of earnings. The only thing to add seems to be that while it is true of property income as of labour income that a change in the magnitude of the produce per head is more important than a change in the proportions in which it is divided, it is not quite so much more important as it is in the case of labour income. This is because, since property has the smaller share, greater possibilities of increase through an increase of the proportion taken by it are open to it than are open to the labour income. If the whole is stationary and the property income is one-third of the whole, it could be increased 50 per cent. (becoming one-half of the whole) by a reduction of labour income by only a quarter, whereas labour income could not be increased 50 per cent. without wiping out the other share altogether. So a change in the proportions is at any rate potentially more important to the property income than to the labour income. But even in regard to the property income, if we are to judge by past history, by far the greater hope of increase is in increase of the total. The general level of property income in modern civilisation is far higher than the general level of property-plus-labour income in mediæval or ancient times.

§ 2. *Inequalities between Different Kinds of Property.*

It is a common practice for the owners of each kind of property to complain that their particular kind is less profitable than some or most other kinds. As profitableness is measured only by the ratio which the income-value of the property bears to the capital-value, the complaint involves the allegation that they could improve their incomes by selling their property and investing the proceeds in one of the more profitable kinds of property. They lay themselves open to the devastating question, "Then why don't you sell and go into the kind of business which, you say, pays so much better?"

The complaint is usually quite groundless and only inspired by a half-wish to "fly from ills we know to those we know not of." But at other times it is true enough that the actual income obtained bears a smaller proportion to the capital-value than is found in case of other kinds of property. This is due, as has been already suggested in chapter ix (above, p. 277) to the fact that "circumstances," as Adam Smith called them, other than the rate of return on capital itself have some influence over persons selecting investments. If a particular kind of property, for example, is made disagreeable to hold by unpleasant risk of loss, or made agreeable to hold by pleasing hope of abnormal gain, the fact that individuals do not give these chances their actuarial or average value will deter or encourage investment in them in a way which will make their average return in the one case higher and in the other lower than the average from all kinds of investments. So too if discredit on the one hand or social distinction on the other is commonly attached to the holding of particular kinds of property, the average return will be higher in the one case and lower in the other than the average return from all kinds of property. For example, in the England of two centuries ago the possession of land conferred a certain social distinction which was supposed, and probably correctly supposed, to make land sought after to an extent which made the return on capital invested in its purchase lower than the average on all kinds of property; while in modern England the abuse showered upon owners of houses let to the poor deters capitalists from building such houses and causes the return on them to be higher.

All this is simple enough. But it does not in any way cover the curious belief, founded probably on impressions inherited from feudal times, and fostered by the Ricardian theory of rent, that land is a form of property which, although it confessedly yields a return lower than that given by other property in consequence of the social distinction conferred by its possession, yet is somehow more advantageous to hold than other property.

One support of this belief was an impression that land was always rising in value, coupled with want of understanding of the manner in which expected future rise in value is discounted in present value. J. S. Mill furnished an example of this state of mind when he proposed to confiscate all future increment in the value of land while giving existing holders no reason to complain by letting them continue to enjoy the present market value ! [1] He quite failed to see that if an expectation of increase in the value of any property is removed by legislation or in any other way, the present market value of the property, which, as

[1] " I see no objection to declaring that the future increment of rent should be liable to special taxation; in doing which all injustice to the landlords would be obviated if the present market price of their land were secured to them; since that includes the value of all future expectations " (*Principles*, ed. Ashley, p. 819).

he himself naïvely admits, "includes the present value of all future expectations," must fall. There is no reason for supposing that future rises in the value of land are usually undervalued in the market prices of the moment. History since Mill's time shows that the future prospects of English agricultural land, which was what he had chiefly in mind, were then not under-estimated but grossly over-estimated—partly, no doubt, in consequence of the erroneous teaching of the Ricardian economists. With good judgment, aided by good fortune, a man may here and there secure great gain by buying land and selling or leasing it later when its value has risen, but some lucky persons make money at the Monte Carlo table and have good judgment enough to make them come away at once. The average land speculator suffers from "the hope deferred which maketh the heart sick"; eventually he generally sells at an advance, but at an advance not nearly great enough to make up for interest lost and expenses incurred. If a large number of those who believe in the future increment of the value of land making land a better investment for a given capital than other property could only be induced to try it, we should soon begin to hear less of their doctrine.

Another support for the belief that land was a better property to hold than any other was found in the confusion of mind which led people to think that landowners were "passive" and owners of other kinds of property were active and abstemious. Mill supposed that the increment which he wished the State to appropriate came to the landlords although they were completely "passive" (*Principles*, ed. Ashley, p. 817), and he said, "political economy has nothing to say in defence of landed property" where the landlords are not improvers (*ib.* p. 231). He forgot that it was true of the holders of many other kinds of property which are increasing in value more certainly than land—say, the 3 per cent. stock of a corporation which has to be paid off at par twenty or thirty years hence—that the holder can become richer while remaining purely passive; and that no one thinks political economy condemns debentures or bonds because the holders do not "improve" them. The land may not "want" any improvement—it may be that no further profitable investment could be made in improving it. In fact, of course, the owner of land usually has to be much more active than the owners of shares, stocks and bonds issued by companies and governments. One holding of particular stock is just like another, whereas every parcel of land is different from every other, and requires individual attention from the owner. To imagine the receiver of rents as uniformly passive and the receiver of dividends who has given orders that they should be paid to his bank as uniformly active, is grossly perverse.

A third and equally rotten prop for the belief in the superiority of land was found in a confusion between the origin and the method of acquisition of property which caused people to think of land as if it was all inherited by its present possessors and of all other property as if its present possessors had acquired it by a course of saving or abstinence. This, of course, may have been reasonable in mediæval times, but is merely ridiculous under modern conditions when land is continually being bought and sold, and immense amounts of the most valuable parts of it belong to companies, and are thus reckoned as stocks and shares rather than land by their owners and everyone else.

These absurdities were enshrined in a precious sentence of J. S. Mill's: "They," that is the landlords, "grow richer, as it were, in their sleep, without working, risking or economising" (*Principles*, ed. Ashley, p. 818). We may well doubt whether, if Mill had been given the choice between a gift of land worth £10,000 and a gift of the same value in stocks and shares issued by government and non-landowning companies, he would have chosen the land in order to save himself the trouble of working, the anxiety of risking, and the pain of economising.

§ 3. *Inequalities between Different Individuals.*

The doctrine that Land was the gift of Nature, whether she was considered bountiful or niggardly in the matter, and that Capital was created by the labour of Man seconded by his Parsimony, Thrift or Abstinence, gave rise to a widespread impression that economics taught that the individual capitalist was always a sort of Dick Whittington who started life with nothing, but scraped together a small capital out of his bare subsistence earnings and added to it by further savings from the profits made on this capital, while the individual landlord was an idle improvident person who inherited all he ever had from a father like himself. So it was natural that inequality of incomes from land should be ascribed entirely to forcible appropriations of Nature's gifts which took place in barbarous times and did not concern the economist, and that inequality of incomes from other property should be ascribed to the fact that men are not all equally gifted with the virtues of providence and self-denial.

The nineteenth-century socialist attack on the existing economic organisation did little towards clearing away these ideas, because it was at bottom founded on the primitive and mediæval prejudice against interest on capital rather than on hostility to inequality of incomes. Exponents of general theory in economics seem to have thought the matter too simple to need treatment in their works. J. S. Mill indeed displayed considerable hostility to very large incomes, and was willing to accept such alterations in the laws of inheritance and in the taxation of inheritances as seemed to him likely to reduce such incomes, but this did not lead him into any general consideration of the causes of large and small incomes from property.

In the article entitled "The Division of Income" which I contributed to the Harvard *Quarterly Journal of Economics* for May 1905 (reprinted in my *Economic Outlook*, 1912), I classified the causes of inequality of incomes derived from property under five heads; namely, differences in (1) providence, (2) judgment in the selection of investments, (3) good fortune in investments, (4) magnitude of income out of which to make savings, and (5) amount received by way of inheritance, bequest or gift. *Wealth*, 1914, suggests a grouping of the causes under (1) differences in the amount received by way of inheritance, bequest and gift, (2) differences in the amount saved, and (3) differences in the history of what has been obtained in these two ways, since both what is received by way of inheritance or gift and what has been got by saving may rise or fall in value. The two classifications are at bottom the same, since the amount saved depends on willingness and ability to save (1 and 4 in the earlier classification), and whether the property rises or falls in value depends on the owner's good judgment and good fortune (2 and 3 in the earlier classification). But the second is, I think, a little the easier to handle, and I shall follow it here.

(1) Inequality of inheritances was at one time attributed largely to the law and custom of primogeniture, but if either the law or the custom was ever of any great importance it ceased to be so, in this country at any rate, a long time ago. The law did not apply at all to anything except land, and even in regard to land it did not prevent a full owner from dividing his land and leaving it to whom he pleased. The custom which prevented full ownership by "settling" land on the eldest son for his life and providing that it should then go to his eldest son, often held great estates together, and thus maintained inequality of area of land inherited, but the inequality of the value of property inherited even in this sphere was much less than would appear at first sight, owing to the charges for relations with which the owner was commonly saddled, and the sphere was after all a limited one which has steadily sunk in comparative importance in face of the increase of other kinds of property.

Restrictions on the liberty of bequest which prevent testators from making very unequal distribution of their property on their decease, such as have long prevailed in most countries, have generally had very little effect, because they only prescribe what the testator would generally do of his own free-will. Probably the most important effect of laws enforcing nearly equal division among children irrespective of sex has been to give women a somewhat larger share of property than they would otherwise have had. But when marriage was more universal than it is now, and husband and wife less separate entities, this made little difference.

Given freedom of bequest and a general inclination to divide equally among children, inequality of inheritance will tend to increase or diminish according as persons with property to leave have small or large families, and according as these children intermarry among themselves or marry other persons with little or no property. Quite recent movements rather suggest that forces tending towards equality are being strengthened. As it is considerations of expense that are the most powerful influence in causing well-to-do but not rich people to restrict the number of their family, and these considerations cannot be supposed to have much influence with the very rich, we may reasonably suppose that the size of the families of the very rich will not diminish so much as that of the less rich owners of property, and as there is growing freedom of intercourse in places of education and elsewhere between young people of the richest and other classes, we may also suppose that marriage between the two classes will become more common.

A more powerful influence is the modern system of collecting large amounts of taxation by means of imposts levied on inheritances. Even if these were levied at the same rate on all amounts, they would be to some extent equalisatory in the scheme of the distribution of wealth as a whole, since they would reduce the advantage of the inheritors over the rest of the society. But a flat rate, even if it were 40 per cent., would leave inequality of the inheritances themselves untouched; an inheritance of £2,500,000 would still be a thousand times as great as an inheritance of £2,500; the taxation would reduce it to £1,500,000, but would also reduce the £2500 to £1500. The graduated rates now common, however, cut down the inequality among the inheritances themselves very drastically. The £2,500,000 taxed at 40 per cent. in England comes down to £1,500,000 as before, but the £2500, taxed at only 3 per cent. comes down only to £2425, so that the big inheritance becomes only 606 times as great instead of a thousand times as great as the little one.

Whether the graduation of rate applies according to the magnitude of the property of the deceased or according to the magnitude of the inheritance received by the individual inheritor makes less difference than might be expected on a first view of the matter. It is easy to imagine strong cases in which it would make a great difference; under the second system a millionaire's property bequeathed in equal shares to a thousand legatees would pay much less than if it was left to one person, and this would tend towards reduction of inequality. But in actual life the large properties ordinarily descend in such large blocks that the persons getting the largest inheritances do, in fact, have to submit to the largest deductions of tax under the first system.

While graduation of rate according to amount tends towards equality, graduation according to or rather in inverse relation to the closeness of kinship between predecessor and successor tends in the opposite direction. A rich person's property when it goes on his death to distant relatives or strangers in blood is as a rule distributed more widely than if it goes to his children—it is easier to have twenty nephews and nieces than twenty children. Consequently graduation against strangers in blood and distant relatives will ordinarily be more favourable to recipients of large as compared with recipients of small inheritances than a flat rate will be.

Differences in amounts of property inherited obviously account for a large amount of the inequalities in the amounts of property owned at any one moment, but it seems probable that we are apt to over-rate the importance of this factor as compared with the other two mentioned above. Accumulation is so rapid in modern Western countries that a very large proportion of the property in existence at any one moment consists of things which have never yet been inherited, but have come into existence by accumulation in the hands of their present owners. The accretion of property may easily be 2½ per cent. per annum, and this doubles the whole in about thirty years. This new property has certainly not gone entirely to the inheritors of property, and that in proportion to their inheritances. On the contrary, we are all acquainted with cases in which men who are now very rich started life with little or nothing, and with cases in which inheritors have either accumulated great additions to their inheritance or have somehow managed to have less now than when their inheritance fell to them.

(2) Unequal savings, with their converse, unequal overspendings, account for much of this. Persons who save a great deal become in time possessed of much property, and persons who spend more than their incomes get rid of part or the whole of the property with which they started. The influences which cause one individual to save more or less than another are fairly obvious to ordinary intelligence. "Providence," or care for the future compared with the present, magnitude of income, and amount of "claims" on that income seem to be the chief things which affect the will and the power to save with different force in the case of different individuals, and they sometimes act all in the same direction, but more often in conflict, two of them tending one way and the third tending in the opposite direction.

Magnitude of income may well be taken first, since it is impossible to save if one's income is only sufficient to support life and meet claims, such as taxation and the support of young children, which cannot be repudiated at will. The whole of the surplus can be saved, so that if claims and providence were the same for all individuals, the comparative amounts saved would depend entirely on the comparative magnitude of their respective incomes.

Whatever the magnitude of income, claims vary enormously as between one individual and another. Of two persons with equal incomes, one may have to support a mother or a sister in an asylum and the other have no such claim to meet; one may have a wife and large family of young children and the other be unmarried or married to a wife with independent income and no children; little generalisation about these "family" claims can be made, except perhaps that among the last generation it was probably true that the smallest incomes and the biggest number of children seem to have gone together, and that in recent times some effort has been made by States to lighten the burden where incomes are small, by remissions of taxation to parents who pay income-tax, and by relieving still poorer parents of some educational expenses.

Of two persons with equal incomes, both large, one may belong to the typical "old rich" class and be practically compelled by the pressure of public opinion to maintain an ancient mansion full of ancestral portraits and other treasures, and perhaps a park open to the inhabitants of the neighbouring village and visitors from a distance, while the other belongs to the "new rich" and can live in a flat in the town and a bungalow in the country in equal or greater comfort and much less expense. Given equal income and equal providence, the old rich will save less than the new rich.

There is one "claim," however, which in quite recent times has begun to work steadily in the opposite direction to magnitude of income. This is progressive taxation of income. In this country little more than thirty years ago, incomes above a low minimum were taxed at a flat rate of a few pence in the pound. Now in 1929 the rate is progressive from nothing at all till it reaches 50 per cent. on the surplus over £30,000. This is an enormous sterilisation of the savings-fertility of the very large incomes, and the scale is an important handicap all the way down.

Lastly, as regards providence, there are great individual differences which it seems impossible to reduce to neat order. We shall never be able to account satisfactorily for the frequent occurrence of cases where, of two brothers with the same upbringing and start in life, one is a large saver and the other a spendthrift. In some instances we explain it by saying, "Jack takes after his miserly great-uncle William," and "Bill wasn't extravagant till he married Delia," but we do not know why Jack should have had this particular "throwback," nor why Bill should have been caught by the careless Delia. Apart from individual idiosyncrasies, we can perhaps say that while the persons already in possession of large assured and continuous incomes have less need for saving than those with smaller or less assured and continuous incomes, they usually have somewhat more providence; the security they already enjoy is valued so highly by them that they are more willing to sacrifice some enjoyment in the present for the sake of still greater security in the future, while the people with small and precarious incomes are less afraid of falling lower than they are. We can also say with rather more confidence that the old rich are generally more provident than the new rich, because the fact of ancestors being known to have long held a good position is conducive to desire that posterity should continue to hold that position.

(3) If everyone's property consisted entirely of cash in the house and money due from banks or other institutions, and money did not vary in purchasing power, each person's property at any moment would be exactly equal to the sum of what he had received by way of gift or inheritance plus what he had saved from income. But in fact most persons' property diverges a good deal from this amount. Even where it consists entirely of money, it is liable to change in value as reckoned in the things the owner is likely to purchase, and for the most part it consists of other things than money, and all of these are liable to become worth more or less than they were worth when acquired. Favoured by good judgment and good fortune, a person who has acquired any property by inheritance, gift or saving from income will not only retain what he has acquired, but will find it increasing in value; hampered by bad judgment and bad luck he will find his property diminishing in value. To

discriminate exactly between what is due to good or bad judgment and what is due to good or bad luck is generally impossible. He who invests five shillings in a lottery ticket and wins a £10 prize is only lucky—in fact he showed bad judgment in giving five shillings for a chance which was not actuarially worth that amount. But if he won £10 by betting on a race-course, you cannot say he was merely lucky unless you are sure that neither he nor anyone whose advice he deliberately chose as good knew nothing at all about the horses except their names. When a person's possessions have risen greatly in value, he congratulates himself on his good judgment in having bought them, or, if he acquired them by inheritance, on his good judgment in having retained them: if they fall in value he deplores his ill luck.

However difficult or impossible it may be to determine how much is due to luck and how much to judgment, it is easy to see that the two together, acting in the same direction (or even in different directions if one has little effect compared with the other), have a great deal to do with inequality of property: some persons have the reputation of turning everything which they touch into gold, while the eggs of others are always addled.

In regard to judgment, beginners in the ownership of property are at considerable disadvantage owing to absence of experience and want of access to sound advice. The gains of promoters of bogus banks, bucket shops and other swindles are mostly made at their expense. The very rich descendants of very rich predecessors are indeed rather apt to become interested in other things than investments, but their want of personal experience is more than counterbalanced by the fact that the largeness of their operations secures for them the best available advice.

Of this welter of influences, sometimes co-operating in the same direction, sometimes conflicting with each other in many different combinations and a great number of degrees of force, it is difficult to discover any broad results, and any such results which might be discerned are liable to be disordered by the perpetual intrusion of new property-owners drawn from the earners.

§ 4. *Inequalities between Different Nations.*

In the pre-Smithian, pre-individualist period, when national wealth was conceived as an aggregate without reference to the number of persons who had a share in it, a comparison of the income from property received by one nation with that received by another would be a comparison of aggregates; and as in that period the holding of property in one country by persons living in another country was uncommon, and in the aggregate unimportant, there was no obvious need to take account of it. Consequently, a comparison of national incomes from property would, if it had been thought of at all, have taken the form of setting the aggregate annual value of all the property situated within one country against the corresponding figure for the other country.

But in our own times we are not impressed by aggregates. It is nothing to us that the aggregate of income or of some particular kind of income is greater in the United States than in Switzerland; we want to know about income per head of the persons receiving it. And it is no longer approximately true that all the property inside each country is owned by persons living inside it. In every civilised country some of the property inside is owned by persons living outside, and some of the property outside is owned by persons inside. The property inside one country owned by persons outside may be land belonging to "absentee landlords," like much of the land of Ireland before the State schemes of transferring it to the tenants came into operation, or any other kind of property owned directly by private individuals; but in quite recent times more important elements are (1) the property of companies whose shareholders and bondholders are all or mostly resident outside the country in which the property lies, and (2) such obligations of the State as happen to be held by bondholders outside the country; these last are not so tangible as Irish land, but so long as they are met, they are just as substantial as the rights of the Irish absentee landlord to his rents.

The want of coincidence between the situation of property and the residence of the owners would be of little importance for our present purpose if the income from the property held by inhabitants of each country outside it approximately balanced the income from the property inside it held by inhabitants of other countries. But in many cases the two incomes do not nearly balance. A few of the old countries, and also the

United States, receive more income than they part with, and most of the new countries and some of the old ones part with more than they receive. Great Britain and Holland, for example, receive more than they part with, while South Africa, with her valuable gold and diamond fields owned largely in Europe, parts with more than she receives, as did Russia also before she repudiated her national or " Tsarist " debts.

As things are, the question whether a nation shall have a large or small income per head from property has thus come to depend on the magnitude of the income owned in the world as a whole by the average inhabitant of the country. What this may be depends on historical circumstances about which it is difficult to generalise. The important practical thing to remember is that inhabitants are movable to a considerable extent, and the owners of property are the most mobile of all inhabitants, and are more and more mobile the richer they become; they will therefore tend to congregate in the countries in which residence seems most desirable, and this fact will have to be taken into account when the relative merits of taxation according to personal residence and according to situation of the source of income have to be considered.

CHAPTER XIV

ASPIRATIONS AND TENDENCIES

§ 1. *For and towards Greater Equality of Economic Welfare.*

It is and probably always has been universally recognised that when a given amount of goods or services is to be distributed among a number of persons, equality modified by differences of need is the best rule if nothing beyond the immediate effects of consumption has to be considered. If it is said that capacity for enjoyment should be taken into account, the answer is that we know too little about this capacity for enjoyment to be able to take it into account except where it is covered by differences of need. We cannot safely say of two persons in sound health that A gets more enjoyment out of spending three pounds instead of two than B gets from spending two pounds instead of one, and that therefore it would be well to divide four available pounds between A and B by giving A three and B only one. We could say that this division might be best if A was hale and hearty, and B was infirm and only able to put on his clothes and sit in the porch, but this may be included under differences of need.

The distribution which results from the incomes from labour and property which we have been discussing in the last three chapters is obviously very far from following the rule of equality modified by differences of need. It is extremely unequal, and its inequalities do not in the least coincide with differences of need—among other instances of this we may note especially the fact that income from work has an inconvenient habit of stopping altogether just when the worker becomes incapacitated and requires expensive tending by nurses and surgeons.

Uninstructed benevolence, thinking only of immediate effects, suggests a very simple remedy for this defect of distribution—those that have more than the average should give the surplus to those that have less. Christ said, " Let him that hath two coats give to him that hath none," and under the influence of the apostles, Peter and John, the early Christians at Jerusalem "had all things in common":—

> "Neither was there any among them that lacked: for as many as were possessors of lands or houses sold them, and brought the prices of the things that were sold, and laid them down at the apostles' feet: and distribution was made unto every man according as he had need."

Even a Levite from Cyprus, called Joses, sold his land and laid the money at the apostles' feet and was surnamed Barnabas, "the Son of Consolation," in commemoration of his action (Acts iv. 32–7). How long this plan enabled the faithful to continue "daily with one accord in the temple," "breaking bread from house to house" and eating "their meat with gladness and singleness of heart" (Acts ii. 46) we are not told, but it is perhaps not without significance that a little later a certain Agabus went from Jerusalem to Antioch and delivered some message to the Christians there which induced them "every man according to his ability," "to send relief unto the brethren which dwelt in Judæa" (Acts xi. 27–30). It seems reasonable to conjecture that the Christians of Jerusalem were suffering from the consequences of their experiment when they were assisted by those of Antioch, who evidently had not followed the Jerusalem example, as they subscribed according to their individual ability, and it is difficult not to feel some sympathy with Ananias and Sapphira's unlucky attempt to keep something back against the evil day which they may have foreseen when the experiment should fail (Acts v. 1–11).

We hear nothing further of this unregulated communism among the early Christians, and St. Paul seems to have been altogether out of sympathy with indiscriminate almsgiving. In the First Epistle to the Thessalonians he told them to "support the weak," which possibly means the economically weak, but in the second he reminded them that when staying with them he had set them a good example by working for his living so that he might not be chargeable to any of them, and that he then "commanded them that if any would not work, neither should he eat." He had heard now that some of them were disorderly and did not work at all, but were busybodies, and he adjured them, "that with quietness they work and eat their own bread" (2 Thess. iii. 7–12).

The Christianity of the mediæval period did not require the rank and file to follow the example of the Jerusalem communists, but it was much less " strict " than St. Paul. It did not concern itself with the conduct of the receivers of alms, but held up for admiration and imitation the indiscriminating almsgiver who gave away all he could to the first beggar he met. It was good for his soul, and he needed not to trouble about whether it was really good for the beggar. This kind of charity, practised directly by individuals and indirectly through the religious houses founded by them—also for the benefit of their own souls—naturally led to the creation of an army of sturdy wandering beggars, while much privation remained unrelieved.

Some kind of " charity organisation " became absolutely necessary, and in England the Tudor poor-law was the result. The Act 27 Henry VIII, ch. 25 provided that the local authorities should support the poor who were incapable of maintaining themselves, and " cause and compel all . . . sturdy vagabonds and valiant beggars to be kept and set to continual labour in such wise as by their said labours they and every of them may get their own living with the continual labour of their own hands." Money for these two purposes was to be raised by collections in boxes from the good Christian people every Sunday or otherwise. At first no one was to be " constrained to any such certain contribution but as their free wills and charities extend," but this was soon found to provide insufficient money, and public exhortation, individual " gentle persuasion," and finally committal to prison were successively brought to bear on the close-fisted, and the poor-rate was evolved. History in other countries proceeded on much the same lines, though the English long nourished a curious belief that their country was unique in having a poor-law.

The four-hundred-years-old idea that the State should " find work " for the unemployed eventually produced the parish workhouse, which, after the parishes were grouped together, became the " Union " Workhouse, and also the system of subsidising wages from the poor-rate. Public opinion held that insufficient pressure was applied to the unemployed, but also that some corporate effort was required to give them what was called a " stock " (*i.e.* a stock of materials) to work on and a place to work in, a " work house," as the seventeenth and early eighteenth centuries called what we call a workshop or factory; if this course was inappropriate to rural conditions, it seemed not unreasonable to pay something out of the rates to get them employed by farmers who did not think them worth ordinary wages.

Recognition of the fundamental fact that very young children are unable to support themselves, aided by the desire for "cannon fodder" which prevailed during the eighteenth century, led to a certain (though according to our standards by no means enormous) liberality in giving "relief" to parents of young families. Townsend and Malthus thundered against this encouragement to the propagation of the poor, but the reform of the Poor-law in 1834 was not founded on any direct invocation of their principles, but came about simply because the administration had become very burdensome to the payers of the rates and very little beneficial to the recipients. The new maxim adopted was that people must be deterrred from becoming eligible for relief and demanding it. The State could not be as "strict" as St. Paul and deny a man food—even skilly—if he did not work, but it could and should say, "If any will not work, neither shall he eat unless he chooses to submit to certain unpleasant conditions," such as the restrictive rules of the union workhouse.

The policy of deterrence might be recommended by a Royal Commission and adopted by a parliament chosen by a middle-class electorate, but the populace never could be brought to admit that it is right. Two great difficulties have always been suggested by the questions, "But how about the children of the man who won't work?" and "But suppose the poor man can't find work. What then?"

Malthus as an author, though probably not in real life as a comfortable member of the professional classes with the very benevolent countenance depicted in his portrait, was quite prepared both to make parents work and to make potential parents abstain from propagation by the fear of pain and suffering not only for themselves but for their children. Modern opinion has never swallowed that policy; it cannot believe that the children of even the most obstinate idler should be starved before his eyes in order to make him and others set to work. On the contrary, it has actually made it a punishable offence for a parent not to apply for poor relief if otherwise his children will go hungry. The principle of deterrence, it holds, must be applied to responsible persons and not to proxies. That, it feels, is only justice, but it is desirable also on the purest economic grounds, since ill-fed children cannot all be trusted to die; some will grow up weak and diseased and become a burden on the stronger members of the next generation. How to combine the principle of making the position of the pauper "less eligible," as the old phrase put it, than that of the poorest independent worker, while at the same time looking on his children as wards of the nation, is generally a difficult and often probably an insoluble problem.

It is not made any easier by the fact that the other question "What if a man can't find work?" may be asked at the same time, and that without any very certain answer being available. When a person wants to sell a particular concrete object already in existence, and complains that he cannot find a purchaser, we usually assume that the demand is indefinitely elastic, and advise him to reduce his price. But we do not feel the same confidence in giving that advice when the thing to be sold is not a concrete object but continuous service. The elasticity of demand may be there, but it may be insufficient to take off the service at a price which will give the man a living, and it is no use to him to sell his services for less than that. And even when the demand is sufficiently elastic to take off the service at a price which would give him more than a subsistence wage, we know very well that modern arrangements for "collective bargaining" and for the legal regulation of wages often stand in the way of his getting employment by offering to reduce his price. It is no use to tell a man who says he cannot get a job at his trade, "Why don't you offer to work cheaper?" if we know very well that neither he nor any employer will dare to conclude a bargain on those terms. In that case the only advice that seems possible is that he should change his trade—offer some different service for which there is still an unsatisfied demand at the current rate. But here again we know that he will encounter great difficulty owing to the fact that those already employed in a trade dislike the competition of intruders from other trades, and make it as difficult as possible for them to become qualified to earn the current rate below which they cannot be employed at all.

It is thus not at all surprising that the principle of deterrence has never been expressly approved by popular opinion. But all the same not only the bourgeois class but also, and perhaps especially, the proletariat class, have always unconsciously assisted the policy of deterrence by making the conditions of relief more unpleasant to self-respecting persons than the legislature or the administration ever intended them to be. They have persisted in maintaining towards the recipients of the relief provided by the State an attitude more contemptuous than that which they display towards other persons equally deserving or undeserving who have failed for good or bad reasons to have incomes sufficient for their own or their family's support.

If anyone doubts this, let him reflect on the curious way in which words used in connection with poor-law administration have acquired " bad " senses, so that their use has come to be regarded in wide circles as almost indecent. " Pauper," once nothing but the Latin equivalent of " poor," and quite innocently used to distinguish the poor who received relief under the poor law from the poor who did not, came to be regarded as a most offensive term, which scarcely anyone will now dare to use. The originally quite respectable " work house " became so offensive that it has been officially replaced by the awkward and uninforming term " Institution " ; the " workhouse infirmary " is now the " poor-law hospital" ; and " poor law " itself, we are told by some authorities, must go and be replaced by " public assistance." The desire to change the name of a thing so that it may smell more sweet is a tacit confession that it does not smell sweet. At bottom the popular mind despises the pauper, and would despise him no less if he were called " a recipient of public assistance." To need assistance which other people do not get because they have been more successful in earning or even in inheriting or cadging from relations and friends is regarded as being in general a mark of failure in life which is not respectable. The man who has to confess openly that he needs poor relief loses caste as surely as, perhaps more surely than, the street beggar, and for the same reason. The fact will not be altered by calling him a recipient of public assistance any more than by calling the street beggar a peripatetic solicitor of gratuities.[1]

The perennial conflict between sympathy with undeserved

[1] See the article "The Stigma of Pauperism," in my *Economic Outlook*.

misfortune on the one side and recognition of the necessity of deterring the idle and wasteful from throwing themselves in shoals upon the provision made by the State has led to the fluctuations in " strictness " which have marked the history of the English poor law. At one period, especially when emotions have been stirred by a great war, the tendency has been towards the laxity now known as Poplarism, while in the next period there is reaction towards the severity of St. Paul. There is no reason to expect an early end to those fluctuations to come from a decisive victory of either Paul or Poplar. Beneath the fluctuations there proceeds and will continue to proceed a fairly steady rise in the material welfare of the class which lives on relief furnished by the State, whether the members of that class are called paupers or recipients of public assistance, but it would be rash to say that the rise is greater than the rise in the material welfare of the rest of the community. The inherent difficulties of the case hinder it, and on the whole it seems fairly certain that nothing very great has come or is to be expected to come from the most direct and obvious plan of promoting greater equality of economic condition—that of giving relief to the destitute.

Within certain limited fields much may be done to improve distribution by expedients which take something from the better-off and give it to some class which does not qualify for the gift by destitution or even indigence, but which is, in fact, likely to be generally indigent, and which cannot have its numbers increased by recruits coming in merely because of the gift. Such an expedient was the scheme of old-age pensions as originally put forward by Charles Booth in the early eighteen-nineties. Persons over sixty-five or seventy are for the most part indigent, and their number cannot be appreciably increased by their being better provided for, since people cannot arrive at these ages at will, but only by the lapse of time; a few would live a little longer than they would have done without the pension, but this would only reflect the improvement in their condition which was the main purpose of the plan. And as all the members of the class were to receive the pension whether they were rich or poor, there would have been no widespread slackening of the desire not to become indigent; here and there an individual might be less industrious or thrifty because he knew that however idle and wasteful he might be, an old-age pension awaited him instead of poor-law relief, but this would have been far outweighed by the more general reflection that it is some use to be careful when you are sure to be able to enjoy any little provision for old age which you have made, as a supplement to the pension, instead of having to face the fact that it will probably be insufficient to live on, and so you will have to use up the capital and come on the poor law in the end after all.

But muddleheaded politicians spoilt the plan when they got hold of it. They could not see the use, they said, quite truly (and more shame to them), of endowing all the persons over the qualifying age with the pension. They therefore confined the full pension of 5*s*. a week to those who had not more than 8*s*. a week from all other sources, including even earnings and allowance made voluntarily by relatives or friends. For each shilling from other sources above 8*s*. they reduced the pension by 1*s*., so that it was useless for anyone to have more than 8*s*. from other sources unless he could be sure of passing right through the zone of indifference and having more than the 13*s*., which was the utmost anyone with a pension could have.

This, of course, degraded the plan into a mere adjunct of the poor law, the only difference being that destitution was necessary for a claim to poor relief, while the pension scheme made the receipts of persons over seventy up to 13*s*. a week if they had already 8*s*. a week or more, and gave the full 5*s*. a week to all of that age who had less than 8*s*. All thrift and industry which increased an old person's income from 8*s*. up to 13*s*. was rendered nugatory, and (except for a relaxation in favour of earnings during the war period) this pernicious principle has been maintained, though the amounts have been increased.

But the importance of the whole scheme has been much reduced by the pensions provided for "insured" persons, which will be dealt with in the next section.

More effective than any of the plans for directly relieving poverty are the indirect methods which tend to "equalise opportunity" by enabling persons who would otherwise be handicapped by their early environment to compete on more equal terms with the others. All civilised and some semi-civilised states now make some attempt to reduce the advantage which the children of well-to-do parents enjoy as against the children of the poor. Though the older pious founders of educational establishments often had other ends in view, the endowments which they left did contribute something towards this end, but the modern states, by supplementing these endowments with immense additional funds and by compelling all parents to allow their children to be put on at any rate the first rung of the educational ladder, have done very much more.

Much also is done towards improving distribution by the modern plan of taxing the rich more heavily in proportion to their means than the poor for the common purposes of government.

Of course, it may be said, the fact remains that the space between the highest and the lowest incomes, and even between the highest net incomes after allowing for taxation and the lowest, continues to grow, and does not appear to show any signs even of a diminished rate of growth. Carnegie was much richer than Crœsus and Crassus, but Ford is much richer than Carnegie. On the other hand, the lowest income is as low as ever it was—it is *nil* now and never was less. But we are not to argue from this that inequality of incomes is increasing. We cannot reasonably say that incomes are more unequal simply because A's income is further removed from Z's; we must think also of the intermediate incomes. If A and Z are both outside the common run and the other twenty-four are more closely grouped together near the middle than they were, we should regard the general tendency as being towards equality in spite of the exceptional A's greater divergence from the mean. This is what seems actually to be happening. To the discomfiture of the school of socialists who taught that riches would concentrate themselves in fewer and fewer hands while a growing proletariat continued on subsistence wages, the trend of history is towards nothing of that sort, but towards an immense preponderance of the middle class.

Moreover, the magnitude of incomes, measured by their value, is not the only thing to be thought of in considering comparative economic condition. The pauper or beggar of to-day has no greater income than Lazarus, and Henry Ford has a much greater income than Dives, but the gap in economic condition between Henry Ford and the pauper or beggar is not nearly so enormous as that between Dives, who "was clothed in purple and fine linen and fared sumptuously every day," and Lazarus, whose many sores were licked by the dogs as he lay craving the crumbs that fell from Dives' table (Luke xvi. 19–21). The condition of the persons whose incomes are *nil* or very small has improved, and is still improving greatly, while the largest incomes have long passed the stage up to which an increase of income adds any appreciable advantage to its possessor.

§ 2. *For and towards Greater Economic Security.*

While an outside observer, say a man from Mars, might suppose it to be better to be rich for the first half of life and poor for the second half than to be poor all the time, popular opinion in our mundane universe, backed by the tragedians of all countries and times, holds that the rich man who loses his riches is much more to be pitied than the poor man who never had any. The surest way to receive compassion from all classes is not to say, "I am and always have been poor," but to say, "I once was rich and could have all I desired, and now I am poor." Hence alongside the aspiration for greater equality of economic condition which we have dealt with in the last section, we find a widespread aspiration for what is sometimes called greater security, for something which will remove, or at any rate mitigate, the effects of sharp falls from comfort into penury.

So far as property is concerned, one way by which an individual can diminish the risk of economic disaster is by spreading his risk. This plan has been known and practised ever since the carriers' maxim, "Don't put all your eggs in one basket," began to be used in its narrowest metaphorical sense. In the *Merchant of Venice* Shakespeare makes Antonio congratulate himself that he had spread his risks among several ships. But this by itself was not enough, as Antonio found. The maxim in time gets a wider interpretation which would be better suggested by "Don't invest your all in eggs, even if they are packed in different baskets."

This improved maxim could not be very thoroughly carried out by individual entrepreneurs carrying on businesses on their own account. The division of labour stood in the way; if you are an egg-merchant, your fortune will be mostly in eggs, just as the fortune of the Venetian merchant was in ships. But the substitution of joint-stock companies for the old individual entrepreneur has completely altered the situation. A man may now manage an enterprise much more specialised than Antonio's without holding more than a trifling portion of the capital of a company which undertakes it, if he is chairman or managing director, and without holding any at all if he is a salary-paid manager. What he possesses outside the company may be spread among a great many other investments.

Let the reader transport himself in imagination back into the sixteenth century, and consider how he would invest any little fortune that he might become possessed of either by saving or by inheriting a money bequest. He might buy a particular parcel of land with houses or other fixtures upon it, or he might lend money on mortgage of some particular property, in both cases subjecting himself to all the possible depreciations and disasters to which the particular property was liable; or he might decide to trade with it himself and take all the risk of the business. Nowadays he can write to his stockbroker, or see the stock-exchange clerk at his bank, and spread his investment, if he chooses, over fifty different enterprises in half-a-dozen different countries, and be fairly secure that no overwhelming loss will occur. The fact that this spreading of investments and consequent elimination of serious risk now commonly takes place, accounts for the ease with which large losses in particular trades are now often borne. Coal or iron or cotton may be extraordinarily depressed, and yet we see persons whom we know to be managing those industries and to have appreciable property in them able to live almost as before.

The weak point about the system of spreading risks is that it is impracticable for the very small investor. There is no difficulty at all about dividing £20,000 among forty or fifty different investments, beyond the slightly greater labour involved in the transfers and in signing orders to have the dividends paid direct to the holder's bank, and a small extra expense when the holder dies and his estate is being wound up. But the man who has only £100 to invest cannot spread it widely, because the extra trouble and expense, though perhaps not much more absolutely than that involved in spreading the £20,000, would be prohibitive in relation to so small an amount. He is consequently driven to single investments, and if he attaches great value to security, he must submit to the lower interest yielded by investments which are reputed to be particularly "safe"; and which unfortunately sometimes fail to live up to their reputation—like the stock of some governments which have either repudiated openly or have reduced the value of the currency in which they paid the interest.

In regard to labour, there is nothing precisely analogous to the joint-stock possibilities of spreading investments and risks. A man cannot practise a number of different trades at one and the same time; to do so would be rejecting the principle of division of labour. The best he can do in the desired direction is to be capable of changing from one occupation to another not subject to the same influences. Whether modern development of technique makes this on the whole more or less possible, seems difficult to decide. Specialism increases, but it is said that the specialism is more often of a kind which enables a person to contribute to the production of several different commodities which are not likely to be subject to the same failure of demand or shortage of raw materials; the idea seems to be embodied in the boast of the fitter, "A fitter's a fitter, all the world over." Moreover, machinery which simplifies the operation to be performed by a person, while it makes that operation a very special one, at the same time makes it easy to acquire the necessary skill for performing it, so that, for example, three weeks' probation is said to be sufficient to make a man an expert workman so far as most operations involved in "assembling" a motor-car while it proceeds on its moving platform are concerned. However this may be, there is no doubt that the kind of general intelligence which is seen at its highest present level in some of the countries which are called "new," is increasing rapidly in the older countries with the greater ease of locomotion and the numerous inventions which are making it possible for the populace to realise conditions remote from their own.

The spreading of risks by the individual being often difficult and sometimes impossible, another plan has been adopted in many directions, the plan of individuals agreeing to pool their losses, which we call "insurance." For pooling is in reality the essence of insurance. It is found, say, that 1 per cent. is the loss by shipwreck on an average in a certain length of time or of voyaging; the owners of the ships and cargoes agree to pay 1 per cent. on the value of their ships and cargoes into a common fund and to take out of the fund enough to repay to the owners who suffer by shipwreck the amount of their losses. Or, say, it is found that the loss of houses by fire is 1 per thousand per annum; the owners agree to pay into a common fund 1 per thousand on the value of their houses and to take out of the fund enough to repay the owners who lose by fires. These are cases of insurance; they are obviously cases of pooling of losses.

The details of the arrangement may differ about the amount to come out of the pool. In fire insurance the arrangement most familiar to the private householder is that he is to recover the whole of his loss up to the amount for which the property is insured. If he had insured the house at £1000, he will not in any case recover more than that, but if his loss is under £1000 he will recover the whole amount of it even if the fire might have done much more damage. But another plan is for the amount recoverable to be limited by the proportion which the amount destroyed or lost bears to the total loss which might have been incurred; so that, for example, if a whole cargo, being really worth £10,000, is insured at £5000 and half of it is lost, the insured will not be able to recover more than £2500. Still another arrangement is that no inquiry shall be made into the actual value of the loss, but that it shall be taken to be the amount insured; here the insured may actually make a gain if the loss occurs, so that he may be said to be betting on the chance of it, but, as he has to pay more into the fund in consequence, it is a losing business for him to declare more than what is the actual value to him, and over-valuation is consequently not likely unless fraud is intended. No man will care to try to make money out of his house being burnt unless he contemplates arson.

Even so-called "life assurance," which is generally intended as insurance against loss to the breadwinner's family in consequence of his untimely death, is a kind of pooling. The time at which a healthy person will die is very uncertain, but there is approximate knowledge of the average length of time persons of a given age will continue to live—their "expectation of life," as it is called—and consequently it is possible to calculate approximately how much a number of persons of given ages must pay into a common fund in order that some particular sum can be paid out of it when each of them dies. Here it seems to be taken for granted that the arrangement must be of the third kind mentioned above. When houses are burnt or ships wrecked, the amount of the loss can be estimated with tolerable accuracy, but to estimate the loss incurred by the family of an insured person is much more difficult, and it would be still more difficult to estimate beforehand what amounts should be paid into a pool in order to make it bear the claims which would be admitted for such losses. Consequently life assurance falls far short of the usefulness it might conceivably have. The amounts paid out of the pool are definite sums payable on the death of the insured, and their only relation to the actual loss incurred is that they are paid as soon as the loss (if any) occurs. This, of course, is better than nothing, but it does not go far enough. If it is impossible to make the payment in each instance fit the individual case (though this is done every day in compensation cases), it might well be possible to make contracts of assurance which would give larger amounts if the assured died at an age when his family was least likely to be self-supporting, and less and less as it took place at a later age.

It must not be supposed that the fact that insurance is usually undertaken not by the insured themselves forming a common fund or pool, but by some other persons undertaking the business for profit, makes any difference to the principle of pooling losses. The cost of administering the arrangement has to be met in any case, and this cost is much the same whether the services required are paid for by a mutual society formed of the insurers themselves. or by a company of other persons. The company, it will be said, will require in addition a profit on its capital, and the rate of dividend paid by old companies is often extremely high; this is true, but the capital is often so small in relation to the business done that the toll taken by the profit is a very small percentage of the amounts paid in, and small also in proportion to the expenses of working the business. Consequently proprietary companies manage to attract business even when in active competition with mutual societies.

Many evils besides fire, shipwreck and death come to be insured against—accidents, hailstorms, theft and burglary, for example. The chief reason which prevents further extension of the principle, as, for example, to loss of health or loss of business, is the well-founded fear of potential insurers that some of the insured may be not strictly conscientious in regard to claims. Take the most honest person we know, and ask him if he will be always quite as careful about putting on his fireguard and quite as reluctant to leave his bicycle or car in the street or his useless silver wedding presents in his uninhabited house when he is insured against fire and theft as when he is not. In these cases a little carelessness does not make very much difference, and the cost of it can be borne; it is heavier in regard to theft than in regard to fire, because fire is generally objectionable to the insured for other obvious reasons in addition to the loss of property. Similarly, although the avoidance of motor accidents depends principally on the good conduct of the driver, motor accidents can be insured against, because there are other disagreeable incidents connected with a motor accident besides pecuniary loss.

But a man cannot insure against the general risk of losing by his business, because it is justly feared that if he is so insured, he will not pursue it with the necessary strenuousness. A man cannot insure against the risk of his becoming a dipsomaniac; if he made the proposal, it would be suspected that he had a tendency in that direction. To insure against suicide is very difficult, if not always impossible, for the same reason.

In recent years there has been some tendency for the European states to become dissatisfied with the extent to which insurance against some risks has been developed by mutual and other voluntary institutions, and therefore to make insurance of these risks compulsory. People can scarcely be compelled to insure in voluntary institutions without the institutions being guaranteed by the State, and this makes it necessary for the State to undertake the task of supervising to some considerable extent the operations of such institutions if not to abolish them altogether. Whether it confines itself to supervision or undertakes the whole business itself, it will have to fix the rates of contribution and the rates of benefit.

In purely voluntary insurance the contributions and the cost of benefits plus administration must approximately balance in the long run in any one class, since people will not in the long run pay much more than the average cost to their particular class, and no voluntary unendowed institution can pay out much more in the long run than it gets in from contributions (plus interest if there is a lapse of time between contribution and payment of benefit). But when the State takes a part in the business, on the one hand, any particular class of people may be compelled to pay indefinitely more than the cost of providing the benefits which are given to that class, and on the other they may be allowed to pay indefinitely less.

To take an instance which so far is purely imaginary, and therefore likely to be regarded with impartiality, the owners of textile factories would not in the long run submit to paying fire-insurance companies much more than what is sufficient to cover the losses and expenses, since it would always be open to them to found a society or company which would take their risks at a cheaper rate; and, on the other hand, no society or company would care to continue to take the textile factories' fire risks at a rate which does not pay. But if the State made fire insurance compulsory, both the textile factory owners and the owners of all the other classes of inflammable property would have to submit to the rates approved by the State, so that it might happen either that the textile factories were compelled to make a contribution for the advantage of other kinds of property, or that they were subsidised at the expense of the other kinds. Thus the payments of the insured may show an element of taxation which may vary greatly in degree. The tendency is for States to incline towards flat rates of contribution, disregarding differences of risk.

In this country we have had two great examples of the State taking over insurance and one small one. The small one was the insurance against air raids undertaken during part of the war of 1914–18. Though in this case the insurance was voluntary, the State charged a flat rate all over the country regardless of the risk being so much greater in its eastern parts than in its western parts, but this was only possible in consequence of the temporary character of the emergency: in course of time (if allowed by the State) institutions would have sprung up for taking western risks at a lower rate, and the State would have had to submit to much less profit than it actually got or else to make the insurance with itself compulsory on all.

The two greater examples are the schemes of insurance officially known by the encouraging name of the "National Health and Pensions Insurance," and the less sweet name of "Unemployment Insurance." Under the original Health Insurance scheme the State took part in a considerable sick-benefit insurance business done by the Friendly Societies, and made it compulsory, not indeed on everyone, but only on persons employed at wages or salaries under a certain figure. Subsequently it has raised the contributions and supplemented the sick-benefit scheme by a scheme of pensions for widows of all ages and for all persons over sixty-five years of age. The contributions are flat rates payable during employment, and the benefits are also flat rates irrespective of need and almost irrespective of length of time of contribution. The benefits to widows are so often so much out of accordance with need that it may be disputed whether this part of the scheme is a real improvement of distribution, but the sick benefit may certainly pass as such. The old-age pensions, being paid, unlike those established by the earlier legislation, without any requirement of comparative indigence, have no tendency to discourage thrift and industry. The really weak point about the scheme is its association with employment at wages and salaries, and there seems to be no good reason why it should not be extended to cover compulsorily all persons with small earned incomes and be made open to all others who wish to come under it.

The Unemployment Insurance scheme is more open to hostile criticism. As has been remarked above, a business man cannot insure against want of success in his business. No society or company, not even the underwriters of Lloyds, who are said to be ready to take any possible risk at a price, would undertake to insure a man who produces and sells articles on his own account against the possibility of his not selling them; the insurers could not be certain that he would offer to sell his goods at a reasonable price: once insured, he might become careless about their quality, or hold out for too high a price. To insure a man against not selling his services to an employer is not always quite so impossible, because in many kinds of employment the quality of the service and the price at which it is sold is in some considerable degree standardised, so that a contract to give certain benefit in case of a man not selling his services could be entered into with an express or implied condition that he should offer to sell services of the usual quality at the standard price. Accordingly, we find that long before the State unemployment insurance scheme came into being, trade unions were to some extent insuring their members against the absence of sale for their services, *alias* "unemployment." But the extent to which they did it was severely limited to a small number of weeks' unemployment—a period which would on the average be well under one per cent. of a man's working life. Each union had its own scheme and conditions, so that the insurers had a good knowledge of the conditions of the trade and were likely to know whether the insured was performing his part of the bargain—that he should offer standard service at standard price. And, further, each of these bodies of insurers had the enormously valuable power of themselves lowering the standard price if necessary, so that when one of them found that many of its members were unemployed and the burden of unemployment benefit was high, it might, if it thought fit, agree to a reduction of the standard price, and thus extend the demand, with the result of a reduction of the unemployment and its liability for out-of-work pay.

The State, in starting its scheme for out-of-work pay, adopted the unions' principle of restricting the benefit to a specified number of weeks, but it lost the advantages which the unions enjoyed in supervision and in being able to vary the price of the different services. As the scheme was to cover all the employed except such as were considered not to suffer appreciably from unemployment (the higher-paid employees in all trades, agricultural workers, and domestic servants), difficulties of demarcation would have made it impossible to make different and appropriate schemes of contribution and benefit for each kind of labour and to put the levy of contributions and the distribution of benefit in the hands of the contributors to each special scheme, so that they should retain the inducement to modify the standard price of service if the burden of unemployed pay became heavy.

So the State scheme provided for a flat rate of contribution and a stereotyped rate of benefit for all trades alike whatever their circumstances.

Under the old system each trade " stood on its own legs," and if it was depressed drew nothing from the more prosperous ones. Adversity burnt the candle, so to speak, at both ends, since it diminished contribution to the unemployment fund at the same time as it increased claims on that fund. Under the more general scheme established by the State, the burden of heavy unemployment pay in any particular trade does not fall specially on the employed members of that trade, but is borne by the general fund. This fact, no doubt, must have some influence in diminishing the readiness of unions to agree to meet a slackening of demand by a reduction of wages in such a trade, though, of course, it must be remembered that unions still pay large amounts of out-of-work benefit to their members.

Further, and this is perhaps more practically important, the fact that the general fund is subsidised by the State from general taxation and that it is always possible for the legislature to increase that subsidy temporarily by lending to it, or permanently by giving to it from the proceeds of general taxation, tends to somewhat stiffen the attitude of the unions taken as a whole when there is any question of reduction of the price of services to be considered.

So far as the individual workers, organised or unorganised alike, are concerned, the fact that unemployment benefit exists, from whatsoever source derived, must of course tend in some degree to stiffen the natural reluctance of the employed to accept what they consider unfavourable terms offered by the employers in their own trade, and also their reluctance to embrace the alternative of leaving that trade for another.

Altogether, then, it would not have been unreasonable to expect some increase of unemployment to be the result of the establishment of the State scheme of insurance against unemployment. Conditions since it was established, however, have been so abnormal that it cannot yet be said with any certainty whether this inevitable effect of the scheme will eventually be considerable or not. But it seems clear that if the scheme as it was projected turns out to be a safe method of promoting security, it will only be so because of its limitations. It does very little; what a man really wants for security is not to know that he will have an allowance which will be paid for the first few weeks of unemployment and then stop, but to feel safe against either being thrown out of employment permanently or having to face all the losses and inconveniences involved in changing his occupation and perhaps his place, or even country, of residence. It would be obviously disastrous to insure every man a substantial income for life so long as he continued unemployed, so that nothing is to be hoped from extension of the present unemployed insurance benefit; but it seems quite possible that something may be done with great advantage in the way of insurance against loss on change of occupation. The Report of the Industrial Transference Board in 1928, and the consequent concerted effort to assist superfluous miners to change their occupation and their residence, suggest that useful and important development in this direction is both possible and probable.

On the whole, in spite of all difficulties, it seems we may safely say that the tendency of modern civilisation is towards the better satisfying of the natural desire for security in the enjoyment of economic position.

§ 3. *For and towards Greater Economic Independence.*

When Vedius Pollio gave a dinner to the Emperor Augustus, he naturally had his best dinner service put on the table. A slave waiter, probably made nervous by the greatness of the occasion, knocked over and broke one of the precious goblets. Vedius, with a hardy old Roman's ideas of how to get good service, promptly gave orders that he should be cut in small pieces and thrown into the pond where the fishes were being fattened for the next banquet. Augustus, however, representing a newer civilisation, was so scandalised at this that he had all the other goblets on the table smashed to atoms, and made Vedius emancipate the offending waiter instead of giving him to the eels.

Modern opinion sympathises with Augustus, and goes further than he in all probability ever went, by believing that the best service is not that of a slave who must do as he is bid under pain of punishment, but that of a free man who feels himself " independent " in the sense of being as little under the dominion of those whom he serves as they are under his.

A tinge of feudalism may be detected in Cantillon's saying that " none but the king and the landlords are independent (*il n'y a que le Prince et les propriétaires des terres qui vivent dans l'indépendance*," *Essai*, p. 55), but in Great Britain at any rate, by the beginning of the eighteenth century or earlier, the farmers, merchants and master-manufacturers were recognised as " independent " by themselves and everyone else, except possibly here and there some old-fashioned squire's dame who might grumble about the village butcher or grocer " getting very independent." By Adam Smith's time even a manual worker—a " manufacturer " in the speech of that day—was taken to be " independent " if he did not work " under a master." [1] It was recognised that " the butcher, the brewer and the baker," to whom we owe our dinner, were induced to supply us by their self-interest rather than their benevolence,[2] but this was not supposed to make them dependent on us any more than we are dependent on them : " we " depend on them for our dinner and have to bargain with them as equals, giving them something which they are willing to take in exchange for what they supply. No distinction in this respect was made between the butcher who did his killing with his own hands and one who employed a journeyman to do it ; and if " we " happened to buy the table-cloth for our dinner from a working handloom weaver, he was as " independent " as the butcher or even a master manufacturer employing a hundred weavers.

Yet down as far as the middle of the nineteenth century, and for some time later, even the foremost economists of the time believed that " dependence " was involved whenever a man took service under another man or body of men for wages instead of selling the product of his work after it was finished, and that a feeling that this dependence was galling caused the services of the " working classes " (identified with persons working for wages and not for profit) to be less willing than they might be. In

[1] " An independent manufacturer who has stock enough both to purchase materials and to maintain himself till he can carry his work to market should gain both the wages of a journeyman who works under a master and the profit which that master makes by the sale of the journeyman's work " (*Wealth of Nations*, Vol. I. p. 55).

[2] *Ib.*, p. 16.

1848 J. S. Mill, considering the "Probable Futurity of the Labouring Classes," could not believe that "notwithstanding the effect which improved intelligence in the working classes, together with just laws," might have in altering distribution, they would be permanently contented with the wage-system:

"To work at the bidding and for the profit of another, without any interest in the work—the price of their labour being adjusted by hostile competition, one side demanding as much and the other paying as little as possible—is not, even when wages are high, a satisfactory state to human beings of educated intelligence who have ceased to think themselves naturally inferior to those whom they serve" (*Principles*, 1st ed., Vol. II. p. 322; Ashley's ed., p. 760 n.).

As time went on, Mill became more rather than less gloomy about the wage-system; in the third (1852) edition he said:

"It is not to be expected that the division of the human race into two hereditary classes, employers and employed, can be permanently maintained. The relation is nearly as unsatisfactory to the payer of wages as to the receiver. If the rich regard the poor, as by a kind of natural law, their servants and dependents, the rich in their turn are regarded as a mere prey and pasture for the poor."

And in the fourth (1857) edition he added:

"We look in vain among the working classes in general for the just pride which will choose to give good work for good wages; for the most part, their sole endeavour is to receive as much and return as little in the shape of service as possible. It will sooner or later become insupportable to the employing classes to live in close and hourly contact with persons whose interests and feelings are in hostility to them. Capitalists are almost as much interested as labourers in placing the operations of industry on such a footing that those who labour for them may feel the same interest in the work which is felt by those who labour on their own account" (Ashley's ed., pp. 761–2 and n.).

All this shows much confusion of mind. The wage-earners, who must be taken to include salary-earners, as the salary-earner works under exactly the same kind of contract as the wage-earner, are identified with "the poor" though they may have several thousands a year, and the employers are identified with the employers for profit though employment for direct consumption is common, and with "the rich" though the poor employers greatly outnumber the wealthy employers. The emphasis on the term "servants" suggests that Mill had not got beyond the mediæval idea of working for wages being a mild form of slavery which no free and self-respecting man would sell himself into, and that he had forgotten that no man other than a hermit who declines all the advantages arising from division of labour can support himself without serving the desires of others.

Imagining that the feeling of dependence and consequent reluctance to give willing and efficient service which he supposed to exist among the "labouring classes" arose from the fact that they worked for wages instead of for profit, Mill, followed by most of the prominent economists of the next fifty years, proposed "co-operative production" and "profit-sharing" as the remedy. Immediately after the last of the passages just quoted, he went on to say that there was a solution of the problem how "to obtain the efficiency and economy of production on a large scale without dividing the producers into two parties with hostile interests, employers and employed, the many who do the work being mere servants under the command of the one who supplies the funds, and having no interest of their own in the enterprise except to fulfil their contract and earn their wages. A solution of this problem," he continues, "is afforded by the extension and development of which the co-operative or joint-stock principle is susceptible. That principle supplies means by which everyone who contributes to the work, whether by labour or by pecuniary resources, may have a partner's interest in it proportionally to the value of his contribution." [1] There is a fine vagueness about "the work"; presumably before the railway amalgamations "the work" to a mechanic in the Great Western Railway workshops at Swindon would include that done by the porters at Paddington and Penzance, but not that done by the dockers in South Wales: after the amalgamations it would include the latter as well as the former. What would be "the work" if an individual happened to own both a colliery and an adjoining iron-foundry is a puzzle.

Regardless of such questions, Mill proceeds to quote at length from Babbage's *Economy of Machinery and Manufactures* a

[1] *Principles*, 1st ed., Vol. II. pp. 323–4. The notes in Ashley's ed., pp. 763–4, do not quite suffice to reconstruct the 1st ed. Mill's alterations must have been maddening to an editor desirous of recording all of them.

scheme under which a dozen workmen accustomed to earn £2 a week and possessing a total capital of £800 are to co-operate. The basic distribution of the proceeds of their undertaking is to be £1 a week to the whole capital (which would give it 6½ per cent. per annum) and £1 a week to each workman; any surplus over this is to be distributed in the same proportions, so that if the workmen got £2 a week as before, the capital would get 13 per cent. per annum. What would happen if the business did not produce the basic £13 a week is not explained. The supposed advantages of the plan are that everyone concerned would do his best, all "real or imaginary causes for combinations" would be removed, and none but the best workmen would be admitted (1st ed., Vol. II. pp. 325–9; Ashley's ed., pp. 766–7 n.). In his third edition Mill rather prudently omitted the quotation from Babbage, and relied only on the example of M. Leclaire, a Paris house-decorator who employed two hundred workmen, paid them ordinary wages, allowed himself a fixed salary and a fixed percentage on capital, and divided the surplus as a uniform percentage bonus on the wages and salaries including his own. How ready Mill was to accept the new "principle" is shown by the fact that he said, "It is to be regretted that we are only in possession of the result of M. Leclaire's experiment in the first year during which it was in complete operation," but instead of regarding this as a reason for caution, he adds, "Already, however, the success had been remarkable." [1] That the labourers' share in the profits was small he regards as no objection. "The essence . . . of a partnership is obtained, since each benefits by all things which are beneficial to the concern, and loses by all which are injurious." [2] Then at the end of the chapter he once more gives free rein to his enthusiasm:

"The value of this 'organisation of industry,' for healing the widening and embittering feud between the class of labourers and the class of capitalists, must, I think, impress itself by degrees on all who habitually reflect on the condition and tendencies of modern society. I cannot conceive how any such person can persuade himself that the majority of the community will for ever, or even for much longer, consent to hew wood and draw water all their lives in

[1] 1st ed., Vol. II. p. 331; Ashley's ed., p. 769, does not notice an alteration here.

[2] 1st ed., Vol. II. p. 331; Ashley's ed., p. 772 n.

the service and for the benefit of others; or can doubt, that they will be less and less willing to co-operate as subordinate agents in any work when they have no interest in the result, and that it will be more and more difficult to obtain the best work-people, or the best services of any work-people, except on conditions similar in principle to those of M. Leclaire. Although, therefore, arrangements of this sort are now in their infancy, their multiplication and growth, when once they enter into the domain of popular discussion, are among the things which may most confidently be expected" (1st ed., pp. 332–3; Ashley's ed., p. 773 n.).

It was not for want of preachers that the new gospel failed to find the prompt acceptance which Mill expected. In the next year, 1849, the Christian Socialists, as they were called, Ludlow, Maurice, Kingsley, Vansittart, Neale, and Tom Hughes, formed a Society for promoting "Working Men's Associations." They talked a great deal, and founded a dozen associations of tailors, shoemakers, builders, piano-makers, printers, smiths and bakers on Babbage's lines, though certain French Associations Ouvrières founded on the same principle were their immediate model.

These associations soon collapsed owing to internal difficulties, but the Christian Socialists could not stop talking, and attached themselves as, so to speak, Honorary Vice-Presidents of the later Co-operative Movement. This did not owe its origin to them, or to any teaching like that of J. S. Mill, but sprang out of the experiments of various workmen who had formed combinations in different parts of England with the view of carrying into effect the voluntary communistic ideas of Robert Owen. One of the plans of such workmen was for a combination to buy goods wholesale and retail them to its members, and when this was coupled with the periodical distribution of the profits among the members in proportion to their individual purchases, it turned out a huge commercial success. It was, of course, co-operation of consumers rather than the co-operation of producers in particular businesses advocated by Mill and the Christian Socialists, but the Christian Socialists till they died lived in hopes that co-operation of producers would emerge from it, and, with Mill (Ashley's ed., p. 790) exhorted the societies to be "faithful to the co-operative principle" by giving their employees a "common interest" in "the work." The co-operative societies themselves did not repudiate the patronage, though they failed to follow the precepts, of Mill and the Christian Socialists, and much confusion prevailed between the old and quite unsuccessful movement and the new and successful one until Beatrice Potter (Mrs. Sidney Webb) cleared up the matter in her brilliant sketch, *The Co-operative Movement in Great Britain*, 1891.

In a cruel footnote (to p. 75) she professed not to know whether those who cried " the mine for the miners " and " the land for the labourers " would add " the school for the schoolmasters " and " the sewers for the sewer-cleaners." The jest brings out the essential point. Up to that time the economists had given far too much attention to the internal difficulties of working a business by an association of all the persons who happen to be reckoned as employed in it, and too little to the undesirability and impossibility of organising production on that principle, even if there were no internal difficulties and each association, taken separately, worked perfectly well and without an atom of friction.

Some of the associations would be more prosperous than others. If we suppose absolute immobility in the labour world, this would inevitably mean that persons doing the same work equally efficiently would have very unequal pay. One association of persons employed working a coal-mine would be getting little or perhaps nothing at all because the seam turned out badly, while another association working an adjoining mine would be getting very high pay because they struck a rich seam. The association working the *Daily Railer* might be rolling in wealth while that working the *Daily Appeaser* might be starving. The apostle of co-operative production has got to say to the coal-hewers, the engine-man and the clerks employed at the unfortunate mine that this serves them right—they ought to have exerted themselves more and then they would have found more coal: and to the compositors, the machine-tenders, the lift-man and the office-boys in the association running the *Daily Appeaser*, that they have only themselves to thank for not having succeeded in tickling the public taste for gossip or satisfying its desire for reliable racing news so well as the staff of the *Daily Railer*.

Such a state of things would be obviously neither just nor expedient. Fortunately it is also impossible. The desire of the persons in the less prosperous associations to leave them and get into the more prosperous would prevent it coming into existence and would destroy it in a week if we could suppose it to have come into existence. The members of the most prosperous associations would not receive the masses of candidates for admission with unmixed gladness. Even Babbage thought of their selecting only the best, and he was thinking of filling up vacancies, not of expansion of their numbers. Even in their trumpery three-year experience the Christian Socialists ran up against this impassable obstacle. In their first and final report (1852) they said:

> "Where the associations are successful, the great danger which they and all who are interested in them have to guard against is exclusiveness. The associates find their own position greatly improved, and fear to endanger it by taking in new members. They are apt, therefore, to make too stringent rules as to admission, and to require payments from new members proportionate to the capital which the society has gained." (Quoted in B. Potter, *Co-operative Movement*, p. 123.)

That is, the candidate for admission was asked to buy the chance of getting the higher remuneration: if he could not make this investment of capital, it was open to the prosperous association to take him on as an ordinary employee at the outside market rate of wages, and we are told that this also happened, as some of the associations "degenerated into the profit-making undertakings of small masters" (*ib.*, p. 124).

The only remedy the Christian Socialists could think of was for working men to "look forward and take a broader and more Christian view of their work" (in the *Report* just quoted). Presumably they imagined that true Christians would admit everyone who asked, so that the most prosperous coal-mine would be filled to the brim with coal-hewers and the *Daily Railer's* office crammed to the door with compositors.

As against this monstrous chimæra of co-operative production, the system of wages and salaries seems eminently effective and in accordance with accepted ideas of justice. The principle of it is that workers should be paid for the work they do, and not for that which somebody else does. If the compositors employed by the *Daily Railer* set up type no better than those employed by the *Daily Appeaser*, neither common-sense nor justice require that the *Daily Railer* compositors should receive more in consequence of the *Daily Railer's* management, with which they have nothing to do, causing it to bring in more money than the less well-managed *Daily Appeaser*. It seems perfectly reasonable that everyone in a particular business should be paid for his special work at the same rate as he could get elsewhere, and then that the person or persons responsible for buying their services as well as everything else required in the business and applying them in a particular way should take the positive or negative difference between receipts and expenses—that is, the profit or loss.

It is now over eighty years since Mill imagined that the wage-paid (and the salaried?) workers would not " much longer consent to hew wood and draw water in the service and for the benefit of others," and that they would " be less and less willing to co-operate as subordinate agents in any work when they have no interest in the result " (above, pp. 436–7). What has actually happened has been not a contraction but an important extension of the sphere of labour remunerated by wages and salaries and having " no interest "—that is, no profit-sharing interest—" in the result "—that is, the success of the particular person or institution to whom or to which the services are sold. Though there is still a very large number of small individual employers who receive remuneration for their labour and capital in the form of profit, the general tendency has been and still is for large businesses to be more and more undertaken by companies and other corporate institutions. It used to be said that such entities had " neither souls to be saved nor bodies to be kicked "; it is also true that they have neither hands to work with nor brains to manage with, so that though they undertake the business in the sense of accepting the profit or loss, they cannot undertake any of the manual or mental work which it requires. In each generation there are indeed a few great individual entrepreneurs such as Andrew Carnegie, William Whiteley, Henry Ford and W. R. Morris, to whom the companies into which they " turn themselves " are mere fictions so long as they are alive and well. But as soon as these pioneers grow too old for work or die or retire, their companies become a reality, the active management passes into the hands of salary-paid servants of the company, and another " divorce of the workman from his means of production " has taken place.

The consequence is that the class of employed—the wage-paid and salary-paid class—has come to include individuals who are much better paid and vastly more influential than the " labourers " or even the " principal clerk," whose work of " inspection and direction " Adam Smith despised (Vol. I. p. 51). The two largest businesses in Great Britain are the Post Office and the L.M.S. Railway, and neither the Postmaster-General and the Secretary to the Post Office nor the Chairman and the General Manager of the L.M.S. get a share in the profits of the Post Office and the L.M.S. any more than the postmen and the porters who are their fellow-servants. But no one thinks of complaining because these mighty men are compelled to " hew wood and draw water " for the whole or any part of their lives " in the service and for the benefit of others."

Moreover, while the growth of company and institutional organisation has thus made it more difficult to conceive the employed as essentially poor, and also oppressed and exploited by their employers, it has at the same time made it more difficult to conceive the employers, in the manner of Mill, as essentially rich. Quite poor people, as taxpayers, are employers of all Civil servants; as ratepayers, they are employers of all persons engaged in municipal service; as co-operators, they are employers of all in the service of co-operative societies; and as shareholders, of all in the service of companies. And whereas the riches of the individual undertaker of business and the magnitude of his undertaking vary pretty closely together, the individual riches of the persons who are members of an employing institution or company have little or no connection with the magnitude of its undertaking; the biggest concern may belong to a vast number of persons with small shares in it.

We may add further that the considerable and rapidly growing publicity of operations and accounts which company and institutional organisation has brought with it makes it much plainer than before to the ordinary apprehension that any irksome " dependence " of which the wage-earner complains, or is alleged by his self-appointed champions to complain, is a dependence not on the employer who takes the profits, but on the ultimate consumers who take the goods. It is, of course, always these consumers "for whose benefit" the wage-earner works, whether his employer is an individual or an institution or company, but it is much easier for him to realise the fact when he knows more about the actual circumstances. Employed by an individual generally (though by no means always) richer than himself, he is ordinarily said to be "working for" that person, and is likely to be told by some sour-faced stirrer-up of strife that he is working "for the profit" of that person, and to leave it at that. Employed by an institution or company whose affairs are even only very roughly known, he is much more likely to grasp the conception of his employer as an agency for selling the product of the business and dividing the proceeds between the various contributors of labour and capital; he may be discontented with the management, with the price obtained, and with the division of the price between him and other sharers, but he will not any longer imagine that working "for" an employer means merely that he is toiling to feed a vampire which battens on his sweat and tears.

He may even be employed, or know others who are employed, by a public institution which borrows all the capital it requires at fixed rates of interest and adjusts its charges for the service so as to cover that and all other expenses without making a profit for anyone, and he cannot fail to see that this makes no difference to the employed. Men employed by the old dock or water companies in London were no doubt told from time to time that they were, in Mill's words, "working for the profit" of the water and dock companies, but it certainly became impossible to tell them that after the businesses were taken over by the Metropolitan Water Board and the Port of London Authority, which distribute profits to no one. Consideration of such a case can scarcely fail to explode the belief that the employed work for the benefit of the employer who sells the product. Possibly the fact that Mill's own employer, the East India Company, was almost in this position was what made him think that his thirty-three years as a "hired labourer" in the India House were a part of his life "given to India" (*Autobiography*, p. 249) rather than a miserable period in which he was exploited by the Company.

While thus a clearer apprehension of the nature of the organisation in which the wage-earner takes his part has tended to remove an imaginary grievance, a real grievance has been in process of being removed by the gradual decay of the traditional conventions, descended to us from the slave ages, which marked the wage-earner as inferior in status to the employer. Already in Mill's time it had become nearly as impossible for the employer to beat the wage-earners he employed as for them to beat him, but " respectful demeanour " was generally expected from the wage-earners towards the " masters," and nothing of the sort from the " masters " to " their men." It can scarcely be said that eighty years later perfect equality prevails in this matter, but we are certainly vastly nearer it.

In considering the " probable futurity of the labouring classes " Mill forgot the domestic servants. No ingenious M. Leclaire had discovered a means for giving the housemaids and cooks in private households a share in the profit of their work. Yet the domestics in the early Victorian four-storey town houses with the only cold-water tap in the basement and a coal-cellar under the street pavement were eminently entitled to be regarded as " drawers of water " and " hewers of wood," or at any rate carriers of coal-scuttles. Whatever judgment may be passed upon their general economic advantages and disadvantages in comparison with other workers, these wage-earners were in Mill's time somewhat behind the rest in regard to the quality of " independence," and they are so still. But they have shared in the general advance, and there is no reason to believe that they have not advanced at least as much as the others, while the condition of the labour market suggests that some of the conventions which at present stamp the class with a badge of inferiority, such as the absurd use of Christian names instead of the usual surname with the prefix " Miss," and the practice of engaging a new maid without showing her where she will be expected to sleep, will soon follow the almost obsolete requirement of attendance at church or chapel.

We may conclude quite safely that the aspiration on the part of the wage-earners for greater " independence " is in process of being satisfied, with the expected result of more willing and efficient service. Mill's description of the working classes of his day as having none of " the just pride which will give good work for good wages," and as making " for the most part " no attempt except " to receive as much and return as little in the shape of service as possible," deliberately inserted in the fourth edition of his *Principles*, may have been over-coloured, but Mill was a philosopher and an economist with a kindly word for gardeners (*Principles*, ed. Ashley, p. 126). Nowadays we should only expect to hear such a condemnation of the working classes from the mouth of some descendant of Vedius Pollio who had just lost her seventh cook in the last six months, or from the mouth of some harried works manager in the middle of a labour dispute. No responsible economist would agree with it further than to admit that the wage-earners, like any other sellers, quite rightly desire to get the best possible price for their goods.

INDEX

www.ingramcontent.com/pod-product-compliance
Lightning Source LLC
LaVergne TN
LVHW011103300926
849160LV00008B/267

9781138218161